Broadcast
Radio and Television
Handbook

Edward M. Noll is an accomplished author of numerous technical books, lessons, articles, and instruction manuals. He also devotes much of his time to circuit design and lecturing. He has taught radiocommunications at the university level and has served on the staff of several broadcast stations. His other SAMS books include: *Linear IC Principles, Experiments, and Projects, Wind/Solar Energy for Radiocommunications and Low-Power Electrical Systems, Oscilloscopes Applications, and Experiments, 73 Dipole & Long-Wire Antennas, Solid-State Circuit Files* (Vol. 1 & 2), *Microprocessor Circuits* (Vol. 1), and *General Radiotelephone License Handbook.*

Broadcast
Radio and Television
Handbook

Sixth Edition

by
Edward M. Noll

Howard W. Sams & Co., Inc.
4300 WEST 62ND ST. INDIANAPOLIS, INDIANA 46268 USA

International Standard Book Number: 0-672-21999-1
Library of Congress Catalog Card Number: 82-50659

Edited by: *Welborn Associates*
Illustrated by: D. B. Clemons

Printed in the United States of America.

Preface

In the more than fifty years since KDKA, Pittsburgh first took to the air, commercial broadcasting has mushroomed at a phenomenal rate. Today that one lonely voice has been joined by more than 8500 am, fm, and television broadcast stations. Broadcasting provides an exciting and vital career. If you desire technical employment in this field learn the fundamentals well. Your employment chances are improved if you have a good electronic background and some understanding of broadcast practices. If you are a current broadcast employee your advancement depends on how well you keep up with equipment and techniques.

There are very strict FCC operational procedures and technical requirements that must be followed. The repair and maintenance of transmitting equipment must be handled by qualified persons. Become familiar with procedures and equipment.

Broadcast Radio and Television Handbook is a basic broadcast text and has two major objectives: (1) to help you acquire a fundamental technical knowledge of broadcast systems and (2) give you an understanding of important operational procedures and technical requirements as mandated by the Federal Communications Commission. Emphasis is on transmitter equipment because proper operation and maintenance are so important in complying with FCC Rules and Regulations. Complete FCC Rules and Regulations are to be found in the publication Volume III, *Radio Broadcast Services* which can be purchased from the FCC office in Washington, D.C. or can be studied at any one of the FCC field offices.

Studio, master control and remote equipment are also covered to give a more complete introduction to broadcasting. Both solid-state and vacuum-tube equipment are covered. The text also provides a review and upgrading study for the present technician and engineer who may already be employed in the broadcast field.

The first seven chapters of *Broadcast Radio and Television Handbook* provide an introduction to broadcasting and a coverage of microphones, studio and control room equipment and facilities as well as remote gear. Chapters 8 and 9 concentrate on am broadcast transmitters and antenna systems. Chapter 10 provides similar coverage of fm transmitters. Stereophonic fm and am broadcasting are treated in Chapter 11. Important transmitter monitor and test equipment is stressed in Chapter 12. A thorough introduction to the commercial television broadcast system is presented in Chapter 13 along with discussions of actual television broadcast equipment. Emphasis is on color-transmission techniques.

Digital and microprocessor electronic systems are commonplace in modern broadcast systems. Digital techniques are especially applicable to control, monitoring, and test applications. Microprocessor systems which involve more advanced digital techniques are used in programming, operational and control activities. Chapters 14 and 15 introduce the fundamentals of digital and microprocessor systems and include some practical circuits and applications related to broadcasting.

Good luck in your broadcast career.

EDWARD M. NOLL

Contents

CHAPTER 12

CHAPTER 13

CHAPTER 14

CHAPTER 15

CHAPTER 1

Introduction

Anyone wishing to enter the technical phase of radio broadcasting or anyone wishing to progress in that field should embark on a suitable study program. The minimum license required for operating a broadcast transmitter is a restricted radiotelephone operator permit. This permit can be obtained without any examination by filling out an application that can be obtained from the Federal Communications Commission. Addresses of local FCC offices are given in Table 1-1. However, your chances of employment are enhanced if you acquire some knowledge of broadcast equipment and operating procedures as well as an understanding of solid-state and high-power vacuum-tube technology.

"Broadcast Radio and TV Handbook" covers broadcast fundamentals, equipment, operating procedures and important FCC technical requirements. Material includes the three facets of radio broadcasting: am, fm, and television. Many broadcast companies operate am and fm stations; some, all three types. Each type is detailed in this handbook. It is important to know how transmitters are monitored. The FCC requires specific monitoring and logging procedures.

Introductory material on maintenance and proof-of-performance requirements is given. Gathering in of all this knowledge is important and will permit you to better understand the responsibilities assigned to you by the technical supervisor. You cannot learn all things about broadcasting from a handbook but, if you learn the fundamentals, you are better prepared to understand the activities that occur once you are employed in a broadcast facility.

This handbook assumes a previous knowledge of solid-state and vacuum-tube fundamentals especially with relation to transmitter circuits. The type of background material referred to can be found in *General Radiotelephone License Handbook*, also published by Howard W. Sams & Co., Inc. In terms of possible employment it might be an excellent idea to obtain a general radiotelephone license. It would look good on your resume. Furthermore such a license is required to install and maintain broadcast remote-pickup stations, broadcast aural

11

STL and intercity relay stations, broadcast low power auxiliary stations, tv broadcast auxiliary stations, tv broadcast translators, fm broadcast translator and booster stations, as well as broadcast experimental and development stations.

Digital and microprocessor techniques are the new kids-in-the-block in broadcasting. Study the fundamentals as applied to broadcasting in this handbook. Additional knowledge can be obtained from the references that follow.

Table 1-1. Addresses of FCC Field Offices

ALABAMA, Mobile
  439 Federal Building &
  U. S. Courthouse
  113 St. Joseph Street
  Mobile, Alabama 36602
  Phone: Area Code 205 690-2808

COLORADO, Denver
  Suite 2925, The Executive Tower
  1405 Curtis Street
  Denver, Colorado 80202
  Office Examinations (Recording)
  Phone: Area Code 303 837-5137
  Other Information
  Phone: Area Code 303 837-5137

ALASKA, Anchorage
  U. S. Post Office Building Room G63
  4TH & G Street, P. O. Box 644
  Anchorage, Alaska 99510
  Phone: Area Code 907 265-5201

DISTRICT OF COLUMBIA
  (WASHINGTON, D.C.)
  1919 M Street N. W. Room 411
  Washington, D.C. 20554
  Phone: Area Code 202 632-8834

CALIFORNIA, Long Beach
  Suite 501
  3711 Long Beach Boulevard
  Long Beach, California 90807
  Office Examinations (Recording)
  Phone: Area Code 213 426-7886
  Other Information
  Phone: Area Code 213 426-4451

FLORIDA, Miami
  919 Federal Building
  51 S. W. First Avenue
  Miami, Florida 33130
  Phone: Area Code 305 350-5541

CALIFORNIA, San Diego
  Fox Theatre Building
  1245 Seventh Avenue
  San Diego, California 92101
  Office Examinations (Recording)
  Phone: Area Code 714 293-5460
  Other Information
  Phone: Area Code 714 293-5478

FLORIDA, Tampa
  809 Barnett Bank Building
  1000 Ashley Street
  Tampa, Florida 33602
  Office Examinations (Recording)
  Phone: Area Code 813 228-2605
  Other Information
  Phone: Area Code 813 228-2872

CALIFORNIA, San Francisco
  323A Customhouse
  555 Battery Street
  San Francisco, California 94111
  Office Examinations (Recording)
  Phone: Area Code 415 556-7700
  Other Information
  Phone: Area Code 415 556-7701

GEORGIA, Atlanta
  Room 440, Masseli Building
  1365 Peachtree Street N. E.
  Atlanta, Georgia 30309
  Office Examinations (Recording)
  Phone: Area Code 404 881-7381
  Other Information
  Phone: Area Code 404 881-3084

GEORGIA, Savannah
  238 Federal Office Building and
  Courthouse
  125 Bull Street, P.O. Box 8004
  Savannah, Georgia 31402
  Phone: Area Code 912 232-4321
  Ext. 320

MISSOURI, Kansas City
  1703 Federal Building
  601 East 12th Street
  Kansas City, Missouri 64106
  Office Examinations (Recordings)
  Phone: Area Code 816 374-5526
  Other Information
  Phone: Area Code 816 374-6155

HAWAII, Honolulu
7304 Prince Jonah Kuhio
Kalanianaole Building
300 Ala Moana Boulevard
Honolulu, Hawaii 96813
Phone: Area Code 808 546-5640

ILLINOIS, Chicago
3935 Federal Building
230 South Dearborn Street
Chicago, Illinois 60604
Office Examinations (Recording)
Phone: Area Code 312 353-0197
Other Information
Phone: Area Code 312 353-0195

LOUISIANA, New Orleans
829 F. Edward Hebert Federal
Building
600 South Street
New Orleans, Louisiana 70130
Phone: Area Code 504 589-2094

MARYLAND, Baltimore
George M. Fallon Federal Building
Room 819 31 Hopkins Plaza
Baltimore, Maryland 21201
Office Examinations (Recording)
Phone: Area Code 301 962-2727
Other Information
Phone: Area Code 301 962-2728

MASSACHUSETTS, Boston
1600 Customhouse
165 State Street
Boston, Massachusetts 02109
Office Examinations (Recording)
Phone: Area Code 617 223-6608
Other Information
Phone: Area Code 617 223-6609

MICHIGAN, Detroit
1054 Federal Building
& U. S. Courthouse
231 W. Lafayette Street
Detroit, Michigan 48226
Office Examinations (Recording)
Phone: Area Code 313 226-6077
Other Information
Phone: Area Code 313 226-6078

MINNESOTA, St. Paul
691 Federal Building
316 N. Robert Street
St. Paul, Minnesota 55101
Office Examinations (Recording)
Phone: Area Code 612 725-7819
Other Information
Phone: Area Code 612 725-7810

TEXAS, Houston
5636 Federal Building
515 Rusk Avenue
Houston, Texas 77002

NEW YORK, Buffalo
1307 Federal Building
111 W. Huron Street at
Delaware Avenue
Buffalo, New York 14202
Phone: Area Code 716 842-3216

NEW YORK, New York
201 Varick Street
New York, New York 10014
Office Examinations (Recording)
Phone: Area Code 212 620-3435
Other Information
Phone: Area Code 212 620-3437

OREGON, Portland
1782 Federal Office Building
1220 S. W. 3rd Avenue
Portland, Oregon 97204
Office Examinations (Recording)
Phone: Area Code 503 221-3097
Other Information
Phone: Area Code 503 221-3098

PENNSYLVANIA, Philadelphia
One Oxford Valley Office Building
Room 404
2300 East Lincoln Highway
Langhorne, PA 19047
215-752-1324

PUERTO RICO, Hato Rey
(San Juan)
Federal Building & Courthouse,
Room 747
Avenida Carlos Chardon
Hato Rey, Puerto Rico 00918
Phone: Area Code 809 753-4567 or
Phone: Area Code 809 753-4008

TEXAS, Dallas
Earle Cabell Federal Building
Room 13E7,
1100 Commerce Street
Dallas, Texas 75242
Office Examinations (Recordings)
Phone: Area Code 214 749-3243
Other Information
Phone: Area Code 214 749-1719

VIRGINIA, Norfolk
Military Circle
870 North Military Highway
Norfolk, Virginia 23502
Office Examinations (Recording)
Phone: Area Code 804-461-4000
Other Information
Phone: Area Code 804 441-6472

WASHINGTON, Seattle
3256 Federal Building
915 Second Avenue
Seattle, Washington 98174

Office Examinations (Recording) Phone: Area Code 713 226-4306 Other Information Phone: Area Code 713 226-5624	Office Examinations (Recording) Phone: Area Code 206 442-7610 Other Information Phone: Area Code 206 442-7653
TEXAS, Beaumont Room 323 Federal Building 300 Willow Street Beaumont, Texas 77701 Phone: Area Code 713 838-0271 Ext. 317	

Broadcasting is a fascinating field. Prepare yourself well and the opportunity for employment will improve. Once employed, keep studying and you will continue to advance.

The references that follow can be of help in advancing your career in radiocommunications or as an aid in better retaining electronic knowledge with practical experience. The latter three references in particular can be of assistance in obtaining practical experience at home or in a school laboratory situation. Reference 1 is more than a general class license handbook. Text concentrates on solid-state fundamentals. Basic and advanced circuits are detailed with emphasis on transmission and modulation techniques. There is vacuum-tube coverage too. References 2 and 3 stress a better understanding of linear and digital integrated circuits by building up low-cost circuits on solderless circuit boards. Knowledge and practical skill in handling these devices are obtained. The fourth reference concentrates on microprocessor circuits and a chip-by-chip series of *Democircuits* permits you to build up a simple microprocessor system.

1. *General Class Radiotelephone License Handbook.*
2. Ed Noll's *Solid-State Circuit Files, Volume I, Bipolar Transistor, FET, and Linear IC Circuits.*
3. Ed Noll's *Solid-State Circuit Files, Volume II, TTL and CMOS Circuits.*
4. *Microprocessor Circuits, Volume I, Fundamentals and Microcontroller.*

Available from:

> Howard W. Sams & Co., Inc.
> 4300 West 62nd St.
> P.O. Box 558
> Indianapolis, Indiana 46206

CHAPTER 2

Station Frequency Assignments and Power-Output Ratings

There are a variety of broadcast stations including am, fm, television, auxiliary, and international broadcast services. Each of these stations is assigned a specific carrier frequency on specific broadcast bands by the FCC. The stations so licensed are legally obligated to operate on their assigned frequency (within a rather close tolerance) and in accordance with the FCC technical standards for the particular type of broadcast service.

Frequency assignments are made in a manner that precludes as much as possible interference among stations operating on the same channel. In general, the same channel or an adjacent channel is not allocated to more than one broadcast station within the same general listening area. However, even careful allocation does not preclude interference; it is not unusual, at times, for two or even more stations to be received at certain settings on the receiver dial.

2-1. AM BROADCAST

The am broadcast band lies between 535 and 1605 kilohertz. Each am channel is 10 kHz wide. (Refer to the carrier-frequency assignments in Table 2-1.) There are 107 am channels available, and am stations are authorized for powers from 250 watts to 50 kilowatts. The three classes of standard broadcast channels are clear (C), regional (R), and local (L) as indicated by Table 2-1.

A *clear channel* is one on which the dominant station, or stations, renders service over wide areas and is cleared of objectionable interference within its primary service area and over all or a substantial portion of its secondary service area. As will be detailed later, Class I and II, A, B, and D stations operate on clear channels and are assigned powers up to a maximum of 50 kilowatts. A *regional channel* is one on which several Class III-A or III-B stations may operate with power

Table 2-1. AM Channels and Assigned Carrier Frequencies*

Freq (kHz)	Class	Channel	Freq (kHz)	Class	Channel
540	C	1	1080	C	55
550	R	2	1090	C	56
560	R	3	1100	C	57
570	R	4	1110	C	58
580	R	5	1120	C	59
590	R	6	1130	C	60
600	R	7	1140	C	61
610	R	8	1150	R	62
620	R	9	1160	C	63
630	R	10	1170	C	64
640	C	11	1180	C	65
650	C	12	1190	C	66
660	C	13	1200	C	67
670	C	14	1210	C	68
680	C	15	1220	C	69
690	C	16	1230	L	70
700	C	17	1240	L	71
710	C	18	1250	R	72
720	C	19	1260	R	73
730	C	20	1270	R	74
740	C	21	1280	R	75
750	C	22	1290	R	76
760	C	23	1300	R	77
770	C	24	1310	R	78
780	C	25	1320	R	79
790	R	26	1330	R	80
800	C	27	1340	L	81
810	C	28	1350	R	82
820	C	29	1360	R	83
830	C	30	1370	R	84
840	C	31	1380	R	85
850	C	32	1390	R	86
860	C	33	1400	L	87
870	C	34	1410	R	88
880	C	35	1420	R	89
890	C	36	1430	R	90
900	C	37	1440	R	91
910	R	38	1450	L	92
920	R	39	1460	R	93
930	R	40	1470	R	94
940	C	41	1480	R	95
950	R	42	1490	L	96
960	R	43	1500	C	97
970	R	44	1510	C	98
980	R	45	1520	C	99
990	C	46	1530	C	100
1000	C	47	1540	C	101
1010	C	48	1550	C	102
1020	C	49	1560	C	103
1030	C	50	1570	C	104
1040	C	51	1580	C	105
1050	C	52	1590	R	106
1060	C	53	1600	R	107
1070	C	54			

*FCC has under consideration some changes in the class assignments.

not in excess of 5 kilowatts. The primary service area of a station operating in any such channel is protected from interference out to a given field-intensity contour. A *local channel* is one on which several Class IV stations operate. The primary service area of a station operating on any such channel may be limited out to a given field-intensity contour to reduce interference among stations. Daytime power may be no greater than 1 kilowatt while the nighttime power is limited to no greater than 250 watts.

A Class I station is a dominant station operating on a clear channel and rendering primary and secondary service over an extended area and at relatively long distance. Its primary service area is free from objectionable interference from the other stations on the same and adjacent channels. Its secondary area is free from interference except from stations on adjacent channels and from stations on the same channel in accordance with the engineering standards of allocation. The operating power of a Class I station cannot be less than 10 kilowatts nor can it be more than 50 kilowatts. The term *dominant station* is applied to any Class I station that is operating on a clear channel.

A Class II station also operates on a clear channel. It renders service over a primary service area which is limited by and subject to interference from Class I stations. It is known as a *secondary station,* which is any station except Class I operating on a clear channel. A Class II-A (an unlimited time) station must operate with a power no less than 10 kilowatts nighttime nor more than 50 kilowatts at anytime. Class II-B (unlimited time) and Class II-D (daytime or limited time) must operate with a power no less than 250 watts or more than 50 kilowatts. Whenever necessary, a Class II station must employ a directional antenna to prevent interference between it and Class I and other Class II stations.

A Class III station operates on a regional channel and renders service primarily to a metropolitan district and to the surrounding rural area. There are two types of Class III stations: A Class III-A station must operate with a power of not less than 1 kilowatt nor more than 5 kilowatts. A Class III-B station must have a power of not less than 500 watts nor more than 5 kilowatts, and not more than 1 kilowatt during nighttime operation.

A Class IV station operates on a local channel and renders service primarily to a city or town and the neighboring rural area. Power must not be less than 250 watts and not more than 1 kilowatt (250 watts nighttime). Its service area is subject to interference in accordance with standards of allocation.

Standard broadcast stations are licensed to operate only within certain time schedules, unless licensed for unlimited time. If a station has a daytime assignment, it can operate only during the hours between the average monthly sunrise and sunset. Some stations are required to share their time with one or more stations using the same channel. Other stations can go on the air during certain hours only, as specified in the license. Some stations operate on a limited-time basis. This is applicable to a Class II secondary station operating on a clear channel. The time of operation assigned depends on the geographical location of the secondary station relative to the geographical location of the dominant station.

2-2. INTERNATIONAL AM BROADCAST

The transmissions of an international am broadcast station are intended for reception by the general public in foreign countries. Such stations are assigned frequencies between 5.95 MHz and 26.1 MHz, within the following bands:

Band	Frequency (MHz)
A	5.95–6.2
B	9.5–9.775
C	11.7–11.975
D	15.1–15.450
E	17.7–17.9
F	21.450–21.750
G	25.6–26.1

International am broadcast stations will not be authorized for a power less than 50 kW. Carrier frequency must be held with 0.0015 percent of the assigned value. Their frequencies and directional-antenna systems are determined by the countries to be covered, and also by the propagation characteristics of the ionosphere. In short-wave transmission the most effective frequency, in terms of coverage, depends on the time of day and year in addition to the ionospheric variables. For this reason, international am broadcast stations are assigned a number of frequencies on the various short-wave bands so they can use the frequency giving the desired coverage at the time.

2-3. FM BROADCAST

The fm broadcast band lies between 88 MHz and 108 MHz. Each fm channel is 200 kHz wide, making a total of 100 available channels. (See Table 2-2.) Fm power assignments are made on the basis of both the effective radiated power and the transmitter power output. The effective radiated power (erp) is equal to the transmitter power delivered to the antenna, multiplied by the antenna power gain:

$$erp = \text{Antenna Input Power} \times \text{Antenna Power Gain}$$

There are two general classifications of fm broadcast stations, commercial and noncommercial. In the commercial broadcast classification, there are Class A, B, and C stations. In the noncommercial there are Class A, B, C, and D stations. The first twenty fm channels shown in Table 2-2 are the noncommercial educational channels. The commercial Class A, B, and C stations are assigned to the remaining 80 channels.

A Class A fm station renders service primarily to a community and the surrounding rural area. It is limited to three kilowatts of effective

Table 2-2. FM Channels and Assigned Carrier Frequencies*

Freq (MHz)	Class	Channel	Freq (MHz)	Class	Channel
88.1	A-B-C-D	201	98.1	B-C	251
88.3	A-B-C-D	202	98.3	A	252
88.5	A-B-C-D	203	98.5	B-C	253
88.7	A-B-C-D	204	98.7	B-C	254
88.9	A-B-C-D	205	98.9	B-C	255
89.1	A-B-C-D	206	99.1	B-C	256
89.3	A-B-C-D	207	99.3	A	257
89.5	A-B-C-D	208	99.5	B-C	258
89.7	A-B-C-D	209	99.7	B-C	259
89.9	A-B-C-D	210	99.9	B-C	260
90.1	A-B-C-D	211	100.1	A	261
90.3	A-B-C-D	212	100.3	B-C	262
90.5	A-B-C-D	213	100.5	B-C	263
90.7	A-B-C-D	214	100.7	B-C	264
90.9	A-B-C-D	215	100.9	A	265
91.1	A-B-C-D	216	101.1	B-C	266
91.3	A-B-C-D	217	101.3	B-C	267
91.5	A-B-C-D	218	101.5	B-C	268
91.7	A-B-C-D	219	101.7	A	269
91.9	A-B-C-D	220	101.9	B-C	270
92.1	A	221	102.1	B-C	271
92.3	B-C	222	102.3	A	272
92.5	B-C	223	102.5	B-C	273
92.7	A	224	102.7	B-C	274
92.9	B-C	225	102.9	B-C	275
93.1	B-C	226	103.1	A	276
93.3	B-C	227	103.3	B-C	277
93.5	A	228	103.5	B-C	278
93.7	B-C	229	103.7	B-C	279
93.9	B-C	230	103.9	A	280
94.1	B-C	231	104.1	B-C	281
94.3	A	232	104.3	B-C	282
94.5	B-C	233	104.5	B-C	283
94.7	B-C	234	104.7	B-C	284
94.9	B-C	235	104.9	A	285
95.1	B-C	236	105.1	B-C	286
95.3	A	237	105.3	B-C	287
95.5	B-C	238	105.5	A	288
95.7	B-C	239	105.7	B-C	289
95.9	A	240	105.9	B-C	290
96.1	B-C	241	106.1	B-C	291
96.3	B-C	242	106.3	A	292
96.5	B-C	243	106.5	B-C	293
96.7	A	244	106.7	B-C	294
96.9	B-C	245	106.9	B-C	295
97.1	B-C	246	107.1	A	296
97.3	B-C	247	107.3	B-C	297
97.5	B-C	248	107.5	B-C	298
97.7	A	249	107.7	B-C	299
97.9	B-C	250	107.9	B-C	300

*FCC is making some changes in the class assignments.

radiated power, and its antenna height cannot exceed 300 feet above the average terrain.

A Class B station renders service primarily to a metropolitan district or urbanized area of a principal city and the surrounding rural area. Class B stations cover the heavily populated northeastern part of the United States (Zone 1) and Southern California below the 40th parallel, Puerto Rico and the Virgin Islands in Zone 1-A. A Class B station is restricted to 50 kilowatts of erp and an antenna height of not more than 500 feet above the terrain. Minimum erp is 5 kilowatts.

A Class C station renders service to a community and a large surrounding Area in Zone II. Zone II covers the less populated areas consisting of Alaska, Hawaii and the area of the United States not included in Zone I. A Class C station is limited to a maximum erp of 100 kW at an antenna height of 2000 feet above average terrain. Minimum erp is 25 kW.

Class D stations are noncommercial educational fm stations. The maximum power output allowed is 10 watts. Class D stations may be assigned to any of the first 20 channels listed in Table 2-2 (Channels 201 through 220).

2-4. TELEVISION BROADCAST

Television broadcast assignments are made on three bands: 54-88 MHz (low-band vhf), 174-216 MHz (high-band vhf), and 470-890 MHz (uhf). As shown in Table 2-3, there are 82 television channels, 12 for vhf and 70 for uhf. Each channel is 6 MHz wide. To provide a more uniform signal level for all channels in a given area, their maximum power output is restricted as follows:

Channels	Effective Radiated Power
2-6	100 kW (20 dBk)
7-13	316 kW (25 dBk)
14-83	5000 kW (37 dBk)

The abbreviation *dBk* refers to the power output related to an output of 100 watts. For example, an output of 100 kW is 20-dBk greater (power-ratio gain of 100) than an output of 1 kW (0 dBk).

Any one of the twelve vhf channels (2-13 inclusive) may be assigned to vhf translator use on the condition that no interference is caused to the direct reception of any television broadcast station. Vhf translator stations for any one of the twelve channels can be allocated for transmitting signal into an area where direct reception of the television-broadcast station is unsatisfactory due to distance or terrain barriers. There are various restrictions as to their use. For example, they can only be assigned if no interference is caused to the direct reception of any television broadcast station operating on the same or an adjacent channel. They will not be authorized to serve an area which is receiving satisfactory service from one or more uhf television stations or uhf translators. Uhf translators with 100-watt peak visual power are assigned to channels 55 through 69.

The upper 14 uhf channels, 70-83 inclusive, were formerly assigned to television translator stations. The FCC has now reallocated these channels to land mobile service. At the present time, the license of these translators is to be renewed only on a "secondary" basis. Channel 37 is reserved exclusively for radio astronomy services.

Television translator stations are operated for the purpose of retransmitting the signals from a television broadcast or another trans-

Table 2-3. Television Channels and Frequency Bands

Freq (MHz)	Channel	Freq (MHz)	Channel
LOW-BAND VHF		**UHF BAND (Cont.)**	
54-60	2	638-644	42
60-66	3	644-650	43
66-72	4	650-656	44
76-82	5	656-662	45
82-88	6	662-668	46
HIGH-BAND VHF		668-674	47
174-180	7	674-680	48
180-186	8	680-686	49
186-192	9	686-692	50
192-198	10	692-698	51
198-204	11	698-704	52
204-210	12	704-710	53
210-216	13	710-716	54
UHF BAND		716-722	55
470-476	14	722-728	56
476-482	15	728-734	57
482-488	16	734-740	58
488-494	17	740-746	59
494-500	18	746-752	60
500-506	19	752-758	61
506-512	20	758-764	62
512-518	21	764-770	63
518-524	22	770-776	64
524-530	23	776-782	65
530-536	24	782-788	66
536-542	25	788-794	67
542-548	26	794-800	68
548-554	27	800-806	69
554-560	28	806-812	70
560-566	29	812-818	71
566-572	30	818-824	72
572-578	31	824-830	73
578-584	32	830-836	74
584-590	33	836-842	75
590-596	34	842-848	76
596-602	35	848-854	77
602-608	36	854-860	78
608-614	37	860-866	79
614-620	38	866-872	80
620-626	39	872-878	81
626-632	40	878-884	82
632-638	41	884-890	83

lator station into an isolated or remote area. This is done by direct frequency conversion and amplification of the incoming signal, without significantly altering any of its characteristics other than frequency and amplitude. In certain geographical locations and on specified channels, translator stations are restricted to peak visual powers of 100 watts vhf, 1000 watts uhf.

Uhf translator signal boosters can be used for retransmitting of uhf translator signals to provide reception to small-shadowed areas within the allotted primary-station service area. The maximum power output cannot exceed five watts.

Vhf and uhf translators and uhf translator boosters cannot be operated in a manner that will cause harmful interference to the reception of other primary commercial or noncommercial stations and the translators of these stations.

In the 6-MHz television channel it is necessary to allocate space for both the picture and the sound signal components. As shown in Fig. 2-1, the picture carrier is positioned 1.25 MHz from the low-frequency end of the assigned television channel, and the sound carrier is 0.25 MHz below the high-frequency end. Note that the upper sideband of the video channel is substantially broader than the lower sideband. This technique, called vestigial-sideband transmission, permits the sending of a high-definition picture in a 6-MHz channel. Thus, video-frequency components of up to 4 MHz and even higher can be transmitted in a channel only 6 MHz wide.

In the transmission of a color picture, a subcarrier is employed to convey the color hue and saturation information. Its position in the bandpass spectrum is also shown in Fig. 2-1. Brightness detail and picture definition of the televised scene are conveyed by the picture carrier.

2-5. AUXILIARY BROADCAST SERVICES

There are several additional broadcast services useful in the pickup and relay of audio and visual programming signals.

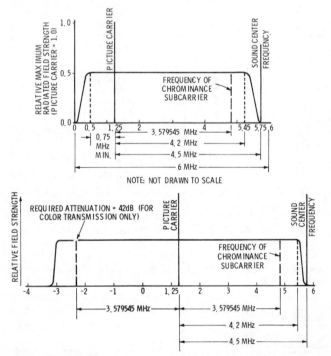

Fig. 2-1. FCC idealized picture transmission amplitude characteristic.

Remote-pickup (am) broadcast stations are used for relaying remote program material. The station (fixed base or mobile) license will specify the maximum authorized power. The allotted power will be no more than required for satisfactory service in the specified frequency band. For the frequency allocations of this service see Table 2-4.

An *aural (am) broadcast stl station* (studio-to-transmitter link) is a fixed-base station for aural transmission between the studio and a remote primary transmitter (other than the transmitter of an international broadcast station). The power limitations are the same as for the remote-pickup (am) station. For frequency allocations, see Table 2-4.

Aural (am) broadcast intercity relay stations retransmit an aural program between two broadcast stations. The same limitations apply to this station as for the aural (am) stl station.

Television remote-pickup stations transmit program material and related communications from a remote to the primary television broadcast station. A *television stl station* transmits program and related communications from a fixed-base remote station to the primary television broadcast transmitter. A *television intercity relay station* retransmits the program and related communications between two television stations. These three categories of stations use the frequencies tabulated in Table 2-4. The license for any one of three types will specify a maximum authorized power that is sufficient for satisfactory service in the

Table 2-4. Auxiliary Broadcast Allocations

Service	Group	Frequencies (MHz unless otherwise specified)
Remote Broadcast Pickup	A	1606 kHz, 1622 kHz, 1646 kHz
	D	25.87, 26.15, 26.25, 26.35
	E	25.91, 26.17, 26.27, 26.37
	F	25.95, 26.19, 26.29, 26.39
	G	25.99, 26.21, 26.31, 26.41
	H	26.03, 26.23, 26.33, 26.43
	I	26.07, 26.11, 26.45
	J	26.09, 26.13, 26.47
	K	152.87, 152.93, 152.99, 153.05, 153.11, 153.17, 153.23, 153.29, 153.35, 161.64, 161.67, 161.70, 161.73, 161.76
	L	166.25
	M	170.15
	N, P, R, S	Assignments are made in the 450-MHz band
Aural Broadcast Studio Transmitter Link (stl)		947.0, 947.5, 948.0, 948.5, 949.0, 949.5, 950.0, 950.5, 951.0, 951.5
Television Remote Pickup, Television stl, Television Intercity Relay	Band A	1990 TO 2500 MHz
	B	6875 TO 7125 MHz
	C	12700 TO 13250 MHz

allotted frequency band. Power cannot exceed 10 percent of the maximum power specified in the station license.

A *television broadcast translator station* is a fixed station that retransmits the initial television program on a different carrier frequency and has been described previously in this chapter under television broadcast stations. A *television broadcast booster station* retransmits the signal of a primary television broadcast station by amplifying and reradiating the incoming signal on the same carrier frequency.

CHAPTER 3

Broadcast Duties and Facilities

This handbook will stress the small am, fm, combination am/fm and tv stations because they outnumber the larger ones, and your chances initially of being employed in a small station are therefore much greater. However, the difference between a large and a small station is a matter of degree; in terms of employment the technical responsibilities initially are not likely to differ to any great extent. So, a thorough knowledge of small-station operation will be of benefit, whether you are employed by a small or a large station.

3-1. LICENSE REQUIREMENTS

Broadcast stations must be operated by persons with a restricted radiotelephone operator's permit or a commercial radio operator license. One operator with the required knowledge and skill must be designated as the chief operator. His responsibility is to keep the station's technical operation in compliance with FCC rules and the terms of the station authorization. The maintenance, repair and measurements of broadcast transmitting equipment are the responsibility of the chief operator and such work must be done by, or under the supervision of, the designated chief operator or another licensed operator designated temporarily when the chief operator is unavailable.

The duty operator must be able to observe and monitor transmitter operations and able to make the necessary adjustments from the normal duty position. It is the responsibility of the station licensee to ensure that each transmitter operator is fully instructed and is capable of performing the associated operator duties that ensure compliance with FCC Rules and Regulations. Such duty operators may perform other station duties provided they do not interfere with the proper operation of the broadcast system.

Typical duty operator observation and/or adjustments involve the following:

1. Those necessary to turn the transmitter on and off.
2. Those necessary to compensate for voltage fluctuations in the primary power supply.

3. Those necessary to maintain modulation levels of the transmitter within prescribed limits.
4. Those necessary to effect routine changes in operating power which are required by the station authorization.
5. Those necessary to change between nondirectional and directional, or between differing radiation patterns, provided that such changes require only activation of switches and do not involve the manual tuning of the transmitter's final amplifier or antenna phasor equipment. The switching equipment shall be so arranged that the failure of any relay in the directional antenna system to activate properly will cause the emissions of the station to terminate.

The operator shall be on duty at the transmitter location, at an authorized remote-control point, or the position at which extension meters are located. The transmitter and required monitors and metering equipment, or the required extension meters and monitoring equipment and other required metering equipment, or the controls and required monitoring and metering equipment in an authorized remote control operation shall be readily accessible to the licensed operator and located sufficiently close to the normal operating locations that deviations from normal indications of required instruments can be observed from that location.

It is the responsibility of the station licensee to ensure that each operator is fully instructed in the performance of all the above adjustments, as well as in the other required duties, such as reading meters and making log entries. Appropriate instructions are usually the responsibility of the chief operator. Printed step-by-step instructions for those adjustments which the lesser-grade operator is permitted to make, and a tabulation or chart of upper and lower limiting values of parameters required to be observed and logged, shall be posted at the operating position.

Some of the responsibilities of the chief operator are the inspection and maintenance on a scheduled basis of the transmitting system including the antenna system and required monitoring equipment, the accuracy and completeness of entries in the maintenance log, as well as the supervision and instruction of all other station operators in the performance of their technical duties. He must make a review of operating logs to ensure compliance with the rules and terms of the station authorization. If the review of any operating log indicates a violation of the rules or terms of the station authorization he must promptly initiate corrective action. Excerpts from important FCC rules and regulations are given at the end of the chapter.

3-2. STATION LOGS

Each broadcast station must maintain program, operating, and maintenance logs. Logs must be kept by persons competent to do so, having actual knowledge of the facts required. The person keeping them must sign the log when going on duty and again when going off duty. They must be kept in an orderly and legible manner in accordance with established procedure and must be made available on request of an authorized representative of the Federal Communications Commission. No portion of the log shall be erased or otherwise obliterated, nor shall the log be destroyed for a two-year period. When the log contains information concerning a disaster or a complaint, it is retained until notified by the FCC. Only the person making the original entry in the log can correct that entry; he does this by crossing out the error, initialing the correction, and indicating the date of the correction.

Operating Log—The operating log is almost always maintained by the operator on duty at the transmitter; sometimes the operator on duty also keeps the program log as well. In other stations the program log is kept by studio and program personnel. Operating log samples are shown in Figs. 3-1 and 3-2. Entries in the operating log are made either manually by a properly licensed operator in charge of the transmitting apparatus, or by automatic devices meeting all FCC requirements. Automatic devices must be accurately calibrated and provide appropriate indications of time, date, and circuit functions. (See also Section 3-5 of this chapter.) Indications of existing operating parameters must be logged prior to any adjustment of the equipment. Where adjustments are made to restore parameters to their proper operating values, the corrected indications are logged and, if any parameter deviation was beyond a prescribed tolerance, the log entry must be accompanied by a notation describing the nature of the correction action. Indications of all parameters whose values are affected by modulation of the carrier must be read without modulation applied. The actual time of observation is included in each log entry. The operating log contains the following entries for all stations:

1. Entries of the time the station begins to supply power to the antenna and the time it ceases to do so.
2. Entries governed by FCC requirements concerning the daily observations of tower lights.
3. Any entries not specifically required in this section, but required by the instrument of authorization or elsewhere in this part.
4. An entry of each test of the emergency broadcast system unless such entries are consistently made in the station program log.

Particular entries for am broadcast stations include the operating constants for determining the dc input power to the last radio-frequency power amplifier, antenna current for nondirectional operation, or common-point current for the directional operation. Such entries must be made at the beginning of operations in each mode of operation and thereafter at intervals not exceeding three hours. Other factors that must be entered are the antenna monitor phase or phase deviation indications for a directional broadcast antenna as well as antenna monitor sample currents, current ratios, or ratio deviation indications.

Fm stations must log the operating constants for determining the dc input power to the last radio-frequency power amplifier of the transmitter and the rf transmission line meter readings when transmitter operating power is determined by the direct method. Entries

RADIO STATION

5000 WATTS D D

1310 KHZ

W G S A

EPHRATA, PA.

DATE:

DAY:

OPERATING CONSTANTS

TIME EST EDT	Frequency Deviation Hertz	Final Ip. Amps.	Final Ep. Volts	Common Point Current	Phase ° Ant 1 : 2	Phase ° Ant 3 : 2	Sampling Loop Ant. 1	Sampling Loop Ant. 2	Sampling Loop Ant. 3

Fig. 3-1. Am

ANTENNA SYSTEM OPERATION

Base Currents

Ant 1 _____ Amps   Ratio 1:2 _____   Deviation 1:2 _____ %
Ant 2 _____ Amps   Ratio 3:2 _____   Deviation 3:2 _____ %
Ant 3 _____ Amps

Remote Currents

Ant 1 _____ Amps   Ratio 1:2 _____   Deviation 1:2 _____ %
Ant 2 _____ Amps   Ratio 3:2 _____   Deviation 3:2 _____ %
Ant 3 _____ Amps

Common Point Current _____   Calibration Time _____   Signature _____

OPERATOR'S SIGNATURE

On _____   Off _____   Carrier On: _____
              Off _____   Program On: _____
On _____   Off _____   Program Off: _____
On _____   Off _____   Carrier Off: _____
                             Log Checked: _____

station operating log.

RADIO STATION   EPHRATA, PA.

50,000 WATTS E.R.P.
HORIZONTAL & VERTICAL   DATE:

105.1 MHZ   DAY:

OPERATING CONSTANTS

Time EST EDT	Frequency Deviation Hz	Pa Plate I Amps	Pa Plate E Volts	% Power Output

STEREOPHONIC OPERATION

Sub Carrier On	PGM on
Sub Carrier Off	PGM off
Sub Carrier On	PGM on
Sub Carrier Off	PGM off
Sub Carrier On	PGM on
Sub Carrier Off	PGM off

Pilot Frequency Deviation:

_____ Hz at _____
_____ Hz at _____
_____ Hz at _____
_____ Hz at _____

SCA OPERATION (67 KHz)

Sub Carrier On	PGM on
Sub Carrier Off	PGM off

Fig. 3-2. Fm

Sub Carrier On — PGM on

Sub Carrier Off — PGM off

Sub Carrier On — PGM on

Sub Carrier Off — PGM off

Sub Carrier Freq. Deviation:
_____ Hz at
_____ Hz at
_____ Hz at
_____ Hz at

Carrier On: _____

Program On: _____

Program Off: _____

Carrier Off: _____

Carrier On: _____

Program On: _____

Program Off: _____

Carrier Off: _____

Tower Light Checked: On _____ Off _____

Log Checked: On _____ Off _____

On _____ Off _____

On _____ Off _____

OPERATOR'S SIGNATURE

station operating log.

must be made at the beginning of operation and at intervals not exceeding three hours.

In the operation of a television station, similar entries must be made at the beginning of operation, and at intervals not exceeding three hours. These include the operating constants for determining the dc input power to the last radio-frequency power amplifier for the aural transmitter and transmission-line meter readings for both the visual and aural transmitters.

A maintenance log must be kept by the licensee of each broadcast station. Entries must be made by or under the supervision of the chief operator. Entries for all stations must include the time and result of auxiliary transmitter tests, calibration check of automatic logging devices, carrier frequency measurements and methods, calibration of extension meters, calibration of indicating instruments at remote control points against the corresponding instruments of the transmitter site, quarterly inspections of the condition of tower lights and associated control equipment, and entries that describe fully any experimental operation.

An entry must be made concerning the date and time of removal from and restoration to service of modulation monitor; transmission-system meter, which is required to be entered in the operating log; and devices for monitoring or generating the EBS attention signal.

In addition, am stations must make entries regarding a variety of antenna-system measurements including calibration checks of remote-reading antenna and common-point ammeters, as well as antenna monitors. For directional antennas, scheduled field-strength measurements must be made and the results entered in the log.

Fm stations must make log entries concerning the calibration of the transmission-line meter used for determining operating power. In addition appropriate subcarrier frequency measurements must be made and recorded for stereophonic and SCA operations.

Entries that must be made by tv stations also include time and date of removal from, and restoration to, service of the visual modulation monitoring equipment and calibration of the transmission line meters used for determining the operating power. In all cases when entries of appropriate maintenance procedures are made it is necessary that the operator sign and date them. More detailed FCC excerpts are given at end of chapter.

3-3. BROADCAST STATION LAYOUT

There are three small broadcast station arrangements. In one arrangement the studio and transmitter can share a common site. In another arrangement the transmitter is separated from the studio. An interconnecting telephone program line links the two. There is an operator on duty at the transmitter site. A third possible arrangement consists of a separate studio and transmitter, with the transmitter being controlled remotely from the studio. In this case the transmitter is unattended and is operated from a studio position.

Three small-station plans as suggested by RCA are given in Figs. 3-3,

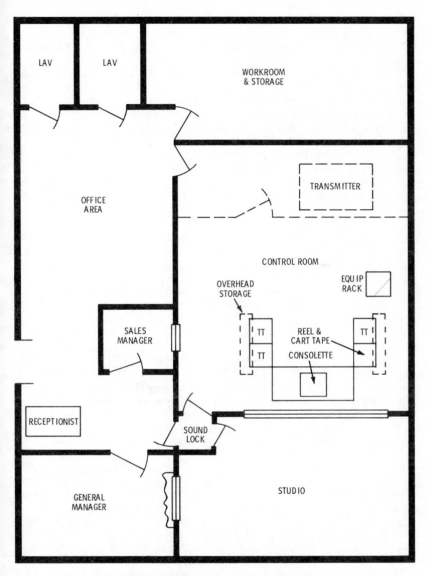

Fig. 3-3. Small broadcast station layout.

3-4 and 3-5. In the plans of Figs. 3-3 and 3-4, the transmitter is part of the studio and control-room facilities. In Fig. 3-5 the transmitter has a different location.

The arrangement of Fig. 3-3 is very compact, with all essential operating equipment located in the control room. The control-room personnel operate the transmitter, make announcements, spin records, play tapes, etc. The equipment rack to the left of the consolette contains the transmitter monitoring equipment. The transmitter itself can be viewed from the control room and its meters are read through a glass pane.

Most small radio broadcast stations do employ a full-time chief operator. Except in a very limited operation, he is excused from spinning records, playing tapes and making announcements. Nevertheless he probably had to do so at one time, so it would not hurt your chances of breaking into broadcasting if you know how to operate various audio devices and do some limited announcing.

Larger stations have a more decided break between program and technical personnel. In such stations the license holder is assigned technical and operating assignments only, but this is no guarantee that he will not be called on, in an emergency, to sub for an ailing "disc jockey," or "tape jockey," or announcer.

In addition to the audio control console or consolette there are turntables and various reel and cartridge tape players and recorders. There is a single studio that can be viewed through a window from the consolette operating position. Some live programming is possible, such as interviews and small discussion groups.

The control-room operator switches and otherwise controls the studio microphones, regulating the absolute and relative amplitudes of the various signals arriving at the console (called "riding the gain"). He is able to observe all studio activities through a soundproof monitoring window.

All station switching operations—changeovers from local announcements, network programs, taped or recorded material, local studio programs, etc.—are made from the console in accordance with the program schedule of the station. If the control-room operator is the only technical person on duty, he is also responsible for the operating logs.

One-man operation of this type, although not uncommon, especially in smaller stations, usually occurs during the late evening and other less active hours when more or less continuous records or tape programs are broadcast. Many modern stations are equipped with automatic record and tape players, and even spot announcements are pretaped or prerecorded and cut in automatically or by pushbutton operation.

A more elaborate studio plan is given in Fig. 3-4. The studio is larger, and there is a separate record room and library containing an audition turntable for previewing records and setting up the program continuity. There is also a separate announce studio.

There is a main control room and a production control room. The main control room contains the consolette, turntables, and tape equipment, plus an equipment rack which is used for the transmitter monitoring gear.

The production control room is used to preview recorded tapes, news, spot announcements, special promotions, commercials, etc., for future broadcast. Inasmuch as the audio equipment in the production control room is identical to that of the main control room, it can serve as an alternate on-the-air control room.

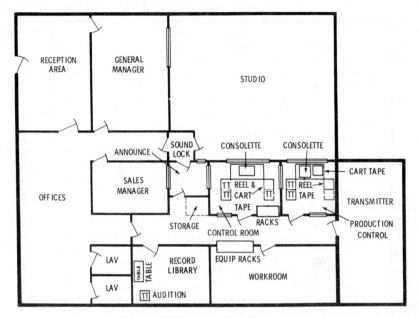

Fig. 3-4. Alternative small station plan.

The station plan of Fig. 3-5 is appropriate for a small am/fm facility. There are separate control rooms for am and fm programming. The equipment lineup is similar, including racks for mounting separate transmitter monitoring equipment or other audio and studio test equipment. Transmitter monitoring equipment is necessary if the station employs unattended remote-control operation. There are separate announce booths and production control rooms and other facilities that can be accommodated by a much larger floor area.

When the studio and transmitter plant are separated from each other and there is a licensed operator on duty at the transmitter, it is not compulsory for the technical personnel of the studio to be licensed. However, the maintenance of the studio equipment and other technical facilities is usually the responsibility of the licensed technical personnel of the station, and in many cases, the control room operator is licensed. Often the technical personnel are rotated between studio and transmitter to give each person an overall background of station operation and equipment.

The transmitter is located at the antenna site. If the antenna is mounted atop a tall building, the transmitter is often located on one of the upper floors. More often the transmitter is located near or outside the city limits. A location is usually chosen to obtain the best coverage. Where feasible, fm antennas and the transmitter building are located on a mountain top, again from the standpoint of securing additional coverage. The audio signals are normally conveyed over common carrier wires between the studio and transmitter. In some installa-

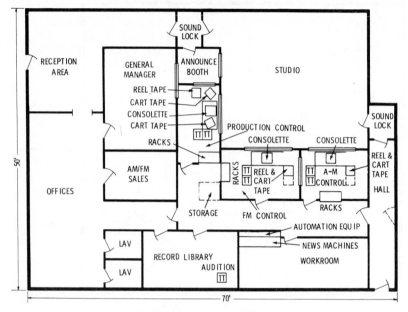

Fig. 3-5. An am/fm studio plan.

tions, especially when the transmitter is on a mountain top or other remote location, a studio-transmitter radio-link operating in the uhf or microwave portion of the radio spectrum is employed.

A suggested transmitter floor plan appears in Fig. 3-6. The transmitter building need not be very large, since it houses only the transmitter and associated equipment, along with the operating personnel. In a separate transmitter building, a licensed operator is usually on duty during air time.

The phasing cabinet in the transmitter floor plan of Fig. 3-6 is not required when the antenna is not directional. The cabinet houses the circuitry that supplies currents of the proper amplitude and phase to the various transmitting towers of a directional antenna system.

The transmitter can be an am or fm type, or a combination of both as in Fig. 3-6. Only a single operator must be on duty.

3-4. REMOTE TRANSMITTER CONTROL

When the transmitter and studio are not in the same room or under the same roof, it is permissible to operate the transmitter by remote control. However, the following stipulations must be met when remote transmitter equipment is attended:

1. The equipment at the operating (studio) and transmitting locations must be so installed and confined that it is accessible only to authorized personnel.

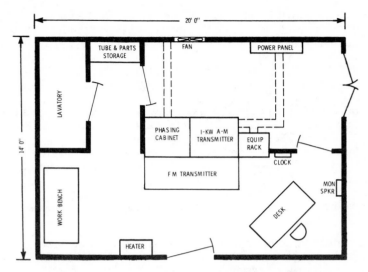

Fig. 3-6. Transmitter floor plan and equipment arrangement.

2. The control circuits from the operating to the transmitting location must provide positive on-and-off control. That is, open or short circuits, grounds, or other line faults must not actuate the transmitter. Moreover, any defect causing such loss of control must automatically "kill" the transmitter.

3. If any part of the remote-control equipment or associated line circuits results in improper control or inaccurate meter reading, the remote-control transmitter operation must cease.

4. All control and monitoring equipment must be so installed that the licensed operator at the remote-control point can perform his functions in an FCC-approved manner.

5. Calibration of required indicating instruments at each remote-control point shall be made against their corresponding instruments at the transmitter site for each mode of operation as often as necessary to ensure their accuracy, but in no event less than once a week. Results must be entered in the station's maintenance log.

6. Remote-control meters shall conform with the specifications prescribed for regular transmitter, antenna, and monitor meters.

7. The negative percentage of modulation indications of the modulation monitor shall be continuously available at the remote-control point.

The broadcast transmitter carrier may be amplitude modulated with a tone for the purpose of transmitting to the remote control point essential meter indications and other data on the operational condition of the broadcast transmitter and associated devices, subject to the following conditions:

1. The tone shall have a frequency no higher than 30 hertz.
2. The amplitude of modulation of the carrier by the tone shall not be higher than necessary to effect reliable and accurate data transmission, and shall not, in any case, exceed 6 percent.
3. The tone shall be transmitted only at such times and during such intervals that the transmitted information is actually being observed or logged.
4. Measures shall be employed to ensure that during the periods the tone is being transmitted the total modulation of the carrier does not exceed 100 percent on negative peaks.
5. Such tone transmissions shall not significantly degrade the quality of program transmission or produce audible effects resulting in public annoyance.
6. Such tone transmissions shall not result in emissions of such a nature as to result in greater interference to other stations that is produced by normal program modulation.

All stations, whether operating by remote control or direct control, shall be equipped so as to be able to follow the procedures of the emergency broadcast system.

A digital remote-control system comprises the control system at the studio or operating point (Fig. 3-7) and a second unit installed at the transmitter which is used for the actual metering and control of transmitter parameters. The link can be by means of telephone lines or a studio/transmitter microwave link.

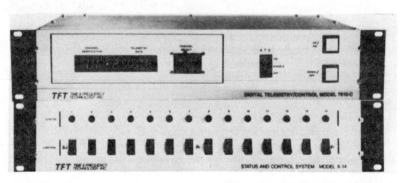

Courtesy Time and Frequency Technology, Inc.

Fig. 3-7. Remote control system.

The TFT system is basically a 10-channel digital system with raise/lower functions and 10 channels of telemetry information. Individual channels are selected using a thumb-wheel switch. Once selected, the channel number is fed back to the control point and displayed on the front panel for verification. The appropriate meter reading is then displayed in digital form. System meter readings are updated three times per second. Control commands can be initiated by pushing the appropriate *raise* or *lower* button on the front panel.

The row of switches and LED indicators at the bottom of the control unit provide direct control of 15 different functions, such as filament voltage, plate voltage, main power, tower lights, program source selection, etc. This is possible without the need for dialing the activities in one at a time. Commands are initiated by the toggle switches. In addition there are fifteen status channels, each with its own independent LED indicator. These can monitor power, voltages, temperatures, intrusion, standing-wave ratio, etc. A built-in beeper alerts the operator if there is an alarm.

3-5. AUTOMATIC LOGGING

Automatic transmitter and program logging has become increasingly popular. Program logging can be handled with tapes and other means acceptable to the FCC. Some highly automatic systems include automatic program switching and automatic control of program continuity along with automatic program logging.

An automatic operating-log recorder must record the transmitter meter readings specified by the license. Accurately calibrated automatic recorders with appropriate time, date, and circuit functions may be utilized to record the entries in the operating log, provided:

1. They do not affect the circuit operation or the indicating instrument accuracy of the equipment being recorded.
2. The recording devices have an accuracy equivalent to the accuracy of the indicating instruments.
3. The calibration is checked against the original indicators at least once a week, and the results obtained from these checks are noted in the maintenance log.
4. Provision is made to actuate automatically an aural alarm circuit located near the operator on duty if any of the automatic log readings are not within the tolerance or other requirements specified in the rules or the instrument of authorization.
5. Unless the alarm circuit operates continuously, devices which record each parameter in sequence must read each parameter at least once during each 30-minute period and clearly indicate the parameter being recorded.
6. The automatic logging equipment is located at the remote control point if the transmitter is remotely controlled, or at the transmitter location if the transmitter is directly controlled.
7. The automatic logging equipment is located in the near vicinity of the operator on duty and is inspected by him periodically during the broadcast day.
8. The indicating equipment conforms with the FCC specifications for indicating instruments, except that the scale need not exceed two inches in length and arbitrary scales may not be used.

3-6. AUTOMATIC TRANSMISSION SYSTEMS (ATS)

The FCC has approved the use of automatic transmission systems. Such a system is self-operating and makes routine observations of transmitter performance. Furthermore it automatically adjusts the transmitter with regard to critical operating parameters. In case of a serious malfunction it will shut down the transmitter. It is required that the transmitting apparatus must be manually activated at the beginning of each broadcast day and operating with a nondirectional antenna system.

The control system must have devices to monitor and control the antenna input power by sampling and evaluating the antenna current. Automatic devices must be included to adjust the antenna input power to the authorized power of each mode of operation within the specified range. If the automatic control device is unable to adjust the antenna input power to a level below 105 percent of the authorized power after three minutes, or a total of three samplings, the emissions of the station will terminate. The ATS system must have a device that will detect and adjust the peak level of modulation. If the modulation exceeds more than 10 bursts of 100-percent negative modulation within a one minute period, or any burst exceeds 125-percent positive modulation as measured at the output terminals of the transmitter, the program audio input signal to the transmitter modulators shall be automatically adjusted downward until these limits are not exceeded.

If a station is authorized or required to operate at more than one antenna input power, or is restricted in its hours of operation, the ATS control equipment must include a timeclock to automatically prevent the station from being signed on prior to the authorized time, perform all required mode-switching operations, and terminate the transmitter radiations at the required time. The system must be designed to provide an alarm signal at an authorized monitoring and alarm point.

The automatic transmission system must incorporate fail-safe transmitter control as related to excessive power output, excessive modulation levels, failure of the mode-switching timeclock, failure of the required alarm system functions or ATS monitoring and alarm point circuits, and loss of ATS sampling functions. The transmitter must shut down automatically if any of the above troubles exist for a period exceeding three minutes.

3-7. EXCERPTS FROM FCC RULES AND REGULATIONS

§ 73.1860   Transmitter duty operators.

(a) Each AM, FM, and TV broadcast station must have at least one person holding a commercial radio operator license or permit of any class except a Marine Radio Operator Permit on duty in charge of the transmitter during all periods of broadcast operation. The operator must be on duty at the transmitter location, a remote control point, an ATS monitor and alarm point, or a position where extension meters are installed under the provisions of § 73.1550.

(b) The transmitter operator must be able to observe the required transmitter and monitor metering to determine deviations from normal indications. The operator must also be able to make the necessary adjustments from the normal operator duty position, except as provided for in § 73.1550.

(c) It is the responsibility of the station licensee to ensure that each transmitter operator is fully instructed and capable to perform all necessary observations and adjustments of the transmitting system and other associated operating duties to ensure compliance with the rules and station authorization.

(d) The transmitter duty operator may, at the discretion of the station licensee and chief operator, be employed for other duties or operation of other transmitting stations if such other duties will not interfere with the proper operation of the broadcast transmission system.

§ 73.1870 Chief operators.

(a) The licensee of each AM, FM, and TV broadcast station must designate a person holding a commercial radio operator license of any class other than a Marine Radio Operator Permit to serve as the station's chief operator. At times when the chief operator is unavailable or unable to act (e.g., vacations, sickness), the licensee shall designate another licensed operator as the acting chief operator on a temporary basis.

(b) Chief operators shall be employed or serve on the following basis:

(1) The chief operator for an AM station using a directional antenna or operating with greater than 10 kW authorized power, or of a TV station is to be an employee of the station on duty for whatever number of hours each week the station licensee determines is necessary to keep the station's technical operation in compliance with FCC rules and the terms of the station authorization.

(2) Chief operators for non-directional AM stations operating with authorized powers not exceeding 10 kW and FM stations may be either an employee of the station or engaged to serve on a contract basis for whatever number of hours each week the licensee determines is necessary to keep the station's technical operation in compliance with the FCC rules and terms of the station authorization.

(3) The designation of the chief operator must be in writing with a copy of the designation posted with the operator license. Agreements with chief operators serving on a contract basis must be in writing with a copy kept in the station files.

(c) The chief operator has the following specific duties:

(1) Conduct weekly (or monthly for stations using automatic transmission systems) inspections and calibrations of the transmission system, required monitors, metering, and control systems; and make any necessary repairs or adjustments where indicated. (See § 73.1580.)

(2) Make or supervise periodic am field monitoring point measurements, equipment performance measurements, or other tests as specified in the rules or terms of the station license.

(3) Review the station operating logs at least once each week as part of the transmission system inspections to determine if the entries are being made correctly or if the station has been operating as required by the rules or the station authorization. Upon completion of the review, the chief operator is to make a notation of any discrepancies observed and date and sign the log, initiate necessary corrective action, and advise the station licensee of any condition which is a repetitive problem.

(4) Make or supervise entries in the maintenance log. (See § 73.1830.)

§ 73.1800 General requirements relating to logs.

(a) The licensee of each station shall maintain logs as set forth in §§ 73.1810, 73.1820 and 73.1830. Each log shall be kept by the station employee or employees (or contract operator) competent to do so, having actual knowledge of the facts required. The person keeping the log must make entries that accurately reflect the operation of the station. In the case of program and operating logs, the employee shall sign the appropriate log when starting duty and again when going off duty and setting forth the time of each. In the case of maintenance logs, the employee shall sign the log upon completion of the required maintenance and inspection entries. When the employee keeping a program or operating log signs it upon going off duty or completing maintenance log entries, that person attests to the fact that the log, with any corrections or additions made before it was signed, is an accurate representation of what transpired.

(b) The logs shall be kept in an orderly and legible manner, in suitable form and in such detail that the data required for the particular class of station concerned are readily available. Key letters or abbreviations may be used if proper meaning or explanation is contained elsewhere in the log. Each sheet shall be numbered and dated. Time entries shall be made in local time and shall be indicated as advanced (e.g., EDT) or non-advanced time (e.g., EST).

(c) Any necessary corrections of a manually kept log after it has been signed in accordance with (a) above shall be made only by striking out the erroneous portion and making a corrective explanation on the log or attachment to it. For program logs, such corrections shall be dated and signed by the person who kept the log or the program director, or the station manager or an officer of the licensee. For operating and maintenance logs, such corrections shall be dated and signed by the person who kept the log or the station technical supervisor, the station manager, or an officer of the licensee.

(d) No automatically kept log shall be altered in any way after entries have been recorded. When automatic logging processes fail or malfunction, the log must be kept manually for that period and in accordance with the requirements of this Section.

(e) No log, or portion thereof, shall be erased, obliterated or willfully destroyed during the period in which it is required to be retained. (§ 73.1840, Retention of logs.)

(f) Entries shall be made in the logs as required by §§ 73.1810, 73.1820 and 73.1830. Additional information such as that needed for administrative or operational purposes may be entered on the logs. Such additional information, so entered, shall not be subject to the restrictions and limitations in the FCC's rules on the making of corrections and changes in logs and may be physically removed, without otherwise altering the log in any way, before making the log a part of an application or available for public inspection.

(g) The operating log and the maintenance log may be kept individually on the same sheet in one common log, at the option of the licensee.

(h) Application forms for licenses and other authorizations require that certain operating and program data be supplied. These application forms should be kept in mind in connection with maintenance of station program and operating records.

§ 73.1820   Operating logs.

(a) Entries shall be made in the operating log either manually by a properly licensed operator in actual charge of the transmitting apparatus, or by automatic devices meeting the requirements of paragraph (b) of this Section. Indications of operating parameters shall be logged prior to any adjustment of the equipment. Where adjustments are made to restore parameters to their proper operating values, the corrected indications shall be logged and accompanied, if any parameter deviation was beyond a prescribed tolerance, by a notation describing the nature of the corrective action. Indications of all parameters whose values are affected by modulation of the carrier shall be read without modulation. The actual time of observation shall be included in each log entry. The following information must be entered.

(1) *All stations:*

(i) Entries of the time the station begins to supply power to the antenna and the time it ceases to do so.

(ii) Entries required by § 17.49(a), (b) and (c) of this Chapter concerning the time the tower lights are turned on and off each day if manually controlled, the time the daily check of proper operation of the tower lights was made if an automatic alarm system is not used, and any observed failure of the lighting system. See § 17.47(a) for daily tower lighting observation or automatic alarm system requirements.

(iii) Any entries not specifically required in this Section, but required by the instrument of authorization or elsewhere in this Part.

(iv) An entry of each test of the Emergency Broadcast System procedures pursuant to the requirements of Subpart G of this Part and the appropriate station EBS checklist, unless such entries are consistently made in the station Program Log.

(2) *AM stations:*

(i) An entry at the beginning of operations in each mode of operation, and thereafter at intervals not exceeding 3 hours, of the following (actual readings observed prior to making any adjustments to the equipment and an indication of any corrections to restore parameters to normal operating values);

(A) Operating constants for determining the DC input power to the last radio frequency power amplifier stage of the transmitter (plate voltage and current or other parameters appropriate for the type of amplifier used).

(B) Antenna current for nondirectional operation or common point current for directional operation.

(ii) When the operating power is determined by the indirect method, the efficiency factor F and either the product of the final amplifier input voltage and current or the calculated antenna input power. See § 73.51(e).

(iii) For stations with directional antennas, the following additional indications shall be read and entered in the Operating Log at the time of commencement of operation in each mode and thereafter, at successive intervals not exceeding 3 hours in duration:

(A) Antenna monitor phase or phase deviation indications.

(B) Antenna monitor sample currents, current ratios, or ratio deviation indications.

(3) *FM stations:*

(i) For each station licensed for transmitter output power greater than 10 watts, an entry, at the beginning of operation and at intervals not exceeding 3 hours, of the following (actual readings observed prior to making any adjustments to the equipment and an indication of any corrections made to restore parameters to normal operation values):

(A) Operating constants for determining the DC input power to the last radio frequency power amplifier stage of the transmitter (plate voltage and current or other parameters appropriate for the type of amplifier used).

(B) RF transmission line meter readings when the transmitter operating power is determined by the direct method.

(4) *TV stations:*

(i) An entry at the beginning of operation and at intervals not exceeding 3 hours, of the following (actual readings observed prior to making any adjustments to the equipment and an indication of any corrections to restore parameters to normal operating values):

(A) Operating constants for determining the DC input power to the last radio frequency power amplifier stage of the aural transmitter (plate voltage and current or other parameters appropriate for the type of amplifier used) if power of the aural transmitter is being determined by the indirect method.

(B) RF transmission line meter readings for visual transmitter, and also for the aural transmitter when the aural transmitter operating power is determined by the direct method.

(b) Automatic devices accurately calibrated and with appropriate time, date and circuit functions may be utilized to record the entries in the operating log provided:

(1) The recording devices do not affect the operation of circuits or accuracy of indicating instruments of the equipment being recorded;

(2) The recording devices have an accuracy equivalent to the accuracy of the indicating instruments;

(3) The calibration is checked against the original indicators at least once each calendar week and the results noted in the Maintenance Log;

(4) Provision is made to actuate automatically an aural alarm circuit located near the operator on duty if any of the automatic log readings are not within the tolerances or other requirements specified in the rules or station license;

(5) The alarm circuit operates continuously or the devices which record each parameter in sequence must read each parameter at least once during each 30-minute period;

(6) The automatic logging equipment is located at the remote control point if the transmitter is remotely controlled, or at the transmitter location if the transmitter is manually controlled;

(7) The automatic logging equipment is located in the near vicinity of the operator on duty and is inspected periodically during the broadcast day. In the event of failure or malfunctioning of the automatic equipment, the employee responsible for the log shall make the required entries in the log manually at that time;

(8) The indicating equipment conforms to the requirements of § 73.1215 (specifications for indicating instruments) except that the scales need not exceed 2 inches in length. Arbitrary scales may not be used.

(c) In preparing the Operating Log, original data may be recorded in rough form and later transcribed into the log.

(d) If required by AM or FM station operator requirements, each completed Operating Log shall bear a signed notation by the station's designated chief operator of the results of the review of that log, and show the date and time of such review.

§ 73.1830   Maintenance logs.

(a) Each AM, FM and TV station must keep a maintenance log. Entries in the log must be made by or under the direction of the station's chief operator, and the entries are to reflect the results of all transmitter inspections, tests, adjustments and maintenance. The following information is to be entered in the log:

(1) *All stations:*

(i) An entry of the time and result of auxiliary transmitter test(s).

(ii) An entry of the calibration check of automatic logging devices when used under the provisions of § 73.1820 (Operating Logs).

(iii) An entry of all carrier frequency measurements, including the date performed and description of method used as required by § 73.1540 (Carrier frequency measurements).

(iv) An entry of the results of calibration of extension meters used against their corresponding regular meters as required by § 73.1550 (Extension meters).

(v) An entry of the results of calibration of indicating instruments at each remote control point against the corresponding instruments at the transmitter site, as required by the rules, for use of remote control (AM, § 73.67; FM, § 73.275; NCE–FM, § 73.375; and TV, § 73.676).

(vi) The entries required by § 17.49(d) of this Chapter concerning quarterly inspections of the condition of tower lights and associated control equipment and entries when towers are cleaned or repainted as required by § 17.50 of this Chapter.

(vii) An entry to describe fully any experimental operation pursuant to § 73.1510 (Experimental operation) and § 73.1520 (Operation for tests and maintenance).

(viii) An entry of the date and time of removal from and restoration to service of any of the following equipment in the event it becomes defective;

(A) Modulation monitor (aural).

(ix) A signed dated statement by the chief operator upon completion of the inspections required by § 73.1580 showing that the inspection has been made. The statement must include details of tests, adjustments, and repairs that were accomplished to ensure operation in accordance with the technical operating rules and terms of the station authorization. If repairs could not be completed, the entry must also include details of the items of equipment concerned, the manner and degree in which they were defective, and the reasons why complete repair could not be made.

(B) Any transmission system meter, the reading of which is required to be entered into the station Operating or Maintenance Log.

(C) Devices for monitoring or generating the EBS Attention Signal.

(2) *AM stations.* In addition to the entries specified in subparagraph (a)(1) above:

(i) An entry of the calibration check of remote reading antenna and common point ammeters against their corresponding regular meters when used under the provisions of § 73.57, including the actual reading of the meters prior to and after calibration.

(ii) For stations using directional antennas, an entry of the calibration of the antenna monitor using procedures specified by the monitor manufacturer's instructions.

(iii) For stations using directional antennas, an entry of the result of field strength measurements made at the specified monitoring points if such measurements are required either by the terms of the station license or § 73.93(e)(4) (Operator requirements).

(iv) For stations using directional antennas, an entry of the following observations (made without modulation if readings are affected by modulation) for each directional radiation pattern. Observations must be made at least three days of each calendar week, not less than 44 hours, not more than 76 hours, apart.

(A) Common point current.

(B) Base currents, their ratios, and the deviations of those ratios, in percent, from values specified in the station authorization.

(C) Antenna monitor sample currents or current ratios and computed deviations of current ratios, in percent, from values specified in the station authorization.

(D) Antenna monitor phase indications and the deviations of those indications, in degrees, from values specified in the station authorization.

(v) Entries specified in § 73.68 (Sampling systems for antenna monitors) or

§ 73.69 (Antenna monitors), for stations using directional antennas, when the antenna sampling system or the antenna monitor is out of service.

(3) *FM stations.* In addition to the entries specified in subparagraph (a)(1) above:

(1) For stations using the direct method of power determination, an entry for each six month period of the results of calibration of the transmission line meter used for determining operating power as specified for FM stations in § 73.267, or for NCE–FM stations, in § 73.567 (Operating power; determination and maintenance of).

(ii) For stations transmitting stereophonic programs, an entry each calendar month of measurements of the stereophonic pilot carrier frequency, including the date performed and description of the procedure used as specified for FM stations in § 73.297 or for NCE–FM stations in § 73.596 (stereophonic broadcasting).

(iii) For stations using SCA, an entry, once each calendar month, of the measurements of each subcarrier frequency, including the date performed and description of the procedure used as required by § 73.295 for FM stations or § 73.595 for NCE–FM stations (Operation under Subsidiary Communications Authorizations).

(4) *TV stations.* In addition to the entries specified in subparagraph (a)(1) above:

(i) An entry of the date and time of removal from and restoration to service of the visual modulation monitoring equipment.

(ii) An entry of the results of calibration of the transmission line meters used for determining the operating power as specified in § 73.663.

(iii) The entries for the measurements required by 73.682(a)(23)(viii) concerning subcarrier frequency measurements and measurements of main carrier modulation by subcarriers.

❋　　❋　　❋　　❋　　❋　　❋

(b) As entries of these maintenance procedures are made, the operator shall sign and date them. In preparing the Maintenance Log, original data may be recorded in rough form and later transcribed into the log.

§ 73.1540 Carrier frequency measurements.

(a) The carrier frequency of each AM and FM station and the visual carrier frequency and difference between the visual carrier and the aural carrier or center frequency of each TV station shall be measured or determined as often as necessary to insure that they are maintained within the prescribed tolerances. However, in any event, each station with an authorized operating power greater than 10 watts shall make at least one measurement or determination each calendar month with intervals not exceeding 40 days between successive measurements for each main transmitter in use.

(b) The licensee of each broadcast station shall determine the method or procedures for measuring or determining the carrier frequency.

(c) The primary standard of frequency for radio frequency measurements is the standard frequency maintained by the National Bureau of Standards or the standard signals of Stations WWV, WWVB, and WWVH of the National Bureau of Standards.

§ 73.1545 Carrier frequency departure tolerances.

(a) *AM stations.* The departure of the carrier frequency of an AM station may not exceed ±20 hertz from the assigned frequency.

(b) *FM stations.* (1) The departure of the carrier or center frequency of an FM station with an authorized transmitter output power more than 10 watts may not exceed 2000 hertz from the assigned frequency.

(2) The departure of the carrier or center frequency of an FM station with an authorized transmitter output power of 10 watts or less may not exceed ±3000 hertz from the assigned frequency.

(c) *TV stations.* (1) The departure of the visual carrier frequency of a TV station may not exceed ±1000 hertz from the assigned visual carrier frequency.

(2) The departure of the aural carrier frequency of a TV station may not exceed ±1000 hertz from the actually visual carrier frequency plus exactly 4.5 MHz.

(d) *International broadcast stations.* The departure of the carrier frequency of an International broadcast station may not exceed 0.0015% of the assigned frequency on which the station is transmitting.

§ 73.1550   Extension meters.

(a) A broadcast station may, without further authority from the FCC, install and use extension meters and monitoring devices provided:

(1) The transmitter is in the same building as the normal operating location of the station's licensed operator and is no more than one floor above or below the normal operating location.

(2) The path from the normal operating location to the transmitter is no longer than 100 feet and provides the operator with ready access to the transmitter.

(3) The required extension meters and monitoring devices are sufficiently close to the operator's normal operating location that deviations from normal indications of such instruments can be observed from that location.

(4) The transmitter is installed and protected so it is not accessible to unauthorized persons.

(5) Each extension meter or monitoring device required for the type of station, pursuant to paragraph (b), shall continuously sample the parameter for which it is installed and constantly indicate that parameter.

(6) Installation and operation of these meters shall be in accordance with the requirements prescribed for their corresponding regular meters and monitoring devices.

(7) Devices used for obtaining extension meter indications do not affect the accuracy of their corresponding regular meters.

(b) Extension metering and monitoring devices shall be installed as follows:

(1) *AM stations:*

(i) Meters for indicating the DC input power of the last radio frequency power amplifier stage of the transmitter.

(ii) A meter for indicating non-directional antenna current or directional antenna common point current.

(iii) The modulation monitor or a percentage modulation meter and peak indicating device which provides continuous and accurate indications of the modulation levels.

(iv) For stations using directional antenna systems, either the antenna monitor or external meters meeting the specifications for accuracy and repeatability prescribed for the monitor itself.

(2) *FM stations operating with transmitter output power more than 10 watts:*

(i) Meters for indicating the DC input power to the last radio frequency power amplifier stage of the transmitter.

(ii) A meter for indicating the relative transmission line voltage, current or power.

(iii) The modulation monitor or a percentage modulation meter and peak indicating device which provide continuous and accurate indications of total modulation levels.

(3) *FM stations operating with transmitter power of 10 watts or less:*

(i) An indicator to show when the transmitter is in operation.

(ii) A percentage modulation indicator or a calibrated program level meter from which a satisfactory indication of the percentage of modulation can be determined.

(4) *TV stations.*

(i) Meters for indicating the DC input power to the last radio frequency power amplifier stages for the aural and visual transmitters.

(ii) Meters for indicating the relative transmission line voltage, current or power for the aural and visual transmitters.

(iii) The aural modulation monitor or a percentage modulation meter and peak indicating device which provide continuous and accurate indications of modulation levels.

(iv) Visual monitoring equipment suitable for monitoring the visual signal so that it may be maintained in accordance with the FCC requirements.

(c) The extension meters required, pursuant to paragraph (b) of this Section, must be calibrated against their corresponding regular meters as often as necessary to insure their accuracy, but in no event less than once each week, and

(1) The results of such calibration shall be entered in the station's maintenance log.

(2) In no event shall an extension meter be calibrated against another remote or extension meter.

(3) Each extension meter shall be accurate to within 2 percent of the value read on its corresponding regular meter.

(4) For AM stations, such calibrations shall be made for each mode of operation.

(d) If a malfunction of any component of the extension metering or monitoring system causes inaccurate readings, the following procedures shall apply:

(1) *All stations.* If the malfunction affects the meters for indicating the DC input power to the last radio stage of the transmitter power amplifier, the indications must be read at the transmitter and entered in the operating log at the same intervals. If the malfunction affects the extended indications of the modulation monitor (aural) the licensee shall, pending repair or replacement, provide other suitable means for monitoring modulation at the extended meter location.

(2) *AM stations.* In addition to (1) above, if the malfunction affects the extension indications of antenna or common point ammeter, the operating power may be determined by the indirect method using the procedures described in § 73.51(e) for a period not to exceed 60 days. Alternatively, the operating power may be determined by the direct method on a continued basis by reading the regular antenna or common point ammeter with indications entered in the operating log once each day for each mode of operation until the defective extension metering is repaired. If the malfunction affects the extended indications of the directional antenna monitor, the pertinent entries required in the operating log must be obtained at the specified intervals at the monitor location.

(3) *FM stations.* In addition to (1) above, if the malfunction affects the transmission line meter, the indications must be read at the transmitter and entered in the operating log at the same intervals.

(4) *TV stations.* In addition to (1) above, if the malfunction affects the transmission line meter(s), indications must be read at the transmitter and entered in the operating log at the same intervals. If the malfunction affects the indications of the visual monitoring equipment, the licensee shall, pending repair or replacement, provide other suitable means for monitoring the visual modulation at the extension meter location.

(e) When a malfunction in the extension metering or monitoring equipment is detected, an appropriate entry shall be made in the station's maintenance log showing the date of the observance and identifying the indicating device(s) affected. A dated entry shall also be made when repair or replacement is completed. If a malfunctioning component cannot be repaired or replaced within 60 days from the date faulty operation is detected, the Engineer in Charge of the radio district in which the station is located shall be notified and request made for such additional time as is needed to complete the necessary repairs or replacement.

§ 73.1560 Operating power tolerance.

(a) *AM stations.* Except as provided for in paragraph (d), the antenna input power of an AM station as determined by the procedures specified in § 73.51 must be maintained as near as is practicable to the authorized antenna input power and may not be less than 90% nor more than 105% of the authorized power.

(b) *FM stations.* Except as provided in paragraph (d), the transmitter output power of an FM station with power output as determined by the procedures specified in § 73.267 (§ 73.567 for noncommercial educational FM stations) authorized for output power more than 10 watts must be maintained as near as practicable to the authorized transmitter output power and may not be less than 90% nor more than 105% of the authorized power. FM stations operating with authorized transmitter output power of 10 watts or less, may operate at less than the authorized power, but not more than 105% of the authorized power.

(c) *TV stations.* Except as provided in paragraph (d), the aural and visual transmitter output power of a TV station, as determined by the procedures specified in § 73.633 must be maintained as near as is practicable to the authorized transmitter output powers and may not be less than 80% nor more than 105% of the authorized powers. The FCC may specify deviation from the power tolerance requirements for subscription television operations to the extent it deems necessary to permit proper operation.

(d) *Reduced power operation.* In the event it becomes technically impossible to operate with the authorized power, a broadcast station may operate at reduced power for a period of not more than 30 days without specific authority from the FCC. If operation at reduced power will exceed 10 consecutive days, a notification must be sent to the FCC in Washington, D.C., not later than the 10th day of the lower power operation. In the event the normal power is restored prior to the expiration of the 30 day period, the licensee must notify the FCC upon restoration of normal operation. If causes beyond the control of the licensee prevent restoration of authorized power within 30 days, an informal written request must be made to the FCC in Washington, D.C. no later than the 30th day for the additional time as may be necessary.

§ 73.1570   Modulation levels: AM, FM, and TV aural.

(a) The percentage of modulation is to be maintained at as high a level as is consistent with good quality of transmission and good broadcast service, with maximum levels not to exceed the values specified in paragraph (b). Generally, the modulation should not be less than 85% on peaks of frequent recurrence, but where lower modulation levels may be required to avoid objectionable loudness or to maintain the dynamic range of the program material, the degree of modulation may be reduced to whatever level is necessary for this purpose, even though under such circumstances, the level may be substantially less than that which produces peaks of frequent recurrence at a level of 85%.

(b) Maximum modulation levels must meet the following limitations:

(1) *AM stations.* In no case shall the modulation exceed 100% on negative peaks of frequent recurrence, or 125% on positive peaks at any time.

(2) *FM stations.* In no case shall the total modulation exceed 100% on peaks of frequent recurrence.

(i) FM stations transmitting stereophonic programs must meet the stereophonic signal modulation specifications of paragraphs (b), and (i) of § 73.322.

(ii) FM stations transmitting multiplex signals for SCA or telemetry purposes must meet the multiplex signal modulation specifications of § 73.319(c).

(3) *TV stations.* In no case shall the total modulation of the aural carrier exceed 100% on peaks of frequent recurrence, unless some other peak modulation level is specified in an instrument of authorization.

(i) [Reserved]

(ii) TV stations transmitting multiplex signals on the aural carrier for telemetry, or Subscription Television Service, must limit the modulation of the main carrier by the arithmetic sum of the subcarriers to not more than 10%, unless some other subcarrier modulation level is specified in the instrument of authorization.

(c) If a limiting or compression amplifier is employed to maintain modulation levels, precaution must be taken so as not to substantially alter the dynamic characteristics of programs.

§ 73.1590   Equipment performance measurements.

(a) The licensee of each AM, FM and TV station, except licensees of Class D non-commercial educational FM stations authorized to operate with 10 watts or less output power, must make equipment performance measurements for each main transmitter as follows:

(1) Upon initial installation of a main new or replacement transmitter.

(2) Upon modification of an existing transmitter made under the provisions of § 73.1690. Modification of transmission systems, and specified therein.

(3) Installation of FM stereophonic transmission equipment pursuant to §§ 73.297 or 73.597.

(4) When required by other provisions of the rules or the station license.

(5) AM and FM stations (except 10 watt non-commercial educational stations). once each calendar year. (One set of measurements must be made during the 4 month period immediately preceding the filing date of the application for renewal of the station license. Successive measurements are to be made at least annually by the anniversary calendar month, and completed within an additional 2 months, with no more than 14 months between measurements.)

(b) *Audio measurements.* Audio equipment performance measurements must be made with the equipment adjusted for normal program operation and must include all circuits between the main studio microphone terminals or amplifier input and the antenna circuit, including any correcting equalizer circuits normally used. Any dynamic audio processing or non-correcting equalizers must be disabled or neutralized. The measurements must yield the following information:

(1) *AM stations.*

(i) Data and curves showing overall audio frequency response from 50 to 7500 Hz for approximately 25, 50, 85 and if obtainable, 100% modulation. A family of curves must be plotted (one for each percentage above) with dB above and below the 1000 Hz reference frequency as ordinate and audio frequency as abscissa.

(ii) Data and curves showing audio frequency harmonic content for 25, 50, 85 and, if obtainable, 100% modulation for the audio frequencies of 50, 100, 400, 1000, 5000, and 7500 Hz (either arithmetical or RSS (root sum square) values up to the 10th harmonic or 16,000 Hz). A family of curves must be plotted (one for each percentage above) with percent distortion as ordinate and audio frequency as abscissa.

(iii) Data showing percentage of carrier amplitude regulation (carrier shift) for 25, 50, 85 and, if obtainable, 100% modulation with 400 Hz tone.

(iv) The carrier hum and extraneous noise level generated within the equipment, and measured throughout the audio spectrum, or bands, in dB below the reference level of 100% modulation by a 400 Hz tone.

(v) Measurements or evidence showing that spurious radiations, including radio frequency harmonics, are suppressed or are not present to a degree capable of causing objectionable interference to other radio services. Field strength measurements are preferred but observations made with a communications type receiver are acceptable. However, in particular cases involving interference or controversy, the FCC may require field strength measurements.

(2) *FM and TV (aural).*

(i) Audio frequency response from 50 to 15,000 Hz for approximately 25, 50 and 100% modulation. Measurements must be made using at least 50, 100, 400, 1,000, 5,000, 10,000 and 15,000 Hz tones. The frequency response measurements made without deemphasis are preferable; however, standard 75 microsecond deemphasis may be used in the measuring equipment provided the accuracy of the deemphasis circuit is sufficient to insure that the measured response is within the prescribed limits.

(ii) Audio frequency harmonic distortion for 25, 50, 100% modulation for the audio frequencies of 50, 100, 400, 1000, and 5000 Hz and audio frequency harmonics for 100% modulation for audio frequencies of 10,000 and 15,000 Hz. Measurements must normally include harmonics to 30,000 Hz. The distortion measurements must be made with 75 microsecond deemphasis in the measuring equipment.

(iii) Output noise level (frequency modulation) in the band of 50 to 15,000 Hz in dB below the reference level of 100% modulation by a 400 Hz tone. The noise measurement must be made using 75 microsecond deemphasis in the measuring equipment.

(iv) Output noise level (amplitude modulation) in the band of 50 to 15,000 Hz in dB below the reference of 100% modulation by a 400 Hz tone. The noise measurement must be made using 75 microsecond deemphasis in the measuring equipment.

(v) If, after type acceptance, any changes have been made in the transmitter or associated equipment (filters, multiplexers, etc.) which could cause changes in its radiation product, data showing attenuation of spurious and harmonic radiation.

(c) *TV visual.* TV visual equipment performance measurements must be made with the equipment adjusted for normal program operation. When practical, the measurements should be made through the video transmission system from the studio program terminal to the transmitting antenna sampling port. The measurements must yield the following information:

(1) Overall attenuation versus frequency response for the visual transmitter.

(2) Field strength or voltage of the lower side-band for a modulating frequency of 1.25 MHz or greater, (including 3.58 MHz for color), and of the upper side-band for a modulating frequency of 4.75 MHz or greater.

(3) Data showing that the waveform of the transmitted signal conforms to that specified by the standards for TV transmissions.

(4) Photographs of a test pattern taken from a receiver or monitor connected to the transmitter output.

(5) Data showing envelope delay characteristics of the radiated signal.

(6) **Data** showing the transfer characteristics between reference black and reference white levels.

(7) If, after type acceptance, any changes have been made in the transmitter or associated equipment (filters, multiplexer, etc.) which could cause changes in its radiation products, data showing the attenuation of spurious and harmonic radiation.

(d) The data required by paragraphs (b) and (c) of this Section, together with a description of the equipment and procedure used in making the measurements, signed and dated by the qualified person(s) making the measurements, must be kept on file at the transmitter or remote control point for a period of 2 years, and on request must be made available during that time to duly authorized representatives of the FCC.

CHAPTER 4

Broadcast Microphones

Dynamic, condenser, and ribbon microphones are the types of microphones employed most often in modern broadcast stations. The dynamic microphone is popular because of its improved design and performance, light weight, small size, ruggedness, and adaptability to modern broadcast techniques.

4-1. TYPES

The three basic microphone movements are shown in Fig. 4-1. The *dynamic microphone* (Fig. 4-1A) employs the moving-coil principle. A wire coil attached to a diaphragm is positioned in a strong magnetic field. Whenever sound waves strike the diaphragm and cause it to move, the coil also moves, and its turns cut the lines of force of the magnetic field. This motion induces a voltage in the coil, the ends of which are connected to a transformer in the microphone.

These coil movements can be made very rugged and can deliver a high output signal level. The output voltage varies with, and depends on, the sound pressure changes on the diaphragm. Microphones in which the output voltage varies with the sound intensity and pressure are referred to as *pressure types*.

The *condenser microphone* (Fig. 4-1B) is also a pressure type. It consists of an aluminum alloy diaphragm and a back plate, with a narrow air space in between. The aluminum diaphragm functions like the movable element of a variable capacitor. A polarizing voltage is applied between the diaphragm and back plate. Any movement of the diaphragm will cause a change in capacitance between the two plates. In turn, a proportional change will occur in the output voltage. Because a condenser microphone has a very low capacitance, the output impedance of its element is very high. In fact, the output voltage is so low and the output impedance so high that the element must be connected directly to the high-impedance input circuit of a transistor audio amplifier, which is often built into the microphone.

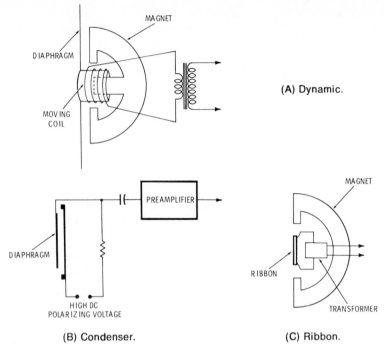

Fig. 4-1. Basic microphone movements.

The *ribbon microphone* (Fig. 4-1C) movement consists of a thin corrugated aluminum ribbon suspended in a strong magnetic field. Any vibration, as a result of sound waves, causes the ribbon to cut the lines of magnetic force. A corresponding voltage is induced into the ribbon, and a current flows through it and into the primary of an associated transformer that raises the extremely low impedance of the ribbon to that of the audio lines and facilities of the broadcast audio equipment. The transformer also steps up the weak ribbon voltage in the primary to provide a usable output across the secondary.

The ribbon itself must be elastic, even though under tension. A ribbon microphone must never be jarred or subjected to intense sounds such as blasting and gunshots, or the ribbon may break. If stretched too tightly, the ribbon may loose its elasticity and shape. As a consequence, the microphone characteristics will be altered. Despite these disadvantages, ribbon microphones are used because of their excellent frequency response and hence quality of performance.

It is interesting to consider the motion of the ribbon when excited by a sound. The ribbon can move backward or forward from its resting position, its motion being a function of the differential sound pressure that exists between its back and front. It will always move in the direction of diminishing sound pressure. Thus, a ribbon microphone is referred to as a *pressure-gradient* type. Its movement responds to sound waves from the front or back—whereas dynamic and condenser movements are strictly pressure types because, regardless of the direction of sound arrival, the diaphragm moves in the same direction. Except for the ribbon types, all other microphones are pressure types.

4-2. MICROPHONE POLAR PATTERNS

Inasmuch as a pressure-type microphone responds to sounds arriving from any direction, it is basically nondirectional. However, it can be made directional through the use of specially constructed baffles and resonant chambers. The pressure-gradient ribbon microphone is basically a directional type. Recall that it responds to the difference in sound pressure between its front and back. However, sound waves arriving from the sides exert the same pressure on the front and back of the ribbon. Consequently, there is no ribbon motion and hence no output. It follows that the polar pattern of the pressure-gradient microphone is a figure-8 (bidirectional). By special construction it is possible to change this polar pattern, or to develop a variety of patterns by using more than one type of microphone movement.

There are three common polar patterns, as shown in Fig. 4-2. Some microphones have only one; others include facilities for changing the pattern to suit the broadcast needs. Although a microphone is a three-dimensional device, normally we are concerned only with its front, back, and side pickup (horizontal directivity).

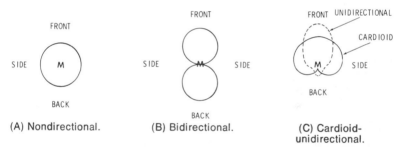

(A) Nondirectional.   (B) Bidirectional.   (C) Cardioid-unidirectional.

Fig. 4-2. Basic microphone polar patterns.

It is apparent that a microphone with a nondirectional pattern (Fig. 4-2A) is preferred when the sound arrives from several directions. For best pickup, such a microphone should be placed at the approximate center of the sound. A microphone with a bidirectional pattern (Fig. 4-1B) is ideal where there are two opposite sound sources (for example, two people seated across from each other at an interview table). It has the added advantage of displaying minimum sensitivity to undesired sounds from the other two sides.

Microphones with unidirectional or cardioid patterns (Fig. 4-2C) are useful when the sound arrives from the same general direction. The cardioid pattern, for instance, can pick up sounds from the wide expanse of a large studio or stage. Its wide angle of pickup improves the balance of an orchestra or choir. At the same time, minimum noise is picked up from the rear (e.g., from the audience) because of the weak pressure from the rear. For more concentrated sources of sound, a microphone having a sharper unidirectional pattern can be used.

In summary, it is apparent that the choice of microphone and pattern hinges on the type of program material. However, the size of the room and the reverberation in it also influence the selection. A general rule is to use a directional microphone wherever there is high reverberation ("live" room) and/or high background noise, and to use a nondirectional microphone for all other programs. In fact, in a highly absorbent surrounding ("dead" room), a nondirectional microphone will provide greater program realism.

4-3. OUTPUT LEVEL AND FREQUENCY RESPONSE

The output level of broadcast microphones usually is rated in dBm, which corresponds to the output in decibels related to 1 milliwatt at a standard sound pressure of 10 dynes/cm². The latter figure is the approximate sound pressure impressed on the microphone by normal conversation when the speaker's mouth is one foot from the microphone. In other specifications the output is often given as so many microvolts/dyne/cm², or in output voltage in dB related to a standard of 1 volt/10 dynes/cm².

Of course, microphone outputs are much weaker than 1 milliwatt or 1 volt. In fact, they are so low that the output level is rated in minus dB—the higher the minus-dB figure, the lower the output level. For example, at a given sound level a microphone rated at −56 dBm has half the output voltage of a microphone rated at −50 dBm.

Frequency response is also an important characteristic. In modern broadcast microphones it extends from approximately 40 Hz to above 12 kHz. Very little program material extends below 40 Hz, and the high-frequency response depends largely on the broadcast service being rendered. High-fidelity fm programs are able to handle the higher-frequency components, whereas many of the highs (as a function of the audio facilities. network lines, and receiver response) are lost in standard am broadcasting. However, even in am broadcasting the high-frequency response may reach as high as 8 to 12 kHz.

The frequency response of a microphone is usually specified between the 6-dB-down points on the low- and high-frequency ends of the frequency curve. Some microphones and their preamplifiers include facilities for setting the frequency response according to the acoustical conditions and audio-line lengths.

Many microphones can also be switched to match one of the three standard impedances of 50, 150, or 250 ohms; lines and facilities are usually terminated in one or more of these three values.

4-4. HUM-PICKUP LEVEL

Another important microphone specification is its *hum-pickup level,* usually given as a minus-dB quantity. The 0-dB reference level is the hum output related to 1 milliwatt when a standard 60-hertz hum field of 0.001 gauss is used. In a microphone with a hum-pickup level of −30 dBm, the amplitude of the hum voltage is twice that of a microphone with a −36 dBm hum level.

A high hum level can reduce the dynamic range of a broadcast. The lowest-amplitude passage (lowest level signal in dB) that can be conveyed satisfactorily depends on how well the signal resulting from this low passage is held above the hum (and noise) levels present in the system.

4-5. TYPICAL BROADCAST MICROPHONES

One widely used broadcast microphone is the *RCA* model shown in Fig. 4-3. It is a ribbon type and has an adjustable acoustical shutter which gives a choice of nondirectional, bidirectional, or unidirectional pattern (Fig. 4-4). Such a microphone can be used for general programming and announcements, or it can be mounted on a television boom. Its characteristics are as follows:

Frequency Response: 50-15,000 Hz
Pattern: 3 choices
Output Level: Nondirectional, −56 dBm
      Bidirectional, −50 dBm
      Unidirectional, −53 dBm
Output Impedance: 250 ohms
Hum-Pickup Level: −128 dBm

Fig. 4-3. RCA ribbon microphone.

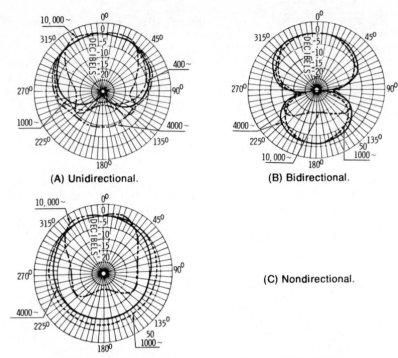

(A) Unidirectional.

(B) Bidirectional.

(C) Nondirectional.

Fig. 4-4. Pattern characteristics of microphone shown in Fig. 4-3.

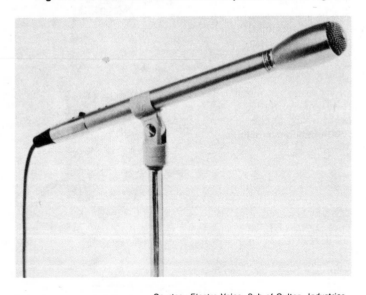

Courtesy Electro-Voice, Sub of Gulton, Industries
Fig. 4-5. Omnidirectional dynamic microphone.

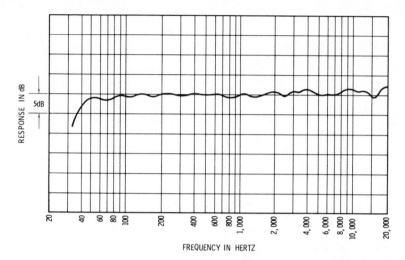

Fig. 4-6. Frequency response of Electro-Voice microphone.

Another popular microphone is the *Electro-Voice* dynamic type (Fig. 4-5). It can be mounted on a stand for general programming and television staging, or carried around during audience-participation shows and interviews. It has a nondirectional pattern and has a low-impedance 150-ohm output. It has an excellent frequency response being very flat up to 20,000 hertz (Fig. 4-6). Its characteristics are as follows:

Frequency Response: 40-20,000 Hz
Pattern: Nondirectional
Output Level: −57 dBm
Output Impedance: 150 ohms

A good-quality broadcast microphone is a complex instrument. A dynamic microphone is more than a magnet and a moving coil attached to a diaphragm. Actually, a resonant circuit is formed by the mass of the diaphragm (which is equivalent to an inductance because it opposes a change in velocity), the compliance of the diaphragm (which can be compared to a capacitance because it opposes any change in the applied force), and the volume of air to the rear of the diaphragm (also a capacitance for the same reason), as shown in Fig. 4-7A. This mechanical resonant effect peaks the response of the microphone at some low frequency. As in any electrical circuit, the Q of a resonant circuit can be lowered and the response flattened by insertion of a resistance (Fig. 4-7B). In a microphone a sound-absorbing felt is employed as a resistance to remove violent peaks in the frequency response.

Still another consideration in microphone design is proper low-frequency response. In a microphone it can be extended by admitting the outside air, through a tube, into the back case of the microphone. In effect, more inductance is added across the resonant circuit of the

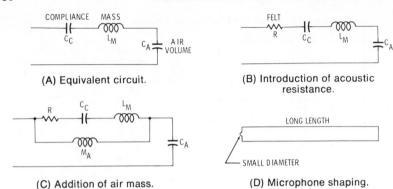

(A) Equivalent circuit.

(B) Introduction of acoustic resistance.

(C) Addition of air mass.

(D) Microphone shaping.

Fig. 4-7. Factors which influence the overall response of the Electro-Voice dynamic microphone.

microphone, as shown in Fig. 4-7C. The combination of this bass-reflex principle and the acoustic resistance of the felt material provides the proper low-frequency response.

The high-frequency response of our hypothetical microphone can be made more desirable by keeping its diameter small and increasing its length (Fig. 4-7D). The long, slim case of the *Electro-Voice* microphone is a good example. The high-frequency response can be further extended by using a frontal resonant cavity between the diaphragm and grille. The cavity and its associated tube are concealed in the grille and form inductive and capacitive elements that extend the frequency response to 15 kHz and up.

An *RCA* uniaxial ribbon microphone is shown in Figs. 4-8 and 4-9. The patterns of Fig. 4-8 are particularly helpful in showing its three-dimensional pickup characteristics (unlike most ribbon microphones,

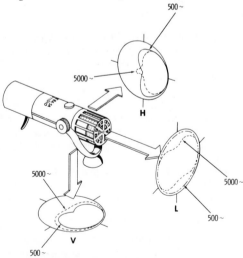

Fig. 4-8. An RCA uniaxial microphone.

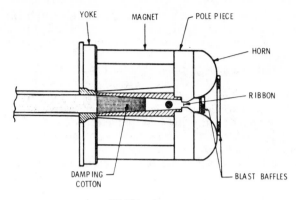

(A) Top view.

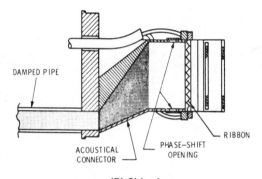

(B) Side view.

Fig. 4-9. Basic construction of the RCA uniaxial microphone.

which are bidirectional). Around its vertical and horizontal axes the microphone has a cardioid pattern. Its longitudinal pattern is nondirectional and becomes compressed at the higher frequencies. The combined three-dimensional characteristics produce a good uniaxial pickup pattern.

The microphone is made to have directional characteristics and to operate as a pressure type by placing an acoustical labyrinth behind the ribbon. The labyrinth is a long folded pipe which is damped by acoustical material along its entire length to eliminate resonant conditions. An acoustical connector links the pipe to the air gap at the back of the ribbon. Two phase-shifting ports establish proper impedance relationships and maintain a uniform frequency response. (See Fig. 4-9.)

The remainder of the circuit consists of a line-matching transformer and an adjustable response compensator. The latter permits additional attenuation of the low frequencies in noisy locations or when the microphone is close-talked (which tends to emphasize the lows). Full-frequency pickup can be used for musical programs.

This style of microphone is particularly adaptable to boom and stand mounting, and for other applications where the microphone must be tilted in the direction of the sound without picking up noises from other directions.

Fig. 4-10 shows a very popular style of broadcast microphone with a characteristic pickup pattern that is directional and uniaxial. This small dynamic type can be held in the hand or worn around the neck on a lanyard. When worn around the neck, such a microphone is often planned to emphasize the high frequencies because of the high-frequency shadow beneath the user's chin. Also, radiation from the user's chest tends to emphasize the lower frequencies.

The characteristics of the personal dynamic microphone are as follows:

Frequency Response: 80-12,000 Hz
Pattern: Semidirectional
Output Level: −67 dBm
Output Impedance: 250 ohms
Hum-Pickup Level: −112 dBm

Modern broadcasting trends emphasize remote pickups in the outdoors and in large amphitheaters. One example would be a small instrumental group riding on a float in a parade. In such applications the microphone must be able to reach out and pick up sounds from a rather concentrated area without picking up surrounding noises.

Fig. 4-10. Miniature dynamic microphone.

Courtesy RCA

A parabolic reflector can be used to further concentrate the directivity of a microphone, as shown in Fig. 4-11A, but it of course has size limitations. The "machine-gun" or "line" type of microphone in Fig. 4-11B is composed of many small tubes varying in length from about two inches to five feet. The open ends act as pickup points, and their opposite ends terminate at the diaphragm of a microphone. All sounds coming directly toward the open ends will travel the same distance to the diaphragm—whether the sounds enter a tube and pass

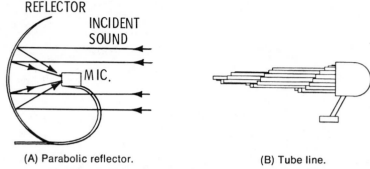

(A) Parabolic reflector. (B) Tube line.

Fig. 4-11. Methods for increasing microphone directivity.

through it, or continue through the air until entering a shorter tube. Since all sounds reaching the diaphragm have traveled the same distance from the source, they arrive at the same time and the diaphragm is activated in phase.

Now let us see why background noises from the sides are not picked up. These side sounds will still enter all tubes at approximately the same time. But the sound entering the five-foot tube must travel almost five feet farther, to reach the diaphragm, than the same sound entering the two-inch tube. For example, a sound 10 feet to the right or left must travel anywhere from 10 feet 2 inches to 15 feet before striking the diaphragm. The sounds arrive at the diaphragm at different times and, being out of phase, the sound waves have a canceling effect and do not cause the diaphragm to vibrate. An even greater phase difference will exist for sounds which originate at points behind the microphone.

The *Electro-Voice* microphone of Fig. 4-12 has high sensitivity, plus a sharp directivity obtained from the combination of line- and cardioid-microphone principles. A cardioid dynamic movement and a single-line tube approximately one foot long are used. A ⅛-inch covered slot in the tube, over its entire length from A to B in Fig. 4-13, displays a linear-taper acoustic resistance. All positions along the slot display equal sensitivity; therefore, equal sound pressures along the line will result in equal voltages being produced by the microphone element. Just as in the "machine-gun" arrangement, signals arriving from the sides and back will be canceled out at the cavity in front of the microphone.

One of the most distracting disturbances in the audio signal in outdoor broadcasting is wind blast and noise. Also the operational-environmental conditions can cause microphone performance to deteriorate prematurely. For instance, in television broadcasting, boom microphones take a considerable beating; they are moved at fast speed from one position to another and are subject to wind-noise pickup. The simultaneous deterioration of the audio signal due to environmental conditions and the impaired quality of microphones has created a demand for an improved microphone.

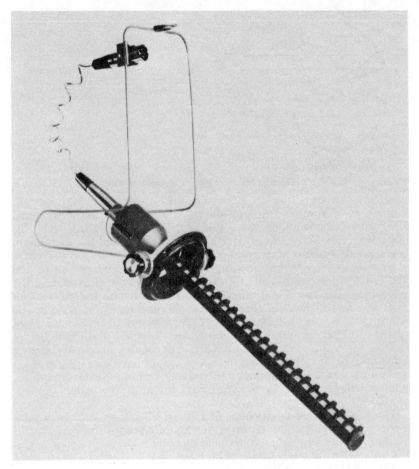

Courtesy Electro-Voice, Sub of Gulton, Industries

Fig. 4-12. Electro-Voice cardiline microphone.

Recently considerable effort has been directed to providing adequate shielding and protection for the boom microphone without disturbing its response. A foam jacket with good acoustical performance serves as an effective windscreen. It also protects the microphone from dust and magnetic particles and minimizes possible damage from being dropped or struck. Such protection is shown for the boom-mounted microphone of Fig. 4-14.

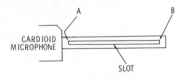

Fig. 4-13. Basic construction of the cardiline microphone.

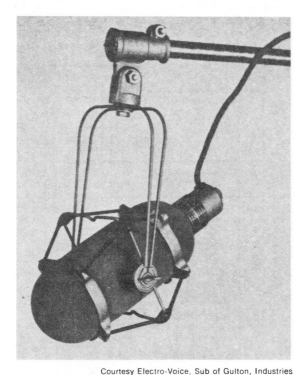

Courtesy Electro-Voice, Sub of Gulton, Industries

Fig. 4-14. A boom-mounted microphone with protective windscreen.

The internal make-up of an *AKG Acoustics* condenser microphone is shown in Fig. 4-15. The condenser element is mounted in the head at the extreme left. A transistor amplifier of high input impedance builds up the amplitude level of the audio signal. The amplifier is followed by an audio output transformer that permits a selection of output impedances.

The high-impedance input of the amplifier is established by the field-effect transistor which is connected in a source-follower configuration.

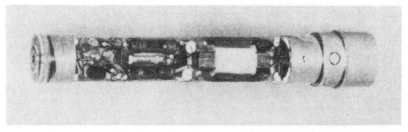

Courtesy AKG Acoustics

Fig. 4-15. Condenser microphone.

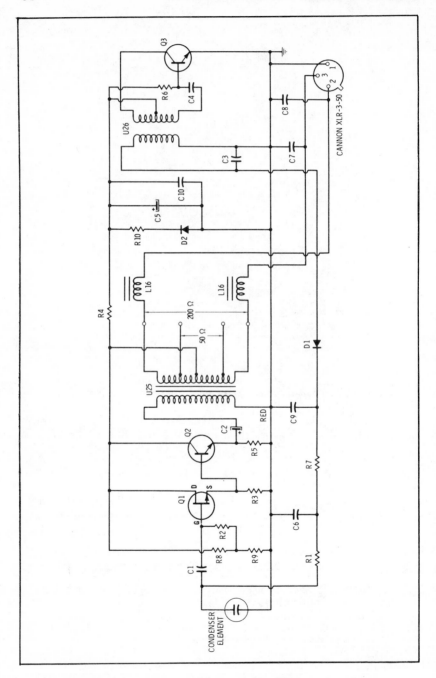

Fig. 4-16. Schematic of AKG Acoustics condenser microphone.

This stage is followed by a bipolar emitter-follower circuit which drives the primary of the output transformer (Fig. 4-16).

The low dc supply voltage for the preamplifier is applied via cable while the high polarizing voltage for the condenser microphone element is developed by an oscillating high-frequency generator. Transistor Q3 oscillates at approximately 1 MHz. The higher voltage output across the secondary is rectified by diode D1. The filtered output of about 60 volts is used as the polarizing voltage across the condenser microphone element.

A popular on-camera mike is the *electret* condenser microphone because of its very small size as well as good sensitivity and frequency response. The *Electro-Voice* version (Fig. 4-17) can be worn lavalier-style or with a tie-clasp bar attached to the user's clothing. A short 6-foot length of miniature cable connects the microphone to a battery/transformer housing that is clipped to the user's belt (Fig. 4-18). The small 1.35-volt battery operates the microphone 1000 hours. A matching transformer supplies a 150-ohm balanced output. In a desk application the battery/transformer housing can be attached to the underside of the desk rather than clipped to the user.

An FET amplifier is housed in the microphone proper. The amplifier acts as an impedance converter, transforming the very-high-impedance output of the electret element to an output impedance of approximately 7000 ohms.

The electret phenomenon is one that places a permanent charge on the condenser-microphone capacitor element. Thus the usual 48 volts or higher need not be supplied as in the case of the conventional condenser microphone. Therefore the only voltage required is the 1.35 volts applied to the FET preamplifier.

The electret effect is an electric field (voltage) set up in certain dielectric materials if they are placed in an intense electric field when they are cooled. In a way the effect is similar to the permanent magnetic field of a magnet. Electret material can be used to form a microphone diaphragm in a condenser microphone. Hence no polarizing voltage is required.

4-6. WIRELESS MICROPHONES

The *wireless* microphone has become a boon to all facets of broadcasting. In television broadcasting in particular it has eliminated the unsightly dangling cord. Stage mobility is improved and the performer is not restricted by microphone cable length. In a multimicrophone installation there are no caught-up or tangled microphone cables. Sound mixing and microphone phasing problems are reduced. Hum and noise pickup is reduced and there are no cable breaks and intermittents.

The *Cetec Vega* (Fig. 4-19) is often seen hand-held by television performers. Note that there is no dangling cord. The compact holder houses the microphone, audio processor, very-low-power transmitter, and antenna. The high operating frequency, 150–216 megahertz, permits the use of a small hidden antenna.

There is a compartment for a 9-volt alkaline battery that provides an

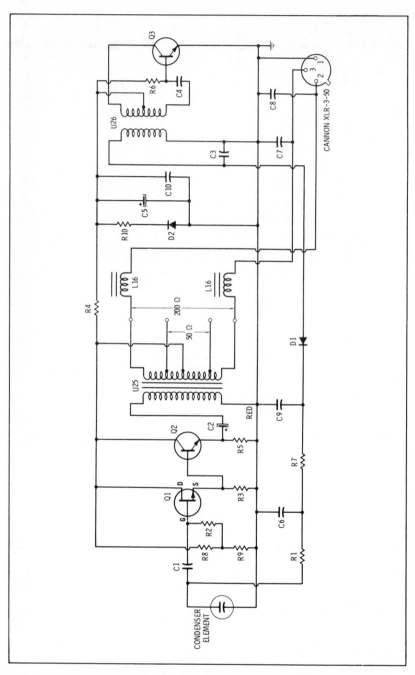

Fig. 4-16. Schematic of AKG Acoustics condenser microphone.

Courtesy Electro-Voice

Fig. 4-17. Miniature electret microphone.

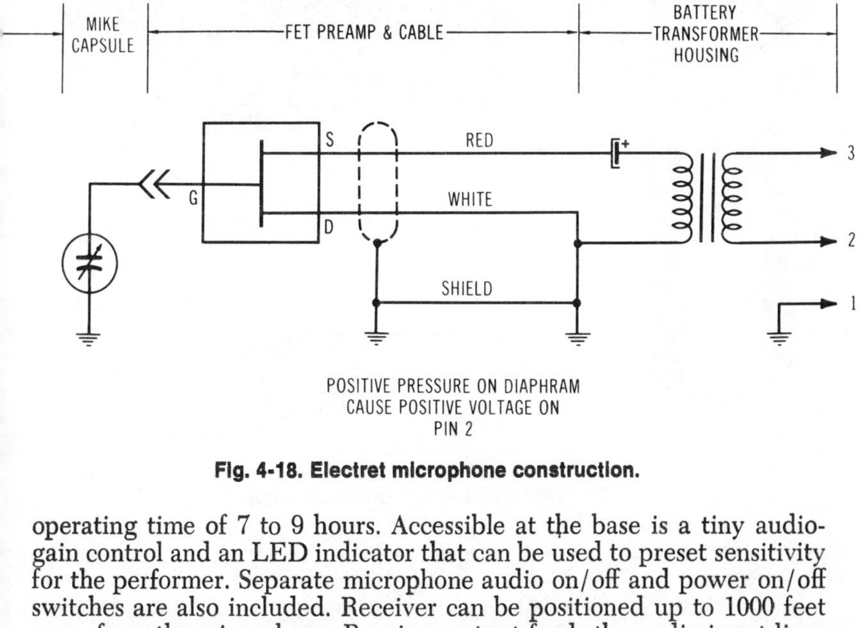

POSITIVE PRESSURE ON DIAPHRAM
CAUSE POSITIVE VOLTAGE ON
PIN 2

Fig. 4-18. Electret microphone construction.

operating time of 7 to 9 hours. Accessible at the base is a tiny audio-gain control and an LED indicator that can be used to preset sensitivity for the performer. Separate microphone audio on/off and power on/off switches are also included. Receiver can be positioned up to 1000 feet away from the microphone. Receiver output feeds the audio input lines of the audio control console.

An example of a *Telex* wireless microphone receiver and belt-attached transmitter is given in Fig. 4-20. The frequency-modulated

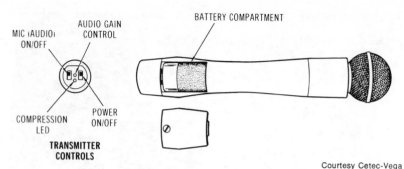

MIC (AUDIO) ON/OFF

AUDIO GAIN CONTROL

BATTERY COMPARTMENT

COMPRESSION LED

POWER ON/OFF

TRANSMITTER CONTROLS

Courtesy Cetec-Vega

Fig. 4-19. Wireless microphone.

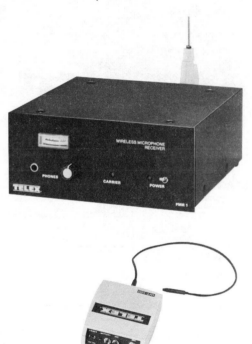

Courtesy Telex Communications, Inc.

Fig. 4-20. Wireless microphone system.

transmitter has a maximum output of 50 mW. Transmit frequency is assigned in the 150–174 MHz band. Receiver sensitivity is less than 1 microvolt for 12 dB SINAD. Consistent operation is obtained over a line-of-sight range of 2000 feet.

The *Telex* system has two special features. A compandor (compression/expansion activity) which provides an improved dynamic range for conveying very-low and very-high sound levels without overmodulation and distortion. In addition, two receiving antennas provide diversity reception to reduce the interaction between direct and reflected signals when the artist roams about with the microphone or when there is other activity between the transmit and receive locations. This technique prevents the dropout of signal or a defect called *picket-fencing* which can cause fast changes in receive signal level. This diversity reception technique uses digital-logic circuits. Further details on the method are given in Chapter 14.

The functional plan of the transmitter is given in Fig. 4-21. Audio signal is applied to the input of the low-noise audio amplifier through potentiometer R5. Signal level is increased by this stage which also includes 50-microsecond pre-emphasis. Audio amplifier output is applied to an integrated circuit compandor. This stage provides dynamic range compression that improves the signal-to-noise ratio. It includes a deviation control. Maximum deviation is ±12 kHz in compliance with FCC transmission type 54F3.

The frequency-modulated transmit oscillator operates in the 16.666–19.555 MHz range. A set of three multiplier/filter stages follow which step up the frequency and deviation by a factor of 9 into the 150–176 MHz range. There is a followup radio-frequency amplifier and an antenna matching system. Antenna is a short quarter-wave piece of flexible wire that can be readily hidden.

The transmitter operates with a 9-volt alkaline battery. An integrated circuit voltage regulator is used to supply a regulated 5 volts to the transmit oscillator. Carrier-frequency stability is 0.005%.

A functional diagram of the receiver is given in Fig. 4-22. Note the two diversity antennas and associated antenna switch. As a function of receive signal-to-noise ratio of the separate signals picked up by the two antennas, a logic system selects the best signal only. The operation of the associated digital circuits is presented in Chapter 14.

The output of the electronic antenna phasor is applied to a helical resonator. This type of resonator has a stable and very favorable response characteristic that passes the desired signal and displays a very high rejection to off-signal frequencies. Details on helical resonators and other types of circuits common to one-way and two-way transmission systems can be found in reference 1 given in Chapter 1.

A radio-frequency amplifier and mixer follow. Local-oscillator injection signal is provided by a crystal oscillator which emphasizes the third harmonic of the crystal frequency and applies it to the mixer. If amplifiers and filters follow. High if frequency is applied to a narrowband fm if/detector—integrated circuit MC3357. This integrated circuit and associated external components include the low-frequency mixer/if amplifier, demodulator, audio processing, and a mute source for squelch operation. Audio output from the U11 integrated circuit is applied to the squelch noise amplifier and the audio amplifier (U7A). The audio compandor (U80) maintains a relatively constant output level with varying signal inputs. Its function is to expand the audio that was compressed originally in the transmitter circuit. Overall signal-to-noise ratio is much improved.

The output of U11 applied to the squelch noise amplifier in conjunc-

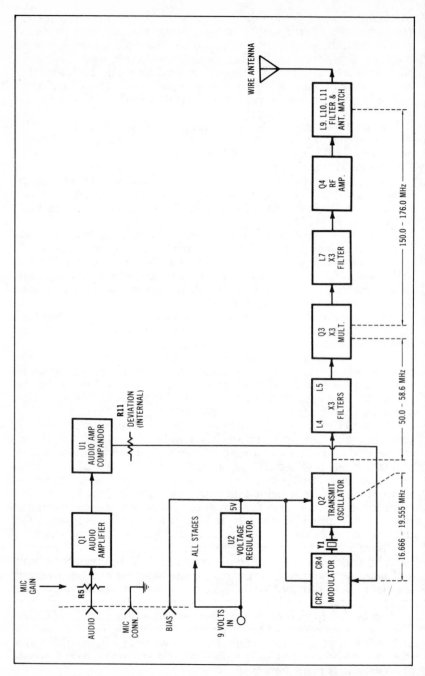

Fig. 4-21. Block diagram of wireless-microphone transmitter.

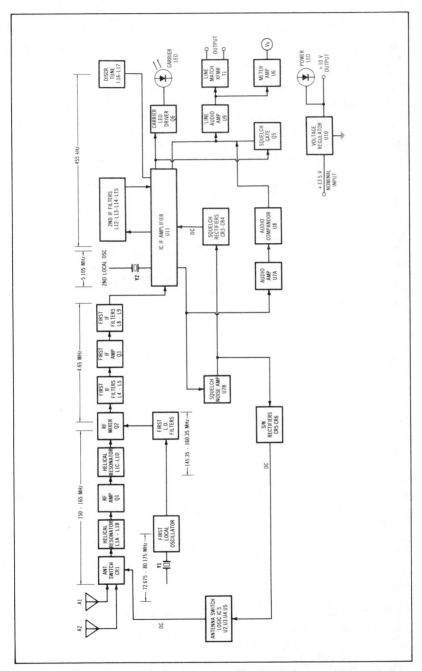

Fig. 4-22. Block diagram of wireless-microphone receiver.

tion with the S/N rectifiers supplies a reference dc level for the antenna digital logic system. It also sets the dc level for the squelch control system by way of the squelch rectifiers (CR3 "and" CR4). The audio output of U8 is de-emphasized and processed ahead of the line audio amplifier (U9). Squelch activity also occurs at this point. The output of the line audio amplifier is applied to an output matching transformer providing an output level of 0 dBm across 600 ohms or −50 dBm across 200 ohms. Output is monitored with a VU meter.

The presence of an rf carrier of proper level will cause the carrier LED to remain on. If the incoming rf carrier is not able to overcome the squelch threshold setting, the circuit will turn off the LED.

4-7. MICROPHONE APPLICATION AND PLACEMENT

It is important that operators have an understanding of proper microphone placement and use. More often than not in a small broadcast station, the program originates from a small enclosure. This can be the control room itself, an announcing booth, or a mobile sound truck. For these applications the cardioid or unidirectional pattern is preferred. In such small enclosures, reverberations are numerous and strong; and acoustical treatment seldom supplies the most desirable correction.

It is characteristic of most announcers to "mug" the microphone. If the announcer will keep at least two feet away from it, better voice quality will result. Television broadcasting, where the microphone must be out of the camera's range, has proved that close-talking is not necessary. This problem can often be avoided by mounting the microphone overhead, as in Fig. 4-23. The table can be sound-treated to minimize reflections.

In a small studio, meeting room, or hall that is highly reflective (high reverberation, or liveness), a directional microphone is usually mandatory—particularly if proper emphasis is to be obtained despite a noisy background.

The nondirectional microphone should be used in highly sound-absorbent broadcast locations, or where liveness and presence are to be added for the listener's benefit. Several factors contribute to this effect of "liveness" in broadcasting. The reverberation time, distance from sound to microphone, and total volume of the studio or broadcast location must be considered. The formula is:

$$\text{Liveness} = \frac{1000\ T^2D^2}{G_PV}$$

where,

T is the reverberation time in seconds,
D is the distance from sound to microphone in feet,
G_P is the directivity of the pickup microphone,
V is the volume of the room in cubic feet.

Of course, the directivity of the microphone (G_P) influences the degree with which the three other factors (T, D, and V) affect the

OVERHEAD
MICROPHONE

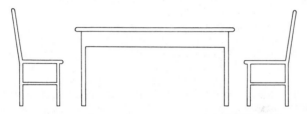

Fig. 4-23. Placement of an overhead microphone.

liveness. In general, a nondirectional microphone enhances the liveness, and a directional type reduces it. If the liveness and background noise of the area are so great that they interfere with the part of the program to be emphasized, a directional microphone should be used or a special accenting microphone in conjunction with a general microphone. In highly absorbent, "dead" locations where liveness must be added to better satisfy the radio listeners, the nondirectional microphone is more useful.

In recent years the small dynamic interview microphone has become increasingly popular. It adds versatility to the usual microphone setup because it can be carried around and thus taken directly to the source of sound. In conjunction with a general-purpose microphone the interview type can be used to sustain interest during many types of gatherings. For example, the general microphone can be placed on stage to pick up the music from an orchestra or band, and the interview microphone taken directly into the gathering—instead of the confusion of having people come up to the microphone on stage. A much more enjoyable program continuity can be maintained with this arrangement.

4-8. MUSICAL PICKUP

To obtain the most pleasurable brilliance and balance between audio-frequency ranges, it is important to avoid placing the microphone too close to the vocalist or solo instrument. In recent years the use of overhead microphones has become increasingly popular. Such a microphone can be positioned above the participant, out of reach, where it is safe from handling, jars, and direct pickup of vibrations.

Successful musical programming is dependent to a great extent on experience gained at rehearsals and during previous pickups from the same location. Adequate rehearsal time permits you to experiment with the microphone positions until the most pleasing and balanced result is obtained. For example, the recommended spacing between microphone and piano is eight feet or more; less spacing upsets the tonal balance. Of course, if the pianist is also a soloist and only one microphone is available, it must be moved closer for the vocal part of the program. But if facilities are available, a separate microphone is preferred for the singing. For a program consisting of a vocalist and a pianist, the microphone should be correctly positioned relative to the piano. Then the vocalist can be placed in accordance with his or her volume and dynamic range. Optimum spacing between pianist and vocalist may be as much as ten feet.

To establish the proper level between a vocalist and a piano, it is sometimes necessary to use a unidirectional microphone to favor the vocalist, and have its minimum-pickup direction toward the piano. A vocalist accompanied by an orchestra must usually be positioned much closer to a single microphone. Rehearsal time is again important in learning beforehand the proper balance between vocalist and musical accompaniment.

A common technique, during musical programs consisting of an orchestra and soloists (instrumentals or vocals), involves the use of one general microphone plus one or several accent microphones which are used only during solo segments of the program. The general microphone is set up to obtain an overall balanced result from the orchestra. Often this microphone is placed overhead and with some sensitivity toward the audience to add liveness to the program. The amount of separation from the orchestra is a function of the liveness factors of reverberation time and volume. Again this is best determined by rehearsal and from experience. If the general microphone is a substantial distance from the orchestra, one must be certain the inherent noise levels around it are not so strong that they are distracting.

Accent microphones are then positioned in the orchestra to pick up the soloist or a small group. If the general microphone is not able to bring out a particular orchestra section adequately, an accent microphone may be employed, even during orchestral selections.

The use of a general microphone some distance away from an orchestra has become increasingly popular in high-fidelity broadcasting.

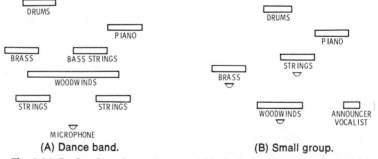

(A) Dance band.   (B) Small group.

Fig. 4-24. Basic microphone placement for dance band and small groups.

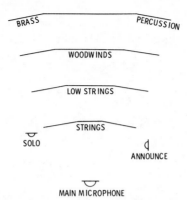

Fig. 4-25. Pickup of a large orchestra.

Of course, accent microphones must be available for the solo, announce, and close-emphasis portions of the program.

Several typical microphone arrangements are shown in Figs. 4-24 and 4-25. With a single microphone, the various segments of the orchestra must be positioned in accordance with each one's amplitude and dynamic range. Usually the small strings are the closest, followed by the woodwinds, bass strings, brass (trombones, trumpets), piano, and drums in that order. If several microphones are available, they can be used to accent individual segments. It is also possible to use the mixer controls of the control amplifier to obtain the most desirable balance among the instrument groups.

In summary, effective placement and use of microphones require a knowledge of microphone characteristics, how the program site acts acoustically, how people respond to a microphone, plus a good listening ear and an understanding of what to emphasize and what is to be background.

CHAPTER 5

Record and Tape Machines

Recorded and taped shows occupy a large percentage of a radio station's total broadcast hours, especially if the station is small or does not have strong network ties. "Disc jockey" shows are at the peak of their popularity. In most stations the DJ is a combination announcer and control-console operator, but not a technical man. He spins records from the studio, a mobile broadcast truck, or remote location set up in department stores, shopping centers, and other locations. Sometimes he may have a permit, a necessity when the transmitter is part of the control-room facilities. The technical staff is responsible for maintaining the record and tape-playing equipment and for setting up remote facilities.

5-1. TRANSCRIPTION DESK AND CONTROL CONSOLE

A transcription desk and control-console combination is shown in Fig. 5-1. From this center the operator can spin records and at the same time control other signal sources such as tape players, studio, network, or remote sources. The switches permit the operator to establish program continuity by turning the various signal sources on and off at the proper times, and the controls allow him to control the amplitudes of the various signals. By watching the needle of the sound-level (volume-unit) meter, the operator can make sure that the signal being supplied to the transmitter is of the proper magnitude.

When a record show is in progress, the operator can place a record on one of the turntables, ready for use, while the second turntable is in operation. In fact, with headphones or a monitoring speaker, he can even listen to the record that he is setting up and position the tone arm to provide a smooth continuity in changing over between turntables. This is referred to as "cuing" the record. A typical sequence follows:

1. While a selection is playing on the left turntable, the operator places another record on the right turntable.

Courtesy WFIL

Fig. 5-1. Turntables and control console.

2. Through the monitoring headphones or speaker he plays the record on the right turntable, listening until he finds the exact spot where the record is to begin, and at the same instant stops the rotation of the record.
3. With the turntable motor still running, he then backs off the record a fraction of a turn and holds it stationary.
4. As soon as the selection is completed on the left turntable, he switches over to the right turntable. With the right turntable now supplying signal to the transmitter, he is free to cue a different record, or to play another selection from the original record, on the left turntable.

In cuing a record an operator, after finding the desired cue spot, turns off the turntable motor and backs the record up a fraction of a turn. At the proper moment, he then switches on the turntable motor. This mode of operation is possible because turntables used in broadcasting are able to reach their normal operating speeds in a fraction of a revolution. If the turntable were slow in building up to maximum speed, the initial part of the selection would be distorted.

The most popular records are the 16-inch, 33⅓-rpm transcriptions and the smaller, 45-rpm records. Approximately fifteen minutes of program time is available on a single transcription. Usually a number of selections, with suitable separations, are recorded on one transcription to permit spot announcements between selections. These transcriptions are sold to radio broadcast stations by numerous transcription services.

Most turntables have two, and sometimes three or four, speeds to handle the large variety of commercial records now available. Likewise, two sizes of stylii are incorporated to accommodate the different record grooves.

WFIL, Philadelphia, Pennsylvania operates on 560 kHz with a power of 5 kilowatts. The switching group and fader controls shown in Fig. 5-1 permit the intermixing and volume level control of the various sound sources. In addition to the phonoplayers there are several cartridge tape players or *cart players* mounted on top of the operating desk. A reel-to-reel tape player is shown at the left.

A remote monitoring and control rack is shown in Fig. 5-2 and is a part of the same room. Switching of the remote monitoring facility

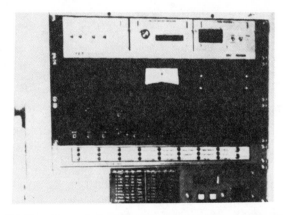

Fig. 5-2. Remote-control and monitoring rack for am station WFIL.

permits a digital readout display of key transmitter and antenna parameters. The remote control function at this point permits adjustment of key transmitter parameters even though the actual transmitter site is miles away. WFIL has a directional transmitting pattern and the patterns themselves differ for daytime and nighttime operations. The transmitter log is kept at this remote-control position in the studios. The rack also mounts the emergency-broadcast-system receiver which must be in continuous operation.

5-2. TURNTABLE AND PREAMPLIFIER

The Harris turntable of Fig. 5-3 has three speeds. It has a rapid start-up time for easier cuing of records. Starting time for the three record speeds is less than ⅙ revolution for 33⅓ rpm; ¼ revolution for 45 rpm and ⅓ revolution for 78.26 rpm. Speeds can be controlled by the slide switch on the front panel. A lever on the tone arm chooses the correct-diameter stylus.

A speed-change mechanism is included for precise setting of turn-table speed when necessary. Usually turntable speed is adjusted with the assistance of a stroboscope disc which usually is operated in con-junction with a neon-lamp light source that is driven by the turntable supply voltage. When using a 60-Hz source the lamp will flash 7200 times per minute. In the stroboscope calibration for 33⅓ rpm there are 216 lines. Multiplied by 33⅓ rpm this corresponds to 7200 lines. Thus if the strobe image lines remain stationary when observed under a 60-Hz light it is an indication there is no speed error. The strobo-scope disc has a 160-line structure for 45-rpm speed adjustment and 92 lines for 78.25 rpm. Again a stationary pattern results when there is no speed error.

Courtesy Harris Communications
Fig. 5-3. Turntable and tone arm.

One function of a phono preamplifier is to increase the level of the phono-cartridge output before it is applied to the control-console input. A second and equally important function is to provide record equaliza-tion. In the recording process the cutting of the grooves is such that the playback output amplitude is not linear with frequency. In fact, the output of the phono cartridge increases with frequency as com-pared to a constant-amplitude input with frequency at the input of a recording-amplifier system.

Response is in the form of a rather irregular curve made in accor-dance with the RIAA (Recording Industry Association of America). This is a standardized recording curve. The frequency response of the phono preamplifier must make a compensation for this curve. This ir-regular response is referred to as the *RIAA equalization curve.* Re-sponse shape is handled by a properly compensated negative feedback network in most phono preamplifiers.

Two phono preamplifiers are shown in Fig. 5-4. These amplifiers can be used for a single stereo phono player or as individual amplifiers for two monophonic (mono) phono players.

Courtesy Harris Communications

Fig. 5-4. Phono preamplifiers.

A schematic diagram of an integrated-circuit phono preamplifier is given in Fig. 5-5. This amplifier has an input impedance of 47K ohms and an output impedance that matches into either 150 ohms or 600 ohms. Its frequency response is within ±1 dB of the standard RIAA curve. Distortion is less than 0.5% over the 50-15,000 Hz audio range.

Output level can be set with potentiometer R18. The input stage is an operational amplifier with signal being applied to pin 3. Output is supplied through the compensating diodes to the bases of the complementary-symmetry output stage. An output transformer provides the appropriate match into either 150 or 600 ohms. A dc-offset adjustment (potentiometer R9) can be set to prevent the input stage from having any influence on the dc biasing of the output transistors.

A network consisting of resistors R1 through R4 plus capacitors C2 and C3 provides a feedback path from output to the second input of the input amplifier. Constants are chosen to obtain the required RIAA equalization.

The power supply consists of a full-wave bridge rectifier and two integrated-circuit voltage regulators that provide output voltage of +15V and −15V.

5-3. TAPE-CARTRIDGE SYSTEMS

The *cart-tape* player (Fig. 5-6) is a popular item in the modern broadcast station. Commercials, station identifications, and other announcements are recorded on the endless tapes that are a part of cartridges that plug into the player. They can be stopped, cued, and started manually, by remote control, or can be made a part of a pro-

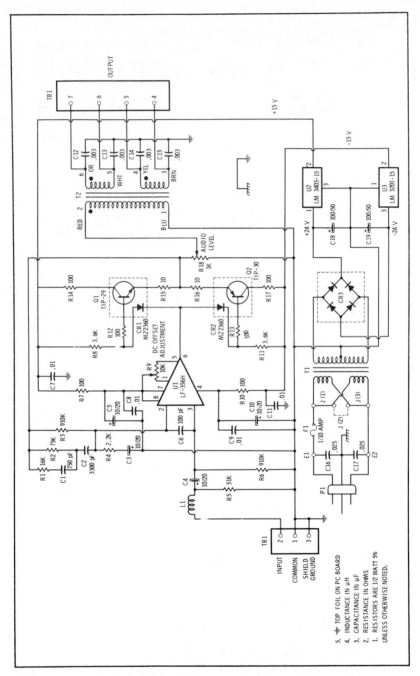

Fig. 5-5. Harris IC phono preamplifier schematic.

Courtesy International Tapetronics Corp.

Fig. 5-6. Cartridge tape player.

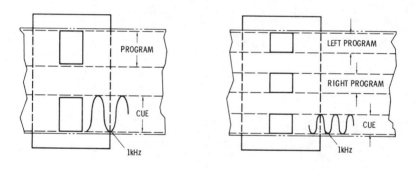

Fig. 5-7. Information tracks on a cart tape.

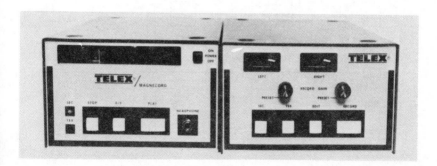

Courtesy Telex Communications, Inc.

Fig. 5-8. Combination player/recorder.

gram automation system. They are simple to operate and preserve good program continuity.

In addition to the program information that can be recorded on the tape (mono or stereo), there is a special cuing track on the tape (Fig. 5-7). Three special cuing tones are used. These cue tones are inserted when the cart tape is being recorded. Thus there are two reproduce heads for a monaural tape player—program and cue. For a stereo version there are three heads provided for left channel, right channel, and cue.

Many cart players also make available a third (tertiary) cue tone of 8 kHz. This tone can also be used to supply information into automated systems or for auxiliary switching activities.

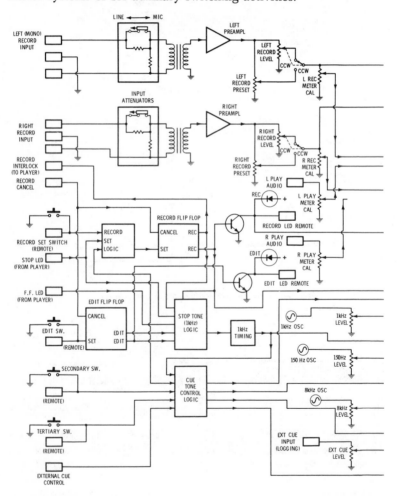

Fig. 5-9. Recorder

Operation of the cart player of Fig. 5-6 requires only the insertion of the cart tape and the use of the stop and start pushbuttons. There is a power indicator lamp that shows the player is connected to ac power. When the cart tape is inserted there is a microswitch that closes the circuit to a "ready" indicator light which is located in the stop switch. This indicates that the tape's transport is ready for starting. Pressing the start switch puts the tape in motion. An indicator light in the start switch indicates that the machine is in "run" condition. The audio message will be reproduced and the tape motion will continue after the message until the primary 1-kHz tone automatically stops the machine, or until the stop switch is pressed.

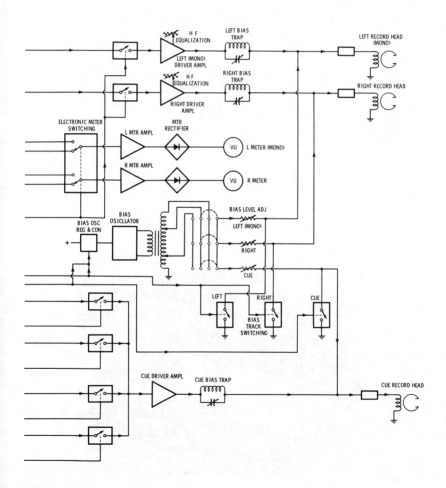

block diagram.

The stop switch can be pressed at any time to stop the tape drive. However, unless the cartridge is allowed to stop automatically it will not be properly cued for the next play.

A combination tape cart player/recorder is shown in Fig. 5-8. The playback segment is on the left; the recorder, on the right. However, components are used interchangeably. For example, the VU meters can be used for both record and playback. The combination is basically a stereo unit. However, the left channel can be used for mono operation.

A functional block diagram of the record activity is given in Fig. 5-9. Linear and digital IC circuits as well as discrete solid-state components are used. The bias oscillator for the three heads (left, right, and cue) is located at the center of the block diagram. This oscillator operates at 100 kHz and develops the individual bias currents for the heads. Each bias level can be adjusted separately. Bias traps prevent the 100-kHz component from feeding back into the individual audio and cue channels.

The primary cue tone is 1 kHz. On the conclusion of a particular audio message the tape continues to advance until a 1-kHz tone is detected, whereupon the cue detector circuit stops the tape drive mechanism. Thus, the tape has been cued automatically and is ready to begin the same or a new message, depending on whether one or more segments of programming have been recorded on the tape. Many cart players also have a high-speed feature. At the conclusion of a given message the tape advances at a much faster speed until it encounters the 1-kHz primary cue tone. This operation is done with a secondary cue tone of 150 hertz which begins at the end of the message. The secondary cue tone cannot only be used for the fast-run mode, if included, but also can be used to actuate relays which indi-

Courtesy Ampex Corp.

Fig. 5-10. Broadcast tape recorder.

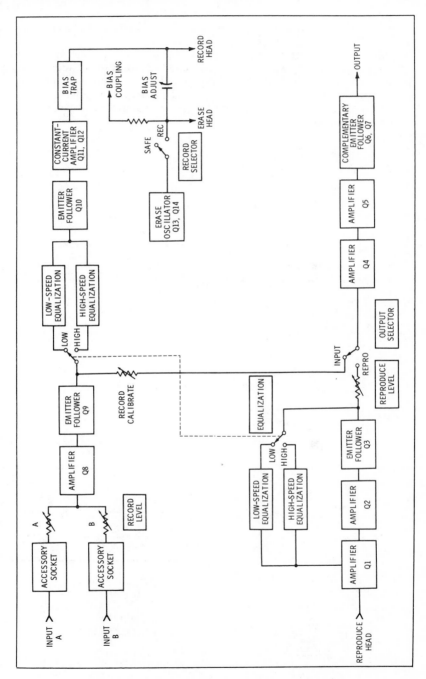

Fig. 5-11. Functional plan of broadcast tape recorder.

cate the end of a specific message, and also switch on a second cart player or other source of program material.

Audio signal inputs are located at the top left and include an input attenuator as well as a switching arrangement for use of audio line or microphone signals. Output of the preamplifiers is conveyed through a record-level control and playback/record electronic switching to the driver amplifiers. Appropriate high-frequency equalization can be set in the driver stages.

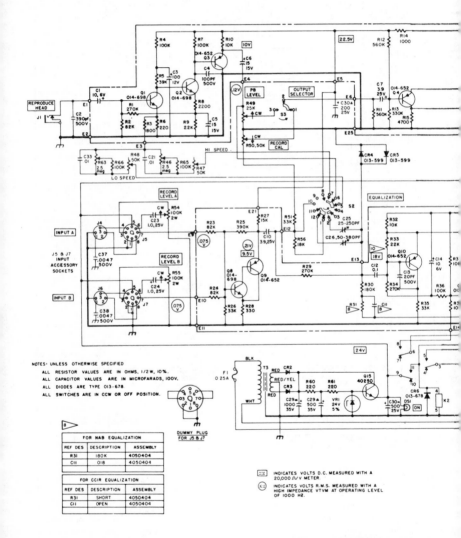

Fig. 5-12. Schematic diagram

A versatile metering arrangement is included. Appropriate logic switching permits the metering circuit to be used on either record or playback modes. Four individual controls are available for meter calibration for each mode. Record preset potentiometers are also located in the output circuits of the preamplifiers.

The three tone oscillators (primary, secondary, and tertiary) are located at the bottom center. A fourth external input is available for inserting a logging cue. The logic switching circuits and controls are

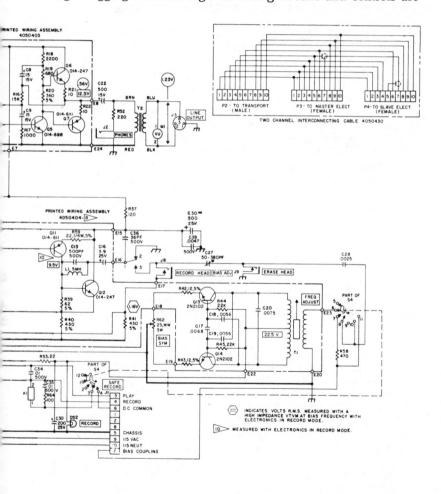

of tape recorder.

located at the lower left. Outputs from the cue tone-control logic circuit switch the appropriate cue signal(s) to the input of the cue driver amplifier which supplies one or more cue signals to the cue record head. The four important operator pushbutton controls are shown at the lower left. These include the record, editing, secondary cue, and tertiary cue switching. These operate through the logic control circuits to set up the appropriate functions for recording.

5-4. TAPED PROGRAM MATERIAL

Magnetic tape recording is an important phase of radio broadcasting. Because of their light weight, tape recorders can be carried around to record interviews, news events, and other programs originating away from the studio. This material can then be played back during a broadcast.

Tape recording systems can also be used to establish fast-moving and interesting program continuity, because it is a simple matter to edit-out the lengthy, uninteresting material. Many stations tape an incoming network program when, for example, a popular local show is on at the same time, and then broadcast the network program at a more convenient time. Complete shows, including music and spot announcements, can be recorded on tape and the entire program then broadcast at the most appropriate time or in accordance with the sponsor's wishes. Automatic spot-tape machines even make it possible to insert taped commericals or other announcements into the program continuity at the proper times.

A compact solid-state broadcast quality tape recorder is the *Ampex* model shown in Figs. 5-10 and 5-11. There are one- and two-channel models. A single-channel model is shown in Fig. 5-10. In the two-channel version there is another identical section at the bottom. The case is slightly larger to accommodate this second module. The latter arrangement can be used for stereo recording and reproduction with appropriate record/reproduce heads.

The RECORD section is shown at the top of the functional block diagram in Fig. 5-11. There is a dual input with separate gain controls. Tape equalization for both speeds is handled between the two emitter followers, Q9 and Q10. Additional amplification follows before the signal is applied to the RECORD head. A 100-kHz bias signal for the ERASE and RECORD heads is generated by the solid-state ERASE oscillator.

The REPRODUCE section is shown at the bottom of Fig. 5-11 and consists of an input voltage amplifier and feedback equalization networks. Through an output-selector switching arrangement, the reproduced signal is passed on to a pair of amplifier stages and an emitter-follower.

The output selector switch also permits the channeling of the incoming RECORD signals to the input of the reproduce amplifier. The path is by way of RECORD calibration potentiometer. From there the signal is passed to a group of amplifiers, and eventually to output transformer T2. (Refer to Fig. 5-12.) The VU meter across the secondary can be used to check the level of the RECORD signals. As a result the amplifier gain controls can be preset before the actual program material is taped.

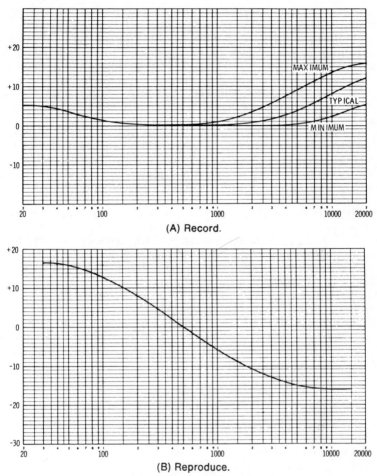

(A) Record.

(B) Reproduce.

Fig. 5-13. NAB response curves.

The same path is also open during the actual recording of the program and audio level can be monitored continuously on the VU meter.

In the REPRODUCE mode, the RECORD section becomes inoperative. The signal taken off the REPRODUCE head is increased in level by a two-stage common-emitter preamplifier, transistors Q1 and Q2. Transistors Q4 through Q7 form a two-stage amplifier and an audio output stage. This output circuit and an appropriate transformer make a match into 600-ohm audio line.

A schematic diagram is given in Fig. 5-12. The two inputs are shown left center. The preamplifier is a direct-coupled common-emitter amplifier and emitter-follower output stage. Note that the second transistor serves as the collector load for the input transistor. The equalization and switching facility follow. After equalization the signal is passed to the input of the emitter-follower transistor Q10. It is followed by a high-gain, constant-current amplifier. The collector output is transferred through capacitor C15, inductor L1, and capacitor C16 to the RECORD head by way of jack J8. The parallel combination of L1 and C15 blocks the bias oscillator (100-kHz) component from the amplifier.

The 100-kHz bias component is generated by a multivibrator consisting of transistors Q13 and Q14. The bias signal is applied to the ERASE head, through the resonant output transformer, and to the RECORD head through the bias-adjustment capacitor C27.

A PLAYBACK signal is transferred to the second amplifier group from the emitter-follower output transistor (Q3) to the gain control and switching section at the input of emitter-follower Q4. The two equalization networks for both low-speed and high-speed operation are connected in the feedback path between the output of transistor Q3 and the emitter circuit of transistor Q1.

The actual RECORD and REPRODUCE responses are given in Fig. 5-13. They are based on the standard NAB (National Association of Broadcasters) responses. In the RECORD mode, high-frequency pre-emphasis is used in maintaining a good signal-to-noise ratio. Proper compensation or de-emphasis is then made in the REPRODUCE curve so as to obtain a linear overall response.

The REPRODUCE signal is built up in level by the second group of amplifiers which drive the output transformer and supply signal to the 600-ohm audio line. A VU meter is connected across the secondary. Headphones can be inserted into the primary circuit of the output transformer. The unit is designed to supply the usual +4-dBm signal to the phone line.

CHAPTER 6

Studio and Control-Room Facilities

The essential features of an am broadcast station are best described by referring to the functional diagram and floor plan of a typical small station. Such a plan is given in Fig. 6-1.

6-1. SMALL STATIONS

The larger dashed-line block at the center of the diagram outlines the console-component functions. At the left of the diagram, you will note the various control-room and studio accessories that include an announce microphone, two turntables, a tape recorder, and three studio microphones. Remote input and network lines are shown on the left side and legend of diagram symbols is shown on the right.

Facilities are provided for three studio microphones. The top three input switches of the console select either the control-room accessories or the studio microphone, and a fourth switch permits a choice between remote and network lines. A jack is provided for inserting a phone into the network line to monitor its signal. Remote input lines are shown at the bottom left.

Preamplifier and mixer gain controls are associated with each of the four console inputs. The two-channel amplifier system includes an audition booster and monitor amplifier plus a program booster and line amplifier. A switching arrangement between the preamplifier system and the dual-channel amplifiers permits either single or mixed incoming signals to be fed to one or the other of the two channels.

An example of possible switching is in relation to the control-room equipment. At the conclusion of a record on turntable No. 1, a changeover from this turntable to the control-room announce microphone may be desired. To do so, the switch of turntable No. 1 is set to the neutral position, and the control-room ANNOUNCE switch is set to position P to

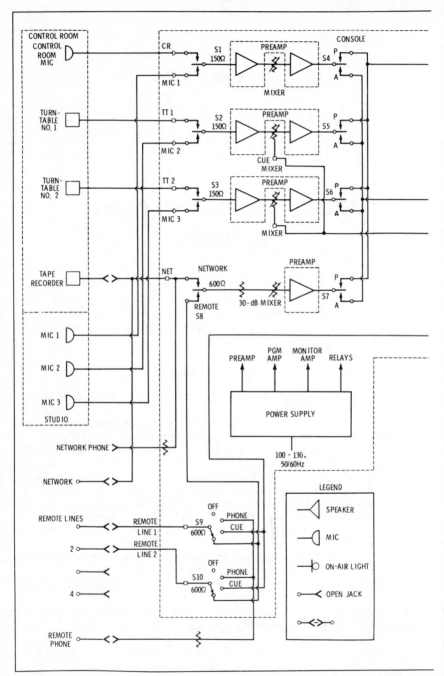

Fig. 6-1. Functional diagram

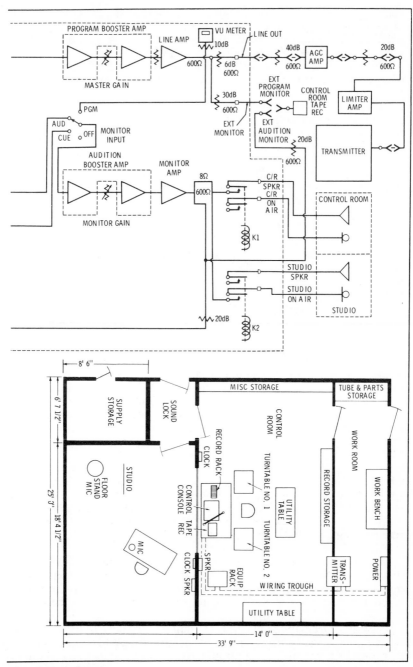

of a small am station.

supply voice signal into the program amplifier. At the conclusion of the announcement, the control-room ANNOUNCE switch is set to its neutral position. Turntable No. 2 may then be switched to the P position, supplying a record signal to the program amplifier.

While the transcription on turntable No. 2 is being played, it is possible to prepare turntable No. 1 for the next selection—perhaps for a recorded spot announcement. The announcement is made ready by using the cue- or audition-booster amplifier. The second channel switch, associated with turntable No. 1, is set to position A. The signal from turntable No. 1 is now being supplied to the audition-booster amplifier, and will reach the control-room speaker when the audition-amplifier input switch is set to the AUD position. In other words, the transcription on turntable No. 2 is supplying signal to the program line and transmitter while the control-room operator is setting up the recorded commercial to be played next on turntable No. 1. When the selection on turntable No. 2 is completed, it is switched off and No. 1 is switched to position P, supplying the commercial announcement to the program-amplifier input.

Also, remote or network signals coming into the console can be switched either into the program line when the signals are to be transmitted, or into the audition channel when they are to be checked or cued. The two switches associated with the remote lines have four positions. The remote-line inputs can be switched for communications (phone), for cuing, to supply signal to the program channel, and also to OFF.

The four preamplifier-mixer controls make it possible to establish the proper relative levels for signals that may be supplied at the same time to either the program and/or the audition channels. For example, it may be necessary to use microphones 1 and 2 in the studio simultaneously during a live program. The input switches to the preamplifiers are set to the microphone No. 1 and No. 2 positions. Likewise, both preamplifier output switches are set to their P positions. Both microphone signals are now being supplied to the input of the program amplifier and have the correct relative signal level.

A monitor speaker in the studio carries the program material except when it is originating "live" from the studio itself. The control-room speaker also carries the program material except when the control room is used for auditions. The studio ON THE AIR light goes on whenever a program is being broadcast from the studio. Likewise, the control-room ON THE AIR light goes on whenever the control-room ANNOUNCE microphone is being used.

The output of the program amplifier supplies signal to a VU meter mounted on the control console. The control-room operator watches the meter to make certain the signal supplied to the line is at the proper level. The operation of the VU meter will be discussed in the following section.

The agc (automatic gain control) amplifier not only relieves the control-console operator from the tedious job of "riding the gain," but also provides a more constant-amplitude signal to the transmitter. As a result, a higher average modulation percentage can be sustained and hence a higher average power output from the transmitter. This is important in obtaining the most reliable coverage over the widest area.

The limiter amplifier prevents the transmitter from being overmodulated by modulation peaks. By so doing, this amplifier also helps maintain a higher average modulation percentage and thus a wider and more reliable coverage.

As shown in Fig. 6-2, the agc amplifier and modulation limiter are mounted in the equipment rack at small stations. When the studio and transmitter are separated, the limiter amplifier is generally part of the transmitter, and the agc amplifier is mounted in the control room. The agc amplifier is discussed later in this chapter, and the limiter amplifier is explained in the chapter on transmitters. A transmitter installation includes a modulation monitor and a frequency monitor. In the small stations these two monitors are mounted in the equipment rack or at the transmitter if it is separate from the studio. These two monitors are discussed in the chapter on monitor equipment.

Notice the jack panel (Fig. 6-2) associated with the equipment rack. Some of the jacks are "normaled through." For example, note that connections have been established between the remote lines No. 1 and No. 2 and their amplifier inputs. The jack (not normaled through) uses open-circuit phone jacks. Patch cords can be used to switch between the various terminations and inputs brought to the jack panel. Let us take two examples of the use of the jack-panel and patch-cord arrangement. Notice that REM 1 and REM 1 IN as well as REM 2 and REM 2 IN are "normaled through," so that connections have already been established between remote lines 1 and 2 and their inputs. Therefore, no patch cord is needed in establishing the connections between these points.

Notice, however, that there is no normaled-through connection between REM 3 and REM 4—the incoming lines terminate at these two jacks. Suppose that REM line 3 must be connected to REM 1 IN of the console. To do so, one end of a patch cord is inserted into REM 1 IN, breaking the connection with REM line 1, and the other end of the patch cord is plugged into REM 3. Incoming REM line 3 is now connected to REM 1 IN of the control console.

A jack-panel and patch-cord arrangement gives added versatility to a station and permits "patch-around" operation in case some unit of the station breaks down. For example, if the agc amplifier failed, it would be possible to bypass it by inserting one end of the patch cord into the 40-dB PAD OUT jack and the other end into the LIMITER IN jack.

6-2. VU METER

The VU meter, which is standard equipment for broadcast use, is designed to follow average speech levels realistically with relation to human hearing. It is underdamped so that the pointer will pause momentarily in its upward swing. It then starts downward more slowly. Erratic vibrations and jumps are thus eliminated, making it possible for the operator to obtain a better "picture" of the audio waves at all times.

The meter is calibrated in volume units (VU), corresponding to the

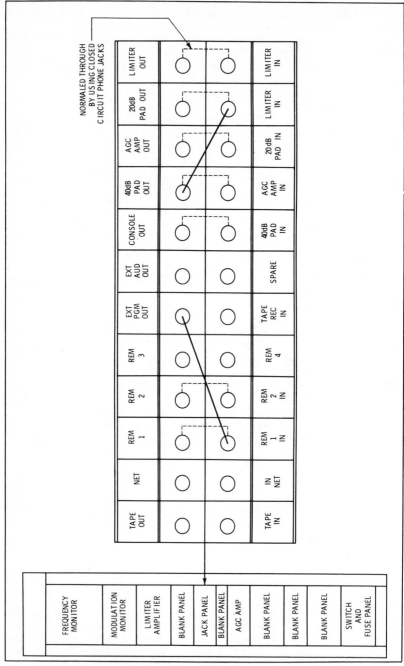

Fig. 6-2. Jack panel and equipment rack arrangements.

number of decibels above a standard reference level of 1 milliwatt across 600 ohms. The 600-ohm value was chosen because it is the standard impedance of remote and network lines. Likewise, 600-ohm lines are generally used for feeding between the various sections of the station—for example, from the output of the program amplifier to the input of the agc amplifier, to the input of the limiter amplifiers, and to the input of the transmitter. Notice, too, that the signal to the VU meter at the program-amplifier output is supplied from a 600-ohm audio line.

The VU meter employs a dc movement and a full-wave copper-oxide rectifier. The meter reads the approximate rms value of an applied waveform. Usually an isolation pad and attenuator are inserted between the line and meter for proper calibration and to prevent the meter from overloading the line. The plan given in Fig. 6-3 is standard. The meter is across a 600-ohm signal source in parallel with the 600-ohm load representing the termination of the line. The combination of the series resistor and attenuator provides a parallel impedance of 7500 ohms. The function of the attenuator is to calibrate the meter to read zero when the correct-amplitude signal level is present on the line. For example, with the component values shown, it is possible to calibrate the VU meter so that its zero reading corresponds to the standard signal level of +4 dBm on a phone line. With suitable resistor pads and attenuators, it is possible to calibrate the meter to read zero VU on other standard signal levels as well. A calibrated meter allows the radio operator to maintain a more constant signal level with only an occasional peak swinging over the ZERO reading. At the same time, the operator can equalize the levels of the various signal sources so that the average sound levels supplied to the line will be adequate and balanced.

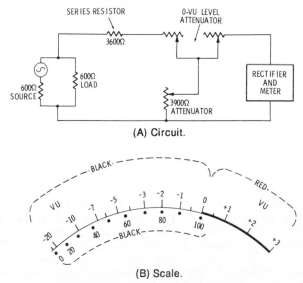

(A) Circuit.

(B) Scale.

Fig. 6-3. VU metering circuit and scale.

The "zero-VU" level is normally set so that a zero-VU reading corresponds to 1 milliwatt across 600 ohms, and the plus and minus VU calibrations correspond to the dB levels above and below this standard.

6-3. ISOLATION PADS AND ATTENUATORS

Television and radio-broadcast signals must be maintained high enough to exceed the background noise level. However, too high a signal level will introduce cross modulation into other lines and into weak-signal circuits. Since most broadcast-amplifier outputs exceed these safe levels, attenuator pads must be used to reduce the signal strength. By maintaining a high degree of isolation between units and by providing good matching characteristics, these pads prevent frequency-response deterioration and crosstalk.

A common form of fixed attenuator is the H-pad shown in Fig. 6-4. The resistor values given in the sample chart are for H-pads that match a 600-ohm input impedance to the same output impedance and provide the dB attenuation indicated on the chart of Fig. 6-4.

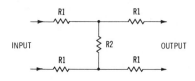

VALUES TO MATCH 600Ω TO 600Ω		
ATTENUATION dB	R1 OHMS	R2 OHMS
1	17.3	5200
3	51	1700
6	100	803
10	156	422
12	180	322
20	245	121
30	282	38
40	294	12

Fig. 6-4. H-pad and sample chart.

Variable attenuators are also used in the broadcast service. A typical example of a variable-T attenuator is shown in Fig. 6-5. As the arm on R1 moves to the right, the arm on R2 moves to the left, and the one on R3 moves toward ground. In the extreme right-hand position of R1, maximum resistance is inserted in series with the line and minimum resistance in shunt. This setting provides maximum attenuation. At the other extreme setting of R1, the series resistance is minimum, and the shunt resistance is maximum. However, at any attenuator setting the impedances inserted across the input and output to the attenuator remain the same. Hence, the proper impedance match is maintained at all times.

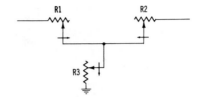

Fig. 6-5. Variable T-attenuator.

6-4. LINE EQUALIZER

In the broadcast services the better-grade lines rented from telephone companies are already equalized up to specific high-frequency limits. Occasionally it is necessary to use an inferior line, and some form of equalizer will be needed to provide a more uniform frequency response up to the desired high-frequency limit. An adjustable line equalizer like the one in Fig. 6-6 can be used. It consists of a parallel-resonant circuit and a series resistance. The lower the resistance, the greater is the compensation. A high resistance lowers the Q of the resonant circuit, reducing the high-frequency emphasis. Switched resistors, instead of the variable resistors R, are often employed which increase the emphasis in 3-dB steps, as shown in the chart.

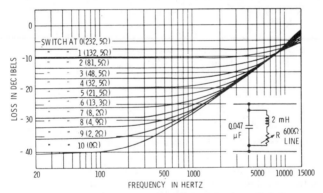

Fig. 6-6. Circuits and characteristics of a line equalizer.

6-5. AGC PROGRAM AMPLIFIER

An agc program amplifier (Fig. 6-7) builds up the level of the program signal, processing it for application to the audio lines that deliver the information to the transmitter. The agc action maintains the average output of the program signal at a nearly constant level despite possible wide variations in input levels. It provides expansion of low-level signals and compression of high-level signals. This is an aid when switching among various sound sources of a broadcast station.

The unit is a solid-state model with a three-stage negative feedback preamplifier, followed by a variable gain-control circuit. The output amplifier is a five-transistor affair which drives a multi-impedance out-

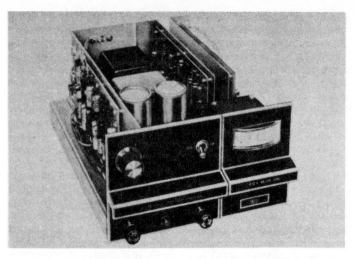

Courtesy RCA

Fig. 6-7. Program amplifier and agc module.

put transformer. This output is supplied to the automatic gain-control amplifier which is in the form of a solid-state module that plugs in on the right (Fig. 6-7).

The agc circuit, when operating under compression, has a fast-attack and slow-recovery characteristic, permitting it to compress fast, high-amplitude audio peaks. It does so without making gain regulation (gain pumping) and background swishing sounds audible.

The input/output agc characteristic is shown in Fig. 6-8. Note that for the first two curves from the left the compression begins when the output level reaches 0 dBm. This is called the "threshold level." Up to this level the amplifier output increases linearly as the input increases.

Above the threshold level, however, the output can no longer keep up with the input. This ratio at which the two increase nonlinearly is called the "compression ratio." The two curves show the above conditions with the amplifier gain control set to maximum and also with the amplifier gain control set for −16 dB attenuation.

In the first two cases the output-level control, shown below the compression meter, was set at maximum. The third curve shows the characteristic when the output-level control is set to its minimum position of −30 dB. Compression now begins when the output level reaches −30 dBm and the input signal level is −70 dBm.

6-6. LARGER STATION FACILITIES

In general the larger station employs the same pieces of equipment as a smaller one, only more of them. Switching facilities are more elaborate at the control consoles because of the increased number of signal sources. There may be various types of automatic players, additional recording facilities, and sound-effects gear.

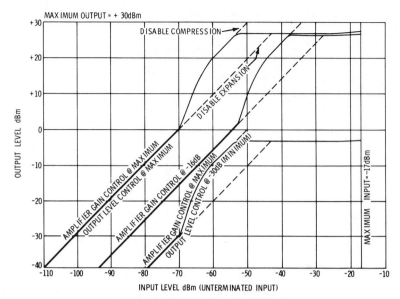

Fig. 6-8. Agc characteristics.

In the plans of Fig. 6-9 and Fig. 3-5 there are separate control rooms for the am and fm programming. There is a third production control room that can be used for prerecording and taping. This control room may also double as an auxiliary control point for either am or fm programming.

Each consolette has a variety of controllable input facilities for microphones, tape players, turntables, network and remote lines, plus spare inputs. Voice signals from the announce booth also terminate at the am and fm control consolettes.

The fm control consolette is designed for stereo transmission and has the required separate left and right channels. The switching facility permits either stereo or monaural operation. The am facility is monaural. Additional outputs are provided for audition or other external monitoring. Each consolette supplies audio to individual control-room, studio, and announce-booth speakers.

Consolette program signals are supplied to an agc/limiter amplifier. The RCA program amplifier can be operated with either an agc output module, limiter module (Fig. 6-10), or a combination of both. The plan of Fig. 6-9 uses three separate program amplifiers with both agc and limiter modules. One of these is used in the path between the am control consolette and the am transmitter. The other two are in the paths of the left and right stereo signals supplied to the fm transmitter.

The functions of a limiter amplifier are to provide abrupt limiting action in the program channels of broadcast transmitters. Such limiters provide an automatic means of holding audio signal peaks at a certain preset level. In so doing overmodulation and overloading of the trans-

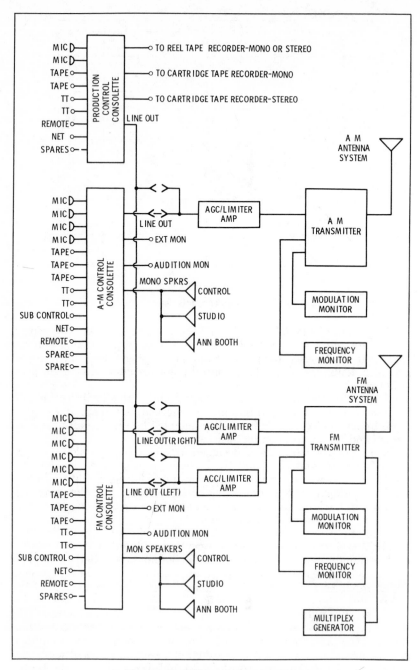

Fig. 6-9. Facilities of a large station.

Courtesy RCA

Fig. 6-10. Program amplifier with limiter.

mitter are avoided. This process reduces distortion and prevents adjacent channel interference.

In addition, by raising the average modulation percentage several decibels, the transmitter power can be used more effectively. As a re-

Courtesy Harris Communications

Fig. 6-11. Program automation system.

sult, overmodulation is avoided on heavy passages of speech or music; at the same time, there is an improvement in signal-to-noise ratio for medium- and low-level audio signals.

Fig. 6-9 also shows the place of the transmitter in the overall broadcast plant. As mentioned previously, the transmitters can be located at the same site as the studio or signals can be carried over common carrier lines to a remote transmitter site. Associated with the am transmitter are modulation and frequency monitors. Similar monitors are required for the fm transmitter. If the station transmits stereo programs or SCA signals the fm transmitter requires a multiplex generator. Transmitters and their associated test equipments are discussed in succeeding chapters.

6-7. PROGRAM AUTOMATION

Automatic programming has become increasingly popular in radio broadcasting. The *Harris System-90* shown in Fig. 6-11 is an example. This system includes a microprocessor that can be used to establish automatic programming over a lengthy period of time. The system controls carts and reel-to-reel tape players as well as other program-source material. The basic system can handle up to as many as 16 sources with the memory bank storing up to 1200 events.

Programming and display are controlled by a small control console (Fig. 6-12). This unit can be located as many as 150 feet away from the computer housing. Not only does it include the controls necessary to set up a specified program series in the computer but, in addition, displays the operating status of the system. A real-time digital clock display as well as a compare-time display using LED readouts are

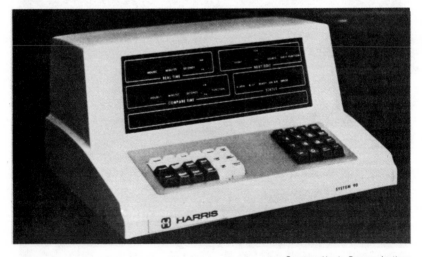

Courtesy Harris Communications

Fig. 6-12. Automation control console.

incorporated in the control console. Thus a comparison between program timing and real time can be made.

Other LED displays can be used for showing which event is occurring and the exact source of program material. This same section can also be used for editing data as related to the source and function programmed for a particular event. There is an alarm LED which comes on when the transmitter is off the air or when two successive sources are not ready, or if there is failure in the logging printer. There is also an indication of whether the next source is ready to be aired..

The major unit (Fig. 6-11) houses the microcomputer and associated circuits as well as monitor and emergency controls that can be used if there is a computer failure. In addition to the power·supply for the system-90 components there is room for the tape and cart decks as well as other necessary items. There is a feedpoint to which an automatic program logger is connected.

Automation control facility is available for a full memory system or for memory use with a live disc jockey. Bulletin insertions can be made. If the disc jockey wishes to leave the control room for brief periods he can also program events to play automatically.

Every on-the-air event can be logged either in clear text or in the form of a numeric high-speed arrangement. In fact, the system-90 can be integrated into automatic billing and accounting systems.

A monitor panel is available for both the program material and for auditioning. Each of four inputs can be monitored if the system is set up for stereo operation. An emergency panel permits operation right from the main unit in case of a computer malfunction.

All audio and control switching is solid-state using a compact enclosure that can house up to 16 source cards. There is a dual-sound sensor card, a fade-out control card, .and a dual-channel line-amplifier card as well. The sensor cards are used for monitoring the system audio as well as the transmitter audio. When the system detects silence it will start the next source. When the transmitter sensor detects silence it will turn on the system alarm indicator and beeper. A *Harris* microprocessor/digital control console is described in Chapter 15.

6-8. AUTOMATED RADIO STATION

Many broadcast station ownerships include both am and fm-stereo outlets. One such successful combination is WGSA-WIOV in Ephrata, Pennsylvania. The fm-stereo outlet (WIOV) live-broadcasts a truckers' and travelers' program from midnight until 9 a.m. Except for special programs, automation takes over for the remainder of the 24-hour day. The country-western program format is set up the evening before. Automatic cartridge racks, reel-to-reel tape player, computer, and control point are shown in Fig. 6-13. Commercials and other announcements are taped on cartridges and inserted into the automatic program sequence. The operating position for live programming on WIOV is shown in Fig. 6-14. Automatic programming panels are shown in the background. The daytime am station (WGSA) is also automated for most of the day.

Fig. 6-13. Cartridge racks, computer, and control point for program automation.

Fig. 6-14. WIOV "live" operating position.

Fig. 6-15. Remote-control, stereo monitoring, and SCA monitor units for fm transmitter.

Fig. 6-16. Directional-antenna monitor for am station.

The fm transmitter and antenna system with an effective radiated power (erp) of 50 kilowatts is located on a nearby ridge. It is operated by remote control. Remote-control unit, stereo monitor, and SCA monitor, shown in Fig. 6-15, can be seen from the operating position.

WIOV also broadcasts sporting events using a uhf airlink to beam the program to the fm transmitter site. From here the signal is sent over telephone lines down to the main operating position where the audio material is coordinated and placed on the program line back to the transmitter.

The am transmitter is located near to the operating position shown in Fig. 6-14. It is a 5000-watt unit and supplies signal to a three-tower directional antenna system. The directional-antenna monitor that indicates phase angle, loop currents, and antenna currents is shown in Fig. 6-16. Although the am station operates much of the day on program automation, there is also a studio and separate control room for WGSA.

CHAPTER 7

Remote Facilities

In order to originate programs at locations other than the studio, am, fm, and television broadcast stations must have remote facilities. In such a broadcast, the terminal facilities are provided by the station and the transmission facilities may be provided by the station or the telephone company.

7-1. THE REMOTE BROADCAST

A common method of handling a remote broadcast is to transmit the program over a pair of rented telephone lines. One line carries the program, and the second line is used for cuing and for communicating back to the studio. In case of trouble on the program line, the spare line could carry the program sound. If only a single line were used, there would be no direct link between remote and studio once the program is on the air. Also, if something happened to the line, the program would go off the air.

The telephone company must, of course, be notified as to when the program is to be aired and also when to install the lines in time for tests or rehearsals. It is advisable to begin setting up the equipment and checking the lines as early as possible. Many remotes are strictly "one-shot" affairs, and the lines are installed in a manner that will permit quick removal. When remotes are held at the same location and at regular intervals, more permanent lines are usually installed.

Many radio stations have remote broadcast trucks equipped with an amplifier, turntables, tape recorders, and other facilities. These trucks often broadcast from local athletic events, parades, or shopping centers. Usually the program is conveyed to the studio over telephone lines.

For some on-the-spot remote broadcasts such as on-the-street interviews or at political conventions, small pack-transmitters are often used. The program material is sent to a remote broadcast center a short distance away. From there it is relayed over telephone lines to the studio.

A third type of remote is the prerecorded pickup, usually taped. Because of its versatility it has become more and more popular, especially with small broadcast stations. Moving around is no problem, since there are no trailing wires or cumbersome equipment to handle. All the interviewer carries is a microphone and a good-quality tape recorder. Another advantage is that the tape can be edited to provide continuity to the recorded program. For example, in covering a parade there often are delays between marching units, and it is difficult to keep up an interesting running commentary.

7-2. CHECKING OUT THE REMOTE

As mentioned previously, it is advisable to set up remote equipment early and to check it thoroughly. As you learned, the studio control-room console has the necessary equipment for auditioning the remote lines. In this way, the microphones and other sound sources at the remote can be checked to make certain their signals are at the proper level.

When a musical program is to be broadcast from a remote location, it is always helpful to set up the line and equipment in time to rehearse the entire program, or at least its musical segments. If the noise level on the line is high while the microphones are open, their cable connections and routing should be checked. Occasionally, fluorescent-lighting fixtures will introduce an arcing noise into the line. Also, electrical equipment which radiates strong fields can feed hum into microphone cables.

Noise on the line while the microphone circuits are closed can mean trouble in the remote amplifier or a high noise level on the phone line. If the latter happens, the phone company should be notified immediately. Just prior to broadcasting time, the system should be checked once more and communications established with the studio control-room, at which time all watches are synchronized and the cue signals reaffirmed.

Microphone placement is often a problem during "remotes." Because of the higher background noise, microphones must be placed as near the sound source as possible, and a unidirectional microphone is almost a necessity. Two microphones can be used—one for announcements and solos, and the other for general pickup—provided the second microphone does not pick up too much background noise to interfere with the first microphone.

7-3. REMOTE AMPLIFIER

Remote amplifiers are light in weight and solid-state construction. The RCA remote amplifier of Figs. 7-1 and 7-2 is an example. The unit weighs 6.5 pounds and can be set up for battery or power-line operation. There are four input channels, one of which can be used as a line amplifier input. This is the fourth input. The channel associated with the first microphone input can also be used as a tone oscillator

Courtesy RCA

Fig. 7-1. Remote amplifier.

which can be helpful in checking a remote line and establishing a reference level.

The four preamplifiers and their individual gain controls are followed by an audio power amplifier and associated master gain control. The power amplifier supplies signal to the audio line as well as a monitoring headset. A VU meter is associated with the power amplifier; it includes a lighted dial when the unit is set up for power-line operation.

The three preamplifiers are quite similar. Each consists of a Darlington pair (Fig. 7-3) which provides good voltage gain as well as a relatively high input impedance. Note that the two collectors are tied together and the emitter of the input transistor is coupled directly to the base of the second transistor. In the second channel the collector load is resistor R15. The microphone level is adjusted with potentiometer R16.

A low-frequency rolloff switch is included in the output. When it is in the circuit, capacitor C13 is placed in series with the signal path and results in a low-frequency rolloff characteristic. When shorted out, there is a low-frequency response that is determined by the larger capacitor (C16).

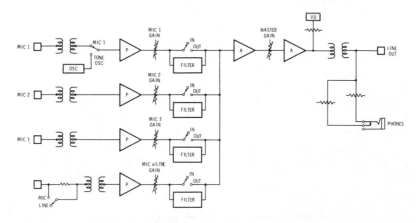

Fig. 7-2. Functional block diagram of remote amplifier.

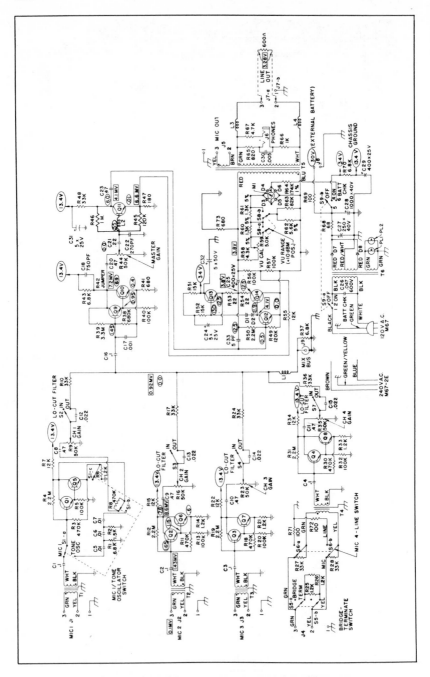

Fig. 7-3. Schematic of typical remote amplifier.

Note switch S1 associated with the first channel. In the tone-oscillator position the stage operates as an RC audio oscillator; the feedback path is via capacitors C5, C6, and C7, along with resistors R1, R2, and the input resistance of the stage. These components determine the frequency of oscillation as well as provide the necessary phase shift to sustain oscillation.

Note that there is a switching arrangement in the input circuit of the fourth channel. This permits this channel to be used either as a microphone input or as an audio-line input. In line operation, it can serve as a line termination, or it can be made to have a higher input resistance for a bridging application.

Transistors Q9 and Q10 serve as an input stage for the main part of the audio amplifier. These two are connected in a Darlington configuration with resistor R43 serving as the collector load. This stage is followed by the master gain control and a common-emitter voltage amplifier. An additional amplifier and the VU-meter circuit are shown at the center right. An output transformer matches the signal into a 600-ohm line.

There is also a utility microphone output winding which can supply signal to a low-impedance microphone line or the low-impedance microphone input of an associated piece of equipment. This is a balanced output configuration with pin 1 serving as the ground connection. Note also that there is a connector (J9) at the bottom center. This can be used to supply a higher level signal to the main amplifier section of the remote unit only.

Another amplifier with a 3-channel input is shown in Fig. 7-4. The three preamplifiers are quite similar. Each preamplifier consists of two common-emitter stages (Fig. 7-4). Referring to the channel 1 preamplifier (which is the basic circuit used in all stages except the power amplifier stage) resistors R1 and R2 provide base-divider bias. Resistors R4 and R5 plus capacitor C3 provide emitter stabilization. Thus the operating-point bias is held essentially constant with circuit and temperature variations. Both dc and ac stabilization is used. Notice that the emitter resistors R4 and R9 are not bypassed. Consequently, there is a limited amount of ac degeneration and an improvement in the ac stability and linearity.

The two stages are direct-coupled, and there is no need for an interstage RC coupling combination, which could introduce low-frequency degeneration and other disturbances. Overall negative feedback for the input amplifier is provided by capacitor C4 and resistor R7 connected between the collector of the second stage and the emitter of the first stage. The generous use of feedback provides a high order of gain stability and permits linear operation with large input signal levels. Thus transistor-parameter variations have a minimum influence on the operation of the preamplifier. The preamplifier is thoroughly decoupled by the RC filters (C2, R6, C5, R11).

The channel 1 preamplifier output is removed at the channel 1 gain control and is supplied, via the isolation resistor R30, to the input of the audio amplifier. This audio amplifier is identical in basic design to the preamplifier. The same feedback arrangements are used to insure

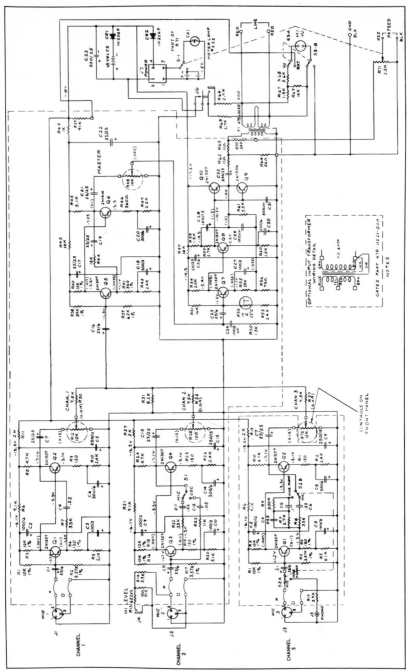

Fig. 7-4. All solid-state remote amplifier.

high operating stability. The audio-amplifier output is removed at the master-gain control and supplied to the audio-power amplifier.

The other two preamplifiers are modified versions of the first-channel preamplifier. The channel 2 preamplifier includes a high-level input. Resistors R13, R14, and R15 provide the necessary attenuation of the high-level signal and an appropriate match into the input of the preamplifier. With the microphone-oscillator switch in the microphone position, negative feedback exists between the collector of the second stage and the emitter of the first stage, just as in the basic channel 1 preamplifier. However, when this switch is set to the oscillator position, there is feedback between the collector of the second stage and the base of the first stage. Rather, there is positive feedback to the input base, and the two stages go into oscillation at approximately 400 hertz. A square wave is generated, and therefore the oscillator signal output is rich in harmonics, providing a good distinctive test signal for transmission over the remote line to the main studio.

The third preamplifier channel is identical to channel 1 with the exception that proper RIAA compensation is provided for a phono signal. A component (R17) is added to the input of the amplifier to provide the correct termination for a magnetic phono cartridge and the necessary high-frequency RIAA equalization. The low-frequency end of the RIAA curve is handled by the feedback network. Notice that the components of the feedback network change when the switch is thrown from the MIC to the MAG PHONO position. The network of capacitors C4 and C5 plus resistors R7 and R9 provide low-frequency boost for RIAA equalization.

The power amplifier is a three-stage, direct-coupled circuit, two voltage amplifiers (Q7, Q8) and a push-pull complementary output stage (Q9, Q10). The last stage operates as a single-ended emitter follower in class B. Therefore, maximum power output can be obtained with a minimum battery drain because the output-stage currents vary with the strength of the audio signals. When no signal is passing through the amplifier, the stages draw very little current, and the battery drain is reduced. Likewise, for lower amplitude passages, they draw less current than for the strong peaks of the program signal.

The bases of the push-pull stage (Q9, Q10) are supplied with an in-phase signal from Q8. Since Q10 is a pnp transistor while Q9 is an npn transistor, the output current of one transistor rises while the output current of the other falls during each half-cycle of signal. However, since the emitter currents are in opposite directions, an effective push-pull output signal is developed across the primary of the output transformer (T1) which supplies the signal to the telephone lines. Signal is also supplied to the phone jack (J6) through isolation resistors R65 and R66. Likewise, an output is derived for operation of the VU meter. Resistors R67, R68, and R69 have values that calibrate the VU meter for a standard signal level and impedance. The values shown are for a zero VU reading that corresponds to +8 dBm across 600 ohms, a standard level of signal for application to a remote telephone line. A 6-dB isolation pad is provided on the primary side of transformer T1 by resistors R62, R63, and R64.

The three-stage power amplifier also includes negative feedback from the emitter of the output stage to the emitter of the input stage via capacitor C29 and resistors R56 and R61. In fact, the dc operating-point stability of the entire amplifier is aided by this feedback path. Note that the emitter current for the push-pull output stage is also present in the emitter resistor (R56) of the input stage. The input-stage (Q7) dc operating bias and, in turn, the dc bias of the following dc coupled stages is held constant with the use of a thermistor (R52) in its base circuit. This thermistor compensates automatically for any change in the conductance of the Q7 base-emitter junction. This activity is also linked to changes in the two succeeding stages because the current through R56 is, in part, contributed by the latter two stages.

To improve the linearity of the amplifier in the handling of a very strong signal, some positive feedback is employed from the emitters of Q9 and Q19 through capacitor C28 to the collector of Q8. This is often referred to as a positive-feedback *bootstrap connection*. What it does

Courtesy McMartin Engineering

Fig. 7-5. Remote radio transmitter.

is increase the effective collector voltage of Q8 in accordance with the amplified signal. Thus, as the amplifier signal voltage rises, the positive feedback to the collector of Q8 aids the linear rise of its collector-output voltage. As a result, adequate linear drive to the output stage is maintained when a high-amplitude signal passes through the remote amplifier.

A 1.5-volt battery and connector (J7) for an external 18-volt (dc) power supply is shown at the top right. It is to be noted that the common return (+18V) for all the stages of the remote amplifier is via the phone jack (J6). Power is supplied to the various stages only when a headset or dummy jack is plugged into J6. As soon as such a plug is removed, the power is disconnected from the unit. The lamp (XA1) will light only when the power-supply mating connector is plugged into the remote amplifier. The mating connector (P7) has a jumper between pins 1 and 3.

7-4. RADIO REMOTE

Electronic news gathering with the use of radio pack transmitters (Fig. 7-5) has become increasingly popular. In this type of installation the announcer can wander about without being impeded by microphone and interconnecting cables. A transmitter of this type has an output of approximately 3 watts on the 150-172 MHz band. Usually the output is frequency modulated with a narrowband deviation of ±5 kHz.

The pack contains a 2.5 ampere-hour rechargeable battery. The unit is especially attractive for radio electronic news gathering and can be used by either an am or fm broadcast station.

The signal from the transmitter is picked up by a receiver in an associated radio van or other type of radio control center. The demodulated signal is then conveyed to the broadcast station over a telephone line or still another higher-powered radio-relay link set up between the control center and the transmitter or control room of the broadcast station.

CHAPTER 8

AM Broadcast Transmitter

The modern low-power am transmitter is a compact and integrated unit with a high order of stability and reliability. Modern broadcast transmitters exceed the FCC requirements for frequency response, frequency stability, carrier-amplitude regulation, distortion, and noise level. In many small stations the transmitters receive a minimum of attention because it is just another unit in a busy control room.

8-1. MAJOR UNITS

Basic designs are somewhat similar among manufacturers. There are some all solid-state transmitters. Most often the low-power stages are solid state while the higher-power amplifiers employ vacuum tubes. There are, of course, many all vacuum-tube transmitters still in operation. The modern RCA transmitter of Fig. 8-1 employs a solid-state exciter and seven higher-powered vacuum tubes are used throughout the transmitter.

Meters at the top of the transmitter read kilovolts applied to the final power amplifier, a multimeter for testing various circuits of the transmitter, and a dc ammeter that reads the current supplied to the final modulated rf power amplifier. The four high-power vacuum tubes of the final rf power amplifier and the modulator can be seen at the top of the rack. Vacuum-tube driver stages are shown immediately beneath.

Fig. 8-2A shows the interconnection plan for the major units of a typical transmitter installation with a remote studio.

In almost all am broadcasting, the program signals from the studio are sent over telephone lines to the transmitter. A minimum of two program lines should be installed, to allow a spare in case of trouble in the other line.

The incoming signal is normally supplied to a booster or line amplifier first, instead of directly to the limiter amplifier. It is advisable to use a booster amplifier, because it can provide additional amplification in an emergency or if the incoming program signal is weak.

Courtesy RCA

Fig. 8-1. One-kilowatt am transmitter.

In the patch panel of Fig. 8-2B, the booster amplifier is normaled-through to the input of the limiter amplifier.

The major function of the limiter amplifier is the compression of the modulation peaks so they will not overmodulate the transmitter. The output of the limiter amplifier feeds the audio-input stage of the transmitter.

Two test units monitor the frequency stability and modulation percentage of a transmitter (Fig. 8-2A). A monitoring amplifier and speaker plus a versatile switching arrangement are part of most transmitters. These facilities permit the transmitter operator to check the program signal at various key locations throughout the transmitter equipment. In the example of Fig. 8-2A, it is possible for the operator to monitor the incoming program line from the phone company, the output of the limiter amplifier, the audio component derived from the modulation monitor, and an auxiliary monitoring input. Some stations use a remote demodulator, located in the antenna field or other point, to pick up some of the radiated rf energy. This rf signal is then demodulated to supply an audio component to the auxiliary-monitor input.

Most stations include a VU-meter panel in the equipment rack. The meter input is terminated at the patch panel, and a patch cord is used to bridge the meter across key points in the program line. Hence, the monitoring facilities include provisions to listen to the program at key points, and a means of measuring the actual sound level as well.

It is very important that the transmitter operator know the general arrangement of his equipment. Once he does, the monitoring facilities will permit him to isolate a point of signal loss more rapidly. Thus, he can quickly find out whether the program signal is missing from the incoming line, or whether the booster or limiter amplifier is out of order. In many instances he could even "patch around" faulty equipment without having to take the station off the air. For example, it would be no problem to bypass the limiter amplifier by connecting a patch cord between the booster-amplifier output and transmitter input.

Usually the accessory equipment at the transmitter is conveniently

Fig. 8-3. A transmitter and associated equipment rack.

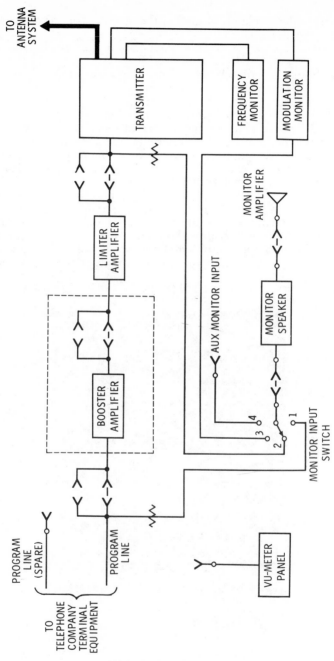

(A) Interconnection plan.

Fig. 8-2. An interconnection plan of the major units

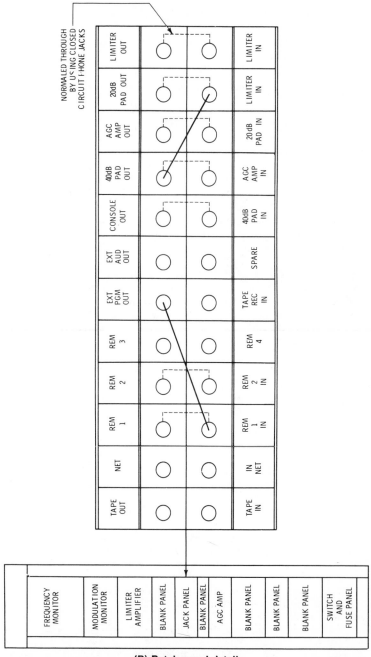

(B) Patch panel detail.

in a typical transmitter installation and a remote studio.

mounted in an equipment rack beside the transmitter. A typical equipment rack is shown to the left of the transmitter in Fig. 8-3. From top to bottom are mounted the modulation monitor, limiter amplifier, and frequency monitor.

8-2. FUNCTIONAL PLAN OF TRANSMITTER

The functional diagram of a transmitter is given in Fig. 8-4. The radio-frequency section starts with a highly stable crystal oscillator. Because of the high quality achieved by modern crystals and their mounts (seldom drifting more than a few cycles with temperature change), some broadcast transmitters no longer include a crystal oven.

The rf signal is built up by a following buffer and intermediate power amplifier. A single power-amplifier stage develops enough rf energy to drive the antenna system at the rated-power output. Most transmitters use a single-ended rf stage with one or more tubes in parallel as is done in Fig. 8-4, the number depending on the power output desired. A push-pull rf power-output stage is rarely used in modern am broadcast transmitters.

Plate modulation is almost universal for the small-station broadcast transmitter. The modulator stage is usually a push-pull class-B or -AB stage. The modulation reactor is separate from the output transformer. This makes it possible to design two small and highly efficient units capable of linear and full modulation of the final rf stage. In some transmitters a small amount of modulation is also supplied to an intermediate power-amplifier stage to improve both the linearity of the transmitter and its ability to handle the modulation peaks. Inverse feedback is used to extend the frequency response of the transmitter, to stabilize the characteristics of the audio amplifier and modulator, and to provide a well-regulated output.

8-3. MAJOR UNITS OF ANTENNA SYSTEMS

A variety of units are associated with the antenna system of the am broadcast station, as shown in Figs. 8-5 and 8-6. The modulated rf signal is usually conveyed over a coaxial transmission line to an antenna tuning unit, the function of which is to tune the antenna to proper resonance and match the transmission line to the antenna (see Fig. 8-5). An antenna-current meter is associated with the antenna tuning arrangement. Although the pickup device is part of the antenna-tuning unit, a remote recording meter is often mounted at the transmitter. This reading gives an excellent indication of the operating conditions of the transmission line and antenna system; it soon indicates any line and antenna-system defect or a decrease in the power output of the transmitter.

The antenna must have suitable lightning protection. Usually it is in the form of a spark gap and a retarding inductor. Also, the power line to the obstruction and beacon lights must be isolated properly in order not to disturb the radio-frequency characteristics of the antenna.

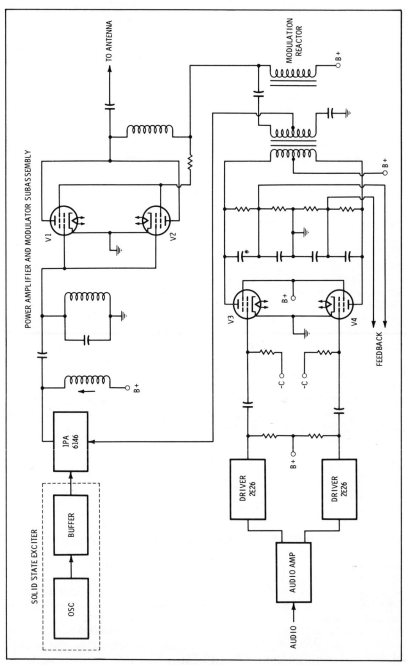

Fig. 8-4. Functional diagram of a typical am transmitter.

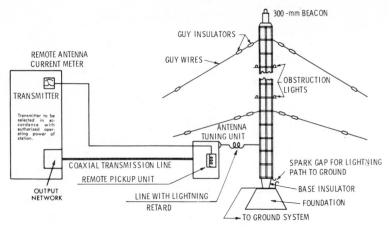

Fig. 8-5. The major units of an antenna system.

These accessories must be protected from lightning damage as much as possible.

Additional units are required for a directional-antenna system. The arrangement in Fig. 8-6 is typical. The directional-antenna pattern is obtained by proper spacing of the antenna towers and by correct phasing between the existing radio-frequency currents. Correct radio-frequency current relationships are established by a phasing unit generally mounted near the transmitter. These phased currents are conveyed on separate coaxial lines to the respective antenna towers and their associated tuning boxes.

A sampling loop, mounted on each radiator, picks up a small amount of rf current and, through its own line, supplies signal to an antenna monitor in the transmitter building. The functions of an antenna monitor are to evaluate the incoming current components from the sampling loops, and to indicate whether correct current and phase relationships have been established at the antennas as well as the antenna base currents. The antenna-tuning houses in Fig. 8-6 also show the chokes which isolate the lighting system from the radio-frequency energy, and also the unit that flashes the beacon light on and off in accordance with FCC requirements.

8-4. DUTIES OF TRANSMITTER OPERATORS

The primary responsibility of the transmitter operator is to monitor the transmitter and its associated equipment. He should respond quickly to any indication that there might be loss of air time. If a specific failure takes the station off the air, he should restore service as soon as possible, even if he must do so at reduced power.

Logging facilities should guide the operator in anticipating possible sources of trouble. Significant drift or erratic meter readings should alert him to possible trouble and/or the need for immediate inspection and maintenance of a particular segment of the transmitter. If the in-

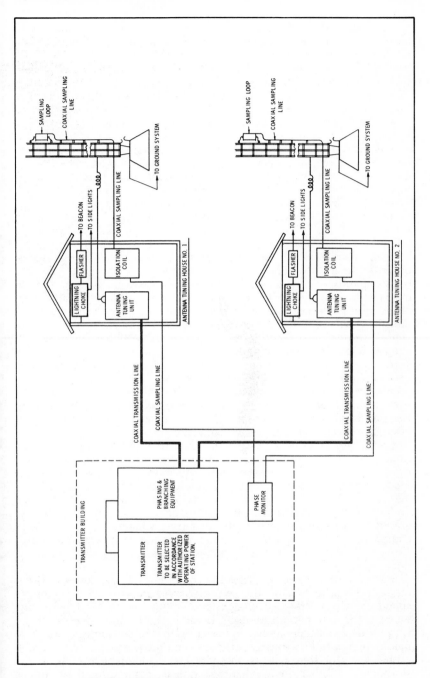

Fig. 8-6. Major units of a directional-antenna system.

spection suggests that the station be taken off the air, he should try to keep the station operating until sign-off, or at least wait until a sustaining (noncommercial) program is being broadcast. However, any trouble serious enough to damage expensive components or violate FCC technical regulations must be corrected as soon as possible, even if it means taking the station off the air. Many stations, particularly the larger, higher-powered ones, have emergency transmitters and/or power supplies that can be pressed into operation in case of trouble in the main transmitter.

A good transmitter operator knows the transmitter and associated equipment down to the smallest detail. He knows the exact location of all stages of the transmitter and its key component parts, or studies instruction manuals and schematics thoroughly until he does. He also knows the wiring plans of the equipment so he can track down power-failure troubles quickly, and learns the switching and patch-panel arrangements so he can "patch-around" a faulty unit of broadcast equipment.

It is a good idea for the neophyte operator to mentally visualize a course of action to follow in certain emergencies. The chief engineer or a capable, experienced operator can give excellent guidance on emergency procedures. It is customary in some stations to call conferences in order to keep all operators informed of possible malfunctions and the repair procedure. Such meetings can do much to build up the confidence of the inexperienced personnel by teaching them how to keep lost air time at a minimum.

In addition to log keeping, the transmitter operator must keep an eye on sound levels. Modern broadcast equipment, with its agc amplifiers and modulation limiters, has made this task easier; and if the operator at the control console does a reasonably good job of riding the gain at his end, the transmitter operator may not even have to readjust the gain from sign-on to sign-off of the station.

The limiter and audio gain should both be adjusted to prevent sustained negative peaks that overmodulate the transmitter. For interview programs, "disc jockey" shows, and small musical groups, the average modulation percentage can be kept high to improve coverage. However, for high-fidelity programs such as concert bands and symphonic orchestras, the modulation should not be nearly as compressed. If low-amplitude passages are overamplified, and high-magnitude passages are compressed too extensively, the program will lose its dynamic range (amplitude separation between loudest and softest sounds) and hence much of its realism.

It is important to realize that the sound-level indication will differ at the transmitter and at the control room. The usual VU meter responds to the average level of sound, following peaks less readily, whereas the volume indicators in the limiter and other sections of the transmitter are usually more responsive. This is important because overmodulation is to be avoided at the transmitter. Occasionally the transmitter operator thinks he is obtaining an inadequate level from the studio; and at other times, when strong peaks come through, he thinks he is getting too much. This differential in meter performance is largely a function of the complex make-up of sound. Some program material has strong peaks and a low average; others are just the opposite. Complex sounds in general have a significantly higher ratio between peak and average than a sine wave has. For a sine wave the ratio between peak and average is always a constant of $1 \div 0.636$, or 1.57 to 1. The ratio for speech or music is generally 10 to 15 dB greater than that of the sine-wave constant, speech usually having the higher ratio.

In summary, the operator must keep a vigil on the sound level to make sure it is not overmodulating the transmitter. At the same time, he must be quite tolerant with the input levels because of the complex make-up of program material.

It is the responsibility of the operator to place the transmitter on the air in the morning, following certain established routines. Usually the operator goes on duty approximately a half hour before air time. Before warming up the transmitter and putting it on the air, he should make certain the program line is not feeding signal to the transmitter. Similar "get ready" procedures are probably taking place at the studio, and signal may inadvertently be fed over the line and be transmitted. Prior to turning the filaments on, many operators thoroughly inspect the transmitter and associated equipment, including the antenna tuning box, to make certain that some obvious defects have not occurred overnight.

Filaments are then turned on, and in some stations the higher-powered filaments are operated at a slightly lower-than-normal voltage for several minutes. After normal filament voltage has been established, plate voltage can be supplied to the lower-powered stages of the transmitter. After a short interval the higher-powered stages are usually turned on, at a reduced power. Any necessary resonance tuning and voltage adjustments are then made for normal low-power conditions. Finally, full power is turned on and fine adjustments made on the transmitter to establish normal operation.

Many transmitter operators are also assigned maintenance duty. Often the workbench is located at the transmitter so that the station equipment can be tested and repaired during the day. A good transmitter operator will familiarize himself with the station equipment so he can lend a hand in solving the inevitable operating and maintenance problems that arise from time to time.

Definite maintenance schedules are followed for the transmitter and its associated equipment. The procedure usually involves a continual round of inspection, cleaning, and tightening. Vacuum-cleaner suction units (or, sometimes, air compressors) help to overcome the ever-present dust menace. Tubes in the transmitter must be checked and spare ones given some operating time occasionally, to keep them from deteriorating on the shelf. Relays and circuit breakers should be watched carefully for signs of sluggishness due to dirt or corrosion. At prescribed intervals, proof-of-performance tests must be made on the station equipment; these various tests will be covered in detail in a later chapter.

8-5. SOLID-STATE BROADCAST TRANSMITTER

The 1-kW broadcast transmitter of Fig. 8-7 is entirely solid state except for the final rf power amplifier. This single-tube transmitter is rated at 1000 watts and has changeover facilities for reducing power to 500 watts for those stations that require daytime to nighttime power reduction. The frequency response is ±1 dB between 20 to 16,000 hertz; distortion is less than 1.5% at 95% modulation. Frequency stability is at least ±2 hertz with a rated carrier amplitude regulation of 3% or less.

Transistors are used in each stage of the transmitter up to the final

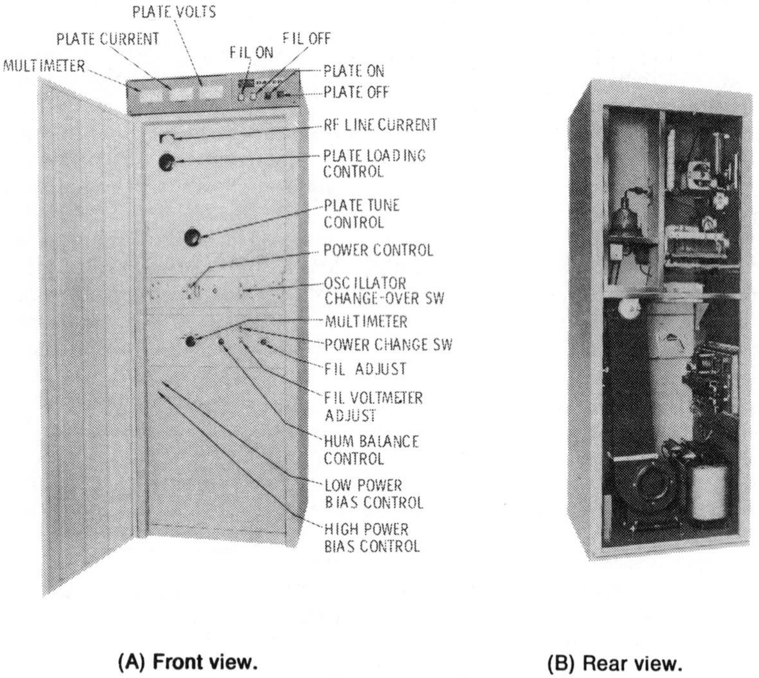

(A) Front view.   (B) Rear view.

Fig. 8-7. Solid-state broadcast transmitter.

rf power amplifier. There are five separate silicon-diode, solid-state power supplies. Two are used by the transistor rf exciter, and there are separate bias, screen-grid voltage and plate-voltage supplies for the vacuum-tube rf power amplifier. The general arrangement of the transmitter including some individual circuit schematics is given in Fig. 8-8.

The three major divisions of the transmitter can be better seen in Fig. 8-7B. The power transformers, chokes, capacitors, relays, control components, and the blower for air-cooling the power tube are mounted at the bottom of the transmitter. At the center is the transmitter exciter

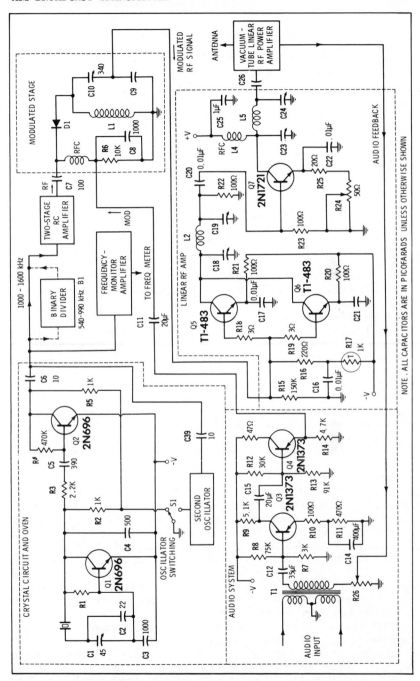

Fig. 8-8. Partial schematic of a solid-state transmitter.

which has been made readily accessible for maintenance and, if necessary, for complete removal. The top part of the transmitter houses the rf power-amplifier stage; the anode connection to the power tube can be seen at the left. The row of meters along the top from left to right are multimeter, pa plate current, and pa plate voltage, respectively. Below the top row of meters is the rf line-current meter.

At the top right center are the filament and plate power switches. Below are the filament and hum-balance controls for the power supplies. The transistor exciter panel includes two controls. One regulates the rf drive to the vacuum-tube rf power amplifier, which determines the power output of the transmitter, and a switch that permits the selection of one of two crystal oscillators.

The transistor crystal oscillator is shown at the upper-left corner of Fig. 8-8. There are two such oscillators and associated amplifiers mounted in the thermostatically controlled oven. A Pierce-type crystal oscillator is used. This stage is followed by a common-emitter buffer amplifier. Capacitor C1 is used to precisely set the crystal frequency. There are no tuned circuits associated with the crystal oscillator (Q1) and its buffer stage (Q2). In fact, the first resonant circuit encountered in the transmitter is in the modulated stage. A second identical oscillator is shown as a block in Fig. 8-8; the oscillator units are selected by completing their respective circuits to ground through switch S1.

For transmitter operation between 1000 to 1600 kHz, the output of the crystal circuit is supplied directly to a two-stage resistance-coupled amplifier. If operation is in the frequency range of 540-990 kHz, the output of the crystal circuit is supplied to a transistorized binary divider that reduces the frequency by a factor of 2. An output from the oscillator buffer stage is also supplied to a frequency monitor amplifier. This transistor amplifier builds up the level of the signal required to drive the station frequency meter.

The two-stage resistance-coupled amplifier employs no resonant circuits. It operates as a straight-through amplifier taking advantage of the high-frequency capabilities of a transistor when used in a resistance-coupled circuit.

A two-stage transistorized audio amplifier (bottom left of schematic Fig. 8-8) builds up the program signal to the level required by a diode modulator for linear modulation of the carrier. The input stage of the audio amplifier is a common-emitter circuit that uses base-divider bias (resistors R7 and R8) and emitter operating point stabilization (resistors R10 and R11 and capacitor C14). Degenerative ac stabilization is provided by the unbypassed resistor R10. The second stage (Q4) of the audio amplifier is an emitter-follower circuit. It provides a high input impedance, and, therefore, maximum voltage gain can be derived from the first stage. At the same time, Q4 has a very low-impedance output and acts as a low-impedance source for the modulating wave applied to the crystal modulator (D1).

A diode modulator operates as a linear modulating circuit when the applied signals are of adequate level and of the proper ratio. In the diode modulator (D1) of Fig. 8-8 the ratio is approximately 3 to 1, or 30 volts of rf carrier input and 10 volts of modulating signal input. A mixing process produces the modulation envelope. If only the rf signal were applied to the diode modulator, the diode current would follow the positive anode alternations. This pulsating current would be filtered out by the output resonant circuit to reconstruct the original rf sine wave. However, when an audio sine wave is applied to the input of the modulator along with the rf wave, a combining action takes place and the peak amplitudes of the peak diode current pulsations depend on the net diode anode voltage at the crest of each radio-frequency cycle. This diode voltage varies up and down with the modulating wave. As a result, the peak diode current varies correspondingly as in Fig. 8-9. The resonant circuit (L1, C9, and C10) because of its energy storing ability reconstructs the opposite alternation of the output voltage variation, forming the familiar am modulation envelope.

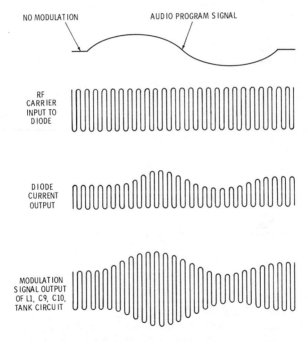

Fig. 8-9. Diode and diode-output tank-circuit waveforms.

The input is the simple combining of two separate signals. However, the output wave results from nonlinear mixing or heterodyning and is composed of three radio-frequency components—the carrier frequency plus two side frequencies.

It is significant that the modulation of the transmitter has occurred at a very low power level. If the modulation envelope is not to be distorted, all following rf amplifiers must be operated as linear class-AB or class-B rf amplifiers.

The two final stages of the exciter are the linear rf amplifiers in the lower right side of schematic (Fig. 8-8). The input stage (Q5 and Q6) consists of two transistors in parallel. Base-divider bias is augmented with a thermistor (R17) that compensates for changes in the conductance of the emitter junctions of Q5 and Q6 with temperature. A pi-network resonant circuit (C18, L2, C19) is employed, providing impedance match between the Q5-Q6 output and the input of the final transistor rf amplifier. The final rf stage (Q7) is operated near class B. However, an adjustable emitter resistor (R24) is used to adjust the power output of the exciter and the drive to the vacuum-tube power amplifier. This control (R24) can be adjusted from the front panel of the transistor exciter. A pi-network (C23, L5, and C24) is used to match the output of transistor Q7 to the input of the vacuum-tube power amplifier.

In the transmitter, feedback is used to stabilize the operating parameters of the transmitter and hold the distortion at a low level. There is a feedback path between the vacuum-tube rf amplifier (V1) and the input to the audio amplifier (Q3) of the exciter. An associated control (R26) is used to set the level of the feedback, which is usually 8 dB.

The output of the transistor exciter is supplied through a parasitic choke (L6) and capacitor (C26) to the control grid of the rf power amplifier (Fig. 8-10). Inasmuch as the rf input signal has an amplitude-modulated envelope, stage V1 must be operated as a linear amplifier. External bias is supplied by a separate power supply and is applied to the control grid via the rf choke (L8).

The positions of the three key meters of the transmitter, antenna current (M3), plate voltage (M2) and plate current (M1) are shown on the schematic (Fig. 8-10). Potentiometer R29 is used for hum balancing in the filament circuit to prevent 60-hertz modulation of the carrier. The multimeter (M4) can be used to measure the following parameters: collector current of the final transistor stage (Q7) of the exciter, grid bias ($-E_c$), filament voltage (Fil), screen-grid voltage (E_{sg}), and screen-grid current (I_{sg}) of the power-amplifier stage (VI).

A pi-T network (L11, C35, C36, L12, C37, L13, and C38) is used to match and transfer power to the antenna system. Inductors L11 (pa tuning) and L13 (pa loading) are continuously variable, and the input-loading coil (L12) uses a shorting tap. Inductor L11 is used to bring the tuned circuit into resonance, while inductor L13 controls the antenna loading and the dc plate current at resonance. If it is not possible to establish the required plate current at resonance, correction can be made by moving the tap on inductor L12.

Capacitor C29 and inductor L9 provide a form of bridge neutralization. Energy for feedback is obtained by mounting a small fixed plate near the air chimney that surrounds the tube in its mounted position. The capacitance removes energy from the anode of the tube and it feeds it back as a neutralization component to the control grid.

A similar takeoff arrangement is used to derive the audio feedback for the transmitter. In this case the energy picked up by the fixed plate near the air chimney is supplied to a diode detector (D2). The audio

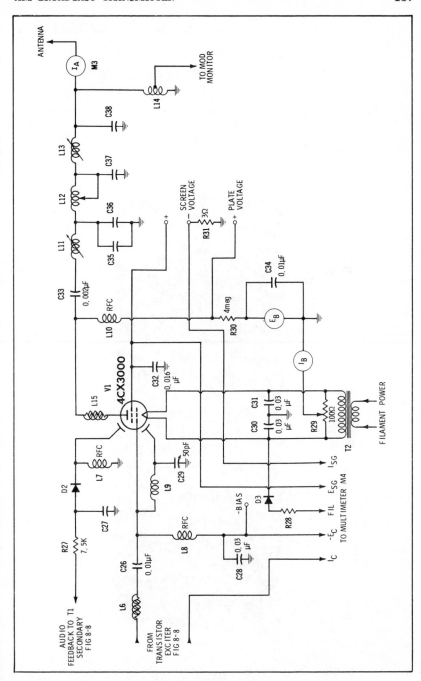

Fig. 8-10. Vacuum-tube amplifier for solid-state transmitter.

output is coupled back to the secondary of the audio input transformer (T1) of the exciter.

8-6. SOLID-STATE 1-kW TRANSMITTER

The *Harris* MW-1A (Fig. 8-11) is an all solid-state 1-kW transmitter. It is capable of an output of 1100 watts and has a 125% positive-peak modulation capability. At the same time overmodulation in the negative direction is avoided and negative peaks do not exceed 100% modulation. Typical efficiency of the transmitter, which uses class-D push-

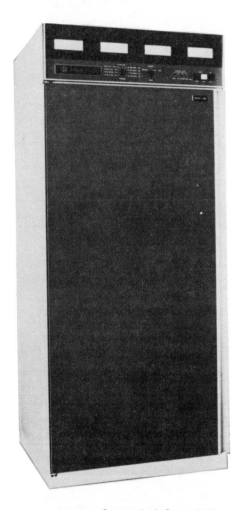

Courtesy Harris Communications
Fig. 8-11. Solid-state 1-kW transmitter.

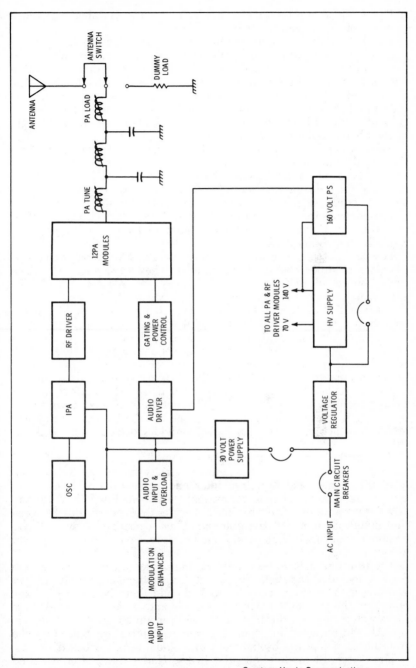

Fig. 8-12. Simplified block diagram of the Harris transmitter.

pull amplifiers (squarewave switching), is 85%. A functional block diagram of the transmitter is given in Fig. 8-12.

The 1100 watt capability for maximum carrier power allows more reserve for driving directional antenna arrays. This am transmitter uses audio processing and the audio signal is first applied to a modulation enhancer. This circuit reduces modulation peaks which have little power and holds down the average audio level. This processing permits a higher average modulation of the transmitter and a more powerful audio level results. This circuit can be disabled when desired, especially when making performance tests.

Audio input and audio driver modules follow. These stages build up the signal to the required level for modulating the transmitter. At the same time a dc-coupled arrangement permits a fixed bias to set the carrier voltage during "carrier-only" conditions. Audio signal is applied to the modulated amplifiers of the transmitter through a gating and power-control circuit. Audio signal, as well as dc level, are supplied over this path. Thus dc carrier level (no modulation) and strength of audio both can be established.

The modulated power amplifier consists of twelve transistor power-amplifier modules connected in parallel. They have an approximate power output of 100 watts each and can supply a maximum of 1100 watts carrier output. In fact, a failure of one module does not affect the transmitter's rated performance. Even if several modules fail the transmitter stays on the air, although at a reduced power level.

The rf driver module that comes ahead of the power amplifier is a similar 100-watt module. Should the driver fail, a pa module can be placed in the rf driver location and the power amplifier allowed to operate with one module short while the rf driver is repaired.

The rf oscillator produces an output frequency which is 2 or 4 times greater than the carrier frequency. This output is divided down to the operating frequency. Rf signal is amplified by the intermediate power amplifier which operates class A and provides drive signal for the rf driver.

Each of the outputs of the 12 power-amplifier modules supplies signal to a 90° network. This arrangement permits the outputs to be paralleled at the same time there is no interaction among the modules. Thus, the loading does not change, for example, if one module fails. Additionally the transmitter output network provides 225° phase shift between the module system and the antenna. Thus a change in the resistive component of the antenna load impedance does not detune the power amplifier stages.

The transmitter includes a built-in dummy load. Also vswr arrangement is included that will recycle the transmitter and provide proper warning if the ratio exceeds 1.2 to 1. Should there be an overvoltage condition the transmitter will also recycle automatically. Should there be repeated overload the transmitter will remain off until manually reset. All the required functions for remote control are built into the transmitter. These are brought out to a single terminal board.

The system of modulation used in the *Harris* transmitter is called progressive series modulation which provides high operating efficiency

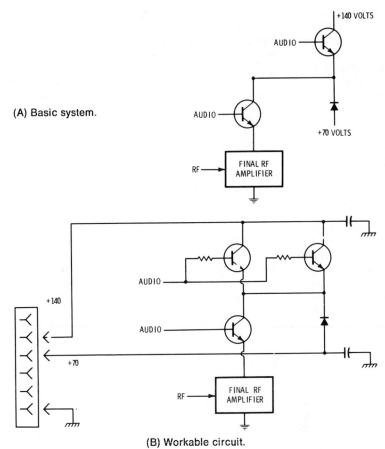

(A) Basic system.

(B) Workable circuit.

Fig. 8-13. Basic plan of progressive series modulator.

and easy to adjust circuitry without the need for a modulation transformer, modulation reactor, power-supply choke, or 70-kHz filter. Control of the transmitter power over a wide range can be accomplished in the low-level stages of the modulator. No adjustment is needed in any of the high-power rf circuits.

A simplified basic plan for progressive series modulation is shown in Fig. 8-13. In circuit A, there are two series-connected transistors along with power-supply voltages of 140 and one-half of this value. Unmodulated carrier occurs whenever the pa voltage is slightly less than the one-half voltage power-supply value of 70 volts. Under these conditions the lower audio transistor conducts and passes the full pa current from the one-half voltage tap through the gating diode. The upper audio transistor is cut off and passes no current.

When there is negative modulation and a swing of the audio away from the zero-carrier value there is a drop across the lower audio transistor. Therefore the pa voltage decreases. As 100% negative modulation approaches, the pa voltage drops to near zero.

On a positive modulation excursion the lower audio transistor is biased at saturation. Now the upper transistor begins to conduct which raises the power-amplifier voltage toward the full supply value of 140 volts. Since the emitter voltage of the upper transistor rises above the one-half voltage value, the gating diode is effectively disconnected. This removes the connection from the 70-volt supply voltage. The current in the upper transistor rises from zero at carrier condition to an instantaneous high value which reaches a peak at the most positive part of the excursion. If this positive excursion is great enough in amplitude to produce maximum modulation, the peak PA supply voltage at that instant will be near 140 volts. The circuit is designed to produce a higher current on the positive excursion than the negative one. The upper transistor works harder than the lower one and does permit the positive modulation percentage to be higher than the negative modulation percentage.

Efficient operation under the above conditions requires that two transistors be connected in parallel in the positive side as shown in Fig. 8-13B. The complete circuit for the modulator and modulated amplifier is shown in Fig. 8-14, which also includes the class-D modulated rf amplifier. Also the driving transistors for the modulator are shown.

The switching type class-D modulated rf amplifier is shown at the bottom of Fig. 8-14. The inputs to the bases are fed by separate secondary windings. The two transistors, however, are in series between the dc supply voltage and ground. The actual rf output is taken from the center connection between the two transistors.

At the center connection between the transistors there is a square-wave voltage that is switched between the supply voltage and the saturation voltage. The circuit arrangement is such that only one transistor is conducting at any instant; there is no overlap in the conduction angle. This overlap is avoided with a small bias developed across the resistor-capacitor combinations in the base circuits. The supply voltage is made to vary at an audio rate in accordance with the previous discussion. In effect, the no-modulation supply voltage is approximately 70 volts. This voltage decreases for negative modulation, dropping toward zero volts. This supply voltage increases for a positive modulating swing rising toward 140 volts. Amplitude-modulated squarewaves are converted to the conventional amplitude-modulated sine waves by a resonant network and filter that follows (Fig. 8-12).

8-7. MAIN/ALTERNATE TRANSMITTERS

In recent years the main/alternate transmitter has become more common. Usually they are designed to operate at the same power and can be two separate and identical transmitters (Fig. 8-15). In association with such an installation there can be an automatic transmitter switcher which in the case of the failure of one transmitter will automatically switch over to the other.

A Collins automatic transmitter switcher is shown in Fig. 8-16. It in-

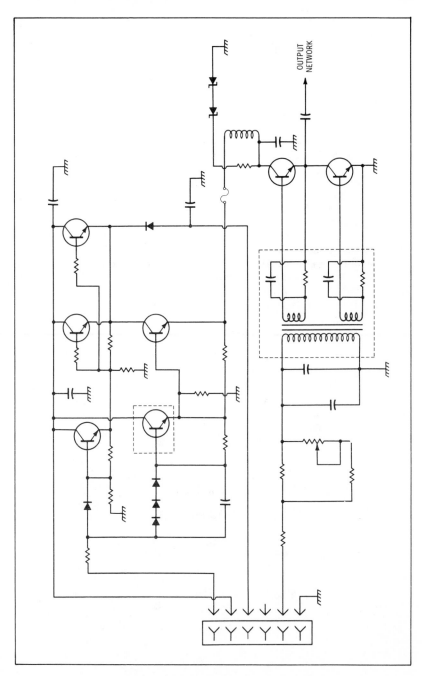

Fig. 8-14. Modulator and modulated class-D rf amplifier.

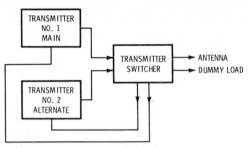

Fig. 8-15. Switching circuit for main/alternate transmitter operation.

cludes the necessary digital circuitry to permit automatic switching of power and antenna system, displaying the particular active routing in the form of an LED flowchart shown on its front panel. Changeover can be made to take place either automatically or by manual operation.

In operation an appropriate sensor determines a failure and the associated digital switching circuit changes state. At this time the plate-off control circuit is actuated and the transmitter interlocks are opened to shut down the transmitter. After switching is complete, interlocks are restored, and the alternate transmitter goes on the air in the event of low power output or outright failure of the main transmitter.

8-8. LIMITING AMPLIFIER

As its name implies, the limiting amplifier keeps the audio output below a predetermined value so that program peaks do not overmodulate the signal. The transmitter can therefore be operated at a higher average-modulation percentage, the limiter acting as a safety valve

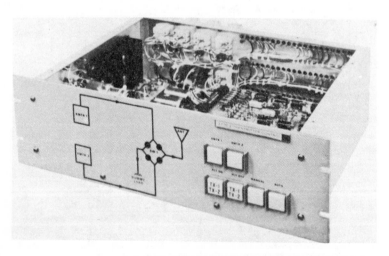

Courtesy Collins Telecommunications, Div. Rockwell Intl.
Fig. 8-16. Automatic transmitter switcher.

against overmodulation with its consequent distortion and splatter (generation of spurious signals). The limiter amplifier must exhibit minimum distortion so that the quality of the program is not impaired, regardless of the amount of limiting (up to the overload point of the limiter amplifier).

If the limiter amplifier is adjusted to introduce substantial suppression, the dynamic range of the broadcast will be limited. Therefore, in the reproduction of concert music and similar program material where considerable dynamic range is desired, the amount of compression should be kept to a minimum.

A Harris modulation limiter is shown in Fig. 8-17. This limiter provides as much as 30 dB of compression. Usually the amount of limiting employed falls between 5 and 10 dB; sometimes between 15 to 20 dB. Negative and positive modulation peaks can be controlled separately with asymmetrical limiting. Negative overmodulation is to be avoided in am broadcast practice. With a 30-to-1 compression ratio the peak negative modulation can be set at 99.5 percent without any danger of overmodulation. At the same time the positive peak modulation can be permitted to rise to 110 or 125 percent without distortion.

Fig. 8-17. Harris modulation limiter.

If the limiter is to be used with an fm transmitter, symmetrical limiting is used because plus or minus peak excursions beyond the maximum permissible fm deviation must be avoided.

The modulation limiter is said to have a fast attack time. This means that when a modulation peak comes along, the limiting action occurs very quickly and distortion or so-called thumping do not occur.

A functional block diagram is given in Fig. 8-18. The incoming signal is first passed through a variable loss circuit. Signal attenuation in this circuit depends on the magnitude of the recurrent modulation peaks. It is here that the control action is exerted. An amplifier section follows which builds up the magnitude of the limited modulating signal prior to its application to the output circuit and on to the transmitter.

A portion of the output signal is applied to the control circuit. The control signal circuit responds to signal peaks and develops a dc control bias that is applied to the variable loss circuit, thus controlling the extent of the signal attenuation.

Positive and negative recurrent peaks are also applied to a comparator circuit. This circuit develops a control voltage that is determined by the relative magnitudes of the positive and negative peaks. Through an automatic peak-phasing circuit the limiter is able to exert an auto-

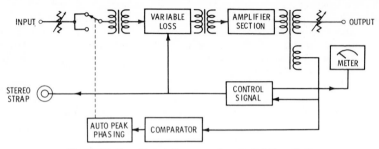

Fig. 8-18. Functional diagram of a modulation limiter.

matic control over the peak polarization that needs the greatest amount of compression.

A schematic diagram is given in Fig. 8-19. The variable loss circuit consists of transistors Q1 and Q2. These two transistors are connected across the secondary of input transformer T1, and the primary of output transformer T2. Their resistances from collectors to emitters are controlled by the dc bias currents applied to their bases. The source of the control bias is the emitter of transistor Q14, center right of the schematic diagram.

The voltage across the Y-WH secondary of limiter transformer T3 is applied through capacitors C14 and C17 to the peak rectifying diodes, CR14 and CR15. Filtering and recovery time is handled by the resistor-capacitor network shown below input transformer T1, at upper left. This same control voltage can also be applied to a second modulation limiter in the case of fm stereo operation.

The control signal is also applied to metering transistor Q13 which, through the front panel meter, indicates the amount of limiting in decibels.

The control signal is amplified by transistors Q14 and Q15, with the emitter circuit of Q14 supplying the control bias current to the bases of variable loss transistors Q1 and Q2.

The relative level of negative and positive peak limiting is a function of the relative biasing of rectifier diodes CR14 and CR15. Equal biasing provides symmetrical limiting; unequal biasing produces asymmetrical limiting. Asymmetrical limiting occurs when S3 is switched to either the 110-percent or 120-percent positions. With program input having a natural imbalance in positive and negative peaks, the unit limits negative peaks to 100 percent, while allowing the positive peaks to reach either 110 percent or 120 percent before limiting occurs.

The limiter includes an automatic peak-phasing circuit. It makes certain, with asymmetrical limiting, that the modulating peaks of the greater magnitude cause positive modulation of the am transmitter. This is done with the relay terminals that are connected in the primary of input transformer T1. Relay coil K1 is connected in the collector circuit of a flip-flop multivibrator (transistors Q9 and Q10). Whether Q9 conducts or is nonconducting depends on whether the positive or negative peaks have the greater magnitude across the Y-WH secondary winding of output transformer T3. The negative and positive peak-

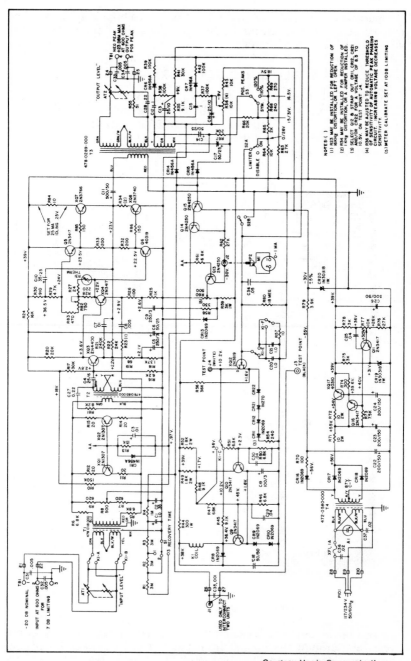

Courtesy Harris Communications

Fig. 8-19. Schematic diagram of a modulation limiter.

comparator diodes are CR6 and CR7. Control voltage is applied to the gate of field-effect transistor Q12. It develops the flip-flop triggering voltage for the multivibrator.

8-9. ALL SOLID-STATE TRANSMITTER

The *Sintronic* transmitter of Fig. 8-20 is completely solid state with a power output of 1 kW and the capability of switching to a lower power of 500 or 250 watts. Frequency stability is an excellent ±0.00005% (±5 hertz at 1 MHz). Modulation capability is 125% on positive peaks; 100% on negative peaks.

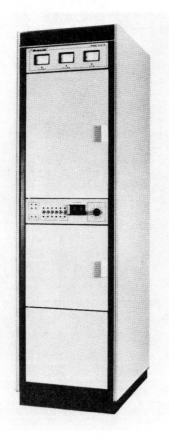

Fig. 8-20. All solid-state 1-kW transmitter.

Courtesy Sintronic

Much of the circuitry is mounted on printed-circuit boards that are accessible through the hinged front panel. Card extender boards facilitate maintenance and troubleshooting; a hinged rear door and removable side panels permit access to internal components and cabling.

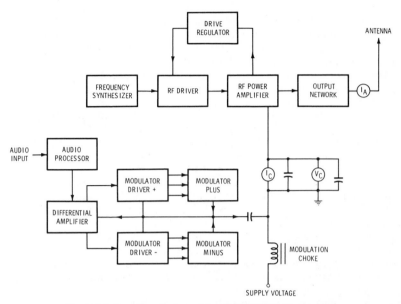

Fig. 8-21. Functional plan of the SINTRONIC transmitter.

A basic functional plan of the transmitter is given in Fig. 8-21. The radio-frequency section begins with a frequency synthesizer. This permits operation on any 10-kHz interval between 540 and 1600 kilohertz. Desired frequency is programmed by a switch selection system mounted on a plug-in card. Proper frequency is maintained with a voltage-controlled oscillator and an associated phase-lock loop system. A 10-kHz reference frequency is established by a digital frequency divider associated with a 4-MHz crystal-controlled clock-frequency oscillator. The output of the frequency synthesizer is a squarewave of the desired carrier frequency which is applied to the rf driver.

The rf driver is a high-efficiency switch-mode rf amplifier and employs VMOS field-effect transistors. A squarewave output with a power level of 70 watts is developed by the driver for application to the rf power amplifier. The rf power amplifier employs five switch-mode amplifier modules. Each module consists of four transistors connected as a class-D full-wave push-pull amplifier. The five outputs are totalized in a broadband transformer-combining network. The high-powered output pulses are supplied to appropriate inductor-capacitor networks with high harmonic attenuation. Thus they are converted to sine waves with an extremely low harmonic content. In fact, the total harmonic distortion is less than 1.5 percent at the 95-percent modulation level.

A drive regulator links the modulated rf power amplifier back to the rf driver. Its responsibility is to adjust automatically the rf excitation for optimum power-amplifier efficiency during the variation of the power-amplifier collector voltage with modulation. It samples a pulse of the squarewave rf modulation envelope at the pa output and compares it with a sample of the modulator audio output. Thus, during the modulating cycle the drive regulator maintains optimum drive to the power-amplifier stage, to ensure a collector efficiency in excess of 95% throughout the modulation process.

High-level collector modulation is employed with the collector voltage varied at an audio rate which ranges from zero during 100-percent negative modulation peaks to twice the carrier level collector voltage at 100-percent positive peak modulation. The individual radio-frequency cycles are squarewaves with their peak-to-peak amplitude varying with the modulating wave. However, after filtering by the followup inductor-capacitor network a conventional amplitude-modulated envelope is developed and is applied to the input of the antenna system.

The output of the modulator is at an extremely low impedance and no modulation transformer is required. A single modulation choke (Fig. 8-21) isolates the audio frequencies from the power supply. The modulator stage consists of five pairs of power amplifiers connected in a complementary-symmetry configuration. Pairs of modulator modules are required to set up the positive and negative portions of the complementary-symmetry arrangement. They are capable of delivering an output level in excess of 1000 watts. The requirement for 100-percent modulation is substantially below this level and a high-modulation percentage can be obtained with minimum distortion.

The modulator driver consists of a complementary-symmetry pair which is in turn supplied with signal from the outputs of a differential amplifier. The differential amplifier is supplied with audio signal from an audio preamplifier/processor.

The radio-frequency modules operate at +200 volts while the modulator, driver and differential amplifier operate at +350 volts. These voltages are supplied from conventional unregulated full-wave bridge rectifier power supplies. Three switch-type 25-volt supplies provide the remaining operating voltages for the transmitter.

The power amplifier dc collector voltage and current, and the radio-frequency output current are displayed on a meter panel at the top of the cabinet. Twenty-three operating and setup parameters are metered by a digital-readout multimeter located on the center control panel.

8-9-1. Synthesized AM Exciter

The carrier frequency of the transmitter is established by the phase-locked frequency synthesizer. The voltage-controlled oscillator is the MC4024 integrated circuit (A1) shown in Fig. 8-22. Carrier frequency is made available at pin 6. One of the outputs is supplied to pin 15 of the A6 combination phase detector and programmable frequency divider. Its responsibility is to divide down the vco frequency to 10 kilohertz. This component is compared in the phase detector portion of the integrated circuit with a reference 10-kHz component applied to pin 18. The phase-detector output is proportional to the time difference between the positive edges of the 10-kHz reference signal and the vco carrier frequency divided by a count which produces a 10-kHz output.

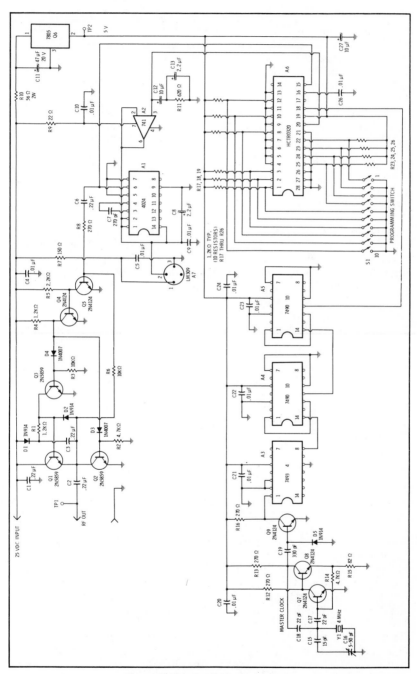

Fig. 8-22. Synthesized am exciter.

When a phase difference occurs, a dc error voltage appears at pin 20 of A6. This signal is fed to input pin 3 of A2, an operational amplifier which operates as a unity-gain low-pass filter that removes any 10-kHz component from the error-correcting dc voltage. The output of the operational amplifier is applied to pin 2 of the vco. In so doing the vco is locked to the desired carrier frequency. This phase-locked loop system holds the carrier frequency within 5 hertz of assigned value.

The highly stable reference signal is generated by the crystal-controlled master clock shown at the lower left. Operating frequency is 4 MHz. Feedback path is from the collector of transistor Q8 and the base circuit of Q7. The output of the oscillator is shaped by diode D5 and transistor Q9 which provides a TTL-compatible squarewave input to the 4-bit binary counter A3. Two successive 10-to-1 dividers follow to obtain a total division of 400. The output at pin 11 of the last counter (A5) supplies the 10-kHz reference component to pin 18 of A6.

The actual carrier division down to 10 kHz is set by programming switch S1. To program the exciter for 1200-kHz operation, for example, switch positions 1 and 8 would be open, the remainder would be closed. If operation were to be on 1220 kHz, switch positions 1, 5, and 8 would open. In the latter case the activities within the A6 would produce a division of 122 to obtain the internal comparison signal of 10 kHz (1220/122).

A 9-kHz incremental frequency operation can be established for export use or if 9-kHz channel spacing is ever used in the United States. In this case, the crystal frequency is 3.6 MHz, and a 9-kHz reference signal must be made available at the phase detector.

The carrier squarewave available at pin 6 of the vco is supplied through capacitor C6 to amplifier transistor Q5. Driver transistors Q3 and Q4 supply signals to output transistors Q1 and Q2 connected in a series-pair circuit, providing a low-impedance squarewave output signal that is supplied through capacitor C2 to the succeeding radio-frequency driver.

8-9-2. VFET Driver

The four VFET driver transistors of Fig. 8-23 operate as a switch-mode class-D amplifier. The output is a 70-watt squarewave at the carrier frequency and made available at outputs 2 and 3. One pair of VMOS transistors provides the positive (above 0) part of the squarewave; the other pair of transistors, the negative part of the square wave (below zero).

Squarewave input at the carrier frequency is applied to transformer T1. Separate secondary windings feed the gates of transistors Q5 and Q8 during one 180-degree cycle of the squarewave input signal. During the other 180-degree portion, the gates of transistors Q6 and Q7 are driven to complete the squarewave. The squarewave output is transformer-coupled to the five separate power-amplifier modules.

The dc supply voltage applied to the driver stage is regulated automatically to a precise level that permits the power-amplifier stages to operate efficiently throughout the modulating cycle.

The efficiency of the five switch-mode class-D power-amplifier combination is related to the drive power supplied to the module inputs. To obtain peak efficiency it is necessary to change the rf excitation to coincide with the varying power demands made when the audio signal is modulating the power-amplifier collector. This is the function of the drive regulator (Fig. 8-21).

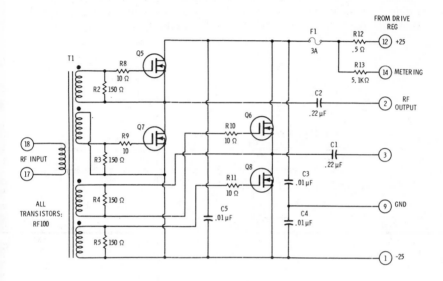

Fig. 8-23. VFET driver.

The drive regulator does so by comparing two modulating wave samples—one taken from the modulating wave applied to the supply voltage line to the modulated power-amplifier and a sample demodulated from the modulation envelope present in the collector circuit of the modulated rf power amplifier. The dc output of the regulator is supplied to the +25 volts applied to the radio-frequency driver. A drive level change results in such a manner that the detected input radio-frequency envelope is kept identically equal to the modulated power-amplifier voltage sample.

8-9-3. Radio-Frequency Power Amplifier

A sample of one of the identical radio-frequency power amplifiers is shown in Fig. 8-24. The radio-frequency input is applied to the primary of transformer T1, input terminals 17 and 18. Individual secondary windings of the same transformer are connected in the base circuits of each of the four power transistors. All of the five input transformers are driven in parallel by the output of the radio-frequency driver.

The supply voltage at terminal 12 is modulated by the output of the modulator. The modulated radio-frequency output is made available at terminals 2 and 3. A sample of this modulated output is removed through attenuating resistor R7 and is applied to the drive regulator from terminal 9.

Again, switch-mode, so-called class-D operation, occurs. Transistors Q1 and Q3 operate for one polarity of the input squarewave; transistors Q2 and Q4 operate for the opposite polarity. Note that there are individual diodes between the base and emitter of each transistor. These diodes are slow-recovery types. They turn on when the appropriate pairs are energized and when the input squarewave changes polarity.

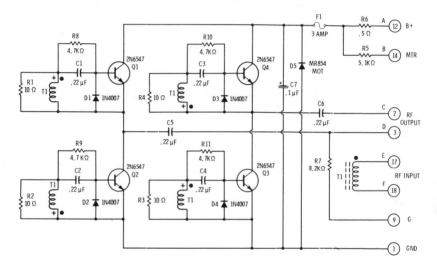

Fig. 8-24. Rf power-amplifier module.

Consequently a given pair of transistors cannot be turned on until its associated diodes have turned off. As a result, opposite transistor pairs cannot be energized simultaneously, and loss of efficiency and short-circuiting are prevented. Each module delivers 220 watts to a radio-frequency output transformer.

8-9-4. Radio-Frequency Output Network

The radio-frequency output network (Fig. 8-25) has a number of functions. The network is resonated to the carrier frequency and converts the modulation envelope composed of carrier-frequency square-waves to radio-frequency sine waves that are modulated in amplitude in accordance with the modulating wave. The output network is basically a pi-section with high harmonic attenuation. The pi-network also provides matching of the output to the antenna system.

The radio-frequency outputs of the five amplifier modules are fed to the individual primary windings of the ferrite-core transformer (T1). The secondary windings are series-connected and supply signal to the pi-network through a current-sensing transformer (T2). The sample

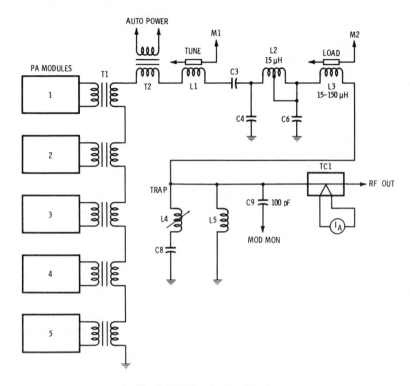

Fig. 8-25. Rf output network.

removed at this location is supplied to the automatic power-control circuit. The pi-network is composed of inductors L1, L2, and L3 plus capacitors C3, C4, and C6. Inductors L1 and L3 are variable with their inductances being determined by the mechanical position of a ferrite core assembly within each inductor. These are the motor-driven tune and load controls of the output network.

A harmonic trap follows the load inductor. Inductor L5 is a static drain choke, acting as a shunt for transients induced in the tower or transmission line by lightning or other static sources. A thermocouple TC1 provides current detection for operation of the antenna current meter.

8-9-5. Differential Audio Amplifier

The differential audio amplifier (Fig. 8-26) supplies a high-voltage audio-frequency signal to the modulator drivers. These two outputs are made available at terminals E and E′ to drive the + driver and − driver individually. The three diodes (D3, D4, and D5) provide a 2-volt differential between the two outputs to minimize crossover distortion. Input signal from the audio preamplifier or processor is applied to the base of transistor Q2 by way of input terminal 1.

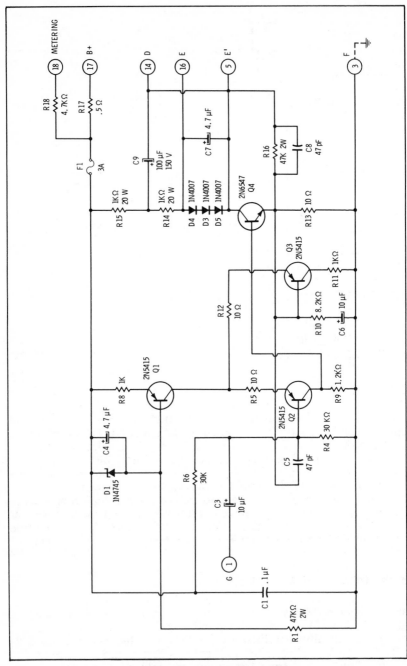

Fig. 8-26. Differential audio amplifier.

This transistor in conjunction with Q1 and Q3 comprises a differential amplifier with audio signal being applied to one input (base of Q2) and feedback from the output of the modulator to the second input (base of transistor Q3). Transistor Q1 operates as a constant-current source. The collector of transistor Q2 is connected to the base of the high-voltage amplifier transistor Q4. This transistor provides the only voltage amplification in the entire modulator. The voltage amplification is limited, being reduced by the feedback loop, and resulting in a very low distortion. However, the audio system and modulator have a very high power amplification. Actually the voltage gain needed to develop a 350-volt peak-to-peak signal is handled by the audio preamplifier and processor (Fig. 8-21).

8-9-6. Modulator Driver

There are two modulator drivers (positive polarity and negative polarity) connected as a complementary-symmetry pair. The plus driver consists of three npn transistors connected in series across the supply voltage (Fig. 8-27). Signal from the differential amplifier is applied at terminal 3, and through resistor R1 is connected to the base of transistor Q3, which operates as an emitter follower to obtain an output that is made available at terminal 2. The other two transistors are

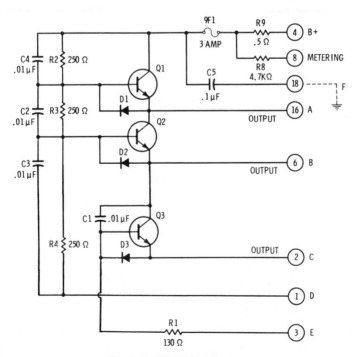

Fig. 8-27. Modulator driver (+).

cascode-connected and develop outputs at terminals 16 and 6. Three individual equal-level outputs are made available for driving the five plus-modulators in parallel.

The modulator driver for the negative side of the complementary-symmetry operation is a similar circuit. The only difference in the two driver circuits is that the negative driver uses pnp transistors instead of the npn types shown in Fig. 8-27 for the plus driver. Resistors R2, R3, and R4 along with their filter capacitors, provide the required base biasing.

8-9-7. Modulator

There are ten modulator modules with five driven in parallel by the plus driver and five driven in parallel by the minus driver. Refer back to Fig. 8-21.

One pair of modulators (plus and minus sections of a complementary pair) is shown in Fig. 8-28. The modulator comprises five such pairs.

The top trio of npn transistors (Q1, Q2, and Q3) are driven by the three outputs of the plus driver. These transistors conduct on the positive alternations of the audio wave producing the positive alternations at the output. The lower trio of transistors (Q4, Q5, and Q6) are driven by the three outputs of the minus driver. These are pnp transistors and conduct during the negative alternations of the audio waves. As a result they produce the negative alternations of the audio information made available at the output. The output is common to that of the

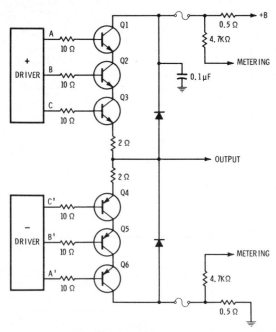

Fig. 8-28. Modulator pair.

other four pairs of the modulator, each pair contributing a like amount, to obtain the total output of the modulator. This output modulates the supply voltage to the radio-frequency power amplifier. Refer back to Fig. 8-21.

8-9-8. Typical Input/Output Readings

The location of the three important meters that can be used to determine input and output is shown in Fig. 8-21. In a typical case the power amplifier dc current is 8.7 amperes and the power amplifier dc voltage is 120 volts. The radio-frequency antenna current is 4.47 amperes. The dc power input becomes:

$$P_{in} = 8.7 \times 120 = 1044 \text{ watts}$$

Assuming that the transmitter is matched to a 50-ohm resistive load, the radio-frequency power output becomes:

$$P_o = (4.47)^2 \times 50 = 999.1 \text{ watts}$$

The efficiency becomes:

$$E_{eff} = \frac{P_o}{P_{in}} \times 100 = 95.7 \text{ percent}$$

8-10. VACUUM-TUBE TRANSMITTER

A typical all-vacuum-tube transmitter of 1-kW level is shown in Fig. 8-29. Note the row of key meters located at the left. These read rf output power, power-amplifier plate current, plate voltage, multimeter checks and line voltage. The multimeter operates in conjunction with the selector switch located below the meters. This switch can then be used to switch the meter into various key circuits of the transmitter to check performance and localize possible defects.

The four large tubes operate in the modulator (right side) and modulated rf power amplifier of the transmitter (left side). The audio preamplifier is located below the power tubes while the radio-frequency exciter is a separate module located at the lower left. It includes its own multimeter. To its right is the power output control along with the right and left modulator bias adjustments. To the left of the rf exciter is a series of circuit breakers which throw out when specific overloads or failures develop in the transmitter. In normal operation the transmitter is controlled by the five pushbutton switches at the bottom of the transmitter. Not shown on the photograph are the power supplies of the transmitter located on a large rack below the control panel.

This Sintronic transmitter uses three radio-frequency stages and two audio stages, Fig. 8-30 and Fig. 8-31. The rf exciter, Fig. 8-30, uses a 12BY7A crystal oscillator followed by a 6146 power amplifier. A third tube is a voltage regulator that holds the screen-grid and plate voltages of the oscillator constant. The oscillator itself is a basic Colpitts circuit and has an untuned output, supplying voltage drive to the succeeding

Courtesy Sintronic

Fig. 8-29. A 1-kW am transmitter.

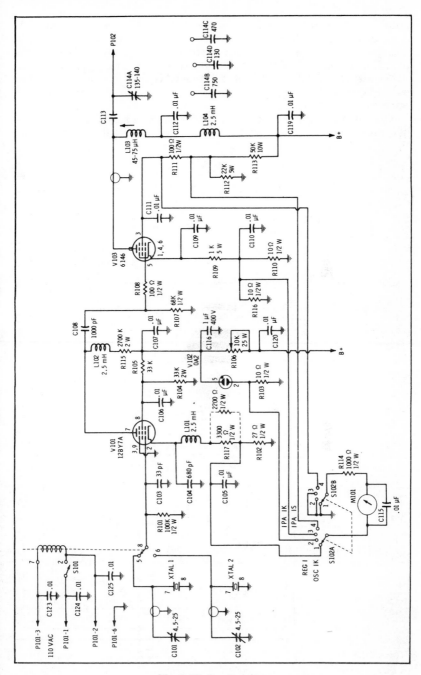

Fig. 8-30. An rf exciter.

amplifier. Four metering positions permit a check of the oscillator cathode current, regulator-tube current, power-amplifier cathode current, and power-amplifier screen-grid current. Observe that the metering circuit takes off a small voltage for measurement from across very low-value resistors (R102, R103, R116, and R111). These resistors are of such low value that switching the meter does not in any way affect the operation of the exciter.

The 1-kW modulated power-amplifier stage, Fig. 8-31, uses two 4-400 tubes connected in parallel. The rf signal from the exciter is ap-

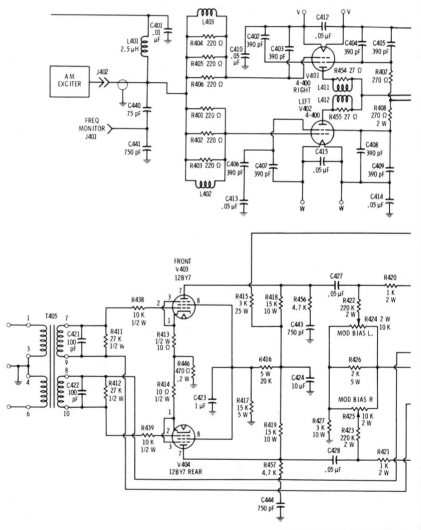

Fig. 8-31. Power amplifier

plied to the paralleled grids through two separate parasitic-suppression networks.

Note capacitors C440 and C441 in the input circuit. At their junction an rf signal component can be removed and applied to the frequency monitor of the station. The plate resonant circuit of the modulated amplifier uses an elaborate pi network with suitable harmonic-suppression components. Parasitic-suppression coils are connected directly to the plate caps of the tubes. These can be seen in Fig. 8-29.

A thermocouple ammeter is located in the coupling circuit between the transmitter output and the antenna. This meter is calibrated to

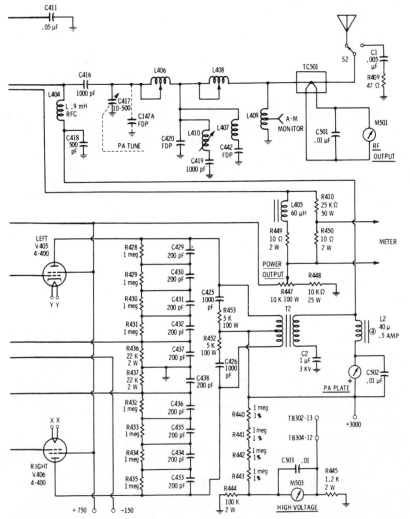

and modulator schematic.

measure the power output ot the transmitter. Likewise a tapped coil (L409) is used to supply a signal component to the am modulation monitor of the station. Although the output resonant circuit includes preset controls there is only one operating control and that is the pa tuning capacitor (C417). This knob is located to the right of the pa plate-current meter on the front panel of the transmitter.

The modulator stages use two 4-400 tubes connected in a push-pull configuration. Modulation transformer T2 matches their output to the input of the modulated amplifier. Notice that the supply voltage to the plate of the modulated amplifier is applied through audio inductor L2. The secondary of the modulation transformer is connected to the same point. Therefore, the plate voltage to the modulated amplifier follows the modulating voltage developed across the secondary of the modulation transformer.

Note that the pa current meter is connected directly below inductor L2. Also the plate-voltage meter is connected into the same circuit. (The supply voltage is +3000 volts.) The +750V source supplies screen-grid voltage to the modulator tubes as well as the screen grids of the modulated amplifier. However, the voltage applied to the screens of the modulated amplifier arrives by way of potentiometer R447. This control is used to regulate the power output of the transmitter by controlling the screen-grid voltage.

The series grouping of resistors and capacitors between modulator tubes and modulation transformer is an elaborate feedback network. Notice that the balanced signal voltages developed across resistors R436 and R437 carry back to the balanced input of the speech amplifier. The 12BY7 input stages function as resistor/capacitor-coupled voltage amplifiers that supply a balanced voltage drive to the modulator tubes. The modulator tubes operate class-AB1 and do not draw grid current. To obtain completely linear operation, separate bias potentiometers are associated with the individual grids of the modulator. These controls can be adjusted, if necessary, on the front panel of the transmitter.

The Sintronic model, as well as most modern broadcast transmitters, also includes a remote-control terminal. From this terminal, lines can be run to a remote-control chassis and then on to a remote-control panel. Such a panel is shown in Fig. 8-32. The Moseley model has a capacity for as many as fifteen separate meter readings that can be taken over interconnecting wire leads. To take a sample of a given current at the transmitter, appropriate relays are activated by pushbutton. This sample will then operate the remote meter, and its reading can be compared with the normal value. In critical circuits a raise-lower control can be used to make necessary adjustments, in order to establish normal operating conditions for particular circuits of the transmitter.

8-11. PULSE WIDTH MODULATION

A simplified functional block diagram of the Collins 5-kW transmitter is given in Fig. 8-33. The efficiency of the power amplifier is approximately 88 percent and delivers a 5.5-kW carrier output operating

Courtesy Moseley Associates, Inc.

Fig. 8-32. Remote control panel.

with a 5000-volt plate-to-cathode voltage and a plate current of 1.25 amperes. Output level can be reduced to as low as 250 watts. Modulation capability is 125% positive and 100% negative with a distortion of less than 2% between 20 and 10,000 hertz. Audio response is ±1 dB between 20 and 10,000 hertz.

The basic carrier frequency is generated by one of a pair of crystal oscillators that feed signal to a solid-state driver. The radio-frequency driver operates at the 500-watt power level, driving the grid circuit of a single-tube high-efficiency rf power amplifier. This power amplifier

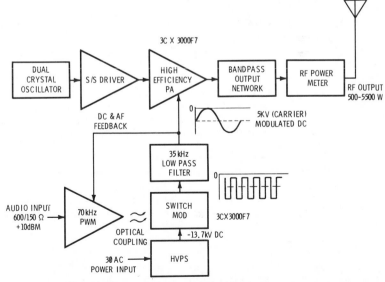

Fig. 8-33. Functional diagram of the Collins 5-kW transmitter.

stage and the switch modulator are the only two tubes in the transmitter.

The drive signal at the power-amplifier grid is a squared wave with a positive pulse that has a duration of 120 degrees. A carrier drive pulse of this duration is favorable for driving the power amplifier which uses a third harmonic resonator in its plate circuit to establish approximate squarewave or switching mode of operation. A sine wave at the carrier frequency is developed across the bandpass output network. From here the signal is applied to the antenna system through an appropriate power meter. Forward and reflected power can be measured.

The power amplifier operates with its plate at dc ground potential. A radio-frequency choke, blocking capacitor, and bypass capacitor are not needed. Instead a negative voltage is applied to its cathode circuit by the high-voltage power supply. A series-regulated modulator is operated in the switching mode and attains an efficiency of about 90 percent.

The high-voltage power supply (HVPS, Fig. 8-33) must provide enough modulating voltage to permit the achievement of 125% modulation on positive peaks and 100% on negative peaks. The proper level for obtaining a 5-kW carrier is about 5000 volts. This occurs when the modulator is switched on for approximately 40 percent of the switching period. Actual time-on interval is varied by the modulation. On a 125-percent positive modulation peak the voltage increases to 11.25 kilovolts with the modulator on nearly all of the time. While in a 100-percent modulation trough the voltage decreases to zero volts and the modulator is off all of the time. This modulator switching occurs at the very fast rate of 70 kHz and is capable of following the audio frequencies from dc to more than 10,000 hertz. A 35-kHz low-pass filter between the switching modulator and the modulated power amplifier prevents the 70-kHz switching signal from modulating the carrier but passes dc and audio modulation.

A typical pulse-width-modulated (PWM) wave as present at the input of the switching modulator is shown in Fig. 8-34. The dashed sine wave in the illustration demonstrates how the width of the 70-kHz pulse varies throughout the sine-wave period. At the peak of the positive crest of the sine wave the pulse duration is maximum. It is minimum at the negative peak in the trough of the sine wave. The PWM waveform of Fig. 8-34 appears inverted in the plate circuit of the switching modulator. Consequently during a long-duration 70-kHz negative pulse a high negative voltage is applied to the cathode of the rf power amplifier and the bursts of radio-frequency plate current are at maximum. Conversely for a short-duration 70-kHz pulse there is minimum negative voltage applied to the cathode of the rf power amplifier and the radio-frequency plate current bursts are of low amplitude. Actually the radio-frequency plate currents vary following the changes of the modulating wave to produce a modulation envelope in the radio-frequency amplifier plate circuit. The 35-kilohertz low-pass filter filters out the 70-kHz component and a modulating sine wave appears at its output and on the cathode of the radio-frequency power amplifier.

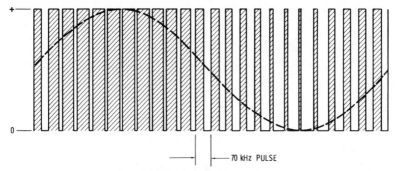

Fig. 8-34. Typical PWM waveform.

The program audio signal is applied to the 70-kHz pulse-width modulator. Here the pulses are generated that vary in duration in accordance with the amplitude changes of the program audio. This PWM signal is transferred to the switching modulator through an optical coupling system. The optical coupling signal permits a very low-powered audio signal to switch an extremely high-powered modulator.

In summary, a number of key operations take place in the PWM modulated broadcast transmitter. A carrier-frequency pulse is generated for application to the radio-frequency input of the vacuum-tube radio-frequency power amplifier. A high-efficiency shaped carrier wave is developed at the output of the power amplifier. This is converted to a high-quality sine wave by the output network of the transmitter. The program audio is first converted to a 70-kHz pulse width-modulated component. This is used to switch a high-powered modulator. The switching modulator applies a changing operating voltage to the radio-frequency power amplifier. The duration of the application of this voltage varies in accordance with the durations of the PWM waveform. Since the modulator is switching at a very fast rate, it follows the audio variations and develops at the output of the low-pass filter a replica of the original program audio, which modulates the cathode of the radio-frequency power amplifier. Thus the instantaneous peaks of the bursts of plate current drawn by the power amplifier follow the amplitude variations of the modulating signal. Therefore an am modulation envelope develops in the power-amplifier output circuit.

8-11-1. Radio-Frequency Exciter

The radio-frequency exciter (Fig. 8-35) contains two separate crystal oscillators that can be selected by a double-coil latching relay and associated pushbutton switches. The crystal oscillator operates at either twice or four times the transmit carrier frequency. If the desired carrier frequency is 1070 kHz or below the oscillators operate at four times the carrier frequency; if the frequency is 1080 kHz or above the oscillators operate at twice the output frequency. An LED indicator shows which crystal oscillator is in operation.

Through the relay contacts the output of the selected oscillator is applied to a buffer amplifier which drives the frequency divider. An

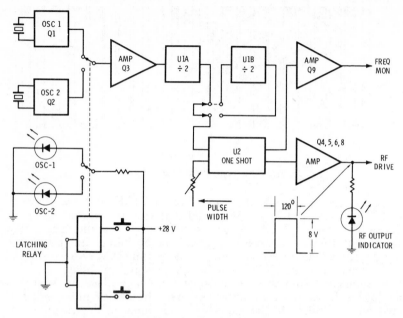

Fig. 8-35. Rf exciter block diagram.

appropriate jumper selects the required two-to-one or four-to-one division required.

The output of the divider turns on a one-shot multivibrator. This circuit includes a pulse-width adjustment that develops an output pulse with a 120-degree duration. Two outputs are derived from the multivibrator, one of which is applied to an isolation amplifier the output of which supplies excitation to the station frequency monitor.

The second output is increased in level by a series of solid-state amplifiers. The exciter final amplifier output is an 8-volt peak pulse. An associated LED indicates the presence of the rf drive signal at the output.

8-11-2. Radio-Frequency Driver and Power Amplifier

The radio-frequency driver consists of eight power transistors connected as a bridge amplifier operating in the switching mode. This stage is driven by a complementary pair of emitter-follower stages which are supplied with signal from the radio-frequency exciter. Output is removed from the common junction of the switching amplifier and is coupled through capacitor C1 to the power amplifier grid transformer (T1, Fig. 8-36).

Overload and underload protection circuits are a part of the driver circuit. If too much drive current is indicated, the driver is shut down after an appropriate delay. If the drive current drops too low, the 70-kHz switching activity is switched off and the high voltage is removed from the radio-frequency power amplifier.

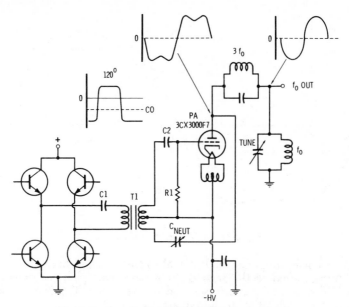

Fig. 8-36. Power amplifier, simplified schematic.

The power amplifier tube is operated class-C with grid bias being developed across the R1-C1 grid combination. The driver transformer operates broadband and has a secondary tap that permits neutralization of the stage by an appropriate neutralization network.

The drive signal to the radio-frequency power amplifier is the 120-degree rectangular pulse. Its third harmonic content is the correct amount and phase to add with the fundamental signal to produce a somewhat squared wave at the power amplifier plate circuit (Fig. 8-37). Note how the fundamental sine wave sums with the third-harmonic component to produce the resultant $f_o + 3f_o$ output wave. This shaping raises the average efficiency of the power amplifier because it maintains a higher average plate voltage during the conducting interval of the power-amplifier tube. There is less plate dissipation for a given power output. In effect, the power amplifier is capable of supplying a 5.5-kW output with a 5000-volt plate-to-cathode voltage and a plate current of 1.25 amperes. Hence the efficiency is 88%.

The dc high voltage is supplied to the power amplifier as a negative voltage on the cathode. The plate circuit operates at dc ground potential. Note that the output tuned circuit is connected to ground in Fig. 8-36.

The output network forms an output sine wave of extremely low harmonic content. It also supplies the appropriate matching between the power amplifier output and the antenna system. The network is referred to as a 4-node, synchronously tuned, bandpass combination. Actually there are four parallel-tuned circuits with 90-degree inductive coupling as shown in the simplified arrangement of Fig. 8-38.

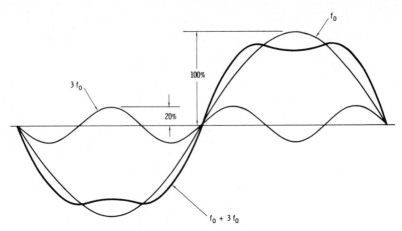

Fig. 8-37. High-efficiency waveform.

The rf power amplifier feeds signal to the resonant first node which is bottom-coupled to the second node pair. This pair is top-coupled to node three, which transfers signal to node four. The final resonant node transfers signal to the antenna system.

The degree of coupling among nodes is determined by the inductor taps and the value of inductor L3. There is also a tap on inductor L5 for connection to a modulation monitor.

The network operates as a bandpass filter with a broad flat frequency response. Thus there is very little attenuation of the sidebands. Furthermore there are steep skirts and no harmonic traps are required.

8-11-3. The Modulation Process

The basic plan of the modulation system is shown by the overall transmitter simplified schematic shown in Fig. 8-39. At the top is the radio-frequency section of the transmitter as described previously. The 13.7 kilovolt high-voltage power supply is shown at the lower left. Note that its positive terminal is connected to ground through the plate current meter as is the output network of the radio-frequency power amplifier. The power amplifier plate voltage is measured between the cathode of the radio-frequency power amplifier and ground.

Negative voltage from the high-voltage power supply is connected to the cathode of the power amplifier through the switching modulator. It is this negative voltage applied to the cathode of the power amplifier that is modulated by the program audio.

The modulator, in effect, is a series regulator that is present between the negative side of the high-voltage power supply and the power amplifier cathode. It operates in a switching mode at a frequency of 70 kHz. The duration of the "on" times of the modulator follows the modulation, which is a function of the PWM drive signal and, therefore, determines the average voltage level of the negative high voltage applied to the power amplifier. The switching modulator plate is connected to the input of a 70-kHz filter (shown as the simplified FL in

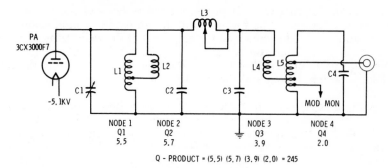

Q - PRODUCT = (5.5) (5.7) (3.9) (2.0) = 245

Fig. 8-38. Output network.

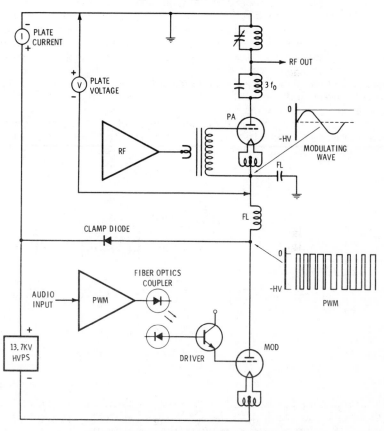

Fig. 8-39. Transmitter simplified schematic.

Fig. 8-39). This filter allows the dc and audio modulation components of the modulator waveform to pass through but stops the 70-kHz switching signal, its sidebands, and harmonics. Thus a replica of the original modulating wave is present at the cathode of the power amplifier and results in the formation of an am modulation envelope.

A clamping diode connected to the output of the modulator provides a current path when the switching modulator tube is biased off. The current in the input coil of the 70-kHz filter flows alternately through the tube when it is on and through the clamping diode when the tube is off.

A more complete schematic of the 70-kHz filter which has an approximate cutoff frequency of 35 kHz is shown in Fig. 8-40. This filter not only has the functions mentioned previously, but is designed to terminate in an impedance of 4000 ohms, which is provided by the properly loaded radio-frequency power amplifier. Proper loading is a requisite to prevent loss in high-frequency audio performance.

Audio feedback is removed at the junction of inductors L10 and L11. This delivers a feedback signal at the proper level to the PWM module. Since the switching modulator and the feedback circuits are direct coupled, the feedback is effective from a high audio frequency down to and including dc. This arrangement provides excellent low-frequency response and provides a simple way of adjusting the power output. In this operation a dc reference voltage is set by a motor-driven potentiometer and the feedback loop can be used to adjust the plate voltage to match the reference.

Program signal is applied to the audio input of the pulse-width modulator, Fig. 8-39. Here the audio signal is used to modulate a 70-kHz triangular waveform. In turn this waveform is converted to a pulse-

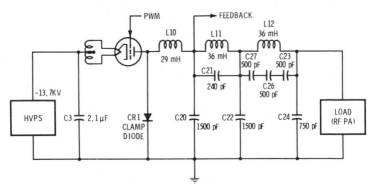

Fig. 8-40. Switching modulator circuit.

width modulated component of constant amplitude but with a width (duration) that varies with the audio signal. Through appropriate inverter, gate, and transistor amplifier the PWM output is applied to a light-emitting diode (LED).

The LED light output is coupled through a fiberoptic cable from the PWM module to the switching driver module. In effect, it is a very low-level signal that is conveyed by the PWM light (ultraviolet) signal via the fiberoptic cable to the photodiode input of the driver which regenerates the original PWM electrical signal. The optical coupling system isolates the low-level voltage PWM circuit from the high-voltage modulator circuit. In fact, a difference of potential of 13,700 volts is isolated by the fiberoptic cable.

The driver consists of an emitter-follower, intermediate amplifier, and high-voltage amplifier. The final stage of the driver is a Darlington switch which turns the control grid of the modulator tube on and off in accordance with the pulse-width modulated waveform. When the Darlington switch is turned on, the modulator grid is driven to +125 volts with respect to the cathode and the modulator conducts. When the Darlington switch is turned off, the modulator grid is connected to −125 volts with respect to the cathode and the modulator is biased off.

The high-voltage power supply is unique in that it has a high ripple frequency which is 12 times the line frequency. The special transformer has a delta-connected primary and two three-phase secondary windings connected in wye circuits (Fig. 8-41). These two secondaries supply

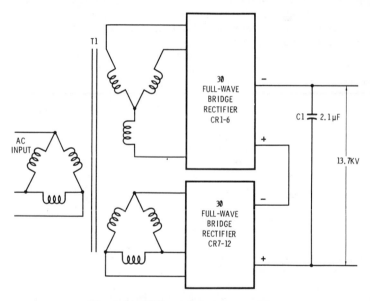

Fig. 8-41. High-voltage power supply.

power to two 3-phase full-wave bridge rectifiers, each operating at half the output voltage and connected in series to obtain the full output voltage. Each section has a ripple frequency 6 times the line frequency. However, the two secondary outputs are 60 degrees related and the additive ripple frequency becomes 720 hertz. This ripple frequency is 40 dB down from the dc output voltage level. Filtering can be handled with a capacitor of appropriate value and no filter choke is required.

8-12. AUTOMATIC TRANSMISSION SYSTEM (ATS)

ATS permits transmitter operation under an automatic control system that senses and monitors key operating parameters. Automatic adjustments are then made. An alarm system must be included as well as an automatic shutdown arrangement that will be activated when necessary. Key operating conditions related to modulation and power are monitored and, if necessary, automatic adjustment is made. If this procedure does not correct the problem, or if certain ATS functions fail, the system sounds an alarm or shuts down the transmitter depending on the nature of the failure.

Stations presently authorized for ATS are nondirectional am stations, directional am stations during nondirectional operating periods, and all fm stations. The transmitting apparatus must be manually activated at the beginning of each broadcast day.

The transmitting apparatus of a station using an automatic transmission system must have devices to monitor and control the antenna input power by sampling and evaluating the antenna current without the effects of modulation. Antenna current is to be sampled at the same point in the antenna circuit as the antenna ammeter but below (transmitter side) the ammeter.

The control system must have devices to automatically adjust the antenna input power to the authorized power for each mode of operation. If the automatic control device is unable to adjust the antenna input power to a level below 105% of the authorized power after three minutes or a total of three samplings, the emission of the station will terminate.

The transmitting system must have a device that will detect and adjust the peak level of modulation. If the modulation exceeds more than ten bursts of 100% negative modulation within a one-minute period, or any bursts exceeding 125% positive modulation, as measured at the output terminals of the transmitter, the program audio input signal to the transmitter modulators shall be automatically adjusted downward until these limits are not exceeded.

If the station is authorized or required to operate at more than one antenna input power, or is restricted in its hours of operation, the ATS control equipment must include a timeclock of specified accuracy and mode switching capability. If there is any failure or interruption in the operation of the clock or clock-controlled switching operation, the ATS mode will terminate until the clock is repaired or reset. The clock must prohibit the transmitter from operating under the ATS mode during hours of directional antenna operation.

In the ATS system the sampling of modulation levels must be on a continuous basis. All other required sampling of transmitting system functions shall be made at intervals not exceeding one minute. It should be possible to test automatic control and alarm devices without interrupting the station transmission.

Automatic transmission systems must include a fail-safe transmitter control capability. It should terminate the radiation from the station in the event of the failure of the automatic power-adjustment circuits if the automatic system does not correct an over-power condition after a three minute period, failure of the automatic modulation adjustment circuits to prevent excessive modulation levels from continuing uncorrected for a period exceeding three consecutive minutes. Termination of transmission shall result automatically if there is any failure of the mode switching timeclock for a period exceeding three minutes, or the failure of the ATS monitoring and alarm point for a period exceeding three minutes. Shutdown shall result if there is any loss of ATS sampling functions for a period exceeding three minutes.

If there is any termination of the station transmission by any failure of the ATS control or alarm function, ATS operation of the station shall not be resumed until all necessary repairs or adjustments have been completed and a notation made in the station maintenance log showing the nature or cause of the ATS malfunction, and a certification entered in the log by the station's chief operator that all required ATS functions are fully restored. Each station operating an automatic transmission system shall be provided with one or more ATS monitoring and alarm points.

At each control point there shall be a means to turn the transmitting apparatus on and off at all times, an off-air monitoring receiver for observing the station's transmitted program signal and an aural alarm system that will be activated if the transmissions of the station are in-

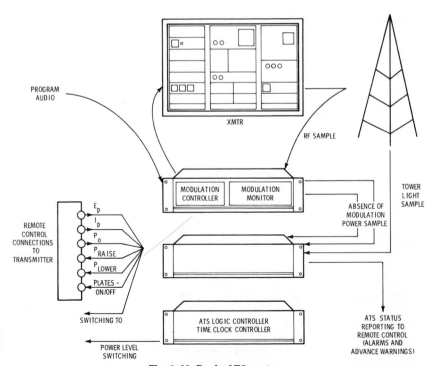

Fig. 8-42. Basic ATS system.

terrupted for a period exceeding three minutes, the transmitter output power falls below 90% of the authorized value if not automatically corrected within three minutes, and an alarm that would indicate any failure of tower lighting equipment.

Whenever an alarm condition occurs the alarm signal shall remain continuously activated until the condition causing the alarm is corrected or manual control of the transmitting system is assumed.

The station employees on duty at ATS monitoring and alarm points shall be fully instructed in procedures to take in the event of a malfunction of the transmission system and receipt of an EBS alert.

A functional block diagram of an ATS system, as suggested by Time and Frequency Technology, Inc., is shown in Fig. 8-42. An rf sample is taken from the antenna tower and is applied to the modulation monitor. Associated with it is the modulation controller which can regulate the level of the audio in accordance with the modulation percentage interpreted by the monitor. Three additional samples are required by the ATS logic controller. These are power output, absence of modulation, and tower light samples. If corrections cannot be made, alarms must be sounded automatically and, if necessary, automatic shutdown of the transmitter must be made. Appropriate status information regarding warnings, alarms and shutdown must be collected. Also shown is the timeclock controller which handles the power level switching of the transmitter.

8-13. AUTOMATIC MODULATION AND POWER CONTROLLERS

The *Delta* power controller and modulation controller of Fig. 8-43, although they have been designed for ATS purposes, may also be used by stations not specifically under ATS control to improve operating conditions.

The automatic power controller senses the operating power of an am station and through its control circuit operates the transmitter's raise- and lower-power control. Thus the operating power is kept within the FCC upper and lower limits. A sensing dc voltage is derived from an external linear rectifier that is driven by a radio-frequency sample derived from the base antenna current. An associated long-time-constant circuit removes the modulation components and averages any carrier amplitude shift. The dc voltage (Fig. 8-44) is compared to two fixed preset low-limit and high-limit references. Through appropriate timing circuits the comparator outputs are used to supply current to either the raise or lower relay driver and relay.

An LED indicator and alarm output is activated when the power exceeds the FCC high limit of 105%. Similar activities occur when the power drops below the FCC low limit of 90%. If the power drops below a selectable low value of 70/80 percent indicating a serious problem the raise relay circuit does not operate. Additional circuits and indicators determine if the FCC power levels are exceeded for three minutes. Relay chatter and hunting is prevented by special digital logic circuits that set the characteristics of the power control activities.

Fig. 8-43. Automatic power and modulation controllers.

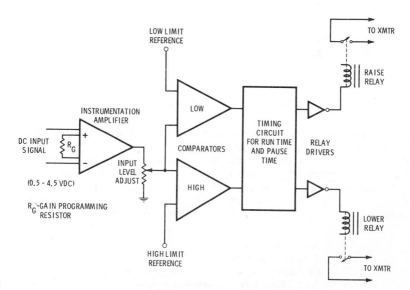

Fig. 8-44. Function diagram of automatic power controller.

The amplitude-modulation controller automatically sets the modulation level of the am transmitter to prevent excessive or undesirably low modulation. It does so despite variations in the audio level between different program sources and variations in transmitter characteristics and supply voltages. The controller continuously samples the modulation level at the transmitter output, comparing these levels with internal preset minimum and maximum modulation thresholds. A digital logic process then adjusts the audio level to the transmitter.

The modulation controller samples the transmitter output and uses this sample to develop both an envelope signal and a dc voltage proportional to the carrier level (Fig. 8-45). The sample is first demodulated by an envelope detector. One output of the detector (E_m) is a signal that has a dc level proportional to the unmodulated carrier and

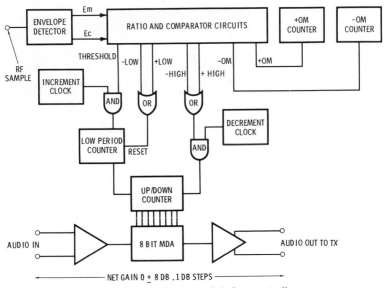

Fig. 8-45. Amplitude-modulation controller.

a superimposed audio component representing the amplitude modulation. The second signal (E_c) is a dc voltage proportional to the carrier level. This component is attenuated by a factor of 25% and sets a threshold level for comparison with E_m.

In fact, seven comparisons can be made simultaneously to establish the following typical modulation conditions. Nominal values are shown, although these can be adjusted to meet the needs of a specific station.

Modulation threshold −25%.
Negative minimum modulation −85%.
Positive minimum modulation +100%.
Negative high modulation −95%.
Positive high modulation +112%.

Negative overmodulation −100%.
Positive overmodulation +125%.

The seven comparator outputs can be seen below the ratio and comparator circuits block in Fig. 8-45. Comparator output signals are TTL logic levels. There is a logic-0 output when the condition for which they are set is not satisfied; a logic-1 output when the condition has been satisfied. The threshold signal determines when modulation of significant level (beyond −25%) is present to activate the controller. When it is, the threshold output logic is used to gate an increment clock.

Pulses from the clock are applied through an AND gate to a low-period counter. The low-period counter also receives negative and positive minimum modulation logic through an OR gate. If this counter is not reset within five seconds of modulation time the increment pulses pass to an up/down counter and cause it to count upward. The up/down counter supplies data to the 8-bit multiplying digital-to-analog converter. This converter adjusts the gain in the program audio channel in 0.1 dB steps over a ±8 dB range. Hence in the previous example the gain will be adjusted upward until the low-modulation thresholds have been satisfied.

When the low-modulation thresholds are satisfied within a five-second period by at least one modulation burst exceeding 85% negative modulation or 100% positive modulation the low-period counter will reset to zero and a new period will begin. Hence, if the low-modulation thresholds have been satisfied during a five-second period, no increment clock pulses will be passed by the low-period counter to the up/down counter. Consequently no gain adjustment will be made.

Let us next consider the activity when the modulation exceeds the nominal −95% or +112% at any time. Under this condition a decrement clock will be gated through an AND gate to the up/down counter. However, this time there will be a down count and the 8-bit information applied to the digital-to-analog converter will reduce the audio level applied to the transmitter until the high-modulation condition has been corrected.

In summary, the modulation controller maintains a high average level of modulation by evaluating preset low- and high-modulation thresholds. The correction activity can be made to operate slowly for the most favorable transmission of classical music. It can be made fast acting to maintain very high average modulation which might be more suitable for stations using more contemporary formats.

The other two thresholds set in the ratio and comparator circuits measure overmodulation conditions, both negative and positive. Logic outputs operate individual positive overmodulation and negative overmodulation counters. These counters display both the accumulating count in the current minute of operation and also display the total count from the preceding minute. These digital displays comply with the overmodulation count signals required by an automatic transmission system.

CHAPTER 9

AM Broadcast Antennas
and Lines

The antenna system of a modern broadcast station consists of the antenna proper, the transmission line, and the associated components needed for tuning and proper lighting of the antenna structure.

9-1. ESSENTIALS OF AM BROADCAST ANTENNAS

The vertical antenna is the type most usually employed in am broadcasting. In addition to being an economical antenna, its horizontal- and vertical-radiation patterns are favorable to broadcast requirements. The horizontally radiated pattern is omnidirectional; that is, the signal is of equal magnitude in all directions of the compass. Thus, the coverage is essentially uniform over the station's service area, as shown in Fig. 9-1.

On the other hand, the low-angle vertical pattern of the antenna concentrates the energy into a ground wave which is the primary medium for supplying signal to the service area. Such a pattern minimizes sky-wave propagation and thus cuts down fading in the secondary service area, where there is the possibility of interaction between sky- and ground-wave components.

An integral part of any antenna system is the tower, since its height is one of the determinants of the range of the system. The two most common tower structures are shown in Fig. 9-2. The self-supporting tower is more costly. For maximum support, the spacing between its base legs should be approximately one-eighth of the tower height.

Broadcast antennas either are grounded or are mounted on insulators. The grounded version is subject to more variables and hence more matching and pattern problems. A common broadcast antenna for small am stations is the guyed vertical type. It is usually mounted on an insulator and is somewhat taller than a quarter of a wavelength. The guy-wire system must be broken up with insulators to avoid any length that

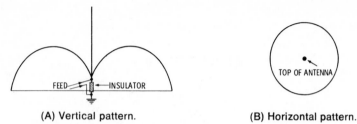

(A) Vertical pattern.   (B) Horizontal pattern.

Fig. 9-1. Basic quarter-wave vertical antenna and radiation patterns.

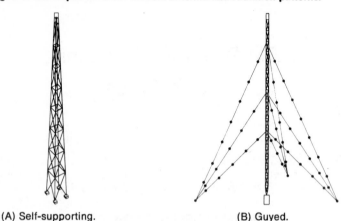

(A) Self-supporting.   (B) Guyed.

Fig. 9-2. Basic tower construction.

may become resonant and adversely affect the characteristics of the radiating element.

To eliminate variables and thereby establish the most favorable operating conditions, a good ground system is essential for a vertical antenna. This is the reason for the system of wires extending like the spokes of a wheel from the base of the tower. The ground must be tied in properly to the tuning system of the antenna.

A combination of vertical radiators is the ideal method of obtaining any reasonable horizontal-radiation pattern. Two or more vertical antennas can be made to concentrate the rf energy in specific areas. At the same time, deep nulls can be inserted into the horizontal-radiation pattern to prevent interference between stations operating on the same or adjacent channels. The major units of a typical directional-antenna system were introduced in conjunction with Fig. 8-6.

9-2. VERTICAL-ANTENNA CHARACTERISTICS

The quarter-wavelength vertical can be considered the basic antenna. Fundamentally it is a half-wavelength antenna, the ground acting as an image quarter-wavelength section, as shown in Fig. 9-3. At an electrical quarter-wavelength, the antenna resistance is theoretically 36 ohms. This "radiation" resistance is not a resistance that can be mea-

sured with an ohmmeter; rather, it is the equivalent resistance required
to dissipate the same power as the antenna. Whether or not it is exactly
36 ohms is a function of the ground system and the conditions below
the antenna. The absolute value is important only in that it must be
correctly matched to the transmission-line system from the transmitter.

The theoretical voltage and current distribution is shown in Fig. 9-3.
At the top of the antenna, the current is zero and the voltage is maximum. The current becomes maximum exactly 90 degrees down (or at
the feed point for a quarter-wavelength vertical). Theoretically, the
impedance at the feed point should be entirely resistive. In practice,
reactive components are often also present and must be balanced out
by the antenna matching system.

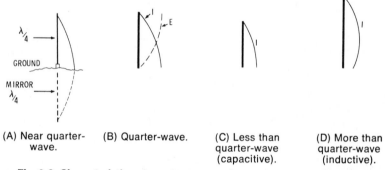

| (A) Near quarter-wave. | (B) Quarter-wave. | (C) Less than quarter-wave (capacitive). | (D) More than quarter-wave (inductive). |

Fig. 9-3. Characteristics of quarter-wave and near quarter-wave antennas.

The current and voltage distribution along a very thin vertical radiator is essentially sinusoidal. Some departure from this sinusoidal relationship will occur, particularly in self-supported towers having a grad-
ually increasing cross-sectional area toward the base. But for most small
stations with their single, uncomplicated verticals, it is safe to assume
an essentially sinusoidal relationship in making performance calcu-
lations.

The broadcast vertical need not be (and usually is not) an exact
electrical quarter-wavelength. The minimum antenna height permitted
a class-IV broadcast station (local) is substantially less than a quarter
wavelength, as shown in Fig. 9-4. Notice that over the entire class-IV
curve (A), the dimensions are shorter than the quarter-wavelength
curve (D). The lower the frequency is, the greater is the height required to obtain a specific minimum field intensity. For class-II and
class-III stations, curve B, the minimum height must be more than a
quarter-wavelength above 1150 kHz. All class-I antennas, curve C,
must be greater than a quarter-wavelength, approaching the half-wavelength electrical dimension of curve E.

When a vertical antenna is less than a quarter-wavelength, it displays
both resistive and capacitive-reactance components, as illustrated in
Fig. 9-3C. The antenna tuning unit must, therefore, introduce an equal
and opposite inductive reactance to balance out the capacitive compo-

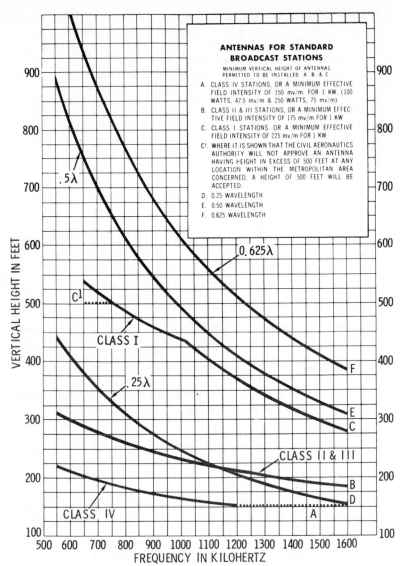

Fig. 9-4. FCC broadcast-antenna dimensions.

nent. As before, the tuning unit must match the transmission line to the resistive component of the antenna.

The impedance of a vertical antenna is usually expressed in terms of the "j-operator." For an antenna of less than a quarter-wavelength the impedance can be written as follows:

$$Z = R - jX_C$$

which can be written:

$$Z = \sqrt{R^2 + X_c{}^2}$$

After the antenna and ground system have been installed, this impedance is usually measured carefully with an impedance bridge. A suitable antenna tuning unit is then designed to permit an ideal match between the transmission-line system and antenna, plus a sufficient tuning range to accommodate any variables.

When a vertical radiator is longer than a quarter-wavelength and less than a half-wavelength it displays inductive reactance, as shown in Fig. 9-3D. This component must be balanced out capacitively by the antenna tuning system. The impedance of such an antenna is usually indicated as follows:

$$Z = R + jX_L$$

Theoretically, an antenna exactly a half-wavelength has resistance but no reactance. Above one-half of a wavelength the antenna again exhibits capacitive reactance, and above three-quarters of a wavelength an inductive component is present.

The antenna height influences the vertical-radiation pattern and, hence, the efficiency of the antenna system. For a small local station, an antenna higher than a quarter-wavelength will provide greater concentration of the radiated energy at low vertical angles. However, the loss in efficiency of a shorter antenna can sometimes be compensated for by boosting the transmitter power, as long as FCC field-strength requirements are met. A shorter antenna reduces the cost of installation —a significant item if the antenna is to be mounted on an existing structure like a downtown building. Antenna height might also be a problem if an airport is nearby.

The antenna resistive component also decreases significantly as the height is made less than a quarter-wavelength. Under these conditions the resistive losses associated with the antenna system, although small, become more significant and absorb a greater percentage of the total transmitter output power. Thus, the efficiency of the antenna system is reduced.

9-3. LONG VERTICALS

Up to now we have discussed the advantages of short antennas. But long verticals have some important advantages, too. In addition to their more efficient radiation of available power, their vertical-radiation pattern concentrates the rf energy at a much lower angle. Typical long-vertical antennas and their radiation patterns are given in Fig. 9-5. Notice how the radiation is concentrated at a lower and lower angle (Fig. 9-5C) between 0.25 and 0.625 wavelength. At 0.625 wavelength a secondary lobe is introduced that begins to direct additional energy skyward. Hence it is advisable to keep antenna heights below this limit.

Most class I and other clear-channel stations have tall vertical antennas. These stations serve not only an extensive area via ground waves, but also a wider area made possible through the use of sky

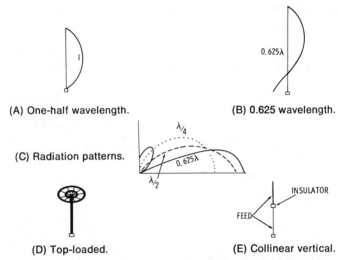

(A) One-half wavelength.

(B) 0.625 wavelength.

(C) Radiation patterns.

(D) Top-loaded.

(E) Collinear vertical.

Fig. 9-5. Long vertical antennas and their radiation patterns.

waves. One might assume that a high-angle sky-wave radiation 0.25-wavelength antenna is preferable to low vertical-angle signals in obtaining an extended coverage. However, the apparent advantage gained by the extended coverage is nullified when the reflected sky waves return to earth near the antenna and cause fading due to interference between the ground waves and sky waves. In fact, long (up to 0.625 wavelength) vertical antennas are often referred to as antifade antennas because they concentrate the radiation at low angles to prevent the sky waves from returning too near the station.

Figs. 9-5D and 9-5E show two common methods used by many clear-channel stations to gain the benefit of greater electrical length from a physically shorter antenna. One is to add an umbrella-like structure at the top of the mast (Fig. 9-5D). Referred to as a *top-loaded antenna* (or "top hat" for short), it includes sufficient radiating area to increase the effective electrical length of the antenna without having to extend its physical height. Suitably dimensioned, such an antenna will display many of the favorable characteristics of a much taller structure, such as more favorable impedance and matching relationships at the feed point, plus better current distribution (which encourages low-angle radiation). A second plan uses a sectionalized tower, usually with one or more insulators to break up the vertical structure into individual radiating elements. Such an antenna is called a *collinear vertical* (Fig. 9-5E), and it is superior to any other antenna if proper impedance and current relationships have been established for the location and coverage desired. In many areas, fading can be reduced substantially with a collinear vertical.

Nevertheless, the short, self-supported vertical is by far the most common for small stations. Also, two or more vertical antennas are employed in directional antenna systems.

9-4. ANTENNA-FEED METHODS

The three most popular feed methods for vertical antennas are given in Fig. 9-6. In many small stations the antenna is just outside the transmitter building (Fig. 9-6A), and only a short transmission line (usually copper tubing) is needed between the transmitter and antenna. The transmission line connects to the antenna at a point which provides an approximate impedance match, and fine tuning of the antenna is accomplished in the output-coupling network of the transmitter.

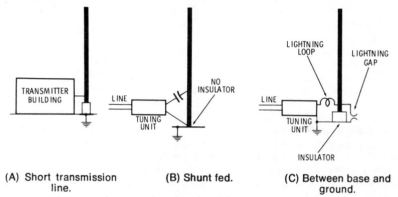

| (A) Short transmission line. | (B) Shunt fed. | (C) Between base and ground. |

Fig. 9-6. Antenna feed methods.

In the shunt-fed (grounded) tower of Fig. 9-6B, the transmitter and antenna are a substantial distance apart; consequently, an impedance-matching antenna tuning unit is associated with the antenna. The slant-wire feed arrangement is connected to the vertical radiator at a point which will provide an approximate impedance match. The fine tuning of the antenna system is then accomplished with the antenna-tuning network.

Fig. 9-6C shows the most popular system of the three antenna feed systems. The antenna is fed between the base of the antenna and ground. The antenna tuning unit matches the impedance of the transmission line to the radiation resistance of the antenna, and also tunes out any reactive components displayed by the latter. For lightning protection, the antenna feed line is looped twice, just ahead of the antenna. The loops act as a choke, presenting a high impedance to a lightning discharge. A second safeguard is the lightning gap, located between the base of the antenna and ground. The gap spacing must be such that a surge of lightning will arc across it but there will be no discharge during modulation peaks in the program.

9-5. TRANSMISSION LINES

The four important operating characteristics of transmission lines are impedance, attenuation, power-handling capability, and ability to withstand weather extremes.

A transmission-line impedance of 50 ohms is almost universal for broadcast transmitters. The power-handling and attenuation characteristics of various lines are given in Table 9-1. Attenuation, a function of the frequency and the distance between transmitter and antenna, is much more important in television and fm broadcasting because of the much higher frequencies, although it also becomes significant in am broadcasting when the use of extremely long transmission lines is necessary.

The five basic transmission lines are shown in Fig. 9-7. The RG/U flexible coaxial lines (Fig. 9-7A), using a solid dielectric of polyethylene, are found in nondirectional am broadcast stations with transmitters rated up to 1 kilowatt. RG17/U and RG19/U are the two most frequently used coaxial cables. The RG19/U has a higher power-handling capability, as indicated in Table 9-1, and in a well-matched system it can be used for powers of up to 5 kilowatts.

The power-rating figures take into consideration the fact that 100-percent amplitude modulation is used. At 100-percent modulation the power peaks of the modulated carrier signal have four times the average power output ($P_{pk} - _{pk} = 2E_p \times 2I_p = 4E_pI_p$) of the transmitter. The power rating is also given with relation to the standing-wave ratio on the line. Of course, the higher this ratio is, the greater is the voltage stress between outer and inner conductors. An average standing-wave ratio (vswr) of 2 to 1 is indicated in Table 9-1.

The semiflexible air-dielectric cable of Fig. 9-7B is widely used in directional am broadcast arrays and by many medium-powered am stations. It consists of outer and inner conductors made of soft-tempered copper and separated by insulators. The $7/8$-inch outside-diameter semiflexible cable is the most used size of coaxial cable and can be used to make reasonable bends in the transmission line path provided it is carefully manipulated to avoid kinks which might disrupt the impedance.

The continuous air-dielectric flexible cable in Fig. 9-7C is a recent

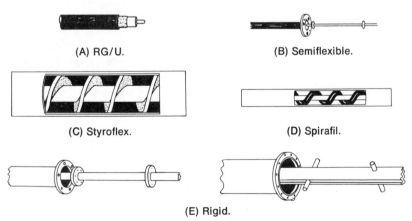

(A) RG/U.   (B) Semiflexible.

(C) Styroflex.   (D) Spirafil.

(E) Rigid.

Fig. 9-7. Broadcast transmission lines.

Table 9-1. Broadcast Transmission Lines

Type	Ohms	VSWR 2/1	
RG			
RG/17U	52	2.9	kW
RG/19U	52	4.25	kW
STYROFLEX			
⅜	50	0.56	kW
½	50	1.12	kW
¾	50	2.52	kW
⅞	50	3.64	kW
1⅛	50	5.99	kW
RIGID COAX			
⅞	50	3.64	kW
1⅝	50	16.25	kW
3⅛	50	52.64	kW
6⅛	50	212.8	kW

entry into the transmission-cable field. It consists of a solid or tubular copper center conductor and a tubular aluminum outer conductor. A *Styroflex* laminated helix and an outer belt of *Styroflex* tape maintain the proper spacing and thus provide a high percentage of air dielectric along the entire line at all times. The helical construction also keeps the spacing uniform, even when the line is bent. As shown in Table 9-1, *Styroflex* lines are available for transmission lines up to 6 kW, with diameter of only 1⅛ inch. The *Spirafil* cable (Fig. 9-7D) has a solid copper center, a tubular outer aluminum conductor, and a solid polyethylene helix.

The rigid coaxial line (Fig. 9-7E) is used mainly by high-powered stations. Tubular inner and outer conductors are employed, along with *Teflon*-disc or *Teflon*-peg spacers. These rigid air-dielectric coax lines are as much as six or seven inches in diameter and are capable of handling several hundred kilowatts or more. They are used for high-powered fm, television, and uhf transmitters because of this power capability and low attenuation. Waveguides are used for high powered uhf stations because of their lower attenuation.

To prevent condensation and the resultant interior arcing, *Styroflex* and rigid coaxial lines are often equipped with dehydrator units. An alternate arrangement is to use pumped nitrogen in pressurized lines. If the flanges and coupling connections are airtight, additional nitrogen is rarely needed after the initial filling. To protect transmission lines from the weather, they are often mounted in troughs.

9-6. GROUND SYSTEM

As you learned earlier, power to the antenna system of most small am stations is fed across the base insulator, the antenna serving as one terminal and the ground system as the other. Theoretically, the ground system should be a perfect conductor in order to establish the most favorable mirror effect for the antenna system. How close this ideal is approached is a function of the length and number of ground radials, along with the size of the ground screen (ground mat) underneath the tower. A typical ground system, shown in Fig. 9-8, consists

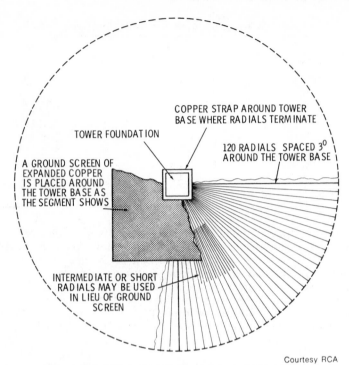

Courtesy RCA

Fig. 9-8. A typical broadcast-antenna ground system.

of 120 radials spaced 3° apart and extending outward the equivalent of at least one-quarter of a wavelength at the operating frequency. Usually the radial system is buried four to twelve inches underground, and a ground screen or additional short radials are used underneath the tower.

The entire system is bonded to a copper bus or strap around the perimeter of the tower foundation. A permanent ground, in the form of a heavy copper plate or strap, must be attached to the bottom of the base insulator and connected (through a heavy copper cable or stray) to a copper-bus ground at the tower base. A similar plan is required for each tower of a directional-antenna system, with copper bus lines or straps forming the junctions between the radial systems. The radial wires, copper screen, base straps, etc., must all be carefully soldered together in order to provide a good, continuous electrical connection.

9-7. TOWER LIGHTING

In most areas all towers over 200 feet must be lighted, and in some locations this ruling applies to even lower towers. For the usual small am station, a beacon light is required at the top and obstruction lights below it, the number depending on the tower height. A photoelectric

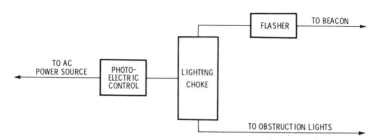

Fig. 9-9. A tower-lighting system.

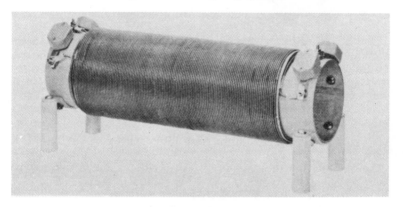

Courtesy Collins Telecommunications, Div. Rockwell Inl.
Fig. 9-10. A Collins lighting choke.

device (Fig. 9-9) can be used to turn on the lights automatically before sunset or during dark days.

It is necessary to block the rf potential of the tower from the power line. This is accomplished with a multisection choke similar to the Collins lighting choke (Fig. 9-10) or an isolation transformer like the Austin ring type (Fig. 9-11). The transformer permits coupling of the low-frequency lighting power, but acts as an isolator to rf potentials because of the wide spacing between its coils.

9-8. ANTENNA-TUNING UNIT

A typical antenna-tuning system is the Harris unit in Figs. 9-12 and 9-13. It has a frequency range of 550-1600 kHz and a maximum modulated carrier power of 1000 watts. The network provides correct matching between the transmission line and a vertical antenna, and it also filters out rf harmonics.

The line from the transmitter is connected to the network by way of a feedthrough insulator at the bottom of the tuning unit (Fig. 9-12); the antenna connects to the insulator at the top right. A heavy copper strap should be connected from a grounding stud (located at the bottom of the unit) to the antenna ground system. The outer conductor of

Fig. 9-11. An Austin ring transformer.

the coaxial line coming from the transmitter must also be grounded to this stud.

The basic part of the tuning unit (Fig. 9-13) is a T-section low-pass filter; key components are the variable inductor L1, C1, C2, and C3. The component values are selected in accordance with the line im-

Courtesy Harris Communications

Fig. 9-12. Antenna tuning unit.

pedance, the type of vertical antenna and its feed method, and the operating frequency. The function of C1 is to block antenna static discharge, which is bypassed to ground via L4. The value of C1 is determined by the antenna reactance; if the antenna reactance is inductive, the reactance of C1 must match. If the antenna is short and displays capacitive reactance, the reactance of C1 is made small enough to be negligible.

The values of C2 and C3 are determined by the transmission-line impedance and the antenna radiation resistance to be matched. For a 90° matching section (comparable to a quarter-wave matching segment), the capacitive reactance must be:

$$X_C = \sqrt{Z_L R_A}$$

where,

Z_L is the line impedance,
R_A is the antenna resistance,
X_C is the total reactance of C2 and C3 in parallel.

Here is the recommended procedure for adjusting an antenna-coupling network:

1. With a bridge, measure the base impedance of the antenna. The coupling unit must match this value to the transmission line. (It is designed with the proper range of adjustments to permit an exact match.)
2. After installing the antenna-tuning unit, connect an impedance bridge across its input. Adjust the tuning unit until the input impedance has a zero reactive component and a resistance equal to the characteristic impedance of the transmission line.
3. Adjust the coil tap at the antenna end of inductor L1 until the resistance at the input to the coupling network equals the characteristic impedance of the line. Next, move the coil tap at the other end of inductor L1 until the input reactance is zero. The transmission line can now be attached to the input of the tuning unit.

A thermocouple meter system or a diode-rectifier meter system can be used to indicate antenna current. In Fig. 9-12 a thermocouple unit can be seen at the right center. In the schematic of this circuit in Fig. 9-13, inductors L2 and L3 and capacitors C4 and C5 act as rf filters. A lead-covered two-pair cable transfers the thermocouple output to the remote meter which is located in the transmitter housing.

In a second arrangement a diode-rectifier meter is connected across meter-switch assembly S1 (Fig. 9-13). The remote meter, M3, or meter M2 at the antenna tuning unit can be switched in or out of the transmission system by S1. L5 and L6 in Fig. 9-13 couple energy from the antenna line. L5 is several turns of tubing at one end of the transmission line. The small field built up around these turns is enough to couple energy into the input circuit of the metering unit.

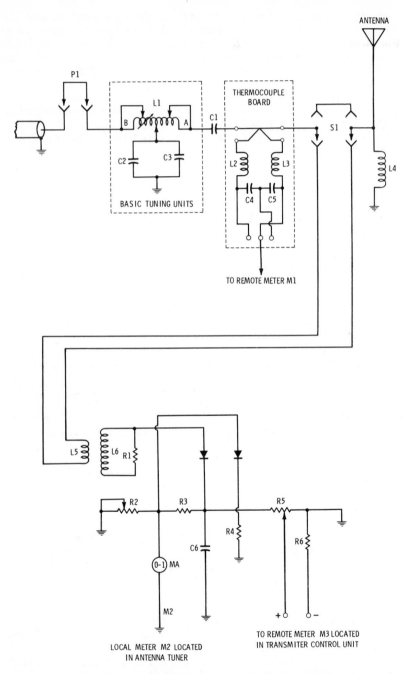

Fig. 9-13. Schematic diagram of an antenna tuning unit.

A common-point impedance bridge that permits continuous monitoring of the operating impedance of an antenna system is shown in Fig. 9-14. Included is an antenna rf ammeter. In operation the sensitivity and tuning knobs on each side of the bridge meter are adjusted to give an on-scale reading near the high end of the scale. The antenna resistance (R) and the antenna impedance (X/F_{MC}) are alternately adjusted for minimum meter reading. As the minimum null point is approached the sensitivity and tuning controls should be advanced to maintain as high an on-scale reading as possible. The bridge is at null when adjustment of R and X dials result only in an increase in meter reading. The resistive component of the antenna system can now be read directly from the R dial. This reading is independent of frequency. The reactive component of the system is found by multiplying the X dial reading by the operating frequency in megahertz.

Courtesy DELTA ELECTRONICS

Fig. 9-14. Common-point-impedance bridge.

Such a bridge permits continuous monitoring of the common-point impedance. In a directional antenna system, separate bridges can be used to measure individual impedances and tower currents.

The bridge (Fig. 9-15) employs the directional coupler principle. A sample of the direct and reflected energy in the transmission line is picked up by a secondary line. Adjustable fixed and variable terminations cause additional wave movement on the secondary line. When these variable terminations are adjusted with calibrated controls they cause equal and opposite waves to be induced from the primary line. As a result a null is shown by the detector and the antenna resistance and reactance values can be taken from the calibrated dials. Potentiometer R1 and capacitor C1 are the controls that balance the bridge. Their calibrated settings are displayed by the R and X/F_{MC} dials on the front of the meter. Capacitor C2 along with resistors R4 and R6 are calibration controls which are initially factory calibrated but can be checked out by a responsible broadcast engineer.

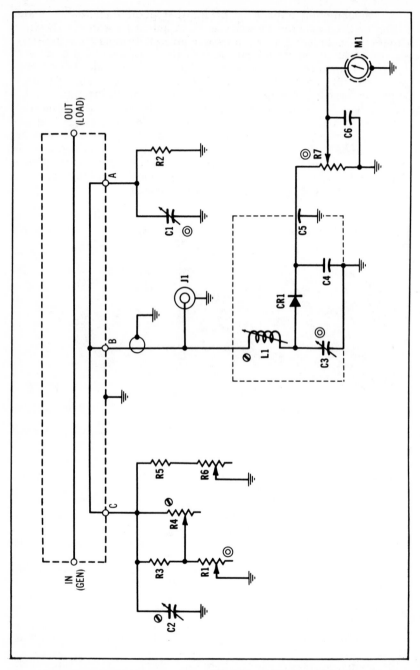

Fig. 9-15. Antenna bridge circuit using directional-coupler principal.

The detector and meter circuit is shown at the bottom center of Fig. 9-15. Capacitor C3 is the tune control and potentiometer R7 is the sensitivity control. Inductor L1 is preset according to the assigned frequency of the am station.

9-9. DIRECTIONAL-ANTENNA SYSTEMS

A directional broadcast-antenna system is used where the rf energy must be concentrated into the service area to be covered. The horizontal radiation pattern is so planned that there is minimum radiation toward the station(s) with which it must not interfere. As mentioned previously, the directional pattern is a function of the number and spacing of the vertical radiators, plus the relative phase and magnitude of their currents. The directivity and general shape of the pattern are determined by the spacing of the vertical antennas and the relative phasing of their currents. The deepness of the nulls is influenced greatly by the relative magnitudes of the radiator currents.

Some stations requiring directional patterns employ only two vertical towers. The technique of obtaining the desired directional pattern from two towers is demonstrated in Fig. 9-16. Let us consider Fig. 9-16A, showing two vertical antennas 180° (one-half wavelength) apart and fed by in-phase currents. The towers in Fig. 9-16A are located in a north and south direction, but they could be located in any direction required by the station location and its service area. The radiation from tower No. 2, in traveling toward tower No. 1, goes through a 180° phase reversal and arrives out of phase with the radiation from tower No. 1. Consequently, the two fields oppose each other, and there is little or no radiation toward the north. The same condition exists toward the south because the radiation from tower No. 2 likewise goes through a 180° phase shift prior to its arrival at tower No. 1.

If the receiver is due east or west from the towers, both signals must travel the same distance to the receiver. Inasmuch as the radiation is in phase, the two components arrive in phase and are additive. Consequently, maximum signal is radiated east and west. This type of horizontal-radiation pattern is indicated by the figure-8 polar drawing. Two antennas spaced 180° apart and fed in phase are often referred to as a *broadside array* because maximum radiation is perpendicular to the plane of the two antenna towers.

Fig. 9-16B demonstrates how the figure-8 pattern can be shifted 90°, just by feeding the two vertical radiators out of phase. With the two towers located the same as before, the radiation from tower No. 2 will arrive in phase with the radiation from tower No. 1 because, in traveling one-half of a wavelength, it has been restored to the same phase as the radiation from tower No. 1. Consequently, the two components will be additive, and maximum signal will be radiated northward. Likewise, there will be maximum radiation in the southerly direction with the arrival of tower No. 1 signal at tower No. 2.

Because the two signals leave the vertical-antenna elements out of phase, any receiver to the east or west of the elements will be the same

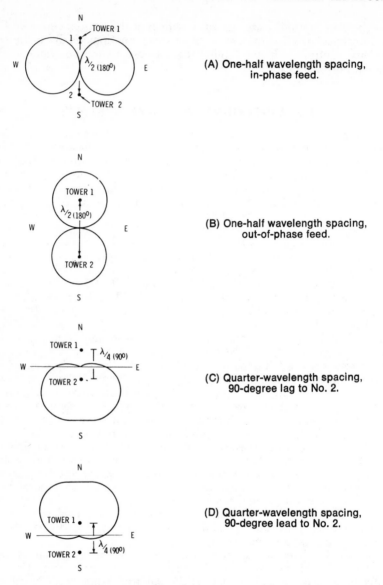

(A) One-half wavelength spacing, in-phase feed.

(B) One-half wavelength spacing, out-of-phase feed.

(C) Quarter-wavelength spacing, 90-degree lag to No. 2.

(D) Quarter-wavelength spacing, 90-degree lead to No. 2.

Fig. 9-16. Basic two-tower spacing and phasing techniques.

distance from both towers. Since the two signal components will have traveled the same distance, they will remain out of phase upon arrival. Consequently there will be minimum radiation toward the east and west. The radiation pattern is again a figure 8, but its maximum direction is now north and south.

Figs. 9-16C and D demonstrate how a unidirectional pattern can be established. The two towers are now separated by only 90°. In Fig. 9-16C, the current supplied to tower No. 2 lags the current of No. 1 by 90°. The energy leaving tower No. 1 and moving toward No. 2 now encounters an additional 90° delay and arrives in phase with the radiation from tower No. 2. Therefore the two signals are in phase, and maximum signal is directed southward.

The radiation from tower No. 2, on moving toward No. 1, also incurs a 90° delay and arrives exactly 180° out of phase with the radiation from tower No. 1. Thus, there is a canceling field and minimum radiation northward. With this method of spacing and phasing, most of the energy is radiated south of the east-west line, with little or none to the north.

In Fig. 9-16D, tower No. 2 is fed a 90° leading current, and so the pattern is shifted through 180°. Now the radiation leaving tower No. 1 will again encounter a 90° delay, but will arrive out of phase with the radiation from tower No. 2. Consequently, there will be minimum radiation toward the south. Tower No. 2 radiation also encounters a 90° delay, but arrives in phase with the radiation from tower No. 1. Hence there will be maximum radiation northward. Now it becomes apparent that most of the energy is forced north of the east-west line, and only a limited amount of energy is radiated south of it.

A wide variety of possible patterns, covering many directional-antenna problems, can be obtained from only two towers, provided they are positioned, spaced, and correctly phased. A typical example appears in Fig. 9-17. The directional pattern shown has been established by spacing two towers 100° apart and by feeding tower No. 2 a lagging 100° current. With this combination most of the radiated energy will be concentrated in the southwest quadrant. The transmitter has been located northeast of the primary area to be covered. The pattern protects other broadcast station service areas approximately north-northeast and another area slightly south and to the east of the transmitter. The depth of these two nulls is a function of the magnitude of the currents. Notice that tower No. 2 is being supplied a lower current (0.8) than the unity current of tower No. 1.

Fig. 9-17. Typical two-tower directional pattern.

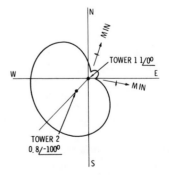

The angle of the minima (Fig. 9-17) can be finely regulated by a phasing adjustment. As the phase difference is increased, the two minima will separate further, as per the small arrows. Conversely, the angle can be reduced by decreasing the phase difference. By repositioning the towers, it is possible to rotate the pattern without changing its shape—to meet a particular geographical situation.

Effective reliable performance cannot be derived from a directional-antenna system unless each tower is properly grounded. Fig. 9-18 shows

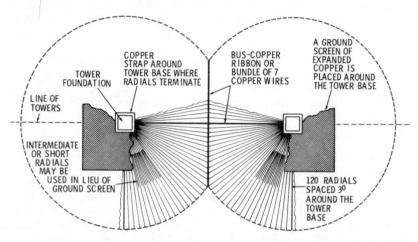

Courtesy RCA

Fig. 9-18. A two-tower ground system.

a typical ground system for a two-tower installation. The same grounding plan of a single tower in Fig. 9-18 is also used for each tower when more than two towers are used for a directional system. Each tower must have its own ground screen and radials. In addition, a copper strap, ribbon, or bundle of wires must link the bases and also the junctions of the radials of adjacent towers.

9-10. POWER-DIVIDING AND PHASING ARRANGEMENT

A two-step process is involved in preparing the excitation for the two or more towers of a directional system. A power divider is needed in each line to establish the proper magnitudes between antenna currents, and a phase-shift network must be included in each line to establish the correct phase relationship between antenna currents. In some two-tower directional systems, the phase-shift network is included in only one of the transmission lines to the towers. The most common arrangement is shown in the block diagram of Fig. 9-19.

One factor in establishing the required phase relationship between currents is the difference in electrical length of the lines feeding the antenna towers. For example, if the current from the first tower travels through an additional 75° of transmission line before reaching the

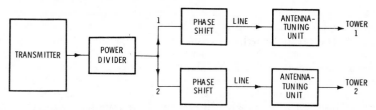

Fig. 9-19. Functional plan of a directional-antenna feed system.

second tower, this 75° must be considered in establishing the overall phase differential required between the currents of the two towers.

In determining the electrical length of a transmission line, its velocity factor (ratio of the speed at which the signal travels along the line, to the speed at which it travels in free space) must be taken into account. The velocity factor of RG17/U is 0.66; in other words, an *electrical* half wavelength of such a cable is 0.66 times the free-space half wavelength. This means that a radio-frequency current traveling along a transmission line which has a *physical* length of one-half wavelength goes through a phase shift substantially greater than 180°.

If the antennas of a two-tower installation are fed over the same length and type of cable, a phasing network must develop the required phase shift. Usually the transmission lines are of different lengths, and the resultant phase difference between the two lines must be considered in the design of the phasing network. Several power-divider arrangements are shown in Fig. 9-20. In Fig. 9-20A, two in-phase signals must be supplied to lines 1 and 2.

From the block diagram in Fig. 9-19 you will notice that the phase-shifting network comes after the divider point and is usually designed

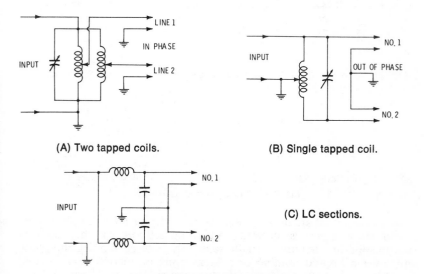

(A) Two tapped coils.

(B) Single tapped coil.

(C) LC sections.

Fig. 9-20. Basic power dividers.

on the basis that the two signals will be exactly in phase or exactly out of phase at the divider output. This arrangement permits in-phase signals to be put on the two lines. Their relative magnitudes can be established with the taps A and B on the output inductors (Fig. 9-20A).

The arrangement in Fig. 9-20B demonstrates how two signals exactly 180° out of phase can be placed on the two lines. Here the relative magnitudes are determined by the position of a single tap on the inductor. This division can also be accomplished with LC sections, as shown in Fig. 9-20C. The constants are selected to establish the proper current division.

Most power dividers are also designed to maintain an impedance match between the transmitter, phasing networks, and/or transmission lines. In more complex arrangements, however, impedance-matching networks must be placed ahead of the power divider. Often the output tuning system of the transmitter can be adjusted to match the input of the power divider.

The phase-shift network follows the power divider as shown in Fig. 9-19. Several typical phase-shift networks are shown in Fig. 9-21. Although the examples show T networks, pi networks can be used for phasing adjustment as well as impedance matching. At the same time, the proper current lag or lead is established by placing inductors or capacitors in the series path to retard or advance the current flow. With inductors, a large-angle lagging network is established; and with capacitors, a large-angle lead network. A combination of the two in the series path permits a small-angle lead or lag, as desired.

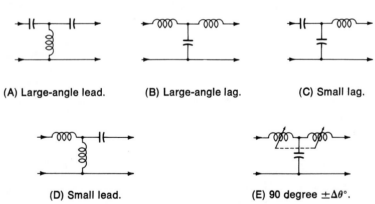

(A) Large-angle lead.   (B) Large-angle lag.   (C) Small lag.

(D) Small lead.   (E) 90 degree ±Δθ°.

Fig. 9-21. Basic phasing networks.

In a directional-antenna system the correct phase relationship is established by proper use of both the phasing networks and the required transmission-line lengths. Usually some means of controlling the phase shift over a limited number of degrees must be incorporated so that variables and other day-to-day fluctuations can be tuned out. A basic

90° phase-shift network, such as that shown in Fig. 9-21, is usually used. A change of several degrees can be accomplished without an adverse influence on impedance matching.

The antenna monitor of a directional-antenna installation allows the operator to constantly keep an eye on the magnitude and phase of the currents. Samples of the current are taken from each vertical antenna, and supplied to the monitor. The readings are recorded periodically in the transmitter log. When suitably calibrated, the phase monitor is useful in tuning and in indicating early trouble in the directional performance of the antenna system.

9-11. MULTIPLE-TOWER SYSTEMS

Three or more directional elements are usually employed by high-powered stations to obtain a particularly complex pattern. Sometimes such highly directional patterns are used in order to concentrate the rf energy and thus provide blanket coverage of the area, even though a less-directional pattern would satisfy the FCC ruling about interference.

A highly concentrated pattern that prevents interference with the radiation of four other stations (A, B, C, and D) is illustrated in Fig. 9-22. It can be obtained with three towers, using the spacing, phasing, and magnitudes indicated. The towers are mounted in a straight line running east and west (90°-270° in Fig. 9-22). The wavelength in degrees between each tower, the current of each tower and their phase angles in relation to tower No. 1 (polar coordinates), and the geographic location of the station towers are given in the lower right corner of Fig. 9-22. Fig. 9-23 is a functional diagram of the phasing equipment required to obtain such a pattern.

Many stations operate directionally during nighttime only, because of the wider coverage at nighttime and hence the greater risk of interference. For nondirectional operation using tower No. 1, switches S1 and S2 must be in the positions shown. The transmitter output will now be supplied directly to tower No. 1.

For directional operation the transmitter output is supplied, through a matching network, to a power divider consisting of L4, L5, and L6 across matching network coil L2. The taps (on L4, L5, and L6) are made in accordance with the currents supplied to the three towers. Tower No. 2 receives the highest current (1.294 amp/135.5°) and No. 1 the lowest (0.382 amp /0°), with tower No. 3 falling in between (0.735 amp /−93.6°), as shown in Fig. 9-22. The angles indicated at each tower are the phase angles of each tower in relation to tower No. 1. The input phase-shift networks (1 and 3) are adjustable to permit a fine setting of the phase to towers 1 and 3. These networks also contribute a certain amount of absolute phase shift and provide an impedance match to the individual transmission lines. Additional phase shifts are contributed by the transmission lines (the line to tower No. 3 supplying the most). However, 90° shifts are also contributed by the matching networks between towers No. 1 and No. 2 and their lines.

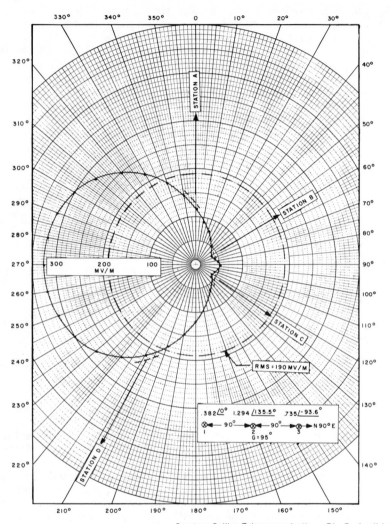

Courtesy Collins Telecommunications, Div. Rockwell Int.

Fig. 9-22. Typical three-tower directional pattern.

A zero phase-shift network is in the path between tower No. 3 and its line.

The power divider and the adjustable segments of the phase-shift networks are usually mounted near the transmitter. Meter M1 is associated with the input to the phase-shift network and measures the total current. M2, M3, and M4 in Fig. 9-23 are located in the respective tuning units of the three towers.

The sensors for remote meters can be installed at the antenna and read at the transmitter-building phase monitor. In addition to a remote

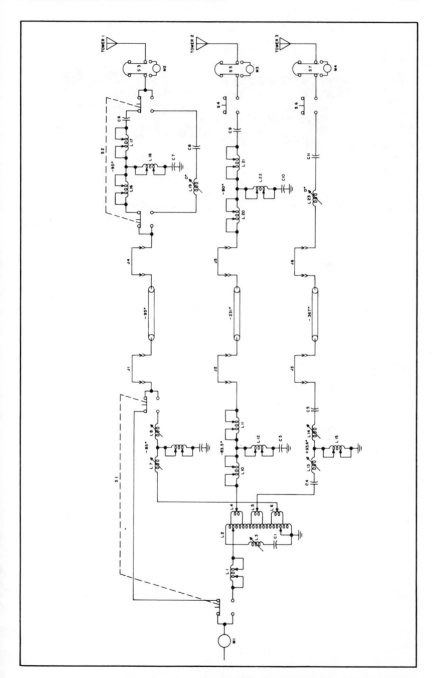

Courtesy Collins Telecommunications, Div. Rockwell Int.

Fig. 9-23. Circuit of a three-tower phasing system.

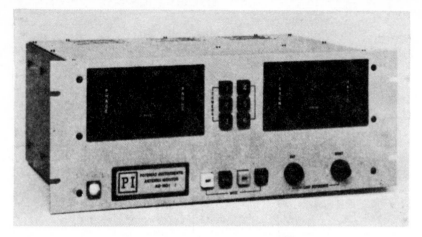

Courtesy Potomac Instruments, Inc.

Fig. 9-24. Directional-antenna monitor.

phase monitor, individual current meters for each line are used in tuning the antenna-coupling networks. During normal operation the antenna-current meters are switched out of the circuit to protect them from being damaged by lightning.

The Potomac directional-antenna monitor (Fig. 9-24) provides a digital readout of loop currents and phase. Up to six towers can be monitored by depressing the appropriate button. The angle of a tower antenna current relative to the zero-angle reference is read on the left.

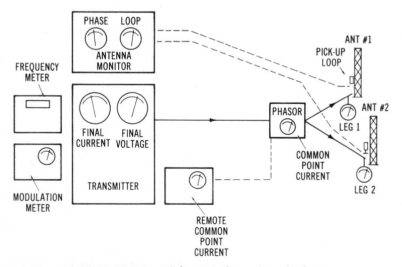

Fig. 9-25. Transmitting metering and monitoring.

The right readout is the current ratio given as percentage. A Delta Electronics digital antenna monitor is described in detail in Chapter 14.

9-12. METERING AND MONITORING SUMMARY

A typical metering and monitoring setup for a two-tower installation is shown in Fig. 9-25. Two important meters of the transmitter read the final power amplifier dc current and dc voltage. The product of these two meter readings is the input power of the transmitter. Associated with the transmitter is a remote common-point antenna current meter. This meter provides a remote indication of the common-point antenna current being supplied to the phasor which is a part of the directional antenna system. This current squared times the resistance of the antenna system is a measure of the transmitter power output.

There is the compulsory modulation meter associated with the transmitter that determines the degree to which the program audio modulates the transmitter output. A frequency meter is used to determine that the transmitter is operating on the FCC-assigned frequency. In modern stations, this meter is common but often is not logged because of the inherent frequency stability of modern transmitters.

The function of the phasor is to properly divide the currents supplied to the towers of a two-tower directional antenna system. Meters are included that can be used to read the individual antenna leg currents. There are also two pickup loops associated with each tower that supply signal back to the antenna monitor. The antenna monitor indicates the relative phase of the two antenna-tower loop currents. At the same time the current ratio is important because relative currents and phase establish the proper antenna pattern.

CHAPTER 10

FM Transmitters

10-1. DIRECT-FM TRANSMITTER

The modern direct-fm broadcast transmitter uses a self-excited vhf oscillator that is frequency deviated by a variable-reactance device such as a voltage-variable capacitor. The voltage-variable capacitor displays a capacitive reactance across the oscillator resonant circuit. Reactance variations follow the audio signal changes causing the frequency-determining circuit of the oscillator to vary in frequency in accordance with the audio.

The limits of the frequency change (deviation) depend on the amplitude of the applied audio signal—the greater the amplitude, the greater the frequency change. The rate of frequency deviation depends on the frequency of the applied audio—the higher the audio frequency, the faster the deviation rate of the vhf oscillator frequency.

In fm broadcasting, carrier frequencies are assigned in the 88-108 MHz band. The maximum permissible deviation is ±75 kHz; this constitutes 100% modulation. The FCC requires that an fm broadcast transmitter must deviate linearly over a 100 kHz range. In so doing a very linear deviation over the ±75 kHz range is ensured.

The FCC requires that the center frequency of each broadcast station be maintained within 2000 hertz of the assigned frequency. Therefore, a means of precise frequency control must be used. This requires an automatic-frequency-control (afc) system which, in the modern fm broadcast transmitter, is in the form of a phase-locked loop. In a modern arrangement (Fig. 10-1) the oscillator operates directly on the assigned vhf frequency.

Stereo fm broadcasting is popular and requires that a multiplex system develop the required fm signals for modulating the oscillator. Also in some fm broadcast stations supplementary SCA (Subsidiary Communications Authority) transmissions are made and an additional modulating signal is also applied to the fm modulator of the vhf oscillator. This signal appears on a subcarrier frequency and its generation will be discussed in detail later in this chapter.

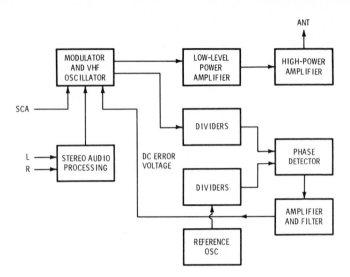

Fig. 10-1. Functional plan of modern fm-broadcast transmitter.

The output of the modulated oscillator is at a very low level and must be increased in magnitude with a low-level power amplifier. In most modern transmitters all but the high-power amplifier stages are solid state. The output of a typical low-level power amplifier might be 10 to 20 watts. This is applied to the high-power amplifier which consists of several stages that build up the signal level to the final transmit power. The final vacuum-tube power amplifier supplies the frequency-modulated signal to the antenna system.

The power output of an fm broadcast station is based on its effective radiated power (erp). This value is the product of the power delivered to the antenna and the antenna power gain or:

$$\text{erp} = P_{ant} \times \text{antenna power gain}$$
$$\text{erp} = (P_{transmitter} - P_{line\,loss}) \times \text{antenna power gain}$$
$$\text{erp} = P_{ant} \times (\text{field gain of antenna})^2$$

Output from the modulated oscillator section is also applied to a frequency divider (Fig. 10-1) which reduces the frequency of the signal to the audio frequency range and applies it to a phase detector. A reference comparison signal is also applied to the phase detector and is developed by a reference crystal oscillator followed by a second frequency-divider chain. If the two frequencies applied to the phase detector are in phase the vhf oscillator is operating on the correct frequency. However, if there is a phase drift, the phase detector develops a dc output voltage that is a measure of the phase differential. This dc error voltage is applied through an amplifier and filter to the vhf oscillator. It applies a correcting voltage to the oscillator bringing on a frequency change that will bring the outputs of the divider chains back in phase.

This feedback system, referred to as a phase-locked loop, is so accurate that the vhf oscillator is held precisely on the assigned channel frequency. Any attempted drift in the center frequency of this oscillator causes the lock system to go into operation and results in a correcting activity that holds the oscillator precisely on frequency.

10-2. FREQUENCY MULTIPLIER CHAIN

Older fm broadcast transmitters operate with self-excited fm oscillators on a lower frequency (Fig. 10-2). In this arrangement it was necessary to multiply the frequency of the oscillator output before it was amplified and applied to the antenna system. Typically the frequency multiplier had a total multiplication of 18 and consisted of two triplers and a doubler as shown.

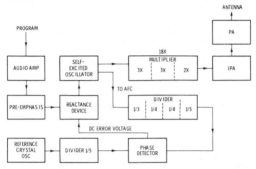

Fig. 10-2. Block diagram of a direct-fm transmitter.

Frequency multipliers were necessary because of the type of reactance modulation used. Only a limited deviation of the self-excited oscillator would produce a linear frequency change. Thus it was necessary to start out at a lower center frequency because the maximum linear deviation may only be approximately 5000 hertz. However, in the multiplication process both the deviation and the center frequency are multiplied by the same amount and with a total multiplication of 18 the final maximum possible linear deviation could be as high as ±90 kHz (5 × 18).

In this system of fm modulation it was also necessary to use an afc system to hold the oscillator on the correct center frequency. Thus a portion of the oscillator output was also applied to a frequency-divider chain and then on to a phase detector. Here it was compared with a signal developed by a reference signal oscillator and a succeeding divider. In the example shown the output of the frequency divider is compared in the phase detector with a frequency that is one-fifth of the output frequency of the reference crystal oscillator. If the center frequency drifts in phase, a dc error voltage is developed by the phase detector and supplied to the reactance device that holds the center frequency of the oscillator to the required value that will produce the channel frequency output after a multiplication of 18 times.

10-3. DEVIATION AND BANDWIDTH

In the fm process a number of sideband pairs are generated according to modulating frequency and deviation. This is unlike the am process, which generates only one pair of sidebands. The number of significant sideband pairs generated is a function of the modulation index, which has the following relation:

$$\text{Modulation Index} = \frac{\text{Deviation (kHz)}}{\text{Modulating Freq. (kHz)}}$$

The higher the modulation index is, the more sideband pairs there are. As shown in Fig. 10-3, the sidebands are displaced from the center

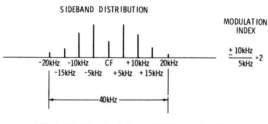

(A) ± 10-kHz deviation, 5-kHz modulation.

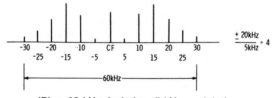

(B) ± 20-kHz deviation, 5-kHz modulation.

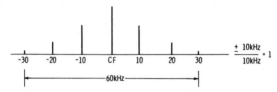

(C) ± 10-kHz deviation, 10-kHz modulation.

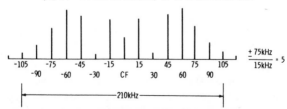

(D) ± 75-kHz deviation, 15-kHz modulation.

Fig. 10-3. Frequency and energy distribution for four values of modulation index of an am signal.

frequency by multiples of the modulating frequency. In comparing Figs. 10-3A and 10-3B, notice that the greater the deviation (increase in the audio amplitude), the more sideband pairs are generated and the greater is the bandwidth occupied by the transmitted fm signal. The higher the audio frequency, the greater is the separation between sideband pairs and the greater is the bandwidth of the transmitted signal (compare Figs. 10-3A and 10-3C).

The *maximum bandwidth* of a transmitted fm signal is a function of the modulation index at *maximum permissible deviation* (100-percent modulation) and *highest audio frequency*. The sideband distribution for a deviation of ±75 kHz and an audio frequency of 15,000 hertz is shown in Fig. 10-3D. For a modulation index of 5, the number of significant sideband pairs is 7. These would occupy a span of frequencies some 210 kHz wide.

The FCC channel assignments are only 200 kHz wide. However, we have considered the bandwidth extreme in the example. Seldom is a maximum-amplitude high-frequency note transmitted in the usual program material. High-frequency components are clipped when too high by limiters and result in a correspondingly lower deviation.

10-4. PRE-EMPHASIS AND DE-EMPHASIS

A major advantage of an fm transmission system is that it can be designed to reject amplitude noise components. Inasmuch as most interference is of the amplitude-varying type, an fm system has a more favorable signal-to-noise ratio. However, noise and interference can also produce fm components, and so the system is not completely noise-free. Usually the deviations of fm signal, caused by the desired modulating wave, are much greater than deviations caused by interference.

In an fm system, according to Fig. 10-4, the noise interference has less effect when it exists at low audio-sideband frequencies near the center frequency. If the interference beat occurs at a higher frequency, a greater unwanted deviation of the fm signal occurs. Thus the noise-rejection characteristics of the fm system decreases in the direction of a higher interference frequency.

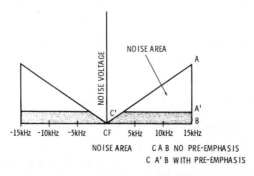

Fig. 10-4. Noise with and without pre-emphasis as related to center frequency.

The noise-rejection characteristic of an fm system can be improved by pre-emphasis of high-frequency audio components. The pre-emphasis circuit, as shown in Figs. 10-1 and 10-2, is inserted in the audio-amplifier section of the transmitter. The pre-emphasis network displays a decreasing attenuation as the audio frequency increases, as in Fig. 10-5. Consequently, higher-frequency components produce a greater deviation of the broadcast signal than lower-frequency components of the same amplitude. By so modulating, the system is made less subject to high-frequency interference because the desired high-frequency modulation now causes a greater deviation of the fm signal. This reduction in high-frequency noise susceptibility produces a flatter overall signal-to-noise relation, as indicated in Fig. 10-4.

The overall frequency response of the fm system is restored to a linear relation by the use of a de-emphasis network in the receiver (Fig. 10-5). This network has an attenuation characteristic equal but opposite to that of the transmitter pre-emphasis circuit. Although the de-emphasis network in the receiver reduces the amplitude of the high-frequency audio components, the noise components are reduced by the same amount.

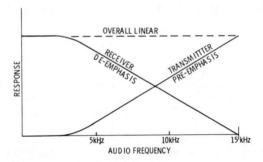

Fig. 10-5. Pre-emphasis at transmitter, de-emphasis at receiver, and overall frequency response.

The pre-emphasis network at the fm broadcast transmitter has been standardized as one having a time constant of 75 microseconds. If a simple RC combination is used as a pre-emphasis network it must have a value of 75 microseconds as obtained from the following formula:

$$TC = R \times C$$

where,

TC is the time constant in microseconds,
R is the resistance in ohms,
C is the capacitance in microfarads.

The de-emphasis network must have the same time constant, but an opposite attenuation characteristic, in order that the exact correction of the frequency response can be obtained when the network is inserted in the circuit.

10-5. SCA FM MULTIPLEX

In a multiplex system, the fm carrier can be modulated by more than one sound signal simultaneously. Multiplex operation is popular among fm broadcasters, especially for supplying background music to markets, department stores, industrial plants, etc. Stereophonic broadcasting also involves the transmission of a separate but related audio signal on the same fm carrier.

In the SCA multiplex system one program will frequency-modulate the fm carrier in the conventional manner. This is the main program channel used for broadcasting to the general public. As shown in Fig. 10-6, a second sound signal can be used to modulate a supersonic carrier. This frequency-modulated subcarrier is then used to frequency-modulate the main carrier. The subcarrier is supersonic so that it does not interfere with the main program channel.

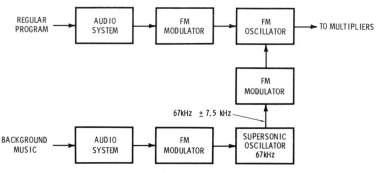

Fig. 10-6. Functional diagram of a multiplex transmitter.

A multiplex process must in no way degrade the regular program material, or adversely affect the operation of standard fm receivers when receiving regular fm broadcasts. The FCC technical standards for Subsidiary Communications Authority (SCA) multiplex operation are:

1. Frequency modulation of SCA subcarriers shall be used.
2. The instantaneous frequency of SCA subcarriers shall at all times be within the range of 20 to 70 kHz. If the station also broadcasts in stereo the instantaneous frequency of SCA subcarriers shall at all times be within the range 53 to 75 kHz.
3. The algebraic sum of the modulation of the main carrier by SCA subcarriers shall not exceed 30 percent. This modulation is limited to 10 percent when the station also broadcasts in stereo.
4. In no case shall the total of modulation exceed 100 percent on peaks of frequent recurrence. This total modulation of the main carrier includes stereo and SCA subcarriers.
5. Frequency modulation of the main carrier caused by the SCA subcarrier operation shall, in the frequency range 50 to 15,000 Hz, be at least 60 dB below 100% modulation. If the station is also

engaged in stereophonic broadcasting the frequency modulation of the main carrier by the SCA subcarrier operation shall, in the frequency range 50 to 53,000 Hz, be at least 60 dB below 100% modulation.

6. The center frequency of each SCA subcarrier shall be kept at all times within 500 hertz of the authorized frequency.

In the example of Fig. 10-6, a 67-kHz subcarrier has been selected. This subcarrier is frequency modulated. Deviation for 100-percent modulation is ±7.5 kHz. The frequency-modulated 67-kHz subcarrier is used to frequency-modulate the main carrier. At no time may the subcarrier frequency modulation of the main carrier exceed ±22.5 (0.3 × 75) kHz.

Insofar as a standard fm receiver is concerned, it operates normally in receiving regular program material. Such a receiver does not respond to the subcarrier frequency because of the latter's supersonic range.

A multiplex receiver includes the necessary channel for removing and amplifying the 67-kHz subcarrier. It will then be supplied to a separate fm demodulator and recovered for distribution over an associated music system.

10-6. DIRECT FM EXCITER

A functional block diagram of a Harris 10-watt direct fm exciter is given in Fig. 10-7. The frequency-modulated oscillator is shown at the top center, and consists of the modulated oscillator and a succeeding buffer plus a dc voltage regulator. The 15-25 milliwatt oscillator output is stepped up to the 10-watt level by a succeeding 4-stage amplifier shown at the top right. The oscillator operates on the FCC-assigned frequency.

The automatic frequency control at right center is also supplied with a signal from the buffer output of the modulated oscillator. Its frequency is dropped down to approximately 6000 Hz and applied to a frequency-comparing phase detector. A reference oscillator which is crystal-controlled operates on an approximate frequency of 1.5 MHz. Crystal oscillator frequency is also divided down to the 6000 Hz range. The divided-down frequency from the modulated oscillator and the divided-down frequency of the reference oscillator are compared in the phase detector. The output of the phase detector corresponds to any phase displacement (frequency difference) between the two components. This reference develops a dc error voltage which is supplied to the modulated oscillator to keep it on the proper center frequency. By FCC regulation, the center frequency may not drift more than 2000 Hz in the fm broadcast service. The automatic frequency control system also includes alarm circuits which indicate functional failures.

The audio module at the center of the diagram contains the pre-emphasis networks and additional circuits needed for processing audio signals for use in stereo broadcasts or SCA transmissions. SCA and stereo generator functional blocks at the left will be described later.

The modulated oscillator (Fig. 10-8) consists of a stable frequency-

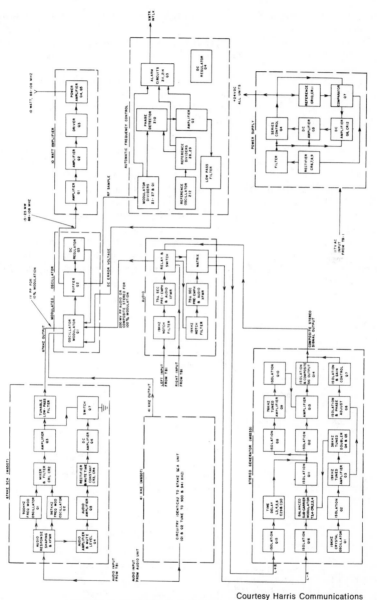

Courtesy Harris Communications

Fig. 10-7. Functional diagram of an fm exciter.

modulated oscillator, an isolating buffer amplifier, and a power supply regulator. The oscillator, transistor Q1, in a common-emitter config-uration is connected as a Clapp circuit. Three pairs of stabilizing ca-pacitors are employed according to the frequency of operation. These capacitors are highly stable, reducing the influence of external capacitance and compensating for any frequency drift resulting from temperature variations. Voltage-variable capacitor diodes, CR1, CR2 and CR3, permit controlled changes in the frequency of operation of the oscillator.

Such diodes have a capacitance that is a function of the dc voltage present across their elements. The capacitance change of diode CR3 is in response to the dc error voltage contributed by the afc unit. Its function is to maintain the oscillator on a correct center frequency. Recall that the dc error voltage is a result of the comparison between the divided frequencies of the modulated oscillator, and the reference frequency of the crystal oscillator in the afc unit. The actual oscillator comparison voltage is removed at the collector of buffer transistor Q2, and is supplied through capacitor C18 to the afc unit.

Diodes CR1 and CR2 produce the actual frequency modulation of the oscillator, deviating the oscillator frequency on each side of center frequency in accordance with the variations of the modulating wave.

The various signal inputs are shown at the left. The two inputs at the top are for the SCA signals (two blocks at the top left of the functional diagram in Fig. 10-7). The fm program signal is supplied to the third terminal. This can be a monophonic or stereophonic signal.

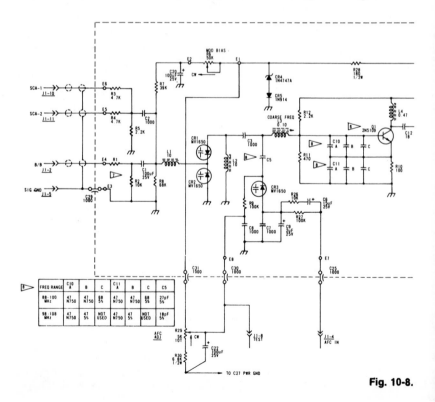

Fig. 10-8.

Program signals are applied to the junction of the two voltage-variable capacitor diodes and cause their capacitances to change in a balanced manner with the program signal variations. Since these capacitances are a part of the resonant circuit of the oscillator there is a linear deviation of the oscillator frequency in accordance with the voltage variations of the program signal.

The frequency of the resonant circuit is also determined by inductor L3 which is used as a coarse frequency adjustment. Two potentiometers, R6 and R29, also have an influence on the modulated oscillator performance. Potentiometer R29 is, in effect, a fine frequency control which sets the dc voltage felt across the voltage-variable capacitor CR3. This provides a fine adjustment of the center frequency of the fm transmitter. Potentiometer R6 applies the proper dc bias to the voltage-variable capacitors to which the program material is applied. Balance is set in such a manner that the diodes respond in a linear manner to the audio variations, thus producing a linear deviation of the oscillator frequency.

The collector output of the modulated oscillator is applied to the base of the buffer through an isolation network. The modulated oscillator supplies a moderately strong output and it can be attenuated and still provide enough drive for the buffer. The attenuator provides good

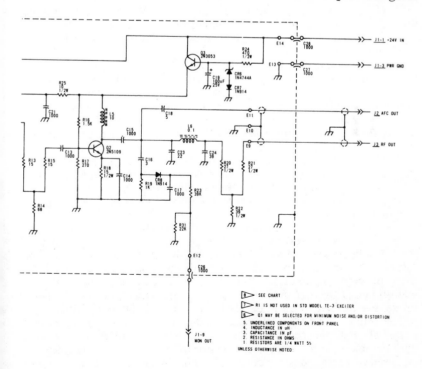

Modulated oscillator.

isolation between the buffer and the oscillator, and prevents changes in circuit operations from influencing the frequency of the modulated oscillator.

The collector output of the buffer is supplied through a low-pass filter (inductor L8 and capacitors C23 and C24) to an output attenuator. From here the frequency-modulated signal is supplied to the input of the succeeding 10-watt amplifier.

The afc output was mentioned previously. Also, diode CR8 rectifies a portion of the output of the buffer. The resultant dc component is applied to the monitor output of the modulated oscillator. It provides a check of the rf output of the modulated oscillator.

Zener diodes CR4 and CR6 provide regulation in the dc bias circuit of the voltage-variable capacitors and in the base of the voltage regulator, Q3. The use of the transistor regulator permits the regulation of the higher currents drawn by the collectors of transistors Q1 and Q2.

The 10-watt amplifier (Fig. 10-9) is a four-stage affair. The output stage uses two transistors connected in parallel to provide a 10-watt output when the input signal power to the amplifier is only several hundred milliwatts. Input signal is applied through an rf drive potentiometer, R11; the setting of R11 determines the rf power output of the amplifier.

The first two stages are reasonably the same and use interstage transformers T1 and T2 which match low-impedance base circuits to the higher-impedance collector circuits. Resonance and impedance-matching adjustments are made with capacitors C4 and C7.

The driver transistor Q3 and the parallel-connected output transistors Q4 and Q5 are vhf types with balanced-emitter configurations. Low capacitances result and permit good stage efficiency despite the high operating frequency. Resonance and impedance matching are handled by inductors L1 and L2, along with capacitors C14 and C15. The output circuit is a modified pi network using inductors L5 and L6, plus capacitors C19 and C20.

Rf samples for monitoring and adjustment are removed by way of capacitor C22. A small rf component is rectified and filtered by diode CR1 and a resistor-capacitor output combination, forming a dc monitoring component that is a function of the rf output level of the amplifier.

The Harris afc unit is shown in Fig. 10-10. The output of the buffer stage of the modulated oscillator is supplied to input receptacle J1 at the top left. A series of seven integrated-circuit flip-flop multivibrators follow. The first four provide an overall countdown of 16; the latter three provide counts of 16, 16 and 4 respectively. Therefore the total countdown is 16,384 ($16 \times 16 \times 16 \times 4$). The output, in the 6-kilohertz range, is supplied to an integrated-circuit phase detector, Z10.

The reference crystal-controlled oscillator uses an integrated circuit, Z12. The first two transistors are connected in multivibrator fashion with common-emitter coupling. The crystal itself is a high-stability unit enclosed in a temperature-controlled oven. Coarse frequency is set with capacitor C27, while a fine frequency adjustment is accomplished with

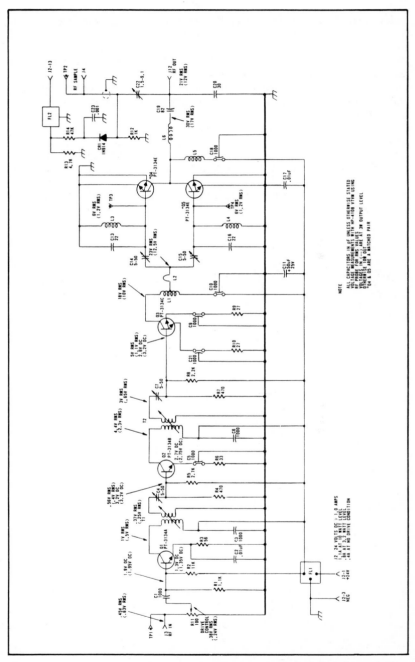

Courtesy Harris Communications

Fig. 10-9. A 10-watt amplifier.

potentiometer R48 which sets the bias for voltage-variable capacitor CR10.

The oven itself is in the form of a solid-state circuit that maintains the oven temperature at exactly 60°C. The arrangement consists of an integrated circuit dc differential amplifier Z13 which responds to changes in the resistance of thermistor RT1. Its dc output, through transistor Q5, determines the current drawn through oven heater resistor R38.

The third transistor of integrated circuit Z12 serves as a buffer, developing the necessary drive for the two counters Z8 and Z9. These counters provide a total countdown of 256 (16 each). The output of the second counter is applied to the phase detector integrated circuit Z10.

If the two signals at the inputs of the phase detector (divided-down center frequency from fm exciter and divided-down frequency from

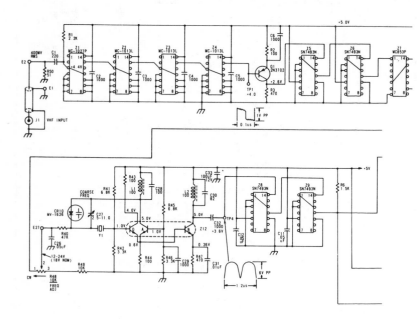

Fig. 10-10.

reference oscillator) are the same, the output of the detector is a square wave with equal positive and negative segments (50-percent duty cycle). This output provides a reference component for application to the amplifier, and detector transistor Q2. Output is filtered to obtain a reference dc voltage.

The duty cycle of the squared wave at the output of the detector is proportional to the difference in the two input frequencies. The dc component of current drawn by transistor Q2 responds to this change in duty cycle, and the dc output voltage shifts above or below the reference value in accordance with any tendency of phase shift between the two incoming frequencies. This *dc error voltage* is applied back to the modulated oscillator to keep the center frequency of the fm broadcast transmitter on its FCC-assigned frequency.

The factors monitored by the alarm system are the outputs of the reference and modulator-oscillator frequency dividers and the so-called

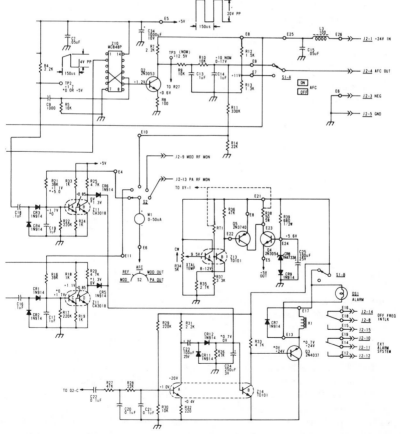

Courtesy Harris Communications

The afc unit.

out-of-lock condition. Output from the reference divider is rectified by diodes CR1 and CR2. The dc component is amplified by integrated-circuit Z11 and applied to the alarm circuit. A similar arrangement exists for monitoring the output of the modulated-oscillator divider chain. Either dc component operates integrated circuit Z14 and turns on transistor Q3 which will draw current through the alarm light and relay coil K1.

If the modulated oscillator should drift out of the frequency control range of the afc circuit there is a large ac component developed at the collector of transistor Q2. This large ac component applied to section A of integrated circuit Z14 is detected by diodes CR12 and CR11. The resultant dc voltage turns on section B of integrated circuit Z14 and transistor Q3, thus setting off the alarm system.

10-7. SCA-SUBCARRIER GENERATOR

An SCA generator permits an fm broadcast station to transmit special background music and other subscription program material in addition to the regular fm program. The SCA generator is a part of the fm exciter, as shown in Fig. 10-7. The most common SCA subcarrier frequency is 67 kHz. Although the fm station is transmitting stereo programs, an SCA signal can be conveyed simultaneously. Another SCA-subcarrier frequency is 41 kHz, which can be used when the station does not transmit a stereophonic fm signal and wishes to transmit two SCA signals.

An SCA generator is shown in Fig. 10-11. This generator permits the selection of either of the SCA-subcarrier frequencies of 41 kHz or 67 kHz. The Colpitts oscillator circuit associated with transistor Q1 operates on 900 kHz, while the circuit of transistor Q2 can be operated on either 941 or 967 kHz. The actual subcarrier frequency is then the difference between the two oscillator frequencies. Note that the two outputs are mixed in the CR1 and CR2 diode mixer circuit. The output filter network selects the difference frequency and attenuates harmonics of the subcarrier frequency and the two oscillator frequencies as well. After amplification by transistor Q3 the signal meets a very elaborate tunable low-pass filter which removes all harmonics of the subcarrier frequencies.

The subcarrier is frequency-modulated by applying the audio variations to the bases of the two oscillators. Such voltage variations at the bases cause corresponding changes in the effective base-emitter capacitance of each of the oscillators. In turn, the capacitance variation deviates the frequency of each of the Colpitts oscillators.

The audio modulation is applied by way of transformer T1. Since the modulating information is fed out of phase to the bases of the two oscillators and the outputs of the two oscillators are in parallel, there is a two-fold increase in the net deviation as compared to the frequency modulation of just one of the oscillators. An audio shaping circuit is present in the primary circuit of the transformer. It controls audio response to obtain a linear deviation and a rolloff of the frequency response above 5 kHz.

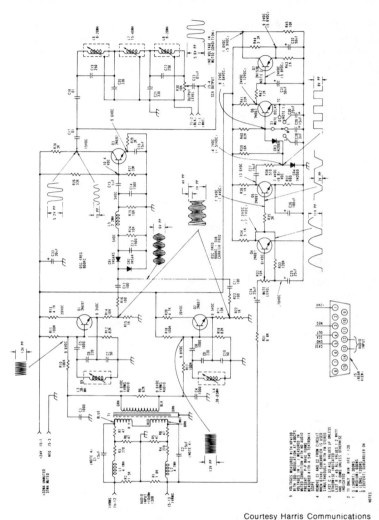

Courtesy Harris Communications

Fig. 10-11. An SCA generator.

The four transistors at the lower right are part of a so-called *muting* circuit. When audio is applied to the input of the generator, the muting control transistor Q7 is nonconducting. The modulated subcarrier signal can be removed at the SCA output. However, when there is no modulating information applied, the control transistor Q7 conducts and places a low resistance shunt to common from the junction of capacitors C17 and C18. This reduces the magnitude of the unmodulated subcarrier signal some 50 to 60 dB.

The arrival of modulating information at the base of transistor Q4 initiates formation of a squared wave. This wave applied to transistor

Q6 establishes a nonconducting state for transistors Q6 and Q7. As a result there is no muting of the output circuit. The removal of the program material removes the squared waves and transistors Q6 and Q7 conduct.

10-8. FM ANTENNA SYSTEMS

The horizontally polarized antenna is universal in fm broadcasting, whereas most am broadcast stations use a vertically polarized antenna. Although an fm broadcast antenna includes a tower, it is only a support for the radiating elements of the antenna; but in am broadcasting, the tower is actually the radiator. In many fm/am stations, the tower serves as both the vertical radiator for am operation and the support for the radiating elements of the fm antenna system. Currently a number of fm stations transmit both horizontally and vertically polarized components. The vertical components improve reception on fm car radios and small fm radios using whip and line-cord antennas.

The radiating elements of an fm antenna are usually modified dipoles, spaced one above the other to provide the desired antenna power gain. Typical gains for the vertically spaced horizontal dipoles used in fm broadcasting are given in Table 10-1. It is these power gains times

Table 10-1. Typical Antenna Power Gains

Bays	Power Gain
1	0.9
2	1.6 − 2
3	3
4	3.7 − 4.1
5	5.1
6	6 − 6.3
7	7 − 7.3
8	7.3 − 8.3

the antenna input power that determines the effective radiated power (erp) of a given fm station.

In fm broadcasting it is advisable to concentrate the vertical radiation at very low angles, to provide the best coverage of the service area. Any vhf energy radiated at high vertical angles represents wasted power because it does not return to earth. The stacking of horizontal dipole elements concentrates the radiated power into low vertical angles. The horizontal- and vertical-radiation patterns of a simple half-wavelength horizontal dipole are given in Fig. 10-12A. The vertical radiation pattern looking into the end of a single dipole is circular. However, by stacking dipoles in bays it can be elongated at low angles (Fig. 10-12B).

The doughnut-shaped radiation pattern of a dipole is a figure 8 in the horizontal plane. This is not desirable for uniform coverage at all compass angles. Two steps can be taken to make the horizontal-radiation pattern more circular. The dipole can be folded around in a circle, as shown in Fig. 10-12C, to make its horizontal-radiation pattern more omnidirectional. In the arrangement of Fig. 10-12D, the dipole is cut for several megahertz higher than its operating frequency. This tends to broaden the lobes of a basic figure-8 pattern, making the antenna more omnidirectional. Forming the dipole into a V-configuration permits additional improvement of the omnidirectional characteristics. The use of stacked dipoles of circular or V shape permits an fm antenna system to have an essentially omnidirectional horizontal pattern and a low-angle vertical pattern.

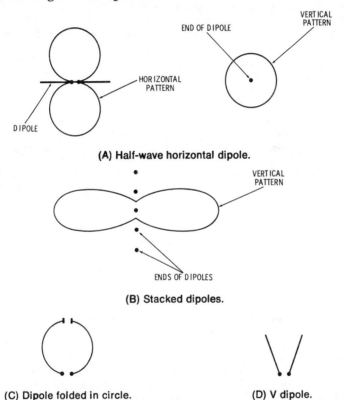

(A) Half-wave horizontal dipole.

(B) Stacked dipoles.

(C) Dipole folded in circle.   (D) V dipole.

Fig. 10-12. Basic fm (dipole) antenna types and radiation patterns.

It is common practice in fm antenna systems to space the dipoles at approximately one wavelength along the vertical axis. They are fed in phase by making certain the transmission-line section between each dipole is exactly one electrical wavelength. Because of the velocity factors of the cable, the dipoles are usually not spaced a full wavelength physically.

The impedance of each dipole is made greater than the transmission-line impedance by the number of bays. For example, if a 50-ohm transmission-line system were being used to feed four bays, the radiation resistance of each dipole would be approximately 200 ohms. Since the four bays are connected in parallel, their total impedance is 50 ohms.

The high velocity factors of the most common forms of fm transmission lines (air-dielectric, rigid, and semiflexible types) permit the bays to be spaced by almost a full wavelength.

10-9. FM ANTENNA TYPES

Three popular fm broadcast antennas are the stacked ringed dipole, curved dipole, and V dipole. Fundamentally, the Collins (Fig. 10-13A) and RCA (Fig. 10-13B) antennas are shunt-fed dipoles as shown by the basic dipole (Fig. 10-13C). The inner conductor of the coaxial

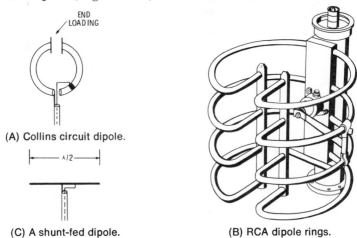

(A) Collins circuit dipole.

(C) A shunt-fed dipole.   (B) RCA dipole rings.

Fig. 10-13. Shunt-fed dipole and two popular antenna types.

cable is attached to a point on one of the quarter-wave sides of the antenna to provide the proper impedance match. Most fm broadcast antennas are pretuned to a specific frequency. The necessary bandwidth is obtained by lowering the Q of the dipole with either a large-diameter circular element (Fig. 10-4) or a multiple-ring attachment (Fig. 10-13B). These types of construction permit the antenna elements to be supported by the rigid coaxial transmission line that feeds the individual dipoles.

To obtain the necessary omnidirectional pattern, the Collins dipole is folded around and end-loaded. The capacitance across the ends provides a more uniform current along the antenna length, the physical length of the antenna being shortened considerably with relation to a free-space half-wavelength because of the presence of the end-loading. Thus there is more uniform horizontal radiation. The capacitive plates at the ends of the Collins circular dipole in Fig. 10-14 are adjustable for critical resonance.

The circularly polarized antenna of Fig. 10-15 avoids the need for separate vertically and horizontally polarized antennas. A simpler transmission-line feeding system and mounting arrangement are pos-

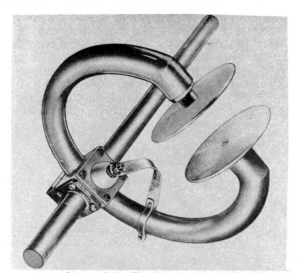

Courtesy Collins Telecommunications, Div. Rockwell Intl.

Fig. 10-14. Collins fm transmitting antenna.

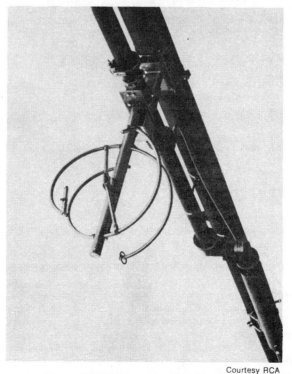

Courtesy RCA

Fig. 10-15. An fm antenna with circular polarization.

Courtesy Harris Communications

Fig. 10-16. A 20-kilowatt fm transmitter.

sible. Equal power is radiated in the horizontal and vertical polarization planes. In effect, the transmitter power can be doubled without exceeding the licensed horizontal plane effective radiated power. The power delivered by the transmitter and transmission-line system is in effect split equally between the two planes of polarization.

Additional effective radiated power can be obtained by increasing the number of bays. Each antenna is shunt-fed through an insulator mounted on a short horizontal section of transmission line. The main vertical transmission line then continues on up to the next bay where there is a similar feed arrangement. The power gain of two bays in both the horizontal and vertical planes is twice the power gain of a single bay; a three bay antenna has approximately three times the power of a single bay, etc.

10-10. A 20-KILOWATT FM TRANSMITTER

The transmitter of Fig. 10-16 is a three-tube affair capable of supplying a 20-kilowatt power output. It can be driven directly by the 10-watt amplifier of the fm exciter (Fig. 10-9). The fm exciter, stereo, and SCA generators mount directly in the transmitter case, with the fm exciter supplying fm modulated drive signal to the first vacuum-tube stage (Fig. 10-17).

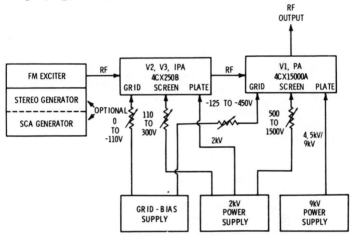

Fig. 10-17. Block diagram of fm transmitter.

The rf signal level is increased in magnitude by the two paralleled tubes of the input stage which develops the input power required by the final power amplifier. Three separate power supplies are included. There are separate plate supplies for the intermediate power amplifier and final power amplifier. These are three-phase supplies using silicon rectifiers. A third silicon-rectifier supply develops the grid bias for both stages.

Four meters at the top of the transmitter monitor filament voltage (both pa and ipa), pa plate current, pa plate voltage and a combination vswr (voltage standing-wave ratio) and power output. A multimeter arrangement inside the doors permits monitoring of the pa grid current and the ipa grid, cathode, and screen-grid currents.

A schematic diagram of the rf stages is given in Fig. 10-18. The two stages are mounted within a shielded rf enclosure. The input stage employs grid neutralization. There are a number of resistors shunted across the input resonant coil which establish the proper bandwidth for the

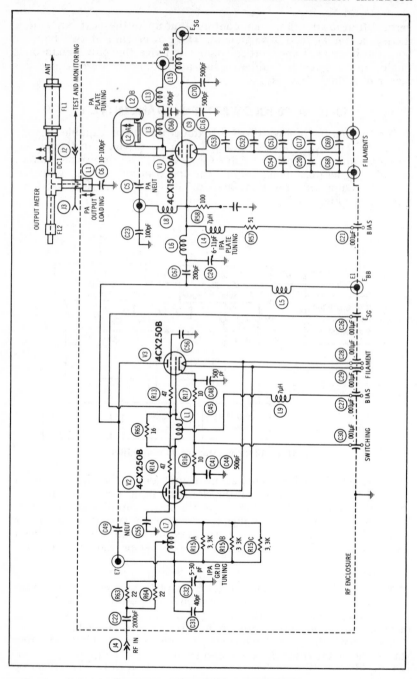

Fig 10-18. Schematic of the rf amplifier.

input circuit. A pi-network links the plate signal to the grid of the power amplifier.

The plate circuit of the power amplifier is a half-wave resonant line. The length of the inner conductor is adjustable and is set for that inductance which, along with the output capacitance of the tube, resonates at the desired transmit frequency. There is both a coarse and a fine frequency adjustment of the resonant line. A capacitive coaxial coupler transfers signal from the resonant circuit to the transmission-line system. Coupling is adjustable and acts as the power-amplifier loading control.

Two filters are included in the output system. Filter FL1 is a coaxial low-pass filter which reduces transmitter harmonic input. There is also a more selective filter (FL2) which provides additional attenuation of the exact second harmonic of the transmitter output. It is referred to as a second-harmonic notch filter. These filters are useful in minimizing interference to television and other radiocommunication services.

CHAPTER 11

Stereophonic Broadcasting

Most fm broadcast stations are now equipped to broadcast stereo programs. Such facilities are a part of a high percentage of the small independent fm stations. Consequently the beginning broadcast technician should know something about stereo broadcast principles because it is quite likely that stereo broadcast gear will be in operation at his first place of employment.

11-1. STEREO BASICS

Stereo broadcast stations use a form of subcarrier multiplex frequency modulation. One audio signal frequency-modulates the fm carrier; the second audio signal amplitude-modulates a subcarrier. The subcarrier, in turn, frequency-modulates the fm carrier, as in the block diagram of Fig. 11-1.

At the receiver, the regular fm detector demodulates one audio signal and the subcarrier fm signal. The subcarrier signal is supplied to an am detector (called a *subcarrier detector*). The output of the subcarrier detector is the second audio signal.

A more detailed functional diagram is shown in Fig. 11-2. In a stereo broadcast system, as in stereo systems in general, there are two fundamental audio signals which correspond to the audio variations picked up from the left and right sides of the program source. These two audio components are commonly referred to as the left-channel and right-channel signals. In stereo reproduction the left and right signals power the left-hand and right-hand speakers, respectively. Thus, the directional sound output is comparable to that which is present at the pickup location.

In a stereo broadcast system the left-channel and right-channel audio signals, L and R, are applied to a transmit matrix circuit. Here the two signals are united in a manner that will produce both sum $(L + R)$ and difference $(L - R)$ components of the audio signals. In the transmitter section of Fig. 11-2, three basic circuits comprise the matrix section. These are called an adder No. 1 $(L + R)$, a phase inverter, and an

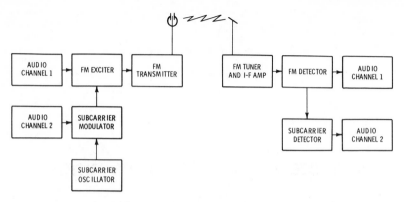

Fig. 11-1. The basic stereo system.

adder No. 2 (L − R). In the No. 1 adder the L and R signals are combined in phase. The output of this adder is L + R component, one of the basic audio signals.

In the phase inverter the polarity of the R signal is reversed. When it is combined with the L signal a difference component will be present at the output of the L − R adder. It is this L − R signal that forms the second basic audio signal.

The L + R signal is used to frequency-modulate the fm transmitter in a conventional manner. It should be understood that the L + R signal is comparable to the audio variations picked up by two microphones, one on each side of the studio. It is basically a monophonic signal of the type formed in conventional broadcasting by using two microphones and combining their outputs in phase in the mixer.

This L + R signal can be handled by a standard monaural fm receiver. It will reproduce as a good monaural program, comparable to that transmitted by any monaural fm broadcast station. This is the important compatibility feature of the FCC-approved method of stereophonic broadcasting. Inasmuch as the L + R signal frequency modulates the fm carrier directly, a standard monaural fm receiver, as shown in Fig. 11-2, demodulates this signal in conventional manner. The monaural L + R signal drives its speaker. The L + R signal is handled in exactly the same manner by a stereo fm receiver, except that the L + R signal at the output of the fm detector is applied to a receive matrix section.

Just how is the L − R signal conveyed from the fm station to the stereo broadcast receiver? The L − R signal at the output of the transmitter matrix is applied to a subcarrier am modulator. In fact, it is applied to a so-called "balanced modulator." The function of the balanced modulator is to cancel out the subcarrier as it forms the subcarrier sidebands. The subcarrier is initiated by an accurate 19-kHz oscillator. A followup doubler forms the 38-kHz subcarrier signal. The 19-kHz oscillator is not only the source of the carrier but also forms a so-called "pilot frequency."

In the balanced modulator, the L − R component and the 38-kHz

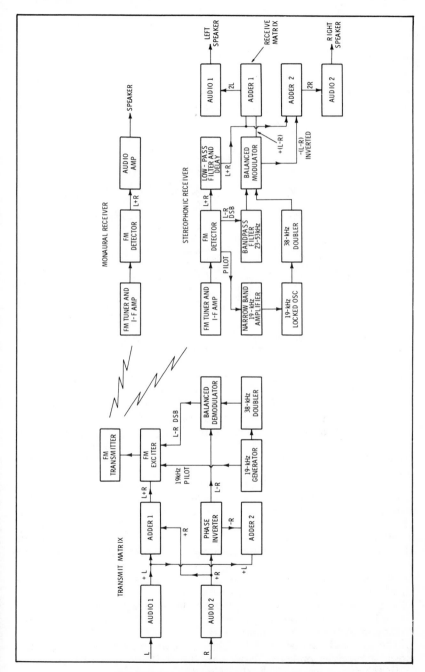

Fig. 11-2. A compatible stereo-fm system.

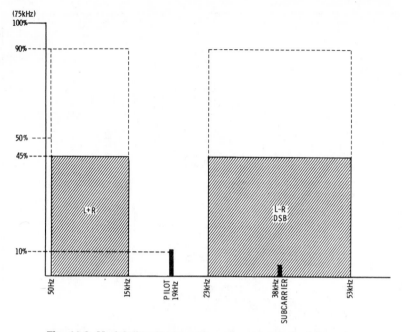

Fig. 11-3. Modulating frequencies and maximum deviations for fm-stereo broadcasting.

component produce am side frequencies on each side of 38 kHz. Since the 38-kHz carrier is cancelled out only the am sidebands are conveyed between the output of the balanced modulator and the fm transmitter. Therefore, the L − R information is in the form of a double-sideband signal (dsb) which, in turn, frequency-modulates the fm transmitter. Its sideband components span outward from the 38-kHz frequency but do not extend into the sideband spectrum of the L + R signal. The spectrum distribution is given in Fig. 11-3.

Why is the subcarrier frequency removed? All of the information conveyed by an am system is contained in the sidebands. Hence the carrier is not needed and the carrier removal means that the substantial amount of power usually contained in the carrier is not required. Furthermore, when there are two carriers present in a common circuit there is a definite trend to heterodyning and the formation of undesired signal components. Since more power can be concentrated in the sidebands by the removal of the subcarrier, there is an overall improvement in the signal-to-noise ratio.

What receiving problem arises with the removal of the subcarrier? To properly demodulate the subcarrier sidebands of their L − R information at the receiver, it is necessary to reinsert a carrier. The stability of the inserted carrier must be high for true demodulation. This imposes a receiver problem. However, the problem is greatly reduced with the transmission of the 19-kHz pilot carrier.

The 19-kHz pilot carrier is generated at the transmitter and is transmitted at low amplitude between the transmitter and each receiver. At the fm stereo receiver, the 19-kHz pilot signal is used to synchronize a 19-kHz oscillator. The output of this oscillator in turn drives a frequency doubler which generates the 38-kHz component used for carrier reinsertion. This component is thus controlled in both frequency and phase by the transmitted pilot signal. Therefore, it forms a stable carrier for the balanced demodulator of the receiver. In the balanced demodulator there is mixing of the $L - R$ subcarrier sidebands and the locally generated 38-kHz carrier; the original audio No. 2 ($L - R$) is extracted at its output.

11-2. RECEIVER ACTIVITY

Three types of information (Fig. 11-3) are conveyed between the stereo broadcast station and each stereo receiver. These are the $L + R$ signal, the pilot frequency, and the $L - R$ subcarrier sidebands. How are these three components deployed at the receiver? All three components, as shown in Fig. 11-2 appear at the output of the fm detector of the receiver. The $L + R$ signal can be applied directly to the receiver matrix. However, it is first passed through a low-pass filter. The responsibility of this filter is to block the 19-kHz pilot frequency and the $L - R$ subcarrier sideband from the $L + R$ channel matrix. The $L + R$ channel also includes a delay circuit that holds up the $L + R$ signal an amount that matches the delay encountered by the $L - R$ information in its more elaborate demodulation process. Thus, the $L + R$ and $L - R$ signals arrive in the same time relationship at the input of the receive matrix as they did at the input of the transmit matrix.

The 19-kHz pilot frequency is applied through a very narrow bandpass filter to a 19-kHz amplifier. As mentioned previously, the 19-kHz output of this amplifier is used to lock in the frequency and phase of the 19-kHz oscillator. The $L - R$ information is applied through a bandpass filter that passes the subcarrier sideband spectrum, but rejects frequency components above and below its range. Hence, only the subcarrier sidebands reach the balanced demodulator.

In the receiver matrix there are two adders and a phase inverter. When the $L + R$ and $L - R$ signals are combined in phase (adder No. 1), the resultant output is the original L signal, since $(L + R) + (L - R) = 2L$. When the $L + R$ and $L - R$ signals are combined out of phase in the second adder, the resultant output signal is the original R signal, since $(L + R) - (L - R) = 2R$.

The individual L and R signals are now amplified in the L and R channels of a stereo audio amplifier as per conventional stereo high-fidelity practice. The two signals drive the separate left- and right-channel reproducers.

11-3. SIGNAL ACTIVITIES

The operation of the stereo broadcast system can be understood in greater depth by considering some typical input and output signals that might be present at the transmit and receive matrices. Let us first assume that a signal is present at the left channel, but none is present at the right.

Assume that a unit of L audio signal is being applied to the input of the transmit matrix as in Fig. 11-4A. Under these conditions, what is the output of the transmit matrix? Without an R signal present there will be half-unit L signals at the L + R and L − R outputs of the transmit matrix. These two half-units of L signal will be transmitted between the transmitter and the receiver. Half-unit L signals will appear at the input of the receiver matrix. Since the output of the left channel of the receive matrix has a value of 2L, its signal level will be unit L ($2 \times 1/2$L). Since the output of the right channel of the receive matrix is 2R, there will be zero R signal output (2×0) because zero R signal has been transmitted.

Let us consider what happens when there is a unit of R signal, without an L signal, at the input of the transmit matrix, as in Fig. 11-4B. Under this condition the outputs of the transmit matrix will be half-units of R with opposite polarity. This will also be their relationship as they are applied to the input of the receive matrix. In the adder (L +

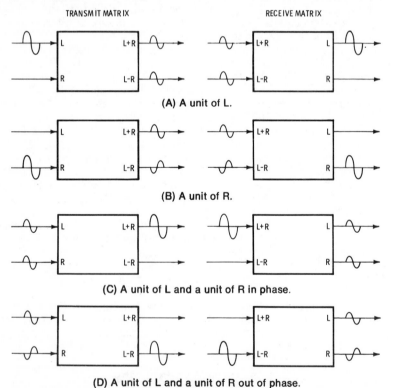

(A) A unit of L.

(B) A unit of R.

(C) A unit of L and a unit of R in phase.

(D) A unit of L and a unit of R out of phase.

Fig. 11-4. Audio signal possibilities at the receiver-matrix input and their transmitter-matrix outputs.

R) of the receive matrix the two components will be of equal amplitude and opposite polarity; L output will be zero. In the adder (L − R), however, the R signal will have been shifted in polarity. Therefore, it will add in phase to produce a unit R output ($2 \times 1/2R$).

Let us next consider two input signal possibilities that may occur on occasion. In Fig. 11-4C, the left- and right-input signals are of equal half-unit amplitude. When combined in-phase assume they produce an L + R output of unit amplitude. When combined out-of-phase (in the L − R adder), they will cancel and there will be no L − R output. The input to the receiver matrix will be a unit-level L + R signal; there will be no L − R signal. The output of the receive matrix, therefore, will be two signal components of half-unit amplitude for both the right and left channels. The relationships are as follows:

$$(L + R) \pm (L − R) = (L + R) + 0$$
L AND R DIVIDE EQUALLY IN-PHASE
OUTPUT IS 1/2 ON L SIDE AND 1/2 ON R SIDE

Hence, the reconstructed voltages at the inputs of the left and right channels correspond to the original signals at the transmit matrix.

The other extreme would be to transmit signals of opposite polarity as in Fig. 11-4D. In this case, there would be no output from the L + R side and a unit output from the L − R side. At the receive matrix only an L − R signal is being applied to the input. As a result, there will be signals of opposite polarity developed at the L and R outputs of the receive matrix. Relations are as follows:

$$(L + R) \pm (L − R) = 0 \pm (L − R)$$
L AND R DIVIDE EQUALLY OUT-OF-PHASE
OUTPUT IS 1/2 L AND −1/2 R

Again the left and right audio channels are driven by reconstructed signals of opposite polarity comparable to those at the input of the transmit matrix.

Of course, actual program material will vary continuously and will seldom match the extremes demonstrated in Fig. 11-4. In actual stereophonic broadcasting it is improbable that one channel will be alive and the other completely dead. Nor is it likely that each channel will carry identical information, either in phase or out of phase. Nevertheless, the consideration of these signal extremes gives you an understanding of the activities for the more practical intermediate-signal conditions.

11-4. SCA BROADCASTING

Many fm stations also transmit SCA (Subsidiary Communications Authorizations) broadcasts in the form of storecast (store background music) or other special music services. These are also transmitted on a mum permissible deviation of a stereophonic and combined stereophonic broadcasting, as shown in Fig. 11-5. The SCA assignment is made in a frequency spectrum higher than the L − R sideband fre-

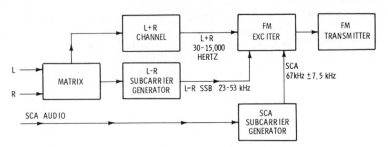

Fig. 11-5. Block diagram of an fm-stereo SCA transmitter.

quencies. The SCA channel uses frequency modulation with a total permissible deviation of ±7.5 kHz about the subcarrier frequency of 67 kHz. The highest audio frequency for frequency modulation of a 67-kHz subcarrier is 8 kHz. Since the modulation index is so low at these limits (7.5 kHz ÷ 8 kHz) the resultant sidebands are confined between 59.5 and 74.5 kHz. Consequently there is no overlap into the sideband spectrum of the L − R (double-sideband) signal. Likewise, sideband components will not exist outside of the 200-kHz bandwidth limitations required by the FCC for an fm broadcast channel.

11-5. DEVIATION CONSIDERATIONS

In an fm system the total deviation of the carrier is considered as the arithmetic sum of the deviations caused by the individual signals and subcarriers that comprise the transmitted information. The maximum permissible deviation of a stereophonic and combined stereo-SCA broadcast carrier is ±75 kHz. The modulation-frequency spectrum chart (Fig. 11-3) shows the frequency distribution of the signals that make up the transmitted data and the maximum deviation values as well, without SCA. The modulating-frequency distribution is shown on the horizontal axis; the maximum permissible deviation as a percentage is shown on the vertical axis.

In the main channel (direct modulation by the L + R signal) the maximum deviation may not exceed 45 percent of the total permissible deviation for a stereophonic broadcast station, assuming that only an L signal (or R signal) is present. Likewise, the modulation of the L − R double sideband channel may not exceed 45%, assuming that only an L signal (or R signal) is present. The L + R or L − R channels have a capability of 90-percent modulation when both R and L signals are present. The pilot subcarrier at 19 kHz (±2 Hz) deviates the main carrier to the limit of 8 to 10 percent. The arithmetic sum (10 percent + 45 percent + 45 percent) of the three deviations approaches 100 percent or full ±75-kHz deviation.

In the case of combined stereo and SCA transmission (Fig. 11-6) it is necessary to reduce the L + R or the L − R subcarrier deviations to a maximum of 18 percent, while the pilot carrier is assigned a 9-percent deviation. SCA subcarrier and sidebands are assigned a maximum 10 percent deviation so as not to cause a maximum deviation greater than

100 percent (10 percent + 9 percent + 40.5 percent + 40.5 percent). Ten percent of 75 kHz is ±7.5 kHz, the maximum permissible deviation of the SCA 67-kHz subcarrier.

In the transmission process, the standard 75-microsecond pre-emphasis and de-emphasis circuits are used. The compensation and correction must be made in both channels. In fact, to minimize cross-modulation between channels the frequency response must be held within 3.5%

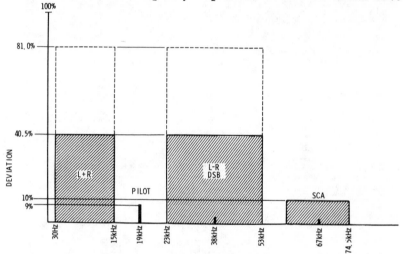

Fig. 11-6. The modulating frequency spectrum of the combined stereo and SCA fm signals.

of unity at all levels of signal and frequency between 50 and 15,000 hertz. Furthermore, the phase difference between the main channel signal and the stereophonic subcarrier sideband envelope shall not exceed ±3% for audio modulating frequencies between 50 and 15,000 hertz.

11-6. STEREO BROADCAST EQUIPMENT

Modern fm broadcast stations include stereo facilities. Usually most programs are broadcast in stereo; others as monaural transmissions. Studios are equipped with a number of stereo signal sources such as stereo phono-player, stereo tape-cart player, and stereo reel-to-reel tape player. A combined stereo recorder and player is shown in Fig. 11-7. Such a stereo tape recorder and associated stereo microphones can be used to prerecord live stereo program material for later transmission by the station. However, most stereo programs are in the form of stereo records and tapes obtained from the various recording sources.

An example of a stereo tape-cart recorder/reproducer is the Ampro model of Fig. 11-8. It is a compact unit that takes the standard NAB cartridges. In addition to the two stereo tracks there is a third control-tone track. Tones can be added during the reproduce mode. There is a 1000-hertz tone referred to as a *stop cue*. After a message has been

Courtesy Midwestern Instruments, Inc.

Fig. 11-7. A stereo tape recorder/player.

played and the tape returned to its starting point this is the tone that stops the tape in cued-in position ready to be replayed.

A 150-hertz *end cue* can also be recorded at the end of a message on a tape. This tone will activate the audio switching system and serve as an automatic start command to another interconnected cart reproducer. It can also be used to initiate a high-speed fast-forward activity for rapid recuing. There is a third 8000-hertz *trip cue* that can be recorded. On reproduce this trip cue can be used for external switching of various types of auxiliary equipment.

A functional block diagram of the reproduce circuits is given in Fig. 11-9. The channel-A and channel-B inputs are shown at the top left followed by preamplifier, switcher, and finally the line amplifier that supplies signal to audio output transformers T2 and T3.

The cue-channel head, also shown at the top left, supplies signal to the tone preamplifier and shaper. Appropriate circuits separate the various cue tones according to frequency—150 hertz, 1000 hertz, and 8000 hertz. The individual detector outputs control the switching operations of the reproduce activity.

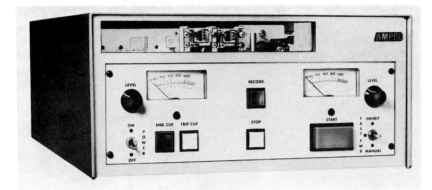

Courtesy Ampro Corp.

Fig. 11-8. Tape cartridge recorder/reproducer.

Power supplies and the various switching circuits are shown at the bottom left. Actually there are three basic modes of operation for the reproduce system. In the ready-mode condition activities begin when the cartridge is fully inserted. The ready indicator light comes on indicating that the system is ready for a playback activity. This activity begins by depressing the start control which, in addition to the mechanical activities, turns on the audio switcher in the playback amplifiers. As a result the prerecorded audio information taken from the tape is built up in amplitude by the associated playback amplifiers.

Another mode is the recue activity. When a prerecorded stop cue is picked up on the cue track the system is automatically stopped, the audio switches are turned off and the system reverts back to the ready mode.

If there has been an end-cue tone recorded there is a faster rerun of the tape to the start position. In this mode of operation the fast-forward activity takes place at the conclusion of the message and then finally the stop-cue signal reverts everything to the ready mode and the message can be repeated when required by depressing the start button.

An example of a stereo main control console for a medium- or small-size fm station is shown in Fig. 11-10. In a large station it may be used for independent programming from a second facility. This *Harris* console has thirteen inputs that can be switched into five mixing channels. As shown at the top left there are two pairs of channels for low-impedance broadcast microphones. These channels include appropriate low-noise preamplifiers. There are three pairs of medium level channels that can be used with stereo turntables, cart players, and reel-to-reel machines, as well as remote, network, or auxiliary program sources. Any of the five pairs of channels can be switched to program-amplifier or audition-amplifier systems. In fact, auditioning or recording of incoming sources can be accomplished without disturbing regular programs. Channels 3, 4, and 5 also have cue positions which provide signals to an amplified cue-system.

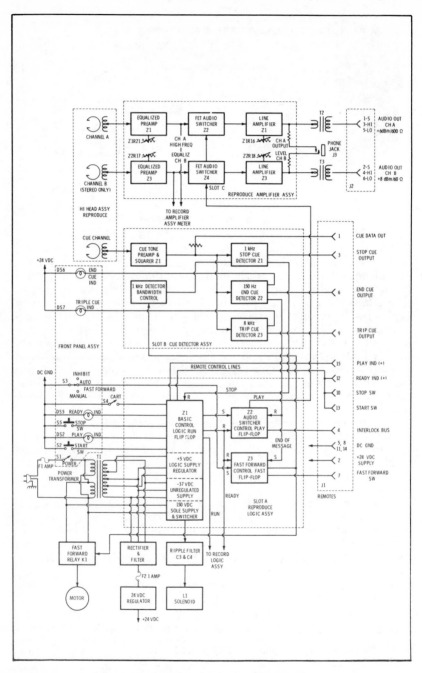

Fig. 11-9. Block diagram of reproduce circuits.

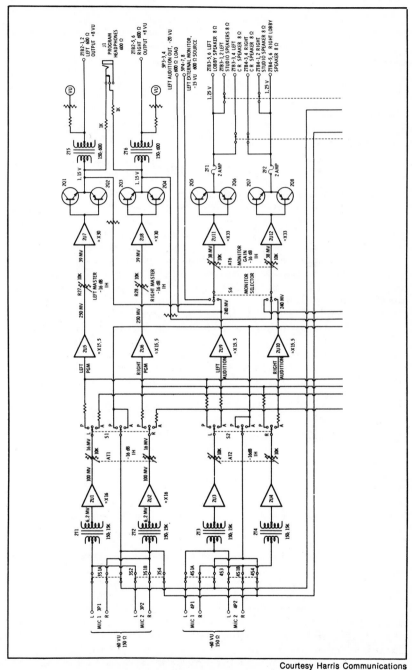

Courtesy Harris Communications

Fig. 11-10. Stereo control console circuits.

The left and right program channels are identical. They include a booster amplifier and an audio output amplifier with individual VU meters. They are usually employed in conjunction with the mixing channel attenuators to establish a reference volume of zero VU (+8 dbm).

The audition and monitor selection system can be used to switch the monitor amplifier to the program circuit, external sources, or auditioning circuit. A protective system of warning lights and speaker muting prevents acoustic feedback and the transmission of a cue signal when live microphones are nearby. A cue amplifier provides drive for cue headphones or cue speaker.

11-7. AUDIO PROCESSING

In fm transmission systems modulation limiters are a requisite. They provide amplitude compression (agc action) as well as peak limiting. In certain types of fm broadcasting, such as in the transmission of beautiful music or classical music formats, only a limited amount of compression is advisable to maintain a good dynamic range and a reasonable average modulation level. In the transmission of modern music with high levels of bass and very-high frequencies as well (as found in rock, disco, and jazz) more compression is preferred, thus increasing loudness. At the same time modulation peaks must be limited to prevent overmodulation. Deviation must not exceed ±75 kHz.

Also in fm broadcasting the technique of pre-emphasis is used to reduce noise. This imposes an additional responsibility on limiters because the very-high frequencies are amplified greatly and overmodulation must be avoided. In the audio processing system this must be done without holding down the mid- and low-frequency ranges. In fact, it is customary in modern limiters to subdivide the audio spectrum into two or three separate ranges for early processing. Additionally there must be two separate like channels to handle the left and right signals of stereo program material. The overall objective of the processing technique is to obtain realism along with maximum signal power and minimum distortion.

The Harris audio processor (Fig. 11-11) has three separate audio ranges. The compression in these three ranges is indicated by the first three meters at the top of the instrument. A fourth meter displays limiting activities while the final meter is the program output indicator. Appropriate switches permit these meters to be used in either the left or right stereo channel.

The blocks of Fig. 11-12 represent a flow diagram among the modules of a single channel. Duplicate modules are used for the second channel. All audio circuits employ linear integrated circuits with no discrete transistors. Balanced or unbalanced signals can be applied to the input circuit of the input/agc module at the top left. There are no input transformers and their associated problems. An input sensitivity switch can be set for either 0 dBm or −2 dBm. There is an additional fine sensitivity adjustment with a range of 20 dB.

The setting of the input-level control depends on station format and market preferences. Depending on settings, the expansion and com-

Courtesy Harris Communications

Fig. 11-11. MSP-100 fm audio processor.

pression can be made to cancel each other during program pauses. In another setting the gain reduction will be almost unnoticeable. The higher the sensitivity setting is the greater will be the gain reduction. In making stereo adjustments of course the left channel can be adjusted first, then the right channel adjusted to match the left-channel operating conditions.

The three agc circuits process the three separate segments of the audio spectrum independently. Adjustments can be made on frequency bandwidth, expansion and compression thresholds, gain control, and attack/recovery time. The farther the agc pointer swings and the faster it moves, the greater is the compression. By setting the expansion and compression thresholds the levels can be made to fit the desired format of the station.

Crossover compensation makes certain the frequency response is free from sharp peaks or dips under dynamic and static operating conditions. There is a low-frequency crossover and a high-frequency one which can be preset with switches. With the low switch set to 95 Hz the low-agc band would be effective only on the deepest bass. Set up to 320 Hz, low agc would handle processing of all bass up into the lower part of the midrange. A setting of 7200 Hz for the high-frequency crossover would result in the processing of mostly overtones and percussives in the high-band agc channel. There would be little effect

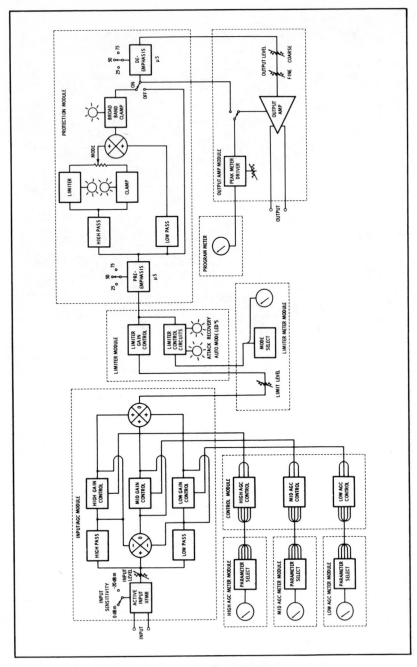

Fig. 11-12. Functional diagram of audio processor.

on voice. The presence range of 3 to 5 kilohertz is processed in the midband agc. The selection of 2450 Hz as the high-frequency crossover would allow significant presence-range processing.

The limiter section (Fig. 11-12) controls the transient peaks and summation errors present in the output of the three-band agc activity. This unit analyzes program content and automatically selects optimum attack and recovery time constants. Thus intermodulation of restricted-bandwidth signals during limiting is minimized. The proper recovery time optimizes the degree to which the dynamic range is reduced according to the nature of the program signal.

The attack and recovery times are monitored by LED indicators. Manual selection of attack and recovery times is available to match the station format and the makeup of the program audio.

The output of the limiter modules is applied through a pre-emphasis network that can be set to one of three time constants; 25, 50, or 75 microseconds. High-frequency energy can cause significant overdrive condition in pre-emphasized systems such as fm, tv sound and SCA broadcasting as well as tape recording. In the protection circuit the signal is modified to eliminate instantaneous overdrive when high frequencies are present. A split-spectrum approach is used. Low-frequency signal components have little overdrive potential but contribute significantly to signal loudness. High-frequency components affect overdrive greatly; therefore, they are controlled to a far more significant degree than lower-frequency ones. In fact, the input signal from the limiter is pre-emphasized and split into two bands above and below 400 Hz. The high-frequency signal feeds a clamp circuit and fast limiter. Then it is recombined with the unprocessed low-frequency signal. A final clamping activity controls transients and summation errors. A followup de-emphasis circuit reduces audible harmonic distortion. LEDs indicate the operation of the limiting and clamping activities.

Output distortion or ringing limitations of transformers are avoided by not using them. There is a 600-ohm balanced output capable of delivering +18 dBm of signal. There are both coarse and fine control level adjustment of the output. The output metering circuit permits observation of peak signal levels both with and without pre-emphasis. Meter sensitivity can be adjusted according to established signal levels.

11-8. FM STEREO GENERATOR

The Harris stereo generator (Fig. 11-13) is a solid-state model. Its functional block diagram is shown at the lower left of Fig. 10-7. At the center of the block diagram is the audio module and the separate left and right channel inputs. The left and right program signal is applied to a 19-kHz notch filter and on to the 75 microsecond pre-emphasis network. The notch filter clears the 19-kHz spectrum because the pilot frequency will eventually be inserted in this region.

Finally, the left and right program signals are applied to the matrix network. Here the signal components are added and subtracted to form the L + R and L − R modulating waves needed for the compatible multiplex system of transmission. Recall that the L + R signal is really a two-channel monaural signal that can be demodulated by a non-stereo fm receiver.

The L + R and L − R signals are applied to the stereo generator through the isolation input stages of the stereo generator, transistors Q15 and Q16 at the left center of Fig. 11-13. The L + R signal is passed through a time-delay network. Intentional delay is necessary to match the delay encountered by the L − R component in the subcarrier process. Individual gain-control facilities are included in the emitter-follower output circuits of the isolation transistors.

The L + R signal is applied to the output level control, potentiom-

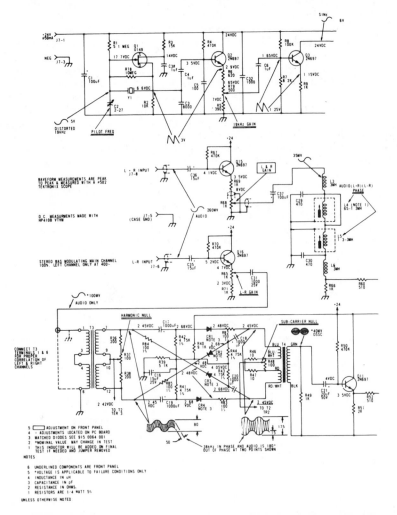

Fig. 11-13. Schematic diagram

eter R53. A three-stage amplifier follows including an emitter-follower isolation stage, transistor Q12; a voltage amplifier, transistor Q13; and the emitter-follower output stage, transistor Q14.

The L − R signal from transistor Q16 is applied to a four-diode-ring balanced modulator. The 38-kHz subcarrier frequency is applied to the same diode modulator arriving at the network of resistors R46 and R47 plus potentiometer R48.

The 38-kHz subcarrier is applied in phase to the balanced modulator while audio components are 180° related. In operation the 38 kHz subcarrier will cancel out and be suppressed. This removal is accom-

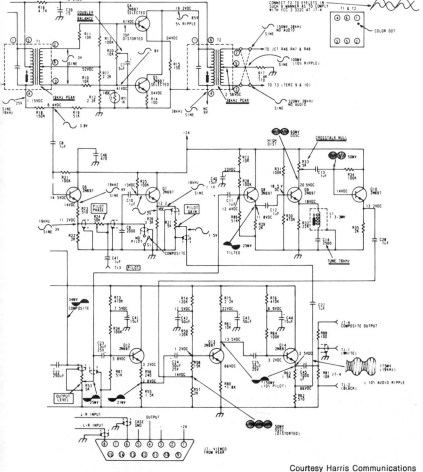

Courtesy Harris Communications

of a solid-state stereo generator.

plished efficiently when the modulator is balanced precisely. Balance potentiometer R48 permits the minimization of the level of the 38-kHz subcarrier in the output.

The operation of the modulator is unbalanced relative to the changes in the L − R audio signal. Therefore sideband frequencies are generated and do develop in the output. In effect the L − R signal has amplitude-modulated the subcarrier frequency. However, the subcarrier signal itself has been removed. A double-sideband and suppressed-carrier signal is developed.

Through the isolation transistor Q11 this double-sideband signal is also applied to output level control R53. Here it combines with the L + R signal.

Let us consider, next, the formation of the subcarrier signal and the pilot-frequency signal. The field-effect transistor Q1 at the top left of Fig. 11-11 is connected in a crystal oscillator circuit. The frequency of operation is 19 kHz. This component is applied to a buffer stage which includes a pilot gain control in its emitter circuit. The output is amplified by transistor Q3 and a 19-kHz sine wave is developed across the primary of transformer T1. Transistors Q4 and Q5 are connected in a push-push doubler circuit. Note that the 19-kHz sine wave is applied in push pull to the bases. However, the collectors are connected in parallel, a favorable manner of connection for developing a strong even harmonic of the 19-kHz signal—this, of course, is 38 kHz. A 38-kHz sine wave develops across the primary of transformer T2. The secondary winding supplies the 38-kHz subcarrier component to the balanced modulator.

A 19-kHz sine-wave component is taken off the primary circuit of transformer T1 and applied through capacitor C8 to the isolation transistor Q6. In the coupling system between transistors Q6 and Q7 the phase of the pilot frequency can be adjusted. This is important because there must be the proper phase relationship between pilot and subcarrier components at the receiver demodulator. The positive rise of the pilot frequency away from the zero axis must match in time the positive rise of the subcarrier component away from the zero axis for alternate subcarrier cycles. This is important to the synchronization of the demodulation process.

The pilot frequency component through the pilot gain control (R27) is applied to the emitter of the composite output transistor (Q14, lower right of Fig. 11-13). Thus, at the output of transistor Q14 the composite stereo-fm signal is present consisting of the L + R component, L − R *dsb* component and the pilot frequency.

A special circuit is included to remove any 76-kHz second harmonic of the 38-kHz subcarrier frequency. Note that a portion of the signal present in the input of transistor Q12 is applied through capacitor C11 to transistor Q8. An out-of-phase component is present across the cross-talk-null potentiometer R33 in the collector circuit of transistor Q9. This out-of-phase component is applied to the junction of resistors R57 and R58 in the base circuit of transistor Q13 through emitter-follower transistor Q10. The function here is to cancel out undesired harmonics including the 76-kHz component. The removal of the second harmonic is particularly important because it falls in the bandpass of the 67-kHz SCA signal. This would cause crosstalk between the stereo and SCA modulating information.

Another method of generating the composite fm signal is to use a switching type modulator (Fig. 11-14). In this circuit the left and right audio signals are sampled momentarily at a 38-kHz rate. This square-wave chopper waveform, which switches between the left and right signals, is generated under the control of a 76-kHz crystal oscillator. The switching technique generates the L + R monaural, as well as the L − R sideband, which cluster about the 38-kHz subcarrier frequency. The combined signal appears at the output of the switching modulator.

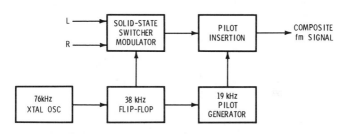

Fig. 11-14. Switching-type stereo generator.

The pilot frequency is generated under control of the output of the 38-kHz flip-flop circuit. It must be inserted at proper amplitude into the fm signal to form the complete composite fm signal consisting of the L + R monaural signal, the subcarrier L − R sidebands, and the pilot frequency.

11-9. DIGITALLY SYNTHESIZED STEREO GENERATOR

A third method of generating the composite stereo-fm signal has been developed by Harris. It includes two special circuits known as the dynamic transient response filter (DTR) and the digitally synthesized modulator (DSM) (Fig. 11-15). These techniques improve the high-frequency separation between left and right signals, reduce the harmonic content, improve the modulation linearity, and reduce SCA crosstalk.

In a stereo system the amplitude and bandwidth characteristics of the left and right audio signals must be constrained to prevent the generated L + R and L − R signals from distorting and producing mutual interference. At the same time it is advisable to keep the loudness level up as high as possible through the use of agc amplifiers, peak limiters, and clippers. Audio processing does add to the harmonic content of the program material and noise or clipping products beyond 15 kHz can result in interference and the loss of stereo separation because of their interference with the pilot or the L − R sidebands. The Harris DTR filter follows the pre-emphasis network and is designed to reduce harmonics above 15 kHz at the same time that the peaks are

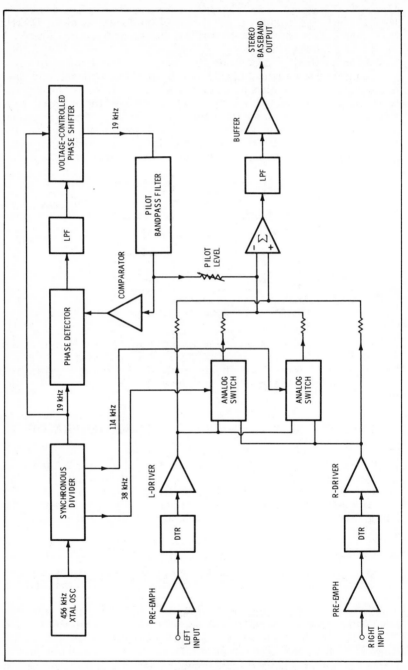

Fig. 11-15. Digital stereo generator.

properly amplitude-limited. Resultant overshoots of the limiting action should not exceed 100% modulation level. Preferred filter characteristics are a frequency response that is flat within ±0.5 dB between 20 hertz and 15,000 hertz at all levels up to 100% modulation. Attenuation above 19 kHz should be a minimum of 50 dB. Overshoots should not exceed 102% modulation. The filter should pass steady-state sine-wave signals with the third harmonic and intermodulation distortion at a level of 0.1% or less. Finally any effects that result from the elimination of the overmodulating overshoots shall be inaudible.

Note from Fig. 11-15 that the processed left and right signals are applied to the analog modulation switcher. The switching waveform for the modulator is derived from a 456-kHz crystal oscillator through a synchronous divider. The 38-kHz component is the actual switching waveform that takes the appropriate samples to generate the L + R and L − R signal components. In the switching process harmonics are generated at 76 kHz and 114 kHz. The 76 kHz components are eliminated by a properly balanced circuit. The third-harmonic components at 114 kHz are eliminated by a cancelling waveform derived from the synchronous divider. Output from the modulator is applied through amplifier, low-pass filter, and buffer.

It is also necessary to add the pilot signal to the composite. Initially it is a 19 kHz pulse component from the synchronous divider which is applied to a phase detector and through a low-pass filter to the voltage-controlled phase shifter. The resultant pilot frequency is passed through a bandpass filter and through the pilot-level control to the pilot-insertion stage. Note that there is a feedback path including a comparator and the resultant automatic phase control system that maintains the 19 kHz sine wave at a constant and proper phase for insertion into the composite signal.

The fm exciter of Fig. 11-16 includes this type of a stereo generator. In addition the *MS-15* exciter includes two SCA channels and even facilities that would eventually permit quadraphonic operation. Also included are 41-kHz and 67-kHz SCA channels. However, the 41-kHz SCA cannot be used when the station is transmitting stereo programming. Automatic circuits prevent the interference that would result from the operation of the 41-kHz SCA and stereo generators simultaneously. Only the 67-kHz SCA channel is operable when transmitting a stereo program. The exciter also includes an rf power amplifier with an adjustable power output that can be set between 3 watts and 15 watts.

11-10. AUTOMATED STATION

Equipment for a highly automatic am/fm facility is shown in Fig. 11-17. It includes a three-section multiple cartridge-handling system that can be organized for multiple program operation, such as am, fm-stereo, and SCA. An included microprocessor can be set up to obtain automatic selection of program material. The same processor can be programmed to self-diagnose error and machine malfunctions. A defect in the IGM *go-cart* will cause operation to cease and an error light

Courtesy Harris Communications

Fig. 11-16. MS-15 fm exciter.

Courtesy IGM

Fig. 11-17. Automated am/fm facility.

will come up on the front panel to illuminate one of seven specific fault indicators.

The rack of equipment immediately to the left of the multiple-cartridge system includes fm modulation, stereo, and SCA modulation monitors. Included is a TFT remote control system.

The far left rack monitors and remote-controls the am transmitter including the associated directional-antenna system. The am transmitter is also remotely controlled. The rack also includes an EBS (Emergency Broadcast System) receiver.

11-11. HIGH-POWER FM TRANSMITTER

The Collins transmitter shown in Fig. 11-18 can supply up to 25 kW to the antenna. The left rack houses the vacuum-tube rf power amplifier and driver stages. It also includes the tuning and loading motors as well as the harmonic output filter. Power-amplifier blower, air switch, and interlocks are also a part of this section.

Courtesy Collins Telecommunications, Div. Rockwell International
Fig. 11-18. Twenty-five kW fm transmitter.

Continuous readout meters for plate current, plate voltage, and output power are located at the top of the center rack along with a dc multimeter that can be used to check out eleven operating parameters. Additionally there is the filament voltage regulator as well as an LED-equipped assembly, with 27 LEDs, that provides a status readout of the protection circuits and control mode. At the center of the center rack is the fm exciter. Various power circuits are located at the bottom.

The major power components are located in the right rack, including controls, as well as the required fuses and circuit breakers. An ac power main meter is located at the top left and will provide readings on each of the three ac voltage phases as well as filament voltage.

Dc voltage control is handled by a 28-volt source. The transmitter is brought up to full power with a safe-start sequence. Automatic power-output control provides a steady constant signal to the antenna.

There are 23 protection circuits for the exciter, vacuum-tube and power circuits, plus air-pressure loss, phase loss, over-temperature safety interlock, etc. There is an automatic overload recycle and an automatic momentary power interruption recycle system. Troubles can be pinpointed with meter readings, circuit breakers, and LED status displays.

11-11-1. Block Diagram

A functional block diagram of the transmitter is given in Fig. 11-19. Required input signal is 10 dBm for monaural, stereo, or SCA operation. The fm exciter can develop one or more of these signals. Exciter output is in the 10–20 watt range on any one of the fm channels between 88 and 108 mHz. The fm exciter is completely solid state.

A two-tube driver with two tubes connected in parallel provides the rf input power required by the high-powered final amplifier. Output is coupled to a 50-ohm antenna system through a low-pass filter and directional coupler. The filter is a tandem type with good harmonic rejection and cutoff frequencies of 130 and 300 megahertz. The directional coupler provides a reading of both forward and reflected power as well as excitation for the automatic power-control circuits. The control circuits remove plate voltage from the power amplifier if an excessive amount of reflected power is detected.

Note the number of power supplies required by a high-powered transmitter. In addition to the filament power supply there are five separate dc power supplies. Three of them furnish plate voltage, screen voltage, and grid bias for the radio-frequency power amplifier. A fourth one develops voltage for the radio-frequency driver stage and the fifth is the 28-volt dc control supply.

A control voltage from the automatic power-control circuit is applied to the power-control unit. This activity regulates the primary voltages applied to the three-phase power transformers associated with the driver, plate, and screen power supplies. Single-phase power is connected to the filament, power-amplifier bias, and control power supplies.

11-11-2. Intermediate and Final RF Power Amplifier

The intermediate power amplifier consists of two tetrodes connected in parallel (Fig. 11-20). The input circuit is a tuned transmission-line section with resistive loading (resistor R1) that provides a wide bandwidth, good stability, and minimizes the influence of plate-to-grid feedback. The short on the tuned line is set according to assigned frequency.

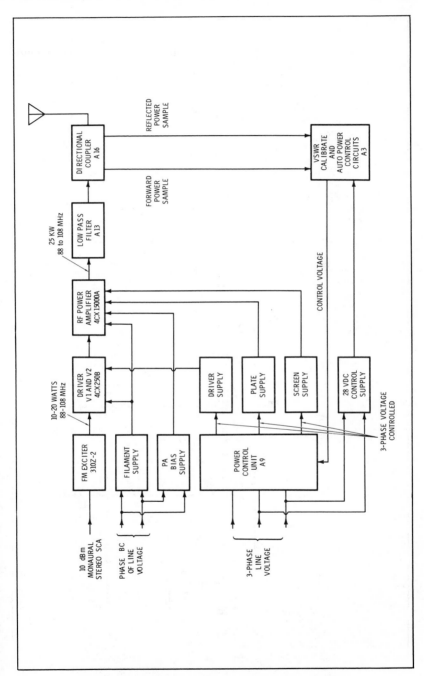

Fig. 11-19. Functional diagram of 25-kW fm transmitter.

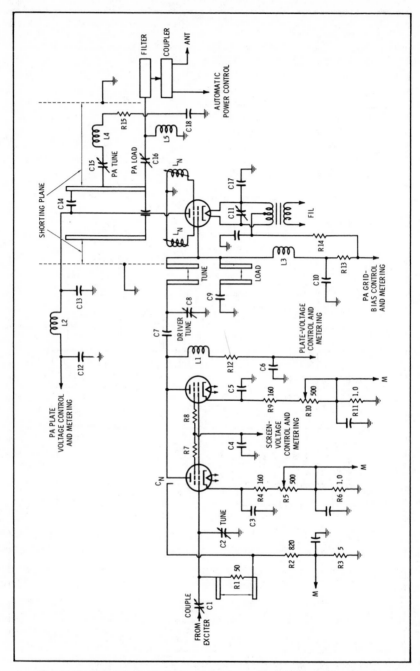

Fig. 11-20. Simplified schematic of rf-driver and power-amplifier circuits.

A tune capacitor (C2) permits a fine adjustment of the input resonant circuit. Excitation is controlled with coupling capacitor C1.

The stage operates class C with appropriate bias being developed across resistor R2 by the flow of grid current. Potentiometers R5 and R10 provide adjustable cathode bias. These are preset for balanced and proper tube currents. All three of the biasing circuits connect back to the metering facility for proper evaluation. A small capacitor C_N consisting of a wire and end paddle is linked to the tank circuit and provides proper neutralization for the stage.

Recall from the functional block diagram of Fig. 11-19 that the driver, plate, and screen power supplies are regulated by a power-control unit. A sample of the screen current flows through a transformer winding associated with a Hall-effect probe. A Hall-effect device responds to a stationary magnetic field and produces an appropriate current through the control-panel meter. Hall-effect devices are used in various supply-voltage circuits for current metering.

Capacitor C8 tunes the plate circuit of the driver. Tuned transmission-line segments provide both tune and load facilities in the grid circuit of the final radio-frequency power amplifier. Capacitor C8 and the tuned transmission-line section also provide impedance matching. The screen grid of the final operates at ground potential. Normal operation is obtained by connecting the cathode to a potential of −750 volts below ground. Cathode-tuning capacitor C11 improves the bypass action at the operating frequency. Two small inductors (L_N) provide neutralization. When an input signal is present, grid bias develops across resistor R13 and other resistors in the grid circuit that are not shown in Fig. 11-20.

The power-amplifier plate circuit comprises a coaxial resonant circuit with the tube mount and its cylindrical assembly serving as the inner conductor. The rectangular shield serves as the outer conductor. This coaxial resonator is tuned by a sliding shorting plane shown at the center of Fig. 11-21. It is coarse-tuned from 88 to 108 MHz by moving it relative to the bottom of the tube shelf.

Two motor-driven capacitors (C15 and C16) provide fine tuning and loading of the coaxial resonant circuit. These capacitors are shown in the simplified equivalent diagram of the output network (Fig. 11-22). These reversible motors are controlled by the raise/lower tuning and loading switches on the control panel. Appropriate takeoffs are provided for obtaining monitoring samples for modulation meter and other instruments. Inductor L4 along with R15 and distributed capacitance C18 act as a suppressor that dampens cavity resonances that may occur near the third harmonic of the output frequency.

11-11-3. Primary Power Distribution

The three-phase primary power is distributed to the various circuits of the transmitter by way of circuit breakers and fuses mounted on the circuit-breaker panel—top of third panel Fig. 11-18. Distribution schematic is given in Fig. 11-23. Primary power is applied at the top left through the ac line circuit breaker. The pa plate power supply breaker to its right serves the delta of the transformer (T1) primary winding.

Courtesy Collins Telecommunications, Div. Rockwell International
Fig. 11-21. Transmitter rf power amplifier.

Through associated breakers it also interrupts power to the pa screen transformer and driver plate transformer. The ac line voltages can be metered by meter M1. A fourth position for the meter is used to monitor the pa filament voltage.

There is a separate breaker for the 28-volt dc power supply. The blower circuit breaker controls the application of primary power to cavity blower and various fans through the filament-on relay. Relay

A19K2 activates when the filaments are turned on by the operator during the equipment turn-on sequence.

Application of primary power to the filament circuits, the exciter, the pa bias power supply, and the pa tuning and loading motors is relay controlled. In fact, the filament-on and the blower-on relays control application of power to the regulated filament circuit through the auto-transformer. Note that this auto-transformer is associated with a variac drive motor and filament voltage regulator. Thus the pa and driver filament voltages are held constant.

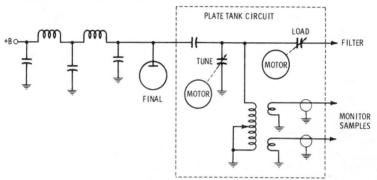

Fig. 11-22. Simplified equivalent of the output network.

Relay A19K1 also controls application of power to the exciter, pa bias power supply, and the pa tuning and loading motors. Power to the exciter and motors is through isolation transformer T4. A time-totalizing meter is placed across the load side of the filament-on relay.

In turning on the transmitter, the filament-on switch of the control panel is pressed. This activates relay K2 and power is supplied to the blower motors. After sufficient air pressure is created an air switch closes and filament-on relay K1 is energized. After a 30-second delay the plate-on switch is pressed and the plate control relay becomes energized activating the power-control amplifier (A9) which applies input voltage to the plate, screen, and driver power supplies. Thus the transmitter is activated through a sequence of blower, filament, time delay, and plate-on automatic steps.

11-11-4. FM Exciter

The fm exciter provides the frequency-modulated 5 to 20 watts of drive signal required by the transmitter. It consists of three major sections as shown in Figs. 11-24 and 11-25. These are the stereo and two SCA modules, the frequency modulator, and the power amplifier. There is an associated power supply. Through two audio-processing stages the left and right program audio is applied to a balanced modulator. Here they are sampled by a 38-kHz switching waveform to develop two outputs. One component is directly proportional to the sum of the two audio signals, producing an L + R signal. The other component is the L − R difference dsb signal. The 38-kHz sampling waveform is de-

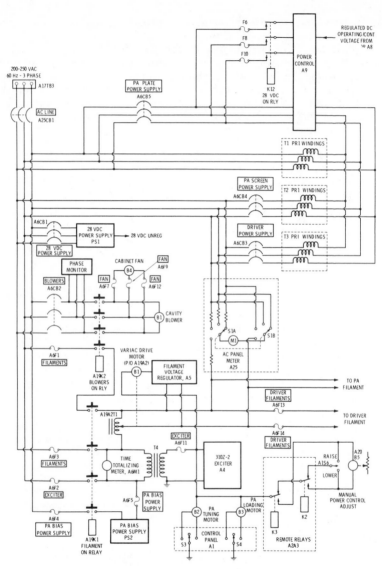

Fig. 11-23. Primary power distribution.

veloped by a 76-kHz oscillator and 2-to-1 divider. An additional 2-to-1 divider is driven by the 38-kHz signal to develop a 19-kHz pilot carrier.

The stereo signal is passed to the output through a 53-kHz low-pass filter. At its output it is combined with the 19-kHz pilot carrier. As a result the stereo baseband signal of Fig. 11-26 is evolved. Note that the L + R signal occupies a band of frequencies between 50 Hz and

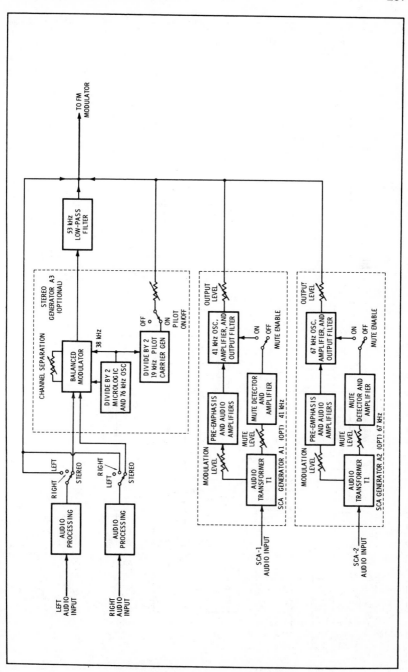

Fig. 11-24. Stereo and SCA generators.

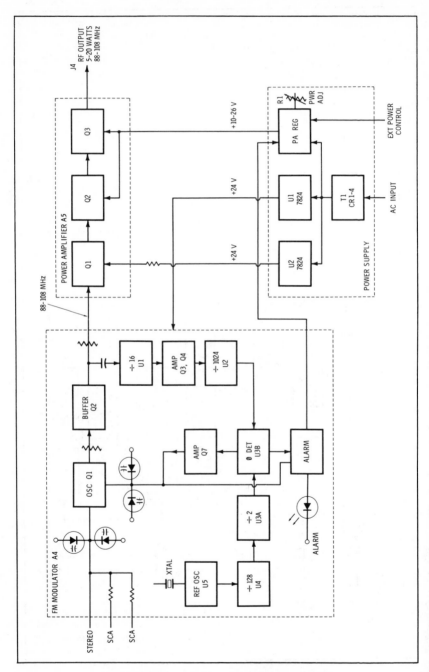

Fig. 11-25. Fm modulator and power amplifier.

15 kHz. The suppressed carrier L − R signal occupies a span of frequencies between 23 and 53 kHz.

If the station also transmits a 67-kHz SCA signal it can also be added to the total baseband signal applied to the frequency modulator. If the station broadcasts two SCA, rather than a stereo fm signal, the two SCA frequencies will be 41 kHz and 67 kHz as shown in Fig. 11-24. The SCA signals are applied through an appropriate pre-emphasis circuit and audio amplifier to the SCA oscillator which is frequency-

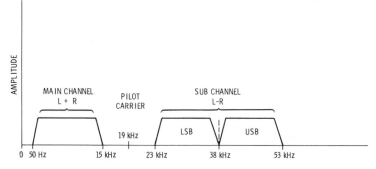

Fig. 11-26. Spectrum of signals in stereo baseband audio.

modulated. In turn the frequency-modulated subcarrier signal is used to frequency-modulate the main carrier oscillator of the transmitter. Each SCA channel is monitored by a carrier-mute circuit. Its responsibility is to remove the SCA output whenever the audio input drops below a selected level.

11-11-5. Stereo Generator

In the Collins stereo generator a time-division multiplex method is used. Samples of the left and right audio channels are switched to the output alternately at a 38-kHz rate. The transmitter and receiver switching rates are synchronized by the transmission of a 19-kHz pilot carrier. Thus the original left and right audio signals are detected and recovered at the receiver. At the receiver the frequency of the received 19-kHz pilot carrier is doubled to generate the 38-kHz demodulating switch.

It is important that the switching frequency in both the stereo generator and receiver be of the same phase to retain the identity and good separation between the left and right audio signals. Actually to maintain a 30-dB channel separation as required by the FCC, the main channel and stereo subchannel signals must have equal peak amplitudes within approximately 0.3 dB. Furthermore the envelope of the subchannel signal must cross the zero level simultaneously with the main channel signal within approximately ±3 degrees.

The schematic diagram of the stereo generator is given in Fig. 11-27. The left and right audio signals are applied through isolating attenuator pads and a 15-kHz low-pass filter to emitter-follower stages Q1 and Q4. Transistors Q2 and Q5 and their associated components oper-

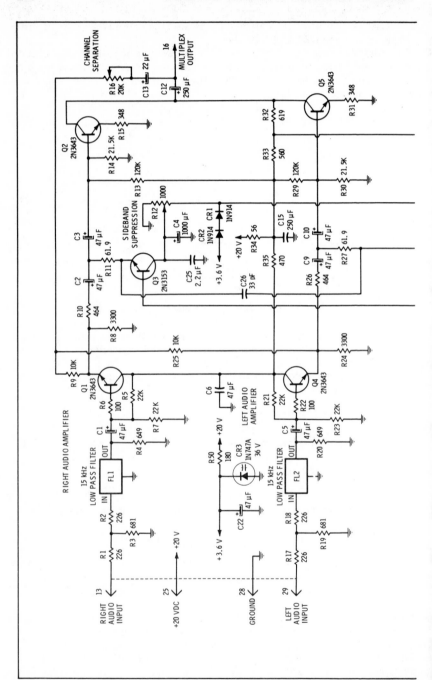

Fig. 11-27.

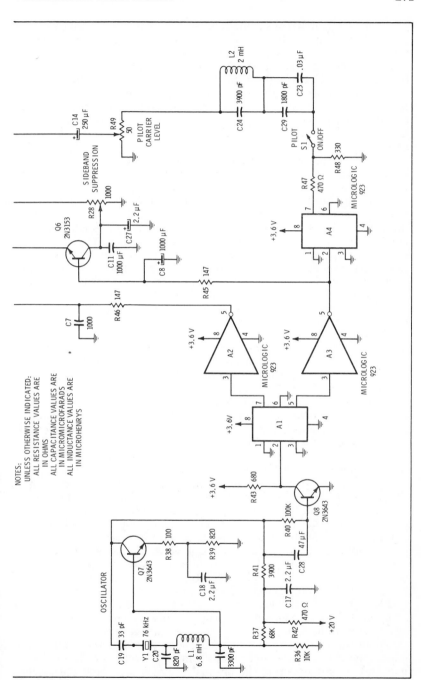

Stereo generator.

ate as a switched balanced modulator. The multiplex output signal is available at their paralleled collectors and is coupled through capacitor C12 to the succeeding fm modulator module.

The 76-kHz generator is shown at the lower left. Its output as developed across collector load resistor R41 is coupled to transistor Q8 which interfaces its output with the input of the digital flip-flop (A1). The logic 1 and logic 0 outputs provide two 38-kHz square waves that are exactly 180 degrees out of phase. One of these outputs is used to trigger another flip-flop through a digital inverter. A phase-locked 19-kHz pilot carrier signal is made available at pin 7 output of digital IC A4. Harmonics of the 19-kHz signal are removed by the filter that follows the pilot on-off switch (S1). Through the pilot level potentiometer the pilot frequency is added to the multiplex output.

Equal-amplitude and opposite-polarity 38-kHz square waves are removed from the two inverter outputs (A2 and A3) and are applied to the bases of transistors Q3 and Q6. These are the modulator switches and because the two 38-kHz signals are of opposite phase, modulator transistors Q2 and Q5 are switched on and off alternately at the 38-kHz rate. Furthermore the phasing results in the cancellation of the 38-kHz subcarrier component at the outputs of Q2 and Q5. Thus the sidebands and not the subcarrier frequency develop in the output. Two sideband suppression controls R12 and R28 can be adjusted for a very minimum of subcarrier and harmonic outputs.

The variable resistor R16 at the output provides a control of the amplitude of the L + R component to make a precise adjustment of channel separation. The waveforms of Fig. 11-28 demonstrate the switching activity. In example A the left and right signals are identical sine waves. On one half-cycle of the square wave switching frequency Q5 conducts and the L signal is sampled. Conversely, on the next half-cycle, Q2 conducts and the right signal is sampled. As shown, the switching frequency is balanced out, and with equal sine wave inputs to both audio channels, no subcarrier sidebands are generated. Only a sine wave L + R signal results. The spikes shown are the result of imperfect switching and are filtered out to obtain a sine-wave output.

When L = 1 and R = 0 combination is applied to the input, both an L + R and a (L − R) dsb component develop. The illustration shows the balanced modulator output as well as the corrections which occur after filtering and after amplitude correction. Amplitude correction is handled in the balance-modulator circuit and is necessary because the peak amplitude of a fundamental sine-wave component of a square wave is $4/\pi$ times the peak amplitude of the square wave itself. Thus the L − R component would be $4/\pi$ times the L + R component.

The waveforms of example C show the relationship when L + R = 0 and L − R = 2. This waveform is the result of equal but opposite audio components since one channel is sampled one-half cycle later than the other. The audio component is removed and only the (L − R) dsb signal remains. The composite signal, after filtering the double-sideband component, is shown in waveform 4. Recovery of the stereo signals and reconstruction of the original L and R signals at the receiver were covered in Sections 11-2 and 11-3.

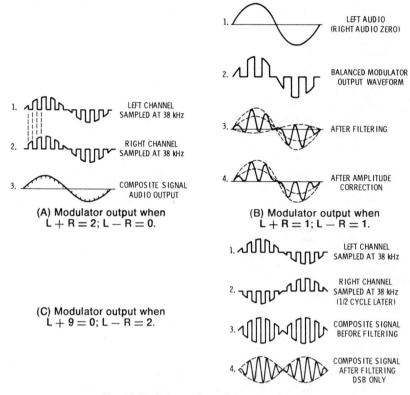

Fig. 11-28. Balanced -modulator waveforms.

11-11-6. FM Modulator and Power Amplifier

The frequency-modulated variable-frequency (Clapp) oscillator operates on the carrier frequency. This is shown as transistor Q1 in the functional block diagram of Fig. 11-25. Four voltage-variable capacitors are used to set the frequency of the oscillator. These devices have a capacitance that is an inverse function of the applied voltage. The input pair is supplied with signal from the stereo and/or SCA generators. They also have an adjustable dc bias that is set for the best linearity of operation as an fm modulator.

Two additional voltage-variable capacitors are used as a part of the phase-locked loop afc system and as a means of making a fine frequency or phase adjustment of the carrier oscillator frequency. Temperature-compensated capacitors are used to reduce frequency drift.

The oscillator is isolated from the followup buffer stage by an isolation pad. The buffer stage itself operates at approximately the 500-milliwatt level supplying that signal to the power amplifier. A sample of the output is taken from the buffer stage and after clipping is supplied to a high-speed frequency divider with a total division of 16.

The output of the divider is amplified and shaped and is applied to a 1024 divider. Thus the combination produces a total division of 16,384 to 1 (16×1024). This component is applied to the phase detector of the pll system.

A reference crystal oscillator operates at 1/64 of the carrier frequency. It is housed in a 75-degree Celsius oven for maximum stability. A vernier control permits a fine adjustment of frequency. Two dividers provide a total division of 256 to 1. The phase detector is clocked by the reference frequency signal. It is then reset by a narrow pulse that has been derived from the last counter of the divided modulated-oscillator frequency. The large division ratio of the modulator divider is effective in removing any phase shift associated with the frequency-modulation process.

The output of the phase detector is a rectangular pulse with a duty cycle that is a function of the time difference of the input clock and reset pulses. It is in fact a function of the phase angle between the modulator and reference oscillator zero crossings. This pulse is amplified and fitered to obtain a dc component. It is applied to the appropriate voltage-variable capacitor of the oscillator to maintain an accurate carrier frequency. For ease of adjustment the dc voltage is also displayed on an appropriate meter as an aid for initial setup and maintenance.

If for any reason the phase lock is lost, a beat note appears at the output detector. This beat note is amplified and a series of constant-amplitude pulses with a repetition rate proportional to the difference frequency is developed. The pulses are rectified and activate an alarm circuit as well as deactivate the exciter radio-frequency output. As a result off-frequency operation is avoided. At the same time, a charge voltage is applied to the fm oscillator, sweeping its frequency through its normal operating range. When the correct frequency is reached the loop is again locked and the charging activity discontinued. At the same time the alarm lamp is extinguished and normal operation of the power amplifier is restored.

The radio-frequency amplifier (Fig. 11-25) is a wideband three-stage circuit. Radio-frequency output power level can be adjusted between 10 and 20 watts. The first stage operates class A while the second and third stages operate as class-C amplifiers. All three stages are set for gain-saturation operation, a permissible condition for fm signal buildup with high efficiency. The radio-frequency output power level is adjustable by regulating the dc voltage applied to transistors Q2 and Q3.

Three separate power sources are made available by the power supply. Two of these are regulated and supply 24 volts to the fm modulator and transistor Q1 of the power amplifier. They also supply the operating voltages for the stereo and SCA generators as well as various audio and meter amplifier circuits.

The driver and radio-frequency amplifier transistors (Q2 and Q3) receive voltage from an adjustable regulated power supply. Voltage can be adjusted between 10 and 26 volts. At the same time an overload protection circuit is included in the event of failure of the regulator.

A silicon-controlled rectifier fires and places a short circuit across the power amplifier power supply. This will blow an appropriate fuse and prevent damage to the power-amplifier transistors.

11-12. STEREO AM BROADCASTING

As in stereo fm, an am stereo system must be chosen that can be handled by a standard monaural am receiver. The system must reproduce as good a monaural program as that transmitted by any monaural am broadcasting station. Thus the left-side and the right-side stereo information is matrixed into L + R and L − R components. The L + R component modulates the am transmitter in conventional manner and, at the receiver, it can be demodulated and reproduced as a monaural signal.

The functional plan of the Magnavox stereo am transmission system is shown in Fig. 11-29. In this system the left and right signals are applied to an audio processor and then on to the matrix which forms the L + R and the L − R components. The L + R and L − R paths must be compensated in terms of frequency response and delay to preserve stereophonic separation throughout the audio range. Thus the two signals will be joined properly at the antenna.

Note that the L + R signal is applied directly to the audio amplifier input of the am transmitter and will amplitude-modulate that transmitter in conventional fashion. Thus the L + R channel operates in the same manner as a regular monaural am transmission system.

The L − R component phase modulates the transmitter. In the arrangement shown in Fig. 11-29 the carrier generator is shown external to the am transmitter. Its output along with the L − R modulating wave is applied to a linear phase modulator. Maximum deviation corresponds to 1 radian (57.3 degrees). In this restricted phase deviation there is no great number of sidebands generated which could possibly interfere with other transmitters or cause distortion in the receiver.

There is no frequency response limitation and, if a station so desires, response can be extended up to 15,000 hertz. Presently the FCC requires that the frequency response of an am broadcast station extend from 100 to 5000 hertz with ±2 dB. However, this can all change with the advent of stereo am because stations are, and have been, permitted to extend their response to 15 kHz.

The Magnavox system also uses a 5-hertz pilot tone which at the receiver will operate a stereo indicator light as well as an automatic system for switching mono-stereo operations in a stereo am receiver. The 5-hertz component serves only in these functions and is not a part of the decoding system as is the 19-kHz pilot frequency of an fm stereo system. The very low 5-hertz frequency is easy to filter out and does not interfere with stereo or monophonic operation of the am receivers.

In the transmitting system the 5-hertz tone component is used to deviate the carrier oscillator ±20 hertz. This happens prior to the application of the carrier component to the linear phase modulator. Thus the output of the linear phase modulator is a composite signal composed of the L − R component and the pilot component. This combination is applied to the conventional intermediate power amplifier

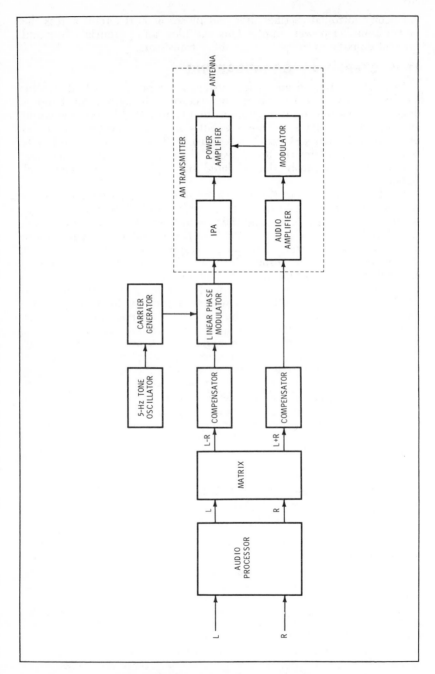

Fig. 11-29. Stereo-am transmission system.

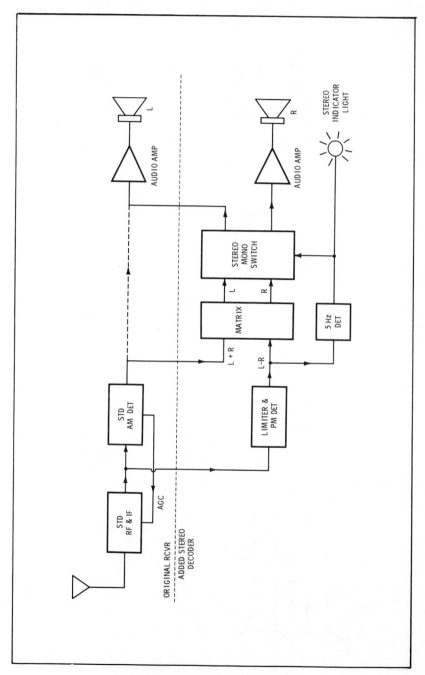

Fig. 11-30. Economy stereo-am receiver.

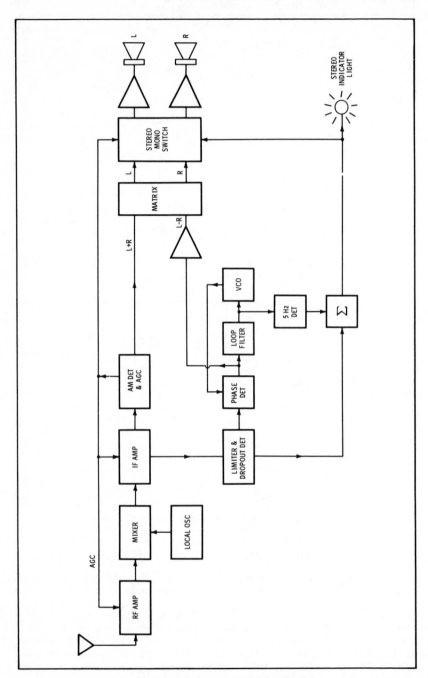

Fig. 11-31. Am-stereo receiver with pll.

input of the am transmitter, and then on to the power amplifier, where it is amplitude modulated by the L + R signal. Combined composite signal is then applied to the antenna system.

In summary, in the am stereo process the sum signal amplitude-modulates the carrier in conventional manner while the difference signal is used to phase-modulate the same carrier. In addition the 5-hertz indicator tone frequency deviates the carrier a small amount.

A functional diagram of a low-cost stereo am receiver is shown in Fig. 11-30. Incoming signal is applied to standard tuner and if amplifier and then on to an am detector. Were this a conventional monophonic am receiver, the output of the detector would be applied to a followup audio amplifier and speaker, as indicated by the dotted line between the detector output and the audio amplifier.

In the stereo am receiver the if signal is also channeled to a limiter and phase-modulation detector. The L − R signal is available at its output and is applied to the receive matrix. Likewise the L + R signal at the output of the standard am detector is applied to the matrix. In the matrix the original L and R (left and right) signals are formed and are applied to the separate left and right audio systems through the stereo/monaural switch.

A detector removes the 5-hertz component from the composite signal at the output of the phase-modulation detector. This component operates the stereo indicator light as well as the stereo-monaural switch. The function of the stereo/monaural switching is to deactivate or mute the L − R channel when a monaural signal is being received.

A good agc system is a requirement of a stereo am receiver if good separation is to be maintained. Both the L + R signal and L − R signal must be held constant for proper matrixing.

A more elaborate receiver is shown in Fig. 11-31. This receiver differs in that a phase-locked loop is used to demodulate the L − R component. This loop is formed by the phase detector, loop filter and voltage-controlled oscillator. The loop filter itself will not follow the ordinary audio modulation but does respond to the 5-hertz tone. Thus it is possible to separate the 5-hertz tone and apply it to the stereo-monaural switch and indicator light. The L − R component is removed at the output of the phase detector and through an appropriate amplifier to the input of the receiver matrix.

Again a good agc system is essential in maintaining constant-level outputs. In addition the agc is used in the stereo/monaural switching arrangement. This circuit too requires the presence of an adequate signal level for smooth operation.

11-12-1. Kahn AM Stereo System

The *Kahn* system, too, uses a combination of amplitude and phase modulation. The L + R components amplitude modulate the transmitter in conventional practice. It is this component that permits monophonic reproduction of a received stereo signal. The L − R component phase-modulates the transmitter. In the modulation process the L + R signal is shifted in phase by −45 degrees, while the L − R component is shifted +45 degrees. Hence there is a quadrature relationship between the two components. The net result is to produce two independent sidebands with the left-side audio information dominating the lower-sideband spectrum; the right side audio information, the upper sideband spectrum. This mode of operation is similar to the phasing method of generating a single-sideband signal with the exception that a single-sideband signal has but one source of audio and, therefore, occupies a spectrum either to the upper side or the lower side of carrier.

A functional block diagram of a typical *Kahn* stereo exciter is given in Fig. 11-32. The L and R signals are applied to a summer, top left, which forms the L + R component. Signal is then passed through a −45 degree phase shifter and, then, on to the audio input of the am transmitter. A low-frequency 15-Hz infrasonic signal can be added at this point to indicate the presence of a stereophonic signal at the receiver and operate the stereo switching and indicator circuits.

The L and R signals are also applied to two low-pass filters. Frequencies below 5 kHz are passed because this range of frequency is all that is required in creating the stereo effect. The L and R signals are passed through a subtractor which forms the L − R component. A +45 degree phase shifter follows. The L − R signal passes on to the summer (the purpose of which will be described later) and, then, to a time-delay circuit. This delay circuit compensates for the time delay involved in the processing of the separate L = R and L − R signals. The phase modulator follows.

The basic carrier frequency is generated by a crystal oscillator which also supplies signal to the phase modulator. Maximum deviation is 0.5 radian. This limited deviation prevents bandwidth extension beyond the FCC bandwidth allocations for am stations. A frequency multiplier follows and then a signal is passed to the low-level radio-frequency amplification section of the transmitter.

In the *Kahn* system the stereo separation is maintained by frequency separation rather than phase separation. If preferred the 15-Hz frequency can be added as a phase-modulation component instead of an amplitude-modulated component to the phase modulator.

By additional control of the phase-modulation component further reduction in signal distortion in the transmission and reception of the am stereo signal can be accomplished by proper processing of the second-harmonic components of the L and R signals after the low-pass filters. As shown in Fig. 11-32 the LPF outputs are first passed to two networks that maintain no phase shift (0 degree) over the desired spectrum. Then the two audio signals are doubled in frequency and combined in a subtractor to produce a second-harmonic L − R component. A variable-gain amplifier follows. This is a so-called leveler circuit that operates under control of the syllabic level of the L − R signal. Note that the output of the +45 degree network is applied to a rectifier that develops the desired dc control voltage for the variable-gain amplifier. The L − R component and the processed second harmonic L − R component are combined in the summer, also passing through the time-delay circuit on to the phase modulator. Optimum operation of this circuit occurs when the frequency-doubled difference signal is approximately 13% of the amplitude level of the stereo differ-

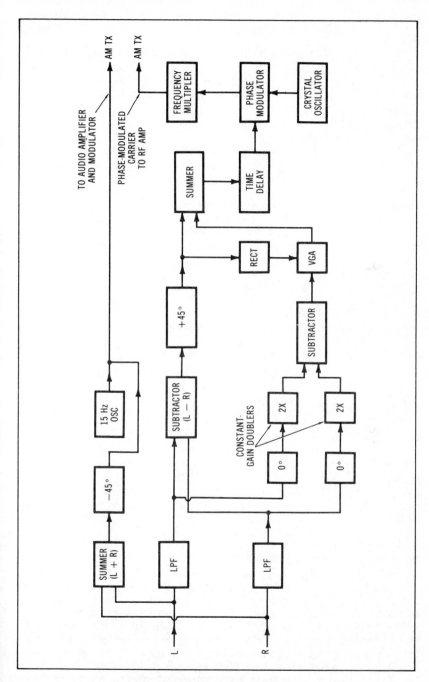

Fig. 11-32. Kahn am stereo exciter.

ence signal at full stereo modulation. The technique minimizes any possible out-of-band interference and distortion in the L sideband spectra.

The functional plan of a top-performing receiver for the *Kahn* system is given in Fig. 11-33. The radio- and intermediate-frequency amplifiers are basically the same as those employed in a conventional good quality am receiver. The L + R component is demodulated by a product detector. An envelope detector such as the conventional diode detector could be used at this spot. However, the product detector provides minimum distortion and the best signal-to-noise ratio. The demodulated L + R component is applied to a +45 degree phase shifter to compensate for the −45 degree shift in the am exciter. From there the signal is applied to the receive stereo matrix.

An output of the rf/if system is also supplied to a local carrier generator consisting of the six small blocks located below the rf/if system block. This is referred to as the *carrier track* system and will be described in more detail later. Nevertheless its output supplies signal for carrier demodulation to the L + R detector, the phase detector, and a system referred to as inverse modulation which will also be described in more detail later.

For the moment follow along the bottom sequence of blocks. The locked-in carried component is first applied to a 90-degree phase shifter, the output of which along with the phase modulation component from the am modulator is applied to the product detector. In fact, the product detector and 90-degree phase shifter operate as a quadrature detector. (This form of detector is used widely in the demodulation section of fm receivers.) The output of the quadrature detector is the L − R component which is transferred through an electronic switch to a −45 degree phase shifter which compensates for the +45 degree shift used previously in the L − R channel of the stereo exciter. Its output is applied to the matrix. Recovered from the matrix are the original L and R stereo signals.

Three special circuits will now be considered. The first of these is the carrier track system. Its purpose is to generate a stable and increased level carrier for demodulating both the L + R and the L − R components. This technique is said to generate an enhanced or exalted carrier. The exalted carrier is particularly effective in the demodulation of the L − R component reducing phase-modulation distortion in the process of removing the stereo difference signal (L − R). It also helps in the suppression of noise bursts that can occur in this channel when the received carrier is fully modulated.

The output of the carrier track system at block X16 is a stabilized version of the carrier portion of the received signal. The generation of the demodulating carrier requires the suppression of the sidebands at the same time the system must follow carrier-frequency errors and drift in the range of ±800 hertz. This is accomplished in the first phase-locked loop A. Next the carrier is divided by a factor of 16. Thus the frequency error is divided by the same amount even though the sideband spacing remains the same. Now additional sidebands are removed by phase-locked loop B which has a passband of only ±50 hertz. This

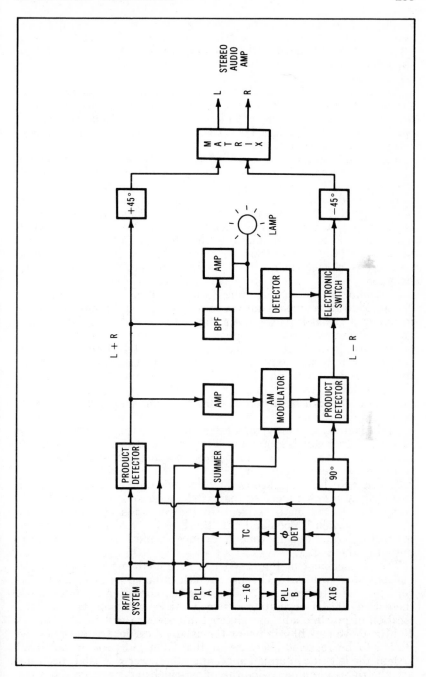

Fig. 11-33. Plan of am stereo receiver.

section acts as the real carrier tracking filter. The X16 multiplier restores the exalted carrier to the original frequency. The actual regenerated carrier is compared to the incoming carrier in the phase detector, the output of the phase detector correcting for phase errors between input and output.

A time-constant TC is used to obtain a slow operation that is able to make the necessary corrections when the equipment is first turned on or if there is a severe carrier fade. In a typical example the exalted carrier voltage level might be 1.5 volts as compared to the 0.94-volt level of the receive carrier.

The technique referred to as *inverse amplitude modulation* of the carrier is represented by the three blocks located between the two product detectors. Its presence results in a further reduction of distortion in the demodulation of the difference frequency component (L − R). The if signal that is to be phase-demodulated comes from the output of the rf/if system and, in the circuit of Fig. 11-33, is applied through a summer and an am modulator to the phase-product detector. If the inverse amplitude modulation system were not included there would be a direct connection between the summer output and the product detector.

In the inverse modulation process, the L + R output of the amplifier is applied to an am modulator via an amplifier. The combination of the incoming if signal from the output of the rf/if system and the newly generated exalter carrier is applied to the summer. It is the summer output that is modulated by the output of the top product detector. By using this technique there is a substantial distortion reduction in the L − R demodulation process. In a typical case, second-harmonic distortion level is reduced to about 0.3%. This circuit can be elaborated on to also obtain a reduction in third harmonic and higher orders of harmonic distortion.

In the stereo indicator system the output of the top product detector is applied to a 15-Hz bandpass filter which removes this infrasonic component and applies it to an appropriate amplifier. Its output level turns on the stereo lamp. A rectified component at the output of the following detector is applied to the electronic switch. Whenever an am stereo signal is being received the switch closes and applies the L − R component to the matrix system. In the reception of a monophonic signal this switch is open and only the L + R signal is applied to the matrix to produce equal-level and identical L and R components at the output of the matrix.

The arrangement of Fig. 11-34 can be added to the output of the matrix shown in Fig. 11-33. This circuit can be added to reduce adjacent channel interference. Recall that in the allocation of am channels there is a 10-kHz separation between carrier assignments. Thus the location of possible adjacent channel interference will be at positions 10 kHz above and 10 kHz below the assigned carrier frequency of the station to be received. Because of the *Kahn* independent sideband system, the left-side information occupies the lower-sideband spectrum, and the right-side information the upper-sideband spectrum. Thus the right-side signal is subject to interference from the adjacent-channel

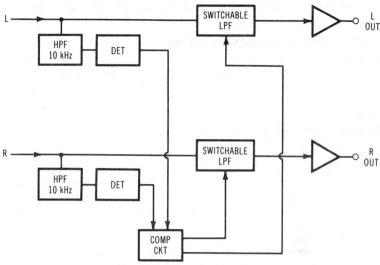

Fig. 11-34. Interference-reduction addition.

carrier located 10 kHz above the desired carrier while the left-side channel is subject to interference by the adjacent-channel carrier that is 10 kHz below the assigned carrier frequency.

In the interference reduction technique both the L and R signals are examined for the presence of carrier interference beats located 10 kHz above and below carrier frequency. Any beat interference present is extracted by the narrow 10-kHz highpass filter and is applied to a detector. These dc components are applied to a comparison detector; outputs of which operate switchable lowpass filters. For example, when there is an interference beat on the L channel, the switching activity will decrease the bandpass of the switchable lowpass filter in the L channel. Thus the beat interference is reduced to a much less annoying level. The same applies to interference that may come from the adjacent channel above the assigned carrier as it appears in the R demodulated signal. In this case the low-pass filter in the R channel is reduced in its bandwidth to cut down the level of the interfering carrier. There may be interference from channels on both sides and the interference reduction system can be made to bring about a controlled reduction in the high-frequency cutoff of both the switchable low-pass filters.

There is another unusual feature of the *Kahn* independent-sideband system that permits a simple process to obtain a stereo output using *two monophonic receivers*. In this procedure one of the receivers is tuned slightly above the carrier frequency, while the other is tuned slightly below the carrier frequency. Thus, one channel will favor the demodulation of the left-side information with its envelop detector, while the other receiver will concentrate on the demodulation of the right-side information. The stereo effect will be quite pronounced but one should not anticipate the performance that can be obtained using a receiver that is designed specifically for the most favorable demodulation of an am stereo signal.

11-12-2. Motorola Compatible QUAM

Motorola in its am stereo system employs *quadrature amplitude modulation* or *QUAM*. However, the quadrature technique is modified in such a way that normal monophonic reproduction is possible without serious distortion. Such is referred to as a compatible QUAM system.

In a basic QUAM system (Fig. 11-35) the transmitter crystal frequency is supplied to two balanced modulators and an output summer. The L + R and L − R signals from the matrix are supplied to separate balanced modulators. The feed to one of the balanced modulators is shifted 90 degrees, which will produce quadrature sideband outputs, but no carrier. The output of the summer consists of a reinserted carrier plus amplitude-varying sum and difference frequencies. The latter are supplied as amplitude modulation to the am transmitter after they are recovered with an envelope detector.

The phase angle component which is related to the relative L + R and L − R levels is derived by first limiting the amplitude variations at the output of the summer. A phase-modulated carrier component is applied to the low-level radio-frequency stages of the transmitter. The controlled angle of the pll if carrier at the receiver when applied to the synchronous detectors or synchronous demodulators of the receiver in conjunction with the demodulating if frequency component produces the separate L and R outputs. It is a phase demodulation process.

At the receiver separate synchronous demodulators recover the L and R signal components. The 90-degree related inserted carriers are derived from the angle information on the incoming signal. The demodulation, in effect, is synchronized by the angular information on the incoming carrier. Although the foregoing system affords an effective means of reproducing stereo, a problem arises when the signal is applied to a monophonic receiver. Distortion and double-frequency components develop because of the dual L + R and L − R amplitude modulation.

In the *Motorola* compatible QUAM system, this problem is overcome by transmitting that which will result in good monophonic reproduction. Such a system intentionally transmits a signal that would reproduce as an improper stereo signal were conventional quadrature reception principles used. However, the system includes circuits that correct the incoming signal in such a manner that distorted outputs are not obtained. Correction circuits change over the incoming stereo data to a standard QUAM structure.

The transmission of a compatible QUAM signal is shown in Fig. 11-36A. The *Motorola* plan shows that only the L + R output of the balanced modulator is applied directly to the am modulator of the transmitter through a suitable time delay. Recall that a time delay is usually needed to time-equalize the separate phase- and amplitude-modulation processes.

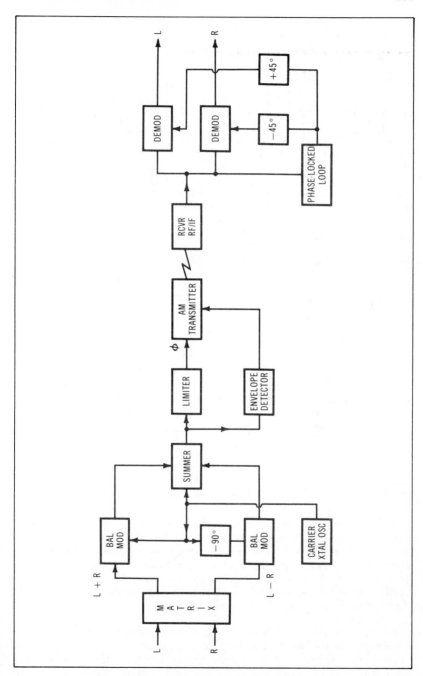

Fig. 11-35. Basic Quam system.

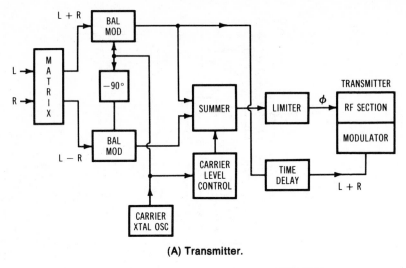

(A) Transmitter.

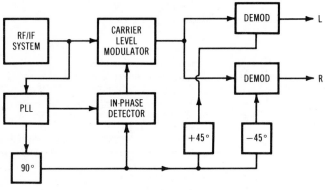

(B) Receiver.
Fig. 11-36. Motorola compatible Quam.

The carrier oscillator, as in any quadrature modulation system, provides in-phase and 90-degree-related components to the balanced modulators. The resultant L + R and L − R radio-frequency sidebands are applied to the summer along with a controlled level of carrier. The resultant output is limited and the angular modulation component is applied to the low-level radio-frequency stages of the am transmitter. The angular deviation is set by the relative levels of the L + R and L − R signals.

In summary, the L + R signal amplitude-modulates the same transmitter and is applied to the low-level audio stages of the modulator. However, contrary to pure quadrature modulation, the L − R component is missing. Inasmuch as the transmitter is amplitude modulated only by the L + R component it can be demodulated by the conventional envelope detector in a monophonic receiver, and provide a non-distorted output.

The absence of the L − R component in the amplitude modulation of the transmitter would result in an improper quadrature demodulation in a stereo receiver. However, in a compatible QUAM receiver (Fig. 11-36B) a component derived from the phase-locked loop circuitry of the receiver can be used to compensate for this absent modulating signal in the phase-demodulation process. This correction takes place at the carrier-level modulator. A carrier component of proper phase is modulated by the received compatible QUAM if signal. As a result the output of the carrier-level modulator is a standard QUAM signal that can be supplied to the synchronous demodulator system.

Injection signal from the pll is supplied through the appropriate phase-shift circuits for operating the two demodulators at the correct angles to recover the original L and R signals.

Phasing relations are quite critical in the operation of an am stereo system. However, this involves no special problem in modern circuit design, thanks to the convenience and stability of integrated circuits. The modulating and demodulating processes along with other essential circuits can be handled by several ICs. Many of these ICs have been designed or are in the design process by semiconductor manufacturers.

11-12-3. HARRIS Variable-Angle Phase Modulation

In a pure quadrature system the phase angle is 90 degrees. However, during stereo programming of high modulation and great separation between left and right channels, the system is not monophonic compatible. However, compatibility can be attained by reducing the angle between carriers in response to high levels of channel separation especially when one or the other of the channels alone reaches up to maximum modulation.

This variable-angle modulation can be accomplished by causing the angle to vary with the separation. Indirectly the same effect can be accomplished by *lowering the magnitude of the L − R modulating component* when there is a rising separation. For most stereo programming an angle between 70 and 90 degrees results in acceptable compatibility. Even with a high amount of separation the angle need not be reduced to any value less than 30 degrees. This compression of the angle by reducing the L − R amplitude can be accomplished at the transmitter. Also a sampling of this angular information can be taken at the transmitter and conveyed to the receiver via the pilot-tone frequency. The information can be used at the receiver to make a suitable correction in the L − R component during the demodulation process. As in the *Motorola* process the system departs from pure quadrature and then is followed by a receiver correction in the interest of maintaining monophonic compatibility.

The basic plan of the system is shown in Fig. 11-37. The L + R component is applied directly as amplitude modulation to the transmitter. The L − R component is passed through a high-pass filter to the analog divider of a compression system. The filter, by removing frequency components below 200 hertz from the L − R signal, prevents that signal

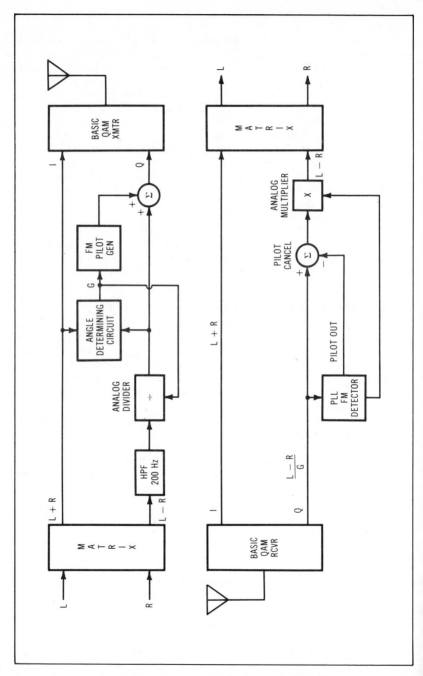

Fig. 11-37. Basic plan of the Harris system.

from interfering with the relatively high frequency of the pilot tone which can be in the 55- to 96-hertz range. Additional filters and a link with the output R channel (not shown) can be used to make compensation for any loss in amplitude at very low audio frequencies.

The suppression of the L − R component is initiated by an angle-determining circuit that evaluates the separation between the L + R and L − R channels. A control output component G regulates the gain of the analog divider, decreasing L − R level in response to an increase in the angle.

At the same time this output frequency modulates the pilot-tone deviating upward from 55 Hz to the maximum indicated above. The level-controlled L − R component and the frequency-modulated pilot tone are summed and applied to the phase-modulated input of the QUAM transmitter.

At the receiver the L + R and the gain-varying L − R component are recovered by the usual synchronous demodulators. The L + R component is applied directly to the receiving matrix. The pilot tone is picked up by a phase-locked loop fm detector. From this detector an output is derived that corresponds to the deviation of that detector by the angle-varying information established at the transmitter. This component controls the gain of the analog multiplier, restoring the L − R component to the relative level it was at the output of the transmit matrix. Thus, a system of transmission compression and receive expansion restores original stereo-difference levels. A pure pilot tone is removed from the detector and applied to a pilot-cancelling circuit which makes certain that the pilot tone itself is removed from the L − R signal information.

In the design of a low-cost receiver the receiver pilot detector and analog multiplier can be eliminated. There is some loss in channel separation in program material that occurs very infrequently for normal program material.

CHAPTER 12

Transmitter Monitor and
Test Equipment

Both am and fm broadcast stations are required by the FCC to monitor their power output and modulation continuously. Appropriate modulation monitors are compulsory. Moreover transmitters must stay within a specified number of hertz of their assigned frequency (20 hertz for am and 2000 hertz for fm stations).

12-1. ESSENTIAL TEST EQUIPMENT

Although frequency meters are no longer compulsory for continuous monitoring because of the inherent frequency stability of modern transmitters, frequency meters independent of the transmitter frequency control must be available and have the high accuracy needed to measure well within the tolerance limits.

In am broadcasting the modulation percentage must be maintained as high as possible consistent with good quality of transmission. It should not be less than 85% on peaks, nor more than 100% on negative peaks of frequent recurrence, during any selection which is transmitted at the highest level of the program. Positive modulation peaks should not exceed 125%. It is the responsibility of the am monitor to continuously indicate the modulation percentage and warn of any sustained overmodulation.

The modulation percentage of fm broadcast stations must be maintained as high as possible consistent with good quality of transmission and good broadcast practice. It should not be less than 85%, nor more than 100% on peaks of frequent recurrence, during any selection which is normally transmitted at the highest level of the program. An fm monitor must be provided to measure the frequency deviation continuously. It must give the operator a suitable indication so he will know if the deviation is in excess of the maximum ±75 kHz. In case of stereo and/or SCA transmissions it is the total of all the modulation components that may not exceed ±75 kHz. The individual deviations

293

of stereo subcarrier and SCA signal must not be permitted to exceed specified values.

Both am and fm stations must maintain their radio-frequency output power as near as practicable to the authorized value. Power may not be less than 90% or more than 105% of the authorized value. Power must be measured continuously by appropriate direct or indirect means. In the case of an am broadcast station that uses directional antennas, an antenna monitor is required to evaluate the individual tower currents and current phases of the directional array.

12-1-1. AM Broadcast Transmitter

A modulation meter must be available for continuous monitoring of the percentage of modulation. A suitable alarm system must be included to give a warning of recurrent overmodulation. An am modulation meter also may include a facility for checking carrier amplitude shift. Some include a built-in frequency meter. Analog or digital displays can be used. Although continuous monitoring of carrier frequency is not compulsory, facilities must be available for making scheduled frequency measurements.

Power output is measured by direct means. Actually the power output is equal to the antenna current squared times the antenna-system resistance. The output meter is calibrated to measure the radio-frequency output in watts. Meters must be included to measure the dc input current and dc supply voltage of the final radio-frequency power amplifier.

The indirect method of power measurement may only be used on a temporary basis in the case of the am broadcast transmitter. Power output in this case is the product of the dc input current and dc voltage of the final power amplifier times an assigned efficiency factor K.

It must also be possible to measure the radio-frequency antenna current at the base of the tower of a nondirectional broadcast antenna. In the case of a directional broadcast antenna using two or more towers, facilities must be included for measuring the common-point radio-frequency antenna current. It should also be possible to measure the antenna current at the base of each individual tower. Moreover, for a directional antenna system, antenna pickup loops must be installed on the individual towers, and supply signal back to the antenna monitor of the transmitter. Here it must be possible to measure the individual loop current and phase. Usually this is done on a ratio basis. Ratios would be the ratio of a given tower current to the reference tower current and a given tower phase to the assumed zero-degree phase value of the reference tower.

An accurate field-strength meter is an important piece of test equipment. It can be taken out in the field and used to measure signal intensity in various directions and at prescribed distances. The field-strength meter is particularly important in checking out the performance of a directional antenna system. It is helpful not only in checking field strength at the various distances and directions but also in making measurements at specific angles for which the station must protect the coverage areas of other broadcast stations.

An audio-frequency generator with an output of extremely low distortion is a requisite in making equipment performance measurements. It should be possible to set the output level and frequency accurately. An associated audio analyzer is also important in measuring the output voltage, harmonic distortion, intermodulation distortion, frequency response, signal-to-noise ratio, and other parameters.

12-1-2. FM Broadcast Transmitter

A modulation monitor is required for an fm broadcast station. It must provide continuous observation of the fm modulation. Overmodulation indicators are included. Most fm modulation monitors also include facilities for measuring the center (carrier) frequency.

A stereo monitor is appropriate for this mode of transmission and can be used to measure both the stereo subcarrier frequency and degree of modulation. Some stereo monitors include facilities for measuring both the right and left channels as well as channel separation and crosstalk. Similar monitors are available for SCA transmissions.

The power output of an fm transmitter can be measured by direct or indirect means. When using the direct method the output meter is calibrated in watts power output. It is customary to rate fm station output in effective radiated power (erp). This quantity is the power delivered to the antenna times the antenna power gain. Often a reflectometer is associated with the output system of an fm transmitter. Such a meter measures direct power and reflected power, indicating the operating conditions of the transmission line and antenna matching. Actual power output would be the difference between the direct-power measurement and the reflected-power measurement.

Two essential meters of the fm transmitter measure the dc input current and dc supply voltage of the final radio-frequency power amplifier. If the indirect method of power measurement is used at the transmitter, the radio-frequency power output equals the product of these two quantities times the assigned efficiency factor K.

A field-intensity meter is important in measuring signal levels for various distances and directions from the transmitting antenna.

A quality audio generator and audio analyzer are also essential for making equipment performance measurements for an fm broadcast station. It should be possible to make the same measurements given under the am broadcast transmitter discussion. For stereo application separate left and right audio-generator outputs should be available. It can be helpful to have both L + R and L − R signals made available. Likewise it should be possible to check both the left and right channels with the audio analyzer. Some instruments include facilities for making phase and ratio measurements.

12-2. AM MODULATION MONITOR

A *Time and Frequency Technology, Inc.* am modulation monitor is shown in Fig. 12-1. The modulation monitor is shown on the right side. The smaller device with digital readout to the left is an accessory item in the form of a radio-frequency preselector which permits remote mon-

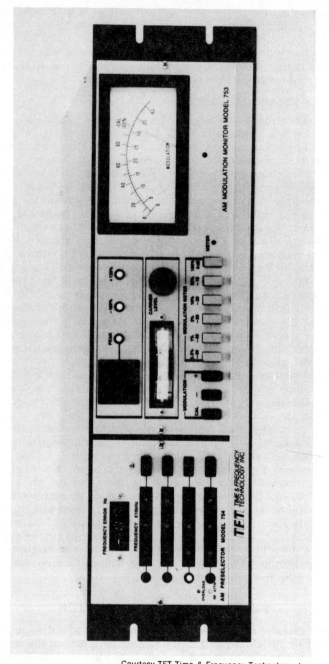

Courtesy TFT Time & Frequency Technology, Inc.

Fig. 12-1. Am modulation monitor with attached frequency meter.

itoring of transmitter modulation and also serves as a carrier-frequency meter.

There are three possible modes of operation. The modulation meter can be excited directly from the modulation meter output of the transmitter. In this case it is mounted near the transmitter. The modulation meter also has remote-meter outputs and a separate remote-meter panel can be purchased and attached. Interconnection is provided by a 6-wire cable and permits the remote operation of the modulation meter, negative 100%-modulation peak flasher, positive 125%-modulation peak flasher, and another peak flasher that can be preset at the modulation meter to flash when the modulation exceeds the preset value. Off-the-air monitoring is also possible using the am preselector and frequency-meter combination.

The modulation meter range extends between 0 and 133 percent, switchable plus or minus. Frequency range is 500 kHz to 4 MHz. Input voltage range extends between 1.0 and 10 volts rms. The instrument can also be used to make various equipment performance measurements according to FCC specifications. A convenient audio output connector permits the attachment of a distortion analyzer.

In operating the modulation monitor after it has been attached to a source of signal it is necessary to adjust the carrier level control at the very center of the meter. To its left is the carrier level meter and the control is adjusted for a center-scale reading. This meter will also indicate if there is any carrier-amplitude shift during modulation. The modulation meter on the right is operated by depressing the plus-or-minus switch on the front panel to measure either positive or negative modulation.

At the top center are two peak flashers which respond to fast transients and peaks that the meter cannot follow. These are preset for 100-percent negative modulation and 125-percent positive modulation, indicating with their flashing whenever the modulation reaches these values. To their left is still another peak flasher which is set by the associated thumbwheel switch to any desired modulation percentage or direction. The peak flasher will then indicate when the modulation exceeds the preset value.

A functional block diagram of the modulation meter is given in Fig. 12-2. Input signal is applied through the carrier-level potentiometer to the am detector. The am detector is a full-wave rectifier which balances out the carrier frequency. This provides a wider bandwidth through the low-pass filter to the meter circuit without allowing the carrier to be passed. However, the output of the am detector does have a dc voltage component which is proportional to the input carrier level. This dc output drives the carrier-level meter shown at the lower left. An amplified version of this dc component can be used to activate an external carrier-alarm circuit by turning on the carrier-fail transistor whenever the output drops below 25 percent on the carrier-level meter.

The audio output of the low-pass filter connects to a voltage-controlled attenuator to keep the modulation meter and flasher calibrated regardless of the carrier-level meter reading. The attenuator is a part of an agc feedback system which holds the dc level at the output constant. Thus, the calibration of the meter and flasher circuits is maintained, even though there may be changes in incoming signal level.

The audio output of the buffer amplifier is fed to the plus terminal of the modulation switch to measure positive modulation peaks, and it is also inverted and applied to the minus terminal of the modulation switch to measure negative modulation peaks. Either of these two outputs can be selected for application to the modulation meter circuit of the programmable peak flasher.

The path to the modulation meter is through an amplifier, adjustable attenuator and a meter detector. The adjustable attenuator has been included to make it possible to read audio voltages in the measurement of residual noise and hum using an external voltmeter.

Whenever the modulation is exceeded in the peak detector circuits an appropriate one-shot multivibrator is activated and turns on the peak LED indicator for approximately two seconds. Thus the LEDs will continue to flash whenever the modulation reaches their preset values.

The audio output of the buffer is amplified and supplies signal to standard audio outputs which are 5 volts rms into 5000 ohms and an

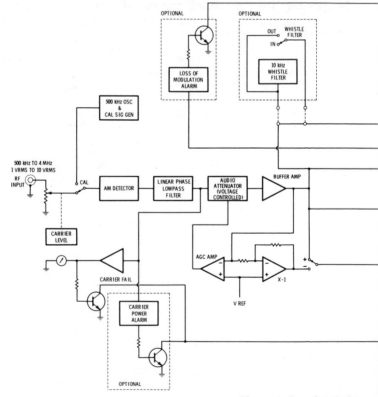

Fig. 12-2. Functional plan

audio monitor output at 0 dBm into 600 ohms. These outputs are used for test and audio monitoring applications.

The output of the audio amplifier also supplies signal to two optional circuits. One circuit is activated and sounds an alarm when the modulation drops below 10% for a specified period of time that can be adjusted between 2-30 seconds. There is also a subaudible output that can be used for telemetry service. Also, as an optional device, a 10-kHz whistle filter is included. This can be placed in the line between the buffer amplifier and the audio amplifier to filter out a 10-kHz tone that may come from a carrier on an adjacent am channel.

A calibration signal generator as shown at the left center is included. This circuit simulates a carrier and modulation of −100% and +125% which has been generated digitally. This is fed to the am detector when the calibration switch is depressed. This signal can then be used to calibrate the modulation meter and peak flashers.

A functional plan of the radio-frequency preselector and frequency meter is given in Fig. 12-3. Signal is applied through an adjustable 50-ohm attenuator and 2-MHz low-pass filter to the first mixer. There is an associated overload circuit and an LED indicator that illuminates

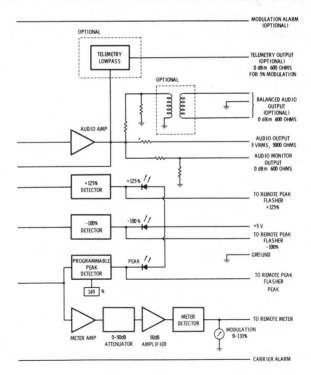

of TFT modulation monitor.

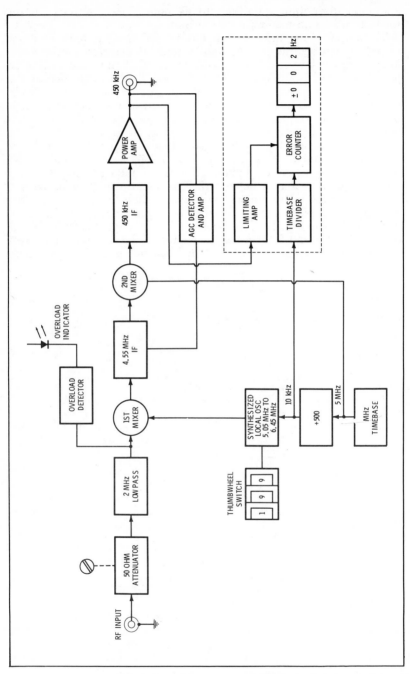

Fig. 12-3. Functional plan of frequency meter.

when the input signal is too strong. The first mixer derives its signal from a synthesized local oscillator, the frequency of which is determined by the setting of a thumbwheel switch. Mixer output is a 4.55 MHz intermediate frequency. A second if mixer and amplifier follow. The 450-kHz output of the power amplifier is applied as excitation to the modulation monitor when it is used at a remote monitoring position. A second output of the amplifier is applied to an agc detector to maintain a constant signal level.

The reference frequency for the synthesizer is a 5-MHz time base which also supplies the injection voltage for the second mixer. A division by 500 results in a 10-kHz output which is supplied to a timebase divider and followup error counter. The output of the power amplifier is also supplied to the error counter through a limiting amplifier. The output of the error counter operates a digital display that reads the number of cycles the incoming carrier is off frequency.

The preselector shown in Fig. 12-1 can actually be pretuned to any four am stations with the associated thumbwheel switches. Thus the carrier frequency of three additional stations can also be checked. Any frequency error will be indicated on the digital display.

12-3. FM MODULATION MONITOR

The *TFT* fm modulation meter is shown in Fig. 12-4. The basic unit is designed for direct transmitter connection. However, it can be used for off-the-air monitoring with the use of a preselector as shown to the left of Fig. 12-4. This preselector can be pretuned to any two fm stations using the thumbwheel switches. Carrier frequency error is indicated on the digital display. Hence the preselector can also be used as a frequency meter.

The modulation meter can read either negative or positive modulation. In addition, two peak flashers, positive and negative, can be adjusted to flash when the modulation attains a value preset by the thumbwheel switch at the top center.

The modulation meter can also be used to measure the percentage of undesired am modulation on the carrier. Appropriate pushbutton switches are included to permit the modulation meter to read very low percentages of modulation. Residual noise as well as other equipment performance measurements can be made. Distortion measurement can be made with a distortion analyzer connected to an appropriate output.

A functional block diagram of the fm modulation monitor is shown in Fig. 12-5. It is basically a superheterodyne receiver capable of measuring accurately the modulation on the fm carrier. An input-level control permits the incoming signal to be adjusted to exactly 1 volt rms. The signal is down-converted by a mixer that receives its injection voltage from a frequency synthesizer which is locked in by an associated crystal oscillator circuit. The signal is then passed through a low-pass filter and limiting amplifier to a one-shot discriminator. If a radio-frequency preselector is being used its output is supplied just ahead of the limiter.

The output of the discriminator develops a pulse output, the fre-

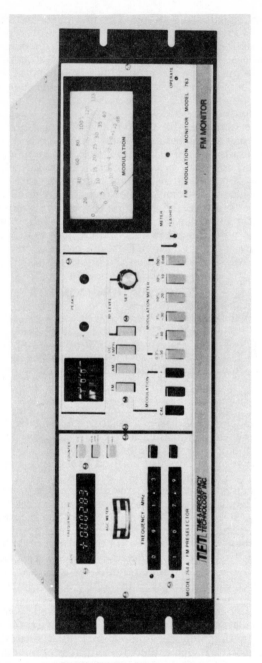

Courtesy TFT Time & Frequency Technology, Inc.

Fig. 12-4. Fm modulation monitor with attached frequency meter.

quency of which is the same as the if carrier. However, it has a fixed pulse width. In fact, the duty cycle of the output pulse train varies with the modulation. The audio is recovered by passing it through a followup low-pass filter. A switch is used to select either inverted or noninverted output, thus permitting the display of either positive or negative modulation peaks for monitoring. Output is supplied through a stepped attenuator amplifier (with or without de-emphasis), and applied to one of two detectors. The peak detector is used when a high percentage of modulation is to be indicated. The other detector is used when low-level signals are to be monitored. Output is supplied to the modulation meter through the meter driver.

The output of the amplifiers that follow the discriminator is also applied to the peak detector circuits, positive and negative. When the modulation peaks reach the preset modulation values they will flash. A pulse stretcher holds them on for approximately three seconds.

Residual am can also be measured. The am detector is shown at the top left and its output is supplied to the am side of the fm/am switch at the right center. From this point the am signal is handled in the same way as the fm audio and is displayed on the modulation meter. The output of the carrier level and am detector is also used to drive a carrier-fail alarm and an optional carrier-power alarm.

Output terminals at the lower right are provided for connection of remote meter and remote flashers if desired. The output of the inverting amplifier is also applied to an audio amplifier at the top right, which supplies signal to a variety of outputs for audio monitoring and making equipment performance measurements. There are also outputs for supplying signal to accessory monitors.

12-4. STEREO AND SCA MONITORS

Stereo and SCA add-on units to the main fm modulation monitor are available. Two such units are shown in the block diagrams of Fig. 12-6. The addition of the stereo monitor permits separate readings of the left- and right-channel modulation. Total modulation is read by the regular fm modulation monitor.

As shown in example A the composite fm signal is applied to the input of the stereo monitor. After amplification the signal takes several paths. A stereo demodulator and phase-locked loop system provide a left- and right-channel output. The left-channel output passes through an associated meter amplifier and detector to the left-channel meter which reads the left-channel modulation continuously. Right-channel output is applied through a step attenuator and amplifier/detector to the second meter which, in the position of the switch shown, reads the right-channel modulation. A stereo pilot indicator is on the front panel.

The right-channel meter can also be used to measure a variety of other modulation and performance characteristics of the stereo signal, such as L + R, L − R, channel separation, crosstalk between main and subchannels, 38-kHz carrier suppression, and 19-kHz injection level. These measurements are selected by a front-panel pushbutton array. Precision attenuators permit the measurement of low-level signals. Remote metering outputs are available at the rear panel. Duplicate left and right modulation meters and 50 feet of cable are supplied.

The SCA monitor shown in example B is also operated in conjunction with the main fm modulation meter. A choice of one of two SCA frequencies can be made using the selector switch associated with the balanced mixer at the input. In addition to modulation of the SCA signal the meter can also be used to measure injection level, signal-to-noise ratio, crosstalk, distortion, and frequency response.

The incoming signal is up-converted to 10.7 MHz and the SCA subchannel is extracted through precision crystal filters. Peak flashers are included to display the plus and minus peak modulation of the SCA

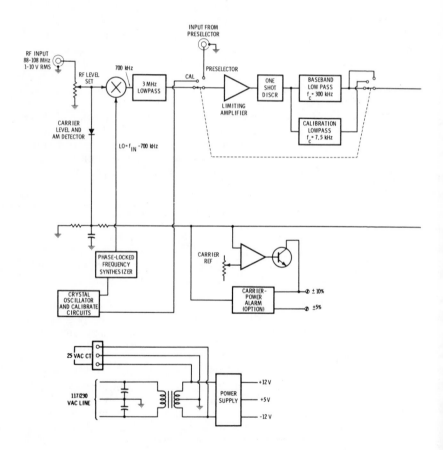

Fig. 12-5. Functional plan of

signal simultaneously. Limits are set from 50-percent to 129-percent modulation by front panel thumbwheel switches.

12-5. EQUIPMENT PERFORMANCE MEASUREMENTS

The FCC requires that broadcast station equipment meet specific performance criteria concerning frequency response, harmonic content, carrier, hum and noise level, spurious radiation, and carrier-amplitude regulation. Scheduled measurements must be made using suitable test equipment. Such data must be obtained and kept on file by the broadcast station in compliance with FCC rules and regulations.

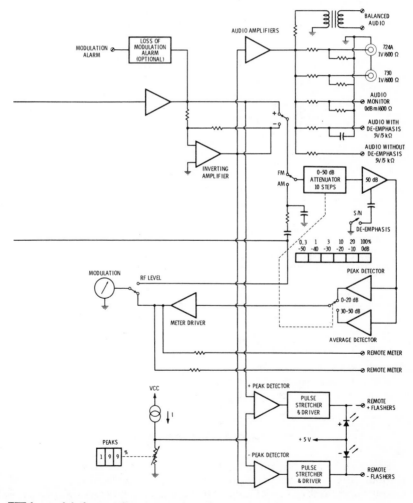

TFT fm modulation monitor.

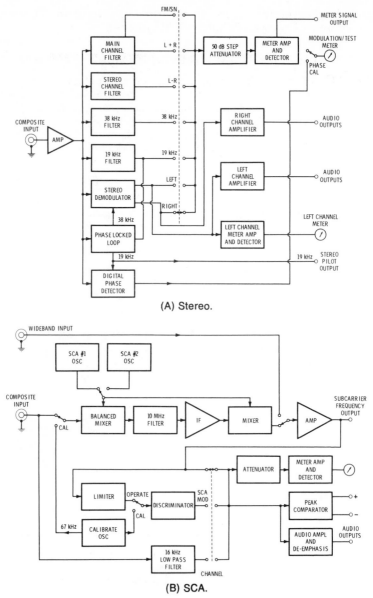

(A) Stereo.

(B) SCA.

Fig. 12-6. Stereo and SCA monitors.

Results also serve as an indication of the overall performance of the station. Measurements disclose signs of deterioration in equipment performance and remedial steps can be taken. Two essential pieces of test equipment are: an audio oscillator (with an appropriate output level gain control system), and an audio analyzer. A radio-frequency pickup probe and diode rectifier combination is required. This unit is connected to a test output associated with the final radio-frequency power amplifier of the transmitter. An optional facility can be the audio output of an am or fm modulation monitor. A typical setup is shown in Fig. 12-7.

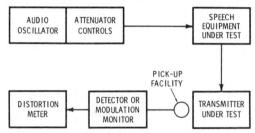

Fig. 12-7. Basic equipment-performance setup.

The audio oscillator should have a fundamental frequency range between at least 30 hertz and 15 kilohertz. Most audio generators used for broadcast test application have a substantially greater frequency range. Output must have a very low harmonic content and a high frequency accuracy. An attenuator system should be included to help in establishing correct signal levels and in making accurate measurements. Proper isolation and matching facilities must be a part of both the audio generator and audio analyzer. Usually, balanced and unbalanced inputs and outputs are made available.

The audio analyzer must have a variety of measurement capabilities. It should be possible to measure ac voltages accurately. Accurate reading of distortion and noise are required. Modulation monitors usually provide low-distortion audio output facilities that can supply signal for an audio analyzer. A panel VU meter is usually an essential unit of a broadcast station and can be used as a volume and output-level monitor for tests. An oscilloscope is useful for analyzing signal waveforms and adjusting test equipment.

Equipment performance measurements are made with station equipment adjusted for normal broadcast operation. All equipment between the microphone and transmitter output should be included in the measurement procedures. The test equipment and broadcast unit should be matched exactly and precautions taken to minimize hum pickup. The chassis of the test instrument should have a good ground connection to the station's ground system. Only short power leads should be used to the test equipment, and these leads should have a power-line filter. Short signal leads are required to supply signal to input stages of the broadcast units that normally operate at low signal levels. At the transmitter the test leads must often be isolated from the radio-frequency energy by appropriate chokes and filter capacitors. In certain performance measurements it is necessary to patch around or deactivate limiter and compression systems of the transmitter.

A field-intensity meter is essential in measuring transmitter fundamental and harmonic outputs and, in particular, in checking the performance of directional antenna systems. A good quality communications receiver can be useful in checking for harmonic and other spurious radiations from the transmitter.

12-6. SOME APPROPRIATE FCC RULES AND REGULATIONS

Typical equipment performance measurements that must be made at scheduled intervals can be found at the very end of Section 3-7 of Chapter 3.

12-7. AUDIO GENERATOR AND ANALYZER

A combination audio generator and audio analyzer is shown in Fig. 12-8. The pair has been designed primarily for commercial broadcast equipment performance measurements and maintenance. They are, of course, packaged separately for measurements requiring physical separation of signal source and signal analyzer as is usually the case in testing broadcast station facilities. The unit can be used for testing both am and fm (monophonic or stereophonic) broadcast stations and the sound facilities of television broadcast stations.

The audio generator has a frequency range that extends between 20 hertz and 200 kilohertz. The unit has an output level accuracy be-

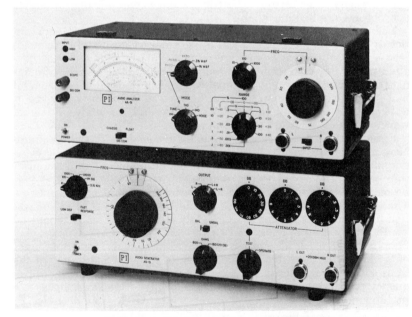

Courtesy Potomac Instruments, Inc.

Fig. 12-8. Audio analyzer and generator.

tween 20 hertz and 100 kilohertz of ±0.2 dB. The attenuator range extends between 0 and 99 dB in 0.1 dB steps. Output level of a sine-wave signal with no attenuation is +20 dBm (7.75V) across a 600-ohm load. Level is 0 dBm across a 150-ohm load.

A front-panel switch permits operation of the audio generator for convenient fast-response operation in making rapid frequency-response measurements. The operator can evaluate frequency response of the device under test with a manual sweep of the frequency dial and multiplier switch. A second low-distortion position of the switch permits accurate signal analysis at any specific frequency. In this latter mode of operation the sine-wave distortion between 50 Hz and 7.5 kHz is less than 0.05 percent, and between 20 Hz and 20 kHz it is less than 0.08%.

The audio generator provides a standard intermodulation test signal as well as a 3.15-kHz test signal for wow and flutter tests.

To handle fm stereo tests separate left and right output connectors are available. Outputs may be switched for left only, right only, left and right in phase (L + R) and left and right in phase opposition (L − R). A switch also permits the generator output level to be reduced to zero, a useful feature during noise measurements.

A functional block diagram of the audio generator is given in Fig. 12-9. The variable Wien-bridge oscillator is shown at the left center. It can be capacitively tuned over a 10-to-1 frequency range. Along with associated decade switch S2 the oscillator serves as a variable sine-wave source from 20 hertz to 200 kilohertz. The control amplifier section at the lower left provides the necessary feedback for the oscillator circuit and ensures a low-distortion output and amplitude stability. The time-constant switch (S3) in this circuit also chooses between fast response and low distortion operation.

The output of the oscillator now passes through step attenuators S8, S9, and S10 and on to the power amplifier. Output signal conditions are controlled by the three switches (S5, S6, and S7) which establish L and R, balanced or unbalanced, 600- or 150-ohm impedances at the two output connectors. An additional stage of attenuation (switch S8) is placed in the left and right channel output line. These stages allow adjustment of the output level in 0.1-dB, 1-dB, and 10-dB steps as an aid in making more rapid calibrated output level changes.

In the test mode setting of switch S4, the output is deactivated, but the maximum voltage output of the inverter is monitored by a comparator system (module A5) and, if correct, the LED indicator illuminates.

The intermodulation signal generator is shown at the top left. It consists of two fixed-tuned 60-Hz and 7-kHz Wien-bridge oscillators with their outputs mixed in a 4 to 1 ratio. A third fixed-tuned Wien-bridge oscillator generates the 3.15-kilohertz signal that is used for wow and flutter testing. Either of these signals can be selected by switch S2 and passed through the attenuators to the output power amplifier.

The audio analyzer (Fig. 12-8) is a multipurpose device that can provide accurate measurements of total harmonic distortion, intermodulation distortion, frequency response, signal-to-noise ratio, wow and flutter, as well as stereo phasing and differential gain. Its ac voltmeter

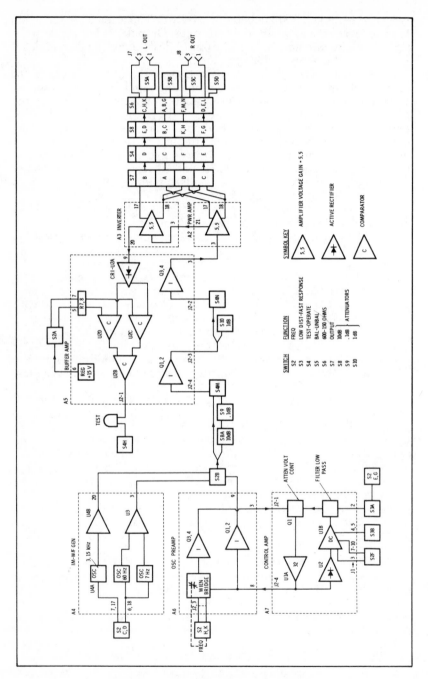

Fig. 12-9. Audio generator block diagram.

has a ±3% full scale accuracy between 20 Hz and 200 kHz. It measures voltage between 1 mV and 100 V rms. Input signals between 0.1V and 80V rms are automatically leveled to the proper reference for distortion measurements. The mode switch has voltmeter, tune, total harmonic distortion, intermodulation distortion, and noise measurement positions.

A functional block diagram of the analyzer is given in Fig. 12-10. In the basic ac voltmeter mode of operation the input signal from either the left or right input connector passes through switch S4 to the A7 voltmeter assembly at the lower right. It is passed to the A7A3 voltmeter buffer for required attenuation and then to the voltmeter amplifier board A7A2. The output is then applied to the meter.

In the noise-measurement mode the same signal path is taken with the exception that the input is bandpass-filtered to remove noises outside the passband 20 Hz to 20 kHz. This is accomplished by high-pass and low-pass filters, U1 on the A7A1 board.

In the measurement of the total harmonic distortion the input signal from the left or right inputs is applied to the A2 leveler circuit at top left. It is suitably attenuated if the signal level is greater than 3 volts rms. The signal is then passed through a current-controlled attenuator which is feedback-controlled to maintain a constant output amplitude from the leveler circuit. This signal is monitored by detector Q1 which operates the HI and LO indicators if there is an improper signal level.

The leveled output of the A2 board is then passed to the null amplifier A6 at the top right. Its responsibility is to suppress the fundamental component of the incoming signal by better than 80 dB. The operation of the analyzer is simplified by the automatic null balancing circuit involving the quadrature detector A4 by analyzing the null amplifier and supplying control signals that maintain proper null tuning. The output of the null amplifier is then applied to the voltmeter assembly A7 for measurement of the remaining harmonic components.

In the measurement of the intermodulation distortion the incoming composite signal of 60 Hz and 7 kHz is also applied to signal leveler A2. This signal is analyzed by the intermodulation demodulator board (A5) at the bottom center. Its responsibility is to remove the 60-Hz component by high-pass filtering. The resultant 7-kHz signal is then evaluated to detect any 60-hertz sidebands introduced by intermodulation. The resultant output signal is then applied to the voltmeter assembly and is read as an intermodulation-distortion percentage.

When making a wow and flutter measurement the appropriate 3.15-kHz signal is applied to a phase-locked loop circuit that is a part of the A5 demodulator board. It detects any frequency variations on the 3.15-kHz signal component. This output is filtered by a 200-Hz low-pass filter and made available at the scope output for analysis. A peak-to-peak rectifier which follows the filter has a specific dynamic response. This output is applied to the meter and can be read on an appropriate scale.

In making a phase comparison of left and right stereo signals applied to the input of the analyzer, the incoming signals are applied directly to the phase and ratio detector module (A3). The two input signals are limited and then compared in phase to produce a dc voltage that is proportional to the phase difference. This signal is applied to the metering circuit. Center scale reading is now 0 degrees. Two operating modes permit either a full-scale ±54-degree or ±180-degree reading scale.

In making a ratio measurement between the two input signals they are again applied to phase/ratio module A3. The L and R signals are peak rectified by linear detectors. They are applied to a circuit which divides the L-channel signal by the R-channel signal level. A dc signal proportional to the ratio of the L and R input amplitudes can then be used to drive the metering circuit.

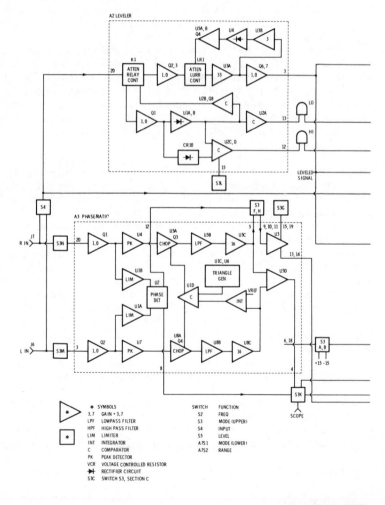

Fig. 12-10. Audio

12-8. FIELD-STRENGTH METER

The *Potomac Instrument* field-strength meter is shown in block diagram form in Fig. 12-11. The am broadcast version operates between 535 and 1605 kHz. Accuracy of calibration is 1%. The field-strength meter can also be used to make signal-ratio measurements.

In making a frequency-intensity measurement the signal is picked up by a loop antenna and applied to a high-quality superheterodyne receiver as shown at the top. The detector output is applied to a calibrated meter shown at bottom center. Detector output is also applied to an audio amplifier and associated speaker or headphone. It can also be applied to a dc amplifier and used to operate a recorder.

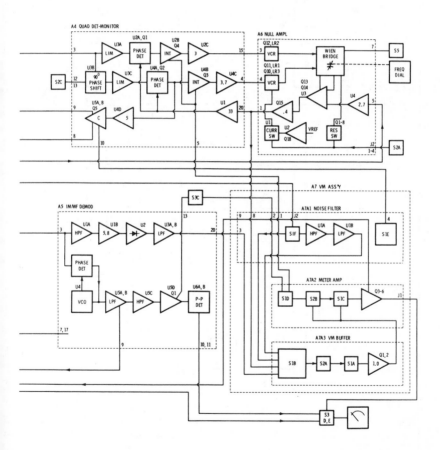

analyzer block diagram.

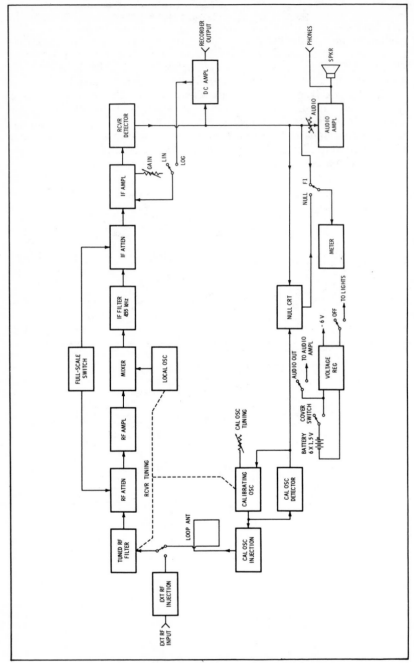

Fig. 12-11. Field-strength meter functional diagram.

The actual meter calibration is set with the output of an accurately calibrated oscillator. In calibrating the meter a precisely determined fraction of the oscillator output voltage is injected into the receiver antenna and is detected by the receiver. At the same time a calibrate detector fed directly by the oscillator output voltage produces a dc voltage for comparison with the receiver detector output. These two components are detected by a null circuit. A meter reading results that drops as the receiver detector voltage approaches the oscillator detector voltage. The reading is minimum when the voltages are equal. Thus the receiver gain value for which the detector outputs are equal is determined by the relation between the rf voltage at the oscillator detector and the rf voltage injected into the antenna circuit. After calibration, the meter can then be used to measure the field intensity of an incoming signal.

CHAPTER 13

Television Broadcasting

Television broadcast stations are more complex than fm and am broadcast stations because of the additional equipment required for video broadcasting. There are two separate signal paths, one from camera to transmitter, and the other from microphone to transmitter. Visual and sound activities must be coordinated. The television transmitter itself is a visual and aural combination that supplies both signals to the antenna.

13-1. GENERAL

Each television broadcast station is assigned a 6-MHz channel. The sound carrier is located at the high-frequency end of the assigned spectrum and is separated from the picture carrier by 4.5 MHz. The sound carrier is frequency-modulated. From microphone to antenna, the sound equipment is comparable to that of an fm broadcast station with the exception that 100-percent modulation constitutes a maximum frequency deviation of ± 25 kHz. Many of the broadcast microphones associated with a television studio are mounted on long booms and are suspended overhead, out of view of the cameras. In some programming, small microphones are hand-held, or hidden on the clothing of the artist. The picture signal information contains both luminance (brightness) and chrominance (hue and saturation) information. The luminance information along with several types of pulses needed to process and synchronize visual information amplitude-modulates the picture carrier. The chrominance information is placed on a subcarrier frequency that is approximately 3.58 MHz above the regular picture carrier frequency. This addition is in the form of double-sideband suppressed-carrier modulation. The subcarrier components also amplitude-modulate the picture carrier frequency. The same antenna radiates both the frequency-modulated sound carrier and the baseband-modulated picture carrier. A device known as a diplexer provides the necessary isolation between sound and picture transmitters.

317

Courtesy RCA

Fig. 13-1. Studio newscasting.

The source of the television picture (video signal) is the camera. The camera contains a lens system and a camera tube that forms a video signal which corresponds to the brightness detail of the image focused on its light-sensitive target. Three separate camera tubes are used to gather the necessary color information. The camera contains other basic circuits which have to do with the amplification and processing of the video signals plus circuits which control the orderly release of this information.

A television studio is a maze of cameras, microphones, cables, lights, and props, as shown in Fig. 13-1. The video signals from the camera and the audio signals from the microphones are supplied to a control room such as the one shown in Fig. 13-2. Separate picture and sound control consoles are integrated as part of the control-room facility. Some of the operations are highly technical and require technical personnel. In addition to the video and audio operators in the control room, there are positions for persons such as directors, producers, and others. There are cameramen, microphone boom operators, and lighting personnel, along with make-up persons and others involved with the artistry of the television program.

Especially in small stations, technicians take on many of the responsibilities of studio and control-room operations. Many of them are licensed and can also operate the television transmitter and its associated equipment.

A high percentage of the broadcast time of a television station is on tape or film (Fig. 13-3). There are numerous studio tape players and

Courtesy RCA

Fig. 13-2. Television control room.

recorders along with television film cameras and slide projectors. The
video and sound information picked up by these devices must also be
channeled into the control room and inserted into the program sequence in a fast, orderly manner.

Lightweight portable television equipment consisting of cameras
and control facilities are essential for making on-the-spot pickups for
taping or direct broadcasting. Quite often a microwave transmitter is
used to transmit the signal to the station for immediate live telecasting.
Electronic newsgathering (ENG) has become an essential part of
newscasting. Complete pickup facilities including cameras and video
tape recorders can be carried by a small van or helicopter. Cameras are
lightweight and can be shoulder supported. Often the live pickup
signal is microwave-relayed to the studio and into the control room.

The control room is an elaborate monitoring and switching center.
Here the various video and sound signal sources—studio, remote, tape
machine, network, projection room, etc., are selected and placed on
the program line to the transmitter. Visual and aural continuity are
handled from here.

Usually the program material is conveyed between studio control and
transmitter over the video cable facilities of the telephone company.
If a transmitter is located on a mountain top or other isolated site, a
studio-transmitter link (stl) conveys the program material over a microwave facility.

Fig. 13-3. Tape and film facilities.

Network programs are carried over microwave links and coaxial-cable systems that operate from coast to coast. Many programs are relayed by satellites. Satellite relaying has been a special boon to world-wide newscasting and live programming from all parts of the world.

The transmitter room houses the combined picture and sound television transmitter along with associated controls and monitoring equipment. A licensed operator must be on duty. Because of the more complex and larger amount of equipment needed at the television transmitter, many tv stations keep more than one operator on continuous duty.

13-2. TELEVISION BROADCAST PRINCIPLES

A thorough discussion of television broadcast theory and equipment is beyond the scope of this handbook. However, the fundamentals of television transmission are presented. This information does cover television transmission principles in the detail needed to help in understanding basic functions necessary for seeking employment in a television broadcast station.

A functional block diagram of a television transmission system is given in Fig. 13-4. Also shown are the basic units of the accompanying sound. The sound transmission will not be elaborated upon because of its similarity to monaural fm broadcasting. Your first introduction to television broadcast techniques will cover the transmission of a *mono-*

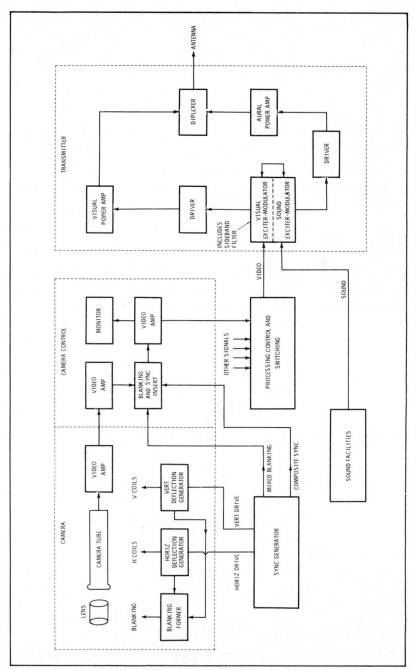

Fig. 13-4. Basic tv transmission system.

chrome (black/white) picture. Although modern broadcast stations transmit color pictures an understanding of the black/white process is a good beginning in gaining an understanding of picture transmission techniques. After the monochrome discussion the added processes required in conveying color information are presented.

The very first step in gaining an understanding of television transmission is to realize that individual television pictures are not sent as an entirety. In modern television broadcasting there are approximately 30 complete pictures sent out each second. However, each of these pictures is broken down into several hundred thousand elements which are sent in a sequential order. The image of a television scene focused on the photosensitive surface of a camera tube is broken up (sampled) by a cathode-ray electron scanning beam, and then reassembled by another scanning beam at the receiver.

The scanning technique is demonstrated in Fig. 13-5A. The camera tube contains a photosensitive area, or target, composed of hundreds of thousands of isolated and light-sensitive elements, on which an optical-lens system focuses the scene into an image. A camera-tube scanning beam moves over this surface, in accordance with a standardized motion, releasing a video signal corresponding to the brightness (luminance) detail of the image. This video signal is released element by element and line by line as the beam moves across the image and down.

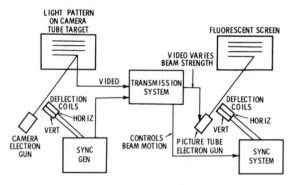

(A) Functional diagram of scanning.

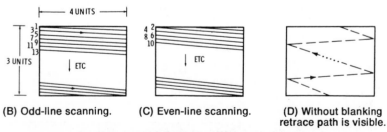

(B) Odd-line scanning.   (C) Even-line scanning.   (D) Without blanking retrace path is visible.

Fig. 13-5. Television scanning at television camera and picture tube.

It is standard to transmit a picture four units wide by three units high —the picture is said to have a 4:3 aspect ratio.

The picture-tube scanning beam in the receiver follows the same motion over the fluorescent screen. As the beam moves across the screen, its electron density is varied by the video signal supplied to the control grid of the picture tube. The fluorescent screen of the picture tube glows in accordance with the strength of the scanning beam striking each individual element. Since the strength of the beam is varied as it scans over the fluorescent surface, the original brightness detail is recovered element by element. In this manner the original transmitted image-brightness pattern is reproduced on the fluorescent screen of the receiver.

It is apparent that if a scene is to be reconstructed exactly, the motions of the picture- and camera-tube scanning beams must be identical—the beams must be synchronized. By so doing, the image will be reconstructed at the picture tube, at the same rate and in the same order that the video information was released from the image focused on the camera tube.

In a television station a sync separator is used to form the pulses that synchronize the motions of the camera- and picture-tube beams. Insofar as the station equipment is concerned, the synchronizing information is sent over a cable directly to the camera circuits that control the motion of the camera-tube scanning beam. Similar pulses are inserted into the television signal that is transmitted. It follows, then, that it is necessary to send not only the video signal from the transmitter to the receiver, but also a group of pulses to synchronize operations at the receiver.

13-3. THE SCANNING TECHNIQUE

It is standard in television broadcasting to transmit thirty complete pictures per second, each picture made up of 525 lines. Thus 15,750 lines (525×30) are transmitted each second. This is referred to as the *line rate* or *horizontal rate* of the television system. However, the 525 lines are not scanned sequentially from the top of the image to the bottom. Rather, there are 262½ lines scanned from top to bottom for a first vertical scan. The scanning action then returns quickly to the top and covers the in-between lines down the screen, as shown in Fig. 13-5. This method of first covering the odd-numbered lines and then returning (retrace) to cover the even-numbered lines is referred to as *interlace scanning*. The *purpose of interlacing* is to reduce *flicker*.

A complete television picture is called a *frame;* it is composed of an odd- and an even-line field. The screen is made to go black during all retraces to prevent spurious bright lines from appearing in the picture. This action is called *blanking*.

The television system used in the USA is referred to as a 525-line and 30-frame system. The field rate is 60 per second; line rate, 15,750 per second. Actually, in modern color television broadcasting, the precise values are 59.94 fields per second and 15,734 lines per second. More on this later.

In a motion-picture theatre, individual scenes are flashed on the screen at the rate of 24 per second. Because of the retentivity of human vision, it is possible to create the illusion of moving pictures. To prevent the screen from flickering, however, each scene is cut on and off twice by the film projector. The more frequent interruption of the motion-picture frames (48 times per second) prevents human vision from observing the light interruption as each new frame is moved into position and the beam is shuttered off for a split second.

If the scanning activities of a television system were shut down to only 30 times per second, there would be a noticeable flicker in the reproduced picture. With the use of interlace and its two shorter vertical-retrace (blanking) intervals for each frame, the brightness is interrupted 60 times per second and flicker is not apparent. The 60-Hz rate of interruption is known as the "field" or "vertical rate" of the television system. It is important to realize, in summary, that 30 complete pictures are sent each second, but that each picture is broken up into two fields.

In the camera circuits a horizontal-deflection waveform causes the electron scanning beam to move from left to right across the sensitive surface, releasing the brightness information along that line. When the scanning beam reaches the right side it is shut off. The retrace period of the horizontal-deflection waveform in the camera now quickly reorients the deflection field from right to left. Hence when the camera-tube beam is turned on again, it starts scanning at the left side of the image.

There is also a vertical-deflection waveform which tends to pull the scanning beam down the image. Consequently when the beam is turned on again at the left side, it will be just slightly below its starting position for the first line described above. Thus, as the scanning activity continues from left to right and back to left at a fast rate, a slower vertical motion of the scanning beam causes a series of lines to be traced from the top of the image to the bottom. Hence the video information is released element by element along each line, and then line by line down the sensitive surface of the camera-tube target.

When the scanning beam reaches the bottom it is turned off. The vertical-deflection field of the camera tube (vertical retrace) is then reoriented as quickly as possible, so that when the scanning beam is turned on again it will appear at the top left of the image, ready to start a new scanning cycle.

The retracing of the field vertically requires a finite amount of time; therefore, during this interval a number of horizontal scanning cycles take place as shown in Fig. 13-5D. However, the scanning beam has been cut off during this time and no horizontal lines are evaluated.

During the motion of the scanning beam, line after line, from top to bottom of the image, the video signal is released. These are referred to as the *active lines* of the television picture. Inasmuch as the horizontal motion during the vertical-retrace interval did not produce any active lines of video, these are called *inactive lines*. In our modern telecasting system there are approximately 525 lines—500 active and approximately 25 inactive lines.

In monochrome telecasting, four basic *rectangular pulses* are conveyed from the sync generator to each camera. There is the *horizontal-sync pulse* (usually called a horizontal-drive pulse in relation to the station equipment), whose purpose is to synchronize the horizontal motion of the scanning beam. A companion *horizontal-blanking pulse* is needed to shut off the scanning beam during the horizontal-retrace interval, to prevent the generation of spurious signals. A *vertical-sync pulse* (vertical-drive pulse) synchronizes the vertical motion of the scanning beam. A companion *vertical-blanking pulse* shuts off the camera-tube beam during vertical-retrace intervals.

Six individual signal components are sent between the transmitter and each receiver. First there is the *video signal,* which conveys the brightness detail of the image. A *horizontal-sync pulse* is sent out to the receiver to time the horizontal motion of the picture-tube scanning beam, synchronizing it with the horizontal motion of the camera-tube scanning beam. A *horizontal blanking pulse* also shuts off the picture-tube scanning beam during horizontal-retrace intervals, to prevent retrace lines on the fluorescent screen. *Vertical-synchronizing pulses* are sent to the receiver to synchronize the vertical motion of the picture-tube scanning beam; a corresponding *vertical-blanking pulse* shuts off the beam for retrace. A sixth signal conveyed between transmitter and receiver is a group of *equalizing pulses.* Their function is to maintain a rigid interlace so that the lines on the receiving picture-tube screen are equally spaced—the even lines exactly midway between the odd lines from top to bottom of the screen.

After signal processing and amplification, *the composite signal* is sent on to a switcher (Fig. 13-4) which acts as a signal source for other camera signals, network lines, remotes, video tape recorders, remote signal sources, etc. The program continuity is controlled from this point and a properly organized and stabilized signal is sent on to the transmitter. Composite television signals can be sent over a coaxial cable or over a microwave studio-to-transmitter link. The accompanying sound must also be conveyed to the aural portion of the television transmitter.

The 6-MHz television channel allocates space for both picture and sound signals. As shown in Fig. 13-6, the picture carrier is positioned 1.25 MHz from the low-frequency end of the assigned television channel. Note that the upper sideband of the video channel is substantially broader than the lower sideband. This technique, called *vestigial-side-band transmission,* permits the sending of a high-definition picture in a 6-MHz channel. Thus video frequency components in excess of 4 MHz can be conveyed in a channel only 6 MHz wide. The required portion of the low-frequency sideband spectra must be removed in the transmitter by a vestigial-sideband filter. Thus low-frequency sidebands that extend more than 1.25 MHz below the picture carrier frequency are not radiated. This filtering activity usually takes place in a low-frequency if range after the modulator. A suitable mixer then steps up the modulated if signal to the transmit frequency. Follow-up linear power amplifiers then build up the signal to the final transmit power level.

The picture and sound signals are now applied to a *diplexer.* This de-

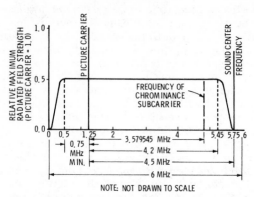

Fig. 13-6. Picture-transmission amplitude characteristics.

vice applies both signals to the antenna system without interaction between transmitters. Thus, both transmitters see a proper load, with sound being kept out of the picture transmitter and video out of the sound transmitter.

13-4. RECEIVER ACTIVITY

At the receiver (Fig. 13-7) a multiplicity of functions are performed on the incoming picture and sound signals. A tuner amplifies and con-

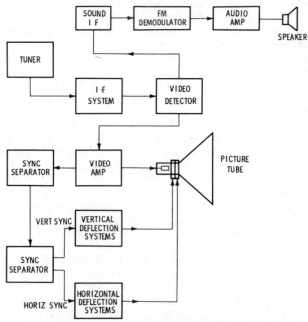

Fig. 13-7. Block diagram of a television receiver.

verts the incoming picture and sound signals to an intermediate frequency in the 40-MHz region. Picture and sound signals are amplified by the if system. A response pattern is shown in Fig. 13-8. Note that the picture if carrier is down approximately to the 50-percent level to compensate for the fact that only a portion of the low-frequency sidebands (vestigial-sideband transmission) was transmitted by the television broadcast station. Thus lows and highs receive the same overall amplification.

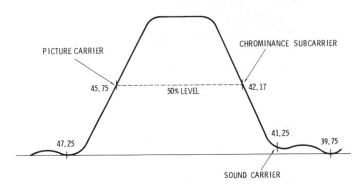

Fig. 13-8. Video if response.

Note also that the frequency separation between the picture and sound carriers is 4.5 MHz (45.75–41.25). Thus at the output of the am detector there is a frequency-deviated 4.5-MHz signal from which the sound information can be recovered. The sound signal is amplified by its own if amplifier and applied to an fm demodulator. Recovered audio is amplified and applied to the speaker.

The composite video signal at the output of the detector takes two paths: one to the video amplifier and picture-tube, and the other to the sync system. A sync-separator circuit removes the combined synchronizing pulses from the composite television signal and segregates them into vertical and horizontal pulses. These pulses are then supplied to the separate horizontal- and vertical-deflection systems of the receiver.

The incoming sync pulses time the horizontal- and vertical-deflection activity. Consequently the waveforms present in the horizontal- and vertical-deflection coils of the picture tube cause the beam motion to follow exactly the scanning activities at the camera tube.

Simultaneously, the video signal which originated at the camera tube is supplied to the control grid of the picture tube. The deflected and modulated picture-tube beam then reconstructs the original image.

A television picture tube (Fig. 13-9) consists of an electron gun and a fluorescent screen that glows in accordance with the number of electrons in the scanning beam from the gun. A focusing system brings the beam to a very fine point at the fluorescent screen. Two deflection-coil systems (horizontal and vertical) are driven by the deflection amplifier

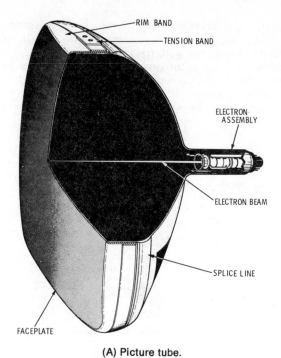

(A) Picture tube.

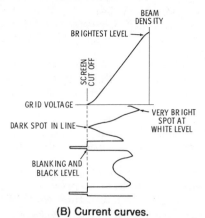

(B) Current curves.

Fig. 13-9. Television picture tube and beam-current curve.

and move the scanning beam from left to right and down the screen in accordance with the previous corresponding beam motion at the camera tube. The beam motion has been synchronized by the arriving sync pulses previously applied to the horizontal- and vertical-deflection systems.

If the scanning beam is of constant strength as it strikes the fluorescent screen, the individual lines that make up the pattern (raster) will be illuminated at uniform intensity by the density and momentum of the electrons hitting the screen. If the scanning beam is modulated so that its density varies, the number of arriving electrons at the screen will change as the beam travels over its established path. Thus the illumination along each line will vary with the changing strength of the beam. The average illumination of the individual lines from top to bottom of the screen will also be a function of the average number of electrons that are contained in the beam throughout the scanning cycle.

The electron-beam current is varied by the video signal supplied to its control grid, as shown in Fig. 13-9B. The signal is applied to the electron gun as a grid-voltage variation. As the scanning beam moves across the fluorescent screen, the individual elements that make up that screen will glow in accordance with the density of the scanning beam at a given instant. Thus the changing video signal on the control grid of the picture tube causes the intensity of the elements along each line to vary, reconstructing the light pattern of the original image line. This restoration occurs for each active line to reproduce the original image completely.

Notice that the blanking pulse (Fig. 13-9B) swings far enough negative on the control grid of the electron gun to reach beam cutoff. This amount of voltage establishes the black, or darkest, spot in the reproduced scene. In fact, the function of the blanking pulses is to shut off the scanning beam during retrace intervals. Likewise the black portions of the scene swing negative to this level to reproduce the black elements that are contained in the scene being televised.

Greater amounts of beam current will flow when the control-grid voltage is made less negative. Consequently, a full range of brightness level is recreated from black, through the gray scale (halftones), to the brightest illumination possible. An extremely bright spot is reproduced when the grid is made the least negative, as indicated by the white spot in Fig. 13-9B. The range of brightness levels between the whitest white and black determines the halftone *contrast* of the reproduced picture. The average illumination of the screen surface is determined by the dc component of the grid bias supplied to the gun, which is adjusted by the brightness control.

13-5. COLOR TELEVISION

An understanding of color transmission requires a knowledge of some of the basic fundamentals of colorimetry. First of all, color is composed of three basic attributes—brightness detail, hue, and saturation. Brightness detail, as its name implies, has to do with the relative brightness among all the elements that make up a scene, regardless of hue and saturation. It is this brightness detail, between white and black over the gray scale, that makes it possible to transmit a black-and-white picture. The black-and-white picture you observe on your monochrome television screen or magazine page is nothing more than a brightness pattern. The breaking up of a scene into many, many elements of differing brightness permits the reconstruction of a scene in detail.

In a color television system it is necessary to convey this brightness detail, just as it is in a monochrome television system. In fact, the brightness detail is conveyed in exactly the same manner as in the monochrome system. By suitable choice of transmission methods this technique permits a color signal also to be reproduced in black and white on the screen of a monochrome receiver.

In transmitting a picture in color, it is also necessary to convey hues and saturation data. Hue is often referred to quite loosely as color, because it represents red, green, yellow, etc. Saturation has to do with how pure a given hue is, and how much it has been desaturated by the presence of white. A pure green is a fully saturated hue, whereas a desaturated green is a pale green because it contains a high percentage of white light. An absolutely pure green is one which contains no white.

The scores of recognizable hues and saturations would at first suggest that it is almost impossible to convey all possible combinations of hue and saturation. If each color had to be transmitted as an entity, color transmission would be extremely difficult—if not impossible. However, human vision is able to interpret bands of colors, and the proper levels of two or more basic colors (primary colors) can be displayed in such a manner that a very useful range of other hues and saturations (secondary colors) can be duplicated. The extremely simplified circle chart of Fig. 13-10 demonstrates this characteristic. In this chart there

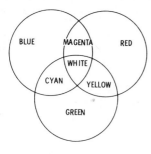

Fig. 13-10. Basic tristimulus color circles.

are the three basic primary colors—red, blue, and green. By mixing equal-intensity levels of red and green, we obtain a yellow; blue and red, a magenta; blue and green, a cyan. Yellow, magenta, and cyan are called secondary colors. The combination of equal intensities of red, blue, and green reproduces white. The use of three primary colors to reproduce an extensive range of hues and saturations is referred to as a *tristimulus* color system or presentation. This tristimulus method of conveying color is used in our color television broadcast system.

A very basic color system, as shown in Fig. 13-11, *would* consist of three camera tubes. A filter, associated with each camera, *would* make certain the camera tube evaluates the color scene with relation to the red, green, and blue ranges. Three signals are formed, one representing the brightness detail in red, the second in blue, and the third in green. Each signal is then conveyed separately from the transmitter to

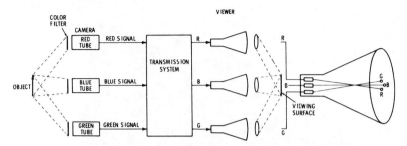

Fig. 13-11. Basic functional diagram of a color-television system.

the receiver. At the receiver the three original color signals *would* be recovered and superimposed on a screen. Inasmuch as all hues and saturations of the original scene have been interpreted in terms of the three primary colors, their superimposition *would* provide a reasonable reproduction of the original color scene.

As shown in Fig. 13-11, the three color images are not exactly superimposed. Rather, each signal excites the proper series of phosphor dots on the picture-tube screen. In this activity the incoming red signal excites only the red dots, the blue signal the blue dots, and the green signal the green dots. Nevertheless the screen is made up of so many hundreds of thousands of dots that, insofar as human vision is concerned, we see them superimposed. Hence we have tristimulus excitation of the eye and are able to perceive a wide range of hues and saturations.

Three separate camera tubes *are* mounted within a color television camera. The camera operates in the manner previously discussed, producing three signals—red, green, and blue. These three signals are processed and used to modulate the picture carrier. At the receiver, the three primary color signals are recovered and presented to their associated guns of the color picture tube (Fig. 13-12). The focusing and deflection system of the color picture tube directs beams to the appropriate color phosphor dots. In this manner the three images are reproduced.

Actually there are three separate close-spaced scanning beams, one for each set of primary color dots. In the front of the screen there is a shadow or aperture mask (Fig. 13-13) with very tiny openings. Alignment of mask, screen and angle of arrival of beams is such that each individual beam strikes only its own corresponding dots. The red beam will only strike the red phosphor dots and not the green and blue ones, and so on.

13-6. THE COLOR TRANSMISSION METHOD

If all three color signals had to be conveyed at full detail on separate carriers, a wide band of frequencies would be needed to transmit a high-resolution color picture. This use of a wide band of frequencies is avoided in modern color telecasting by breaking up the three signals into basic color attributes before transmission.

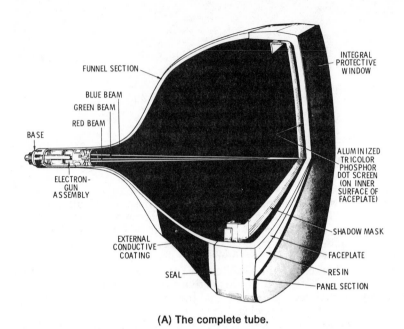

(A) The complete tube.

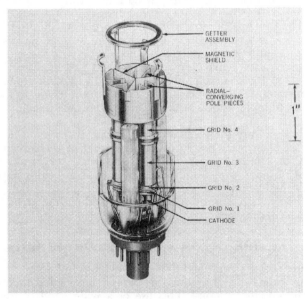

(B) Electron-gun assembly.

Fig. 13-12. A color picture tube.

Fig. 13-13. A portion of the picture-tube screen showing the arrangement of dot trios behind the mask.

As shown in Fig. 13-14, a block diagram of the major units of a color broadcast system, the three signals are broken up by a matrix circuit into brightness details, hue, and saturation. The one signal that conveys the brightness detail is transmitted at full bandwidth. It is this signal component that determines the resolution of the reproduced picture, because definition is related directly to brightness detail whether color or a monochrome picture is being transmitted. In color television broadcasting this is referred to as the *luminance* (Y) signal because it has to do with brightness detail.

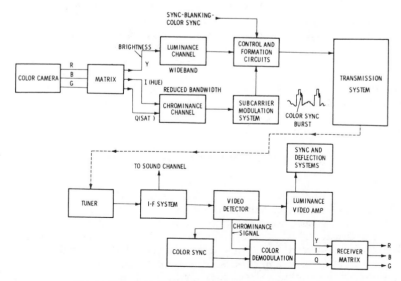

Fig. 13-14. Block diagram of a color-television system.

Hue and saturation are less directly related to detail; consequently, they can be sent between transmitter and receiver with less brightness detail. Therefore, not as wide a frequency response is needed. In fact, the hue and saturation (I and Q signal components) are combined into one signal, called the *chrominance* signal, and used to modulate a sub-carrier frequency much as a second sound signal can be used in a mul-tiplex arrangement to modulate an fm broadcast carrier with two sepa-rate audio signals. In television broadcasting the subcarrier frequency of 3.58 MHz is modulated by the chrominance signal, and the modu-lated subcarrier in turn amplitude-modulates the main video carrier. The frequency position of the chrominance subcarrier can be seen on the transmitted signal and receiver video-if response in Figs. 13-6 and 13-8.

The sync and blanking pulses, and the luminance video signal, mod-ulate the video transmitter carrier in the same manner as in mono-chrome television practice. Hence, in the color transmission a multi-plex system is employed, with brightness detail and synchronizing in-formation being conveyed in the conventional manner, and hue and saturation conveyed by way of subcarrier.

The modulation system is so designed that saturation is determined by the amplitude of the resultant chrominance subcarrier. The hue is present on the subcarrier as a phase-modulated resultant between the I and Q components. In effect, there has been a dual modulation of the subcarrier with saturation and hue data.

It is necessary to synchronize the receiver color circuits with the color activity at the station. Consequently, one additional signal com-ponent must be transmitted—a color sync burst at the 3.58-MHz sub-carrier frequency is placed on the horizontal-blanking pulse. Except for a very slight departure in horizontal and vertical frequencies, the same type of horizontal and vertical sync and blanking and the same equalizing pulses are used in color as in monochrome telecasting.

At the receiver, the color-sync burst is removed and used to synchro-nize the color demodulation activity. Here the hue and saturation com-ponents are recovered and are then broken down into copies of the orig-inal three primary color signals. The red signal is applied to the red gun, the green signal is applied to the green gun, and the blue signal is applied to the blue gun. The color picture is then reproduced on the screen.

13-7. FORMING THE COMPOSITE SIGNAL

The sync generator is the timing center of a television system. Refer back to Fig. 13-4 and Fig. 13-14. Notice the horizontal and vertical drive pulses that are sent to the horizontal- and vertical-deflection sys-tems of the camera. Blanking pulses (mixed horizontal and vertical) are also sent to each camera to shut off the scanning activities during horizontal- and vertical-retrace intervals. The video signals are in-creased in amplitude and processed in such a manner as to make cor-rections for the nonlinear frequency characteristics of camera tube and picture tube. In the case of a color system the individual red, blue, and green primary signals must be matrixed or encoded to produce the required Y, I, and Q luminance and chrominance signals.

To the above described video signal must be added the transmitted blanking and sync pulses. Reference to Fig. 13-4 shows a point of addition to be a blanking and sync insert block which is a part of the camera control unit. In the example of Fig. 13-14 for a color system note that the sync and blanking as well as the color-synchronization information are added in the control and formation circuits.

The addition of horizontal and vertical blanking and sync are demonstrated in the waveforms of Fig. 13-15 and Fig. 13-16. After the ad-

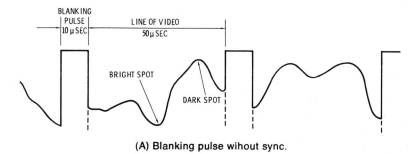

(A) Blanking pulse wihout sync.

(B) Sync pulses added.

Fig. 13-15. Addition of horizontal blanking and sync.

dition of blanking the combination of horizontal blanking and lines of video are shown in Fig. 13-15A. At the end of each video line a horizontal-blanking pulse is inserted. Approximate durations are shown. Each line of video is about 50 microseconds long—the blanking interval, 10 microseconds. Specific durations will be calculated later.

Note on the first line of video that a bright spot and a dark spot are indicated. The nearer the video signal level reaches up to the level of the blanking signal the darker the picture information. A bright spot occurs when there is the greatest separation between the blanking level and the instantaneous video signal level. Of course, in each frame of television picture there are approximately 500 of these active lines of video, which include both the luminance and chrominance video variations.

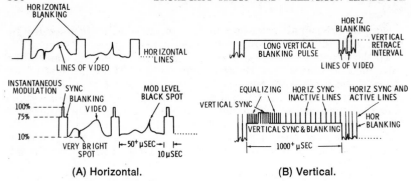

(A) Horizontal.   (B) Vertical.

Fig. 13-16. Addition of blanking and sync to video signals.

The next step in forming the composite television signal is to add the horizontal- and vertical-synchronizing information. The addition of the horizontal-sync pulse and the color-sync burst are shown in Fig. 13-15B. Note that the sync pulses which are shorter than 5 microseconds in duration sit on top of the horizontal-blanking pulses. The sections of the horizontal-blanking pulse ahead of and behind the horizontal-snyc pulse are known as the *front* and *back porches* respectively. Eight cycles of the color-sync bursts of the 3.58-MHz color subcarrier frequency appear on the back porch. Recall that it is this subcarrier burst that synchronizes the chrominance demodulation or decoding activity at the color receiver.

At the conclusion of the last line of each television field a vertical-blanking pulse must be inserted. This is a long-duration pulse of more than 1000 microseconds because of the greater time required to retrace the scanning beams from the bottom of the raster back to the top and begin the tracing of the video lines of the next field. The illustrations of Fig. 13-15A and Fig. 13-16A have shown the addition of the horizontal- and vertical-blanking pulses in the formation of the composite television signal.

Vertical synchronizing information must also be added to the signal as demonstrated in Fig. 13-16B. Actually the vertical synchronization is handled by six individual vertical-sync pulses as shown soon after the start of the vertical-blanking interval in Fig. 13-16B. After the start of the vertical-blanking pulse there are six equalizing pulses followed by the six, longer-duration, vertical-sync pulses. Following the vertical-sync interval there are six more short-duration equalizing pulses.

The vertical-blanking pulse is of long duration and, during this long retrace time, the system must not lose control of horizontal synchronization. Consequently during the remainder of the vertical-blanking pulse, regular horizontal-sync pulses must be added. This considerable interval of time during which the screen is blanked constitutes the so-called inactive lines. As mentioned previously, there are approximately 25 inactive lines that occur during the vertical retrace interval.

For the same reason the vertical sync instead of being a single long-duration pulse is serrated and comprised of six individual pulses. The pulses are so timed that there is no loss of horizontal synchronization.

There are two sets of equalizing pulses which along with the serrated vertical-sync pulses occur at a frequency which is twice the line rate. These equalizing pulses are important in producing an interlaced scanning pattern. On one field the horizontal synchronization is taken care of by the odd-numbered equalizing pulses. At the conclusion of the next field the synchronization is taken over by the even-numbered equalizing pulses. It is this process that maintains tight control of horizontal synchronization and inserts the even-numbered lines at the exact midpoint between the odd-numbered lines of the approximately 500 scanning lines that you can see from top to bottom of your television screen.

In summary, Fig. 13-15B demonstrated the addition of the horizontal-sync pulses and the color-sync bursts. The example of Fig. 13-16B shows the addition of the vertical-sync pulses, the horizontal-sync pulses needed during the vertical retrace interval to prevent loss of horizontal control, and the equalizing pulses needed to establish an interlaced scanning pattern.

The standardized FCC composite television signal is shown more completely in Fig. 13-17. Expanded portions of the line intervals, equalizing and vertical pulses, and horizontal-synchronizing periods are shown in Fig. 13-18. Table 13-1 presents a series of notes that are referenced to the waveforms of Figs. 13-17 and 13-18.

At the top left of Fig. 13-17 are shown the last four video lines of the second field of the last frame of picture. At their conclusion time at the bottom of the picture the vertical blanking begins followed by the first set of equalizing pulses, the vertical-sync pulses, and the last set of equalizing pulses. Next are the horizontal-sync pulses that occur during the remainder of the vertical-blanking interval and constitute inactive lines. The three lines of field shown at the right represent the first three lines (odd-numbered lines) of the first field of the next picture frame. Color-sync bursts are present on the back porches of the horizontal blanking pulses.

Return again to the top left and note the voltage levels. The very sync tip represents maximum voltage and, therefore, 100-percent modulation of the transmitter. The blanking level corresponds to 75% of peak voltage level. The actual reference black level of the transmitted video signal occurs at about 7.5% below the blanking level. The reference white level of the video information occurs at about 12.5% above the zero-carrier level of the transmitted television signal.

Refer now to the ② waveforms of Fig. 13-17. The lines of video represent the last four lines of the first field of the new frame of picture. At the bottom of the picture the vertical blanking begins, followed again by the equalizing, vertical sync, equalizing, and horizontal synchronization during the remaining time of the vertical blanking pulse. The four video lines shown at the right of ② are the first four lines of the second field (even-numbered lines) that now fall interlaced between the lines set down during the first field.

One thing to note about the equalizing pulse intervals for both ① and ② is the timing activity. Note in ① that equalization begins with the first equalizing pulse and synchronization occurs on alternate equalizing and vertical-sync pulses as demonstrated by the time intervals

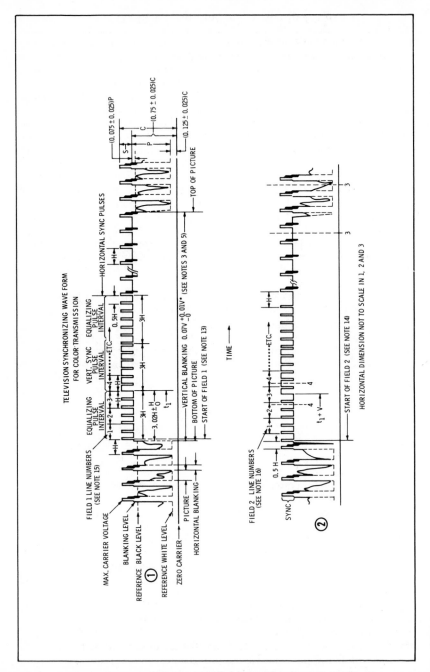

Fig. 13-17. Composite color-television signal for fields 1 and 2.

Table 13-1. Notes for Figs. 13-17 and 13-18

1 H = Time from start of one line to start of next line.

2 V = Time from start of one field to start of next field.

3 Leading and trailing edges of vertical blanking should be complete in less than 0.1H.

4 Leading and trailing slopes of horizontal blanking must be steep enough to preserve minimum and maximum values of (x − y) and (x) under all conditions of picture content.

5 Dimensions marked with asterisk indicate that tolerances given are permitted only for long time variations and not for successive cycles.

6 Equalizing pulse duration must be between 0.45 and 0.55 of the duration of the horizontal synchronizing the pulse duration.

7 Color burst follows each horizontal pulse, but is omitted following the equalizing pulses and during the broad vertical pulses.

8 Color bursts to be omitted during monochrome transmission.

9 The burst frequency shall be 3.579545MHz. The tolerance on the frequency shall be ±10 hertz with a maximum rate of change of frequency not to exceed 1/10 hertz per second.

10 The horizontal scanning frequency shall be 2/455 times the burst frequency.

11 The dimensions specified for the burst determine the times of starting and stopping the burst, but not its phase. The color burst consists of amplitude modulation of a continuous sine wave.

12 Dimension "P" represents the peak excursion of the luminance signal from blanking level, but does not include the chrominance signal. Dimension "S" is the sync amplitude above blanking level. Dimension "C" is the peak carrier amplitude.

13 Start of Field 1 is defined by a whole line between first equalizing pulse and preceding H sync pulses.

14 Start of Field 2 is defined by a half line between first equalizing pulse and preceding H sync pulses.

15 Field 1 line numbers start with first equalizing pulse in Field 1.

16 Field 2 line numbers start with second equalizing pulse in Field 2.

marked ①, ②, ③, and ④. Now drop down to ② drawing. Note that the horizontal synchronization begins with equalizing pulse 2 and follows the alternate equalizing, vertical, and equalizing pulses in this order. Thus synchronization is on alternate pulses that differ from those shown in the drawing of ①. It is this activity that results in an interlaced scanning pattern.

Note in Fig. 13-7 the letters H and V. These two quantities refer to the line and field intervals as indicated by notes 1 and 2 of Table 13-1. Knowing the exact values for H and V, various timing intervals can be calculated for the entire composite color television waveform.

Since there are 15,734 lines transmitted per second, the quantity H refers to 63.56 microseconds.

$$H = \frac{1}{15,734} = 63.56 \times 10^{-6}$$

The term V refers to the field period which is 16,683 microseconds.

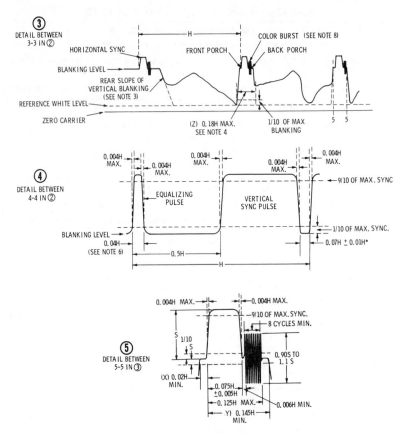

Fig. 13-18. Details for horizontal periods, vertical sync and equalizing, and horizontal sync and blanking.

$$V = \frac{1}{59.94} = 16{,}683 \times 10^{-6}$$

These figures tell us that it requires 63.56 microseconds to transmit one complete line including video and blanking; 16,683 microseconds to transmit one field of the two-field picture frame.

Note from the top right of Fig. 13-17 that the separation between the leading edges of the horizontal sync pulses is H or 63.56 microseconds. The duration of the vertical sync interval and the two equalizing-pulse intervals is 3H. This corresponds to 190.68 (3 × 63.56) microseconds. The separation between each equalizing pulse or serrated vertical-sync pulse is 0.5H which is to be anticipated because these pulses occur at twice the line-frequency rate.

The duration of the vertical-blanking pulse is 0.07V. This corresponds to 1168 (0.07 × 16,683) microseconds. This is the total time allocated for vertical-retrace intervals.

More details about timing can be obtained from the detailed ③, ④, and ⑤ illustrations of Fig. 13-18. In ③, check that for the time of the rear slope of vertical blanking you must refer to note 3 of Table 13-1. This indicates that the leading and trailing edges of vertical blanking should be complete in less than 0.1H. This corresponds to 6.356 (0.1 × 63.56) microseconds.

As shown in ④ and ⑤ the leading and trailing edges of the horizontal-sync pulses, vertical-sync pulses, and equalizing pulses should be 0.004H. This edge time corresponds to 0.254 (0.004 × 63.56) microseconds. Other values that can be found are duration of horizontal-sync pulse, equalizing pulse, vertical-sync pulse, etc.

13-8. COLOR ENCODING AND DECODING

In the previous section the construction of the composite television signal for color transmission was detailed. Section 13-8 emphasizes the complex makeup of the line-by-line video variations that occur between adjacent horizontal blanking pulses of the active lines of transmission. Each line conveys luminance and chrominance information in the form of three signals.

Y — Brightness detail

I — Hue

Q — Saturation

The plot of Fig. 13-19A is known as a *chromaticity graph*. The horseshoe curve referred to as the spectrum locus outlines the region of realizable or possible colors in a tristimulus color presentation. The hue wavelength calibrations are in millimicrons (one micron is one millionth of a meter).

The x and y terms are referred to as *trichromatic coefficients* of the chromaticity diagram. Within the spectrum locus, point W represents a location where trichromatic functions x and y equal 0.3333 and correspond to white light. If we now draw a straight line from W to, let us say, the yellow wavelength on the spectrum locus, we delimit the range of yellows from very light to very deep. At the point where the line crosses the locus we have the saturated yellow, while approaching point W we have increasingly light pastel yellows (or tints) with correspondingly large percentages of white dilution. Thus the diagram indicates both the so-called dominant wavelength of the color as well as the degree of saturation or purity—purity being measured over a range from zero at point W to one (unity) at the spot where the line crosses the spectrum locus.

For example, with the chart it is possible to decide the dominant wavelength and purity for a point such as A. First a line is drawn from W through A until it crosses the spectrum locus at 530 millimicrons. This point of intersection represents the wavelength of green and, inasmuch as point A is half the distance between W and the intersection point, the degree of saturation or purity is represented by the factor 0.5. It is not possible for a color television system to transmit the entire range or gamut of colors enclosed by the spectrum locus. The color television gamut approved by the National Television Standards Committee (NTSC) is enclosed within the triangle shown in Fig. 13-19B. Notice that it is not possible to transmit saturated blues and greens, although it is possible to transmit reasonably saturated colors in the yellow-to-red spectrum range. The NTSC decision was made because of the tendencies to greater saturation in nature over the yellow-to-red range.

The levels of the red, green, and blue primary signals that make up the individual Y, I, and Q signals locate the I and Q color axes on the diagram (Fig. 13-19B). (This signal makeup will be described in more detail later in this section.) Both axes pass through illuminant W at respective angles that are a function of the color difference each signal conveys. The I axis is known as a wideband one and extends from orange on the right side of the triangle to cyan (blue-green) on the left side. The eye is better able to distinguish the color differences along this axis in terms of color detail. Hence the I channel should have

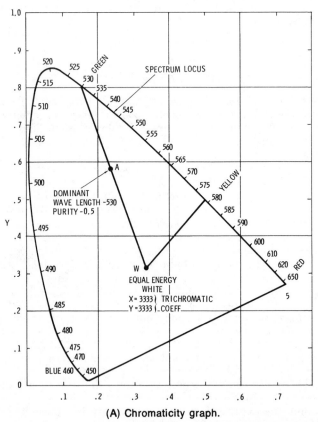

(A) Chromaticity graph.

Fig. 13-19. Chromaticity diagrams

a wider frequency bandwidth. The Q channel can have a narrower bandwidth. Its axis extends from purple to green. Along this axis the eye has very little resolving power in terms of color detail.

13-9. NTSC COLOR TRANSMISSION

The functional plans of the NTSC color system are presented, in conjunction with the block plan of Fig. 13-20. Details of the system and standards will be discussed. At the transmitter a three-color camera arrangement is used to pick up the three basic color primaries. These primaries are applied first to a signal mixer or matrix unit. It might at first be thought proper to transmit all three colors at equal amplitude levels. However, it is a fact that the human eye is more sensitive to some colors than to others, and it has been found advisable to change the relative levels of the colors prior to transmission. These changes permit a method of transmission known as constant luminance, which will be discussed in more detail shortly.

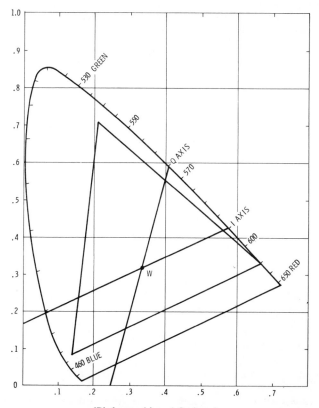

(B) Axes of I and Q signals.

and axes of I and Q signals.

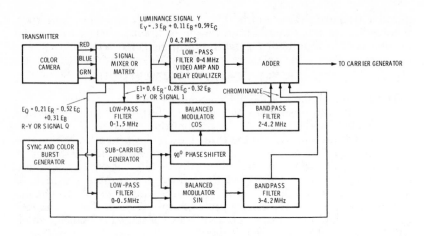

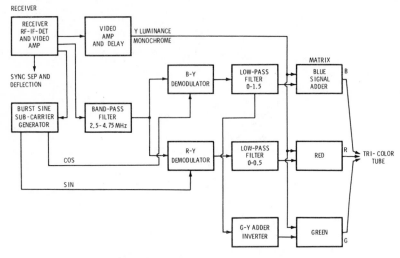

Fig. 13-20. Block plan of NTSC color system.

There are three signals available at the output of the matrix unit. First, there is the luminance signal consisting of red, blue, and green signal components in proper proportions. Used to convey picture detail and brightness variations it is referred to as the Y or luminance component. In addition to information pertaining to luminance, we must transmit the hue and saturation information or chrominance data. The second output from the matrix unit is a B−Y (I signal) component, or blue-chrominance component, which is first applied to a low-pass filter and then to a balanced modulator. A third component, referred to as the R−Y (Q signal), or red-chrominance component, is applied also to a separate low-pass filter and balanced modulator. These two signal components, B−Y and R−Y, contain the chrominance information that is to be transmitted. It must be pointed out here that it appears as though only red and blue chrominance information, in the form of B−Y and R−Y signals, is supplied. However, as will be discussed in greater detail shortly, it is possible to combine the R−Y and B−Y signal components, thereby forming a green resultant signal at the receiver. Thus, in these two signals we have the chrominance information necessary for the three primary colors.

These two chrominance signal components are used in modulating a subcarrier frequency that is located near the high-frequency end of the video spectrum of the NTSC color signal (Fig. 13-21). The frequency chosen has been made high enough to prevent the appearance of any interference pattern on the receiver screen but low enough to permit optimum operation when a picture is to be reproduced in monochrome. The subcarrier frequency (approximately 3.58 MHz) and its sidebands occupy a span of frequencies between 2 and 4+ MHz above that of the picture carrier. The chrominance information in this span of frequencies is interspersed with the luminance information in a frequency interlace form.

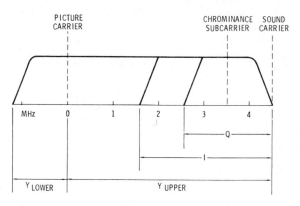

Fig. 13-21. Distribution of signal components for color transmission.

The simultaneous pair of chrominance components amplitude-modulate the sidebands of a pair of suppressed subcarriers in quadrature, which have a common frequency near 3.58 MHz (actually 3.579545 MHz). In modulating one of the subcarrier sine waves the I component has a bandwidth of approximately 1.5 MHz, and its energy is concentrated on the low-sideband side of the subcarrier signal. The Q chrominance signal modulates the second subcarrier sine wave (90 degrees related to the first) but has a more limited bandwidth, approximately .5 MHz, and forms a double-sideband signal. In this double sine-wave modulation system, the color saturation is determined by the amplitude of the modulation and the hue by the phase relationship between the subcarrier sidebands. As modulation takes place the actual subcarrier is suppressed and is not transmitted. The subcarrier is again inserted by a proper sine-wave generator at the receiver.

Thus, in the transmitter section of the block diagram (Fig. 13-20), we notice the I component is first applied to a low-pass filter (upper limit of 1.5 MHz), then to a balanced modulator, and finally to the bandpass filter which allows only the sideband components between 2 and 4 MHz to reach the output. The Q component is applied to a second low-pass filter with an upper limit of only .5 MHz and then to a balanced modulator and bandpass filter output circuit. Associated with the modulaton section is a subcarrier generator whose timing is under the control of the sync generator of the station. It forms the subcarrier frequency that is modulated by the Q component. This subcarrier frequency is also passed through a 90-degree phase shifter to the balanced modulator at which it is modulated by the I chrominance signal. The luminance and chrominance signals are combined in an adder or mixer stage. At this mixer system, the composite sync waveform is also introduced. The remainder of the transmission process continues as per conventional techniques except for the closer tolerances in regard to bandwidth, phase response, and other performance criteria.

The color signal is also received as per conventional practice which uses the superheterodyne principle, employing tuner, if amplifier, video detector, and video amplifier. The luminance, or Y-signal, component is applied to a video amplifier, which has delay characteristics suitable for timing the luminance signal properly with respect to the two chrominance signals and also for adjusting the time delay of the low- and high-frequency components of the signal properly with respect to each other.

The chrominance signal components are applied through a suitable bandpass filter to the I and Q demodulators. In the demodulators the chrominance information is arranged in proper order for release and is demodulated under control of an inserted subcarrier sine wave. This sine-wave burst which rides on the back porch of the received horizontal-sync pulses synchronizes the regeneration of the chrominance subcarrier by the subcarrier generator (Fig. 13-20). Two 90-degree related sine waves are generated and demodulate the I and Q chrominance signals. The output of each demodulator is applied through a low-pass filter to a signal adding stage (Fig. 13-20). The outputs of the two filters are also applied to a G−Y adder and phase-inverter, which form the G−Y signal data from the B−Y and R−Y components. Into each of three separate stages (one for each primary color) the luminance or Y signal is introduced. As a result, the adder output circuit contains the same three individual primary colors which were originally picked up at the color camera.

13-10. CONSTANT LUMINANCE

Let us now consider in more detail some of the individual functions and characteristics of the NTSC color system. In constant-luminance transmission the color signals control the chromaticity of the reproduced image but do not influence its luminance, which is controlled only by the Y signal. The application of the theory of constant luminance has done much to reduce flicker and the effect of noise and interference on the quality of the color picture or monochrome version of the color picture. This method was adopted because the influence of crosstalk and interference is more apparent to the eye when it affects the brightness or luminance of the color picture and is less apparent when it alters the hue of the color picture. By proper choice of relative red, blue, and green signal levels, the luminance factor can be held constant in the chrominance channels.

In a symmetrical chrominance color system, there are equal levels of red, blue, and green primaries that make up the luminance signal. Likewise, the response of the chrominance channels would be symmetrical with respect to each of the primary colors. Thus the three primary color signals (spaced at 120-degree intervals) have equal susceptibility to noises and interference entering the chrominance channels. Inasmuch as the channels are equal in response and 120 degrees apart, the presence of noise creates an equal disturbance in each primary color channel (Fig. 13-22A). The symmetrical chrominance vector indicates that noise would affect each primary color signal equally in terms of voltage disturbance, and it would at first seem possible to have a net interference cancellation at the fluorescent screen of the color picture tube. However, the response of the human eye is not linear in terms of the brightness of the three primary colors. Rather, visual sensation is illustrated in vector B (the eye is twice as sensitive

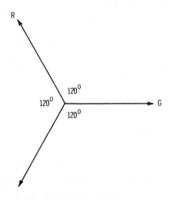

(A) Symmetrical chrominance signal.

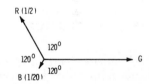

(B) Eye sensation with symmetrical chrominance.

(C) NTSC plan for chrominance signals.

Fig. 13-22. Constant luminance concept.

to green as to red and approximately 20 times more sensitive to green than to blue). Accordingly, in terms of net visual sensation, the symmetrical chrominance signal does create an apparent noise pattern on the color screen because visual sensation responds differently to equal noise-voltage changes in each of the primary colors.

In the NTSC color system (Fig. 13-22C) the type of arrangement of the relative levels of the three primary color signals produces equal visual sensation, rather than equal voltage variations at the output of the chrominance channel. Therefore, in the chrominance channel there is a higher amplification in the red channel than in the green and a still higher sensitivity in the blue than in the green. Consequently, the presence of noise in the chrominance channel creates a greater voltage change in blue than in green. However, when this differential is applied to the color tube and then viewed by human eyes, no brightness change will be observed—the change, in terms of visual perception, having been equalized. Thus differing degrees of noise variations in the chrominance channel will reproduce as equal brightness changes in terms of visual sensation, and produce a net cancellation of the disturbance. Noise in the chrominance channel will not be apparent because of the constant luminance response to noise variations. Instead, noise components in the chrominance channel will cause changes in hue and saturation, which are far less noticeable in terms of visual sensation, producing a perceived brightness change of zero.

Equal brightness response by the chrominance signals is obtained not only by proper relative sensitivity to the three basic colors but also by proper choice of angles. One can control net brightness by means of the timing of signal application as well as the strength of the applied signal. Thus perception of equal brightness can be effected without making the relative voltage ratios among the various primary colors excessive.

13-11. FORMATION OF NTSC CONSTANT-LUMINANCE SIGNAL

The luminance portion of the NTSC color signal contains proportions of signal from the red-, green-, and blue-sensitive cameras required to form a signal that is representative of the brightness variations of the transmitted scene. These proportions are also chosen to correspond to the spectral-brightness characteristics of the eye in order that the monochrome presentation of the scene will have a true gray or neutral scale. The combination of color signals most representative of luminance as a function of visual sensation, color sensitivity of the television system, and phosphor dot response is as follows:

$$E_Y \text{ or } Y = 0.30E_R + 0.59E_G + 0.11E_B$$

The color signal is developed with the use of three separate camera tubes, special color filters, and mirrors (Fig. 13-23). A single-lens system supplies the color information to two special dichroic mirrors. These dichroic mirrors allow the passage of green light but reflect red and blue. The reflected blue information passes through a suitable filter

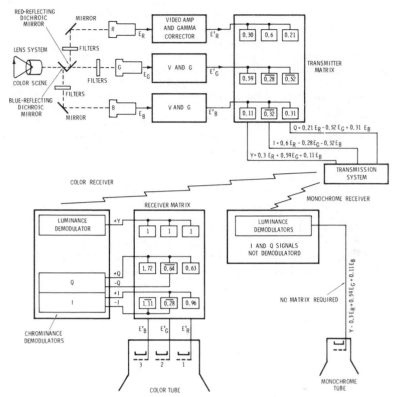

Fig. 13-23. Matrixing of Y, I, and Q signals.

arrangement to a conventional mirror that reflects the blue information into the so-called blue camera tube (a conventional monochrome camera tube that is responding to the luminance information of the blue light). The red information is reflected from a red dichroic mirror to a reflecting mirror and thence into the red camera tube. The green information passes through the red and blue dichroic mirrors directly to the green camera tube.

The signal voltage output of each camera is approximately linear with respect to the luminance information presented to its photosensitive circuit. However, the television system and, in particular, the color picture tube have a nonlinear characteristic in terms of brightness information. Thus it is necessary to alter or predistort the color signal at the output of the camera tube to permit an overall linear response for the color television system. The picture tube has an approximate square-law response to brightness, and consequently an inverse power law is used in the amplifiers that follow the camera tube to obtain an overall linear brightness response. This is referred to as *gamma correction* and occurs before the signal is applied to the matrix unit for formation into a constant-luminance construction.

One of the functions of the matrix unit is to combine the three color signals in the ratios of 59 percent green, 30 percent red, and 11 percent blue, thus producing the constant luminance signal indicated by the previous formula. Inasmuch as this signal represents luminance and not chrominance information, it is actually a monochrome signal and can be applied without any change directly to the grid of a monochrome picture tube. This is the compatibility feature that permits a color picture to be reproduced in monochrome on the screen of a conventional black-and-white picture tube. Furthermore, the signal percentages contributed by the primary colors develop proper signal voltage variations at the grid of the monochrome picture tube. These variations produce brightness differences on the screen which correspond to the special brightness characteristic of the eye, reproducing a true, gray-scale, or neutral, image of the original color scene.

The chrominance information is contained in the two color-difference signals or so-called I and Q signals. The relative levels of the primary color signals in the I and Q chrominance components are determined by the necessity of retaining a constant-luminance signal and the proper location of the I and Q color axes in the color gamut of the system. The I and Q voltages can be represented as color-difference signals or in terms of their relationship with respect to the primary color voltages from the camera as follows:

$$E_Q \text{ or } Q = 0.41(E_B - E_Y) + 0.48(E_B - E_Y)$$
$$= 0.21E_R - 0.52E_G + 0.31E_B$$
$$E_I \text{ or } I = -0.27(E_B - E_Y) + 0.74(E_R - E_Y)$$
$$I = 0.60E_R - 0.28E_G - 0.32E_B$$

The three basic equations are:

$$Y = 0.30E_R + 0.59E_G + 0.11E_B$$
$$Q = 0.21E_R - 0.52E_G + 0.31E_B$$
$$I = 0.6E_R - 0.28E_G - 0.32E_B$$

If the camera output is producing equal voltages of each color, as it would in the transmission of white, the substitution of one (1) in each equal would produce a luminance summation of one, while the summation of the two chrominance voltages would equal zero:

$$Y = 0.30E_R + 0.59E_G + 0.11E_B$$
$$Y = 0.30 + 0.59 + 0.11 = 1$$
$$Q = 0.21E_R - 0.52E_G + 0.31E_B$$
$$Q = 0.21 - 0.52 + 0.31 = 0$$
$$I = 0.6E_R - 0.28E_G - 0.32E_B$$
$$I = 0.6 - 0.28 - 0.32 = 0$$

when,

$$E_R = E_G = E_B = 1$$

If we are to transmit a yellow, the green and red voltages would be represented by one; the blue voltage would be zero because equal levels of red and green are required to transmit a yellow. The luminance formula would have a sum of 0.89 while the I and Q signals would be 0.32 and −0.31 respectively:

$$Y = 0.30E_R + 0.59E_G + 0.11E_B$$
$$Y = 0.30 + 0.59 + 0 = 0.89$$
$$Q = 0.21E_R - 0.52E_G + 0.31E_B$$
$$Q = 0.21 - 0.52 + 0 = -0.31$$
$$I = 0.6E_R - 0.28E_G - 0.32E_B$$
$$I = 0.6 - 0.28 - 0 = 0.32$$

when,

$$E_R = E_G = 1$$

and,

$$E_B = 0$$

It is the function of the transmitting matrix to form the three NTSC color signals from the R, G, and B signals from the camera.

If only monochrome pictures were to be observed on the color television screen, the luminance signal itself would provide all the information required. However, in the presentation of the color picture the luminance and chrominance signals combine—after the chrominance signals have been passed through the proper matrixing unit, whose function is to restore the color signal to the same respective blue, green, and red primary voltage levels that existed at the output of the gamma corrector at the camera. The output of the matrix unit is in the form of color-difference signals that, when combined with the luminance signal, produce the original primary-color signal voltage levels.

When a gray or neutral tone is to be conveyed over the color system, the equal primary voltage levels at the camera produce the constant luminance Y signal as well as the chrominance I and Q components. However, because of the standards chosen in the formulation of the chrominance signals, the outputs of the chrominance channels reduce to zero for neutral colors, and only a monochrome presentation appears on the color-tube screen (equal excitation of the phosphor dots). Likewise, if a monochrome presentation of a color signal is to be made on a color picture-tube screen, it can be produced by turning off the chrominance signals and allowing the luminance signal to provide equal brightness excitation of the phosphor dots.

13-12. SUBCARRIER CHROMINANCE-MODULATION SYSTEM

In the NTSC-approved color system the chrominance information is present on a subcarrier frequency, the phase of which determines the hue of a color while the amplitude determines the color purity or saturation. The choice of the chrominance subcarrier frequency is important.

1. The chrominance subcarrier must be chosen to be an odd harmonic of one-half the line rate to obtain proper "frequency interleaving" and prevent crosstalk between chrominance and luminance channels. It is possible, because of the spectrum distribution of a typical television signal, to position within the video spectrum a subcarrier of chrominance information without interference arising between the two signal groups. Spectrum analysis of a typical video signal shows that the energy and information in that signal are concentrated at frequencies which are whole harmonics of the line rate. Consequently, the video information in the television signal is grouped at harmonics of the line rate throughout the entire video spectrum. In between these harmonics, all through the video spectrum there is no useful signal information. Thus it is conceivable that, with the proper location of a subcarrier, additional information can be conveyed within the same frequency spectrum. Accordingly, a subcarrier frequency which is an odd harmonic of one-half the line rate (always located halfway between two adjacent line-rate harmonics in the video spectrum) is chosen. If this subcarrier is now modulated with video information, its own sidebands will position or "interleave" themselves between the line-rate harmonics of the initial information (Fig. 13-24) and thereby fill in the gaps with useful picture information whose transmission will then require no increase of the necessary bandwidth. This process is also referred to as *frequency interlacing*. In summary the use of a more restricted bandwidth for the transmission of the chrominance information and choice of a proper subcarrier frequency permit not only the transmission of a color picture within a 6-MHz channel but the same quality of picture resolution possible in a standard monochrome transmission. The chrominance information is so positioned that it does not interfere with the normal brightness and luminance data which carry picture detail and resolution.

The insertion of chrominance information at odd harmonics of one-half the line rate (Fig. 13-24) also prevents the appearance of a dot pattern, which can be caused by interaction between the chrominance and luminance signals. Such a disturbance would make itself apparent as a dot pattern on a monochrome rendition of the color signal. Although the crosstalk does exist it is cancelled by the frequency interlace action that results from choice of a subcarrier frequency that is an odd harmonic of one-half the line rate.

The luminance information (picture detail) occurs at integral harmonics of the line rate, and consequently, if information exists at this frequency rate (Fig. 13-25) there would always be a number of full cycles existing during a single-line interval. For example, if the video information along line number 25 were bunched at the third harmonic of the line rate, there would be

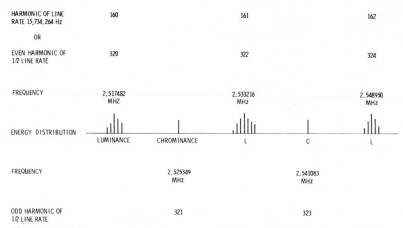

Fig. 13-24. Sideband components over a small section of the video spectrum.

three complete cycles of this information occurring during the line time. Exactly one frame later, or at line 550 (line 25 of next frame), the same three cycles would exist and reinforce one another. Now, if we had chrominance information that existed on a frequency five times the half-line frequency (chrominance information occurs at odd harmonics of one-half the line rate), there would be 2.5 cycles of information included in the line. Exactly 525 lines later the same 2.5 cycles would occur, but then they would be opposite in polarity. A possible brightness variation along the line caused by the chrominance signal is effectively cancelled and dot structure is far less apparent. Pattern is not re-

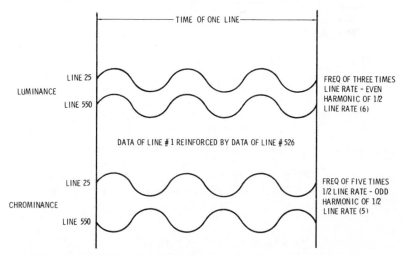

Fig. 13-25. Frequency-interlace cancellation of chrominance components in the luminance channel.

moved completely in dark areas because of the cutoff characteristic of picture tubes. However, dot structure is not discernible
at normal viewing distance.

2. A subcarrier frequency must be chosen such as will minimize interference between the two chrominance components. The proper
choice of subcarrier frequency, use of a narrowband axis and a
wide-band axis, proper filters, and use of one vestigial-sideband
chrominance channel minimize the possibility of crosstalk between
chrominance components. Over the frequency range of ± 0.6 MHz,
which corresponds to the symmetrical double-sideband range of
the Q signal, no crosstalk can enter into the I channel, provided
that suitable filters are present in the Q channel to prevent any
sideband components higher than 0.6 MHz. The I signal channel
also has symmetrical sidebands over the same frequency range,
and therefore, because of the quadrature-phase relationship of
the two subcarrier sine waves, there is no crosstalk into the Q
channel. However, over the range from 0.6 MHz to 2 MHz the
I channel incorporates vestigial-sideband transmission, and there
is a possibility of crosstalk. Again, crosstalk between I and Q
channels is minimized even in this range because of the special
filtering circuit in the Q channel that rejects frequencies above
0.6 MHz which would be within the range of possible interference from the I channel.

3. The subcarrier frequency is positioned at the high end of the
video spectrum and thereby minimizes interference with the luminance components because any pattern that might exist from interference will then be as fine as possible. Interference will also
be minimized by the limited attenuation in the receiver at the
high end of the video passband. The subcarrier, however, must
be low enough to permit the transmission of the upper sidebands
of the subcarrier chrominance signals that convey some color
detail.

4. The subcarrier frequency must be spaced properly with respect
to the sound-carrier frequency, because insufficient attenuation of
the 4.5-MHz sound carrier in a receiver can sometimes cause a
beat between the sound carrier and chrominance subcarrier.
Again, the principle of frequency interleaving minimizes this disturbance. It is necessary to choose a possible interference frequency that occurs at an odd multiple of one-half the line rate.

In the NTSC choice of carrier frequencies the separation between
picture and sound carriers is 4.5 MHz. However, this picture-carrier
minus sound-carrier difference frequency was made to be the 286th
harmonic of the line rate. Thus the horizontal frequency becomes:

$$\text{line frequency} = \frac{4.5 \times 10^6 \text{ Hz}}{286} = 15,734.26 \text{ Hz}$$

Consequently, the field frequency, instead of being 60 Hz, becomes:

$$\text{field frequency} = \frac{15,734.26}{262.5} = 59.94 \text{ Hz}$$

The subcarrier frequency for the chrominance information must, of course, be an odd harmonic of one-half the line rate. In the NTSC standards the harmonic chosen was the 455th, which produces a color subcarrier frequency of:

$$\text{subcarrier frequency} = 455 \times \frac{15{,}734.26}{2} = 3.579545 \text{ MHz}$$

Now if we subtract this subcarrier frequency from the 4.5-MHz sound-carrier frequency, the resultant beat-interference frequency will be the 117th harmonic of one-half the line rate:

$$4.5 \text{ MHz} - 3.579545 \text{ MHz} = 0.920455 \text{ MHz}$$

or,

$$\frac{920455}{.5 \times 15{,}734.26} = 117\text{th harmonic}$$

Therefore, frequency interleaving will exist, and the disturbance will be less apparent.

A functional block diagram of the chrominance modulation system (Fig. 13-26) demonstrates the basic circuits required in the transmission and synchronization of the chrominance channels. At the transmitter the I and Q chrominance signals from the matrix unit are applied to the balanced I and Q modulators. It is necessary to introduce into the modulation system a subcarrier sine wave. This subcarrier sine wave—under control of the sync generator—forms the modulated subcarrier frequency. It is applied through an amplifier and a phase-shifting circuit to ensure a 90-degree relationship between the I and Q subcarriers. The output of each modulator is simply the sideband components of modulation that result from the presence of the subcarrier sine-wave frequency and modulation. The video modulation itself and the actual subcarrier frequency are suppressed and do not exist at the modulator output. The amplitude of the output of each modulator is a function of the amplitude of the chrominance video information applied as modulation.

The two outputs of the I and Q modulators combine in a succeeding bandpass amplifier. The resultant chrominance signal has a phase determined by the relative amplitude and polarity of the two subcarrier frequencies that form the signal. The phase angle, which can exist anywhere between zero and 360 degrees, determines the hue of the color information. The amplitude of the resultant chrominance signal is determined by the amplitudes of the two subcarrier components that form the resultant, individual amplitudes which were determined by the original video I and Q modulation. The amplitude of this resultant chrominance signal determines the purity or saturation of the color information.

To demodulate the chrominance information accurately it is also necessary to transmit a synchronizing signal that will permit the proper timing of a subcarrier frequency generator at the receiver. The receiver subcarrier generator forms a subcarrier signal which substitutes for the

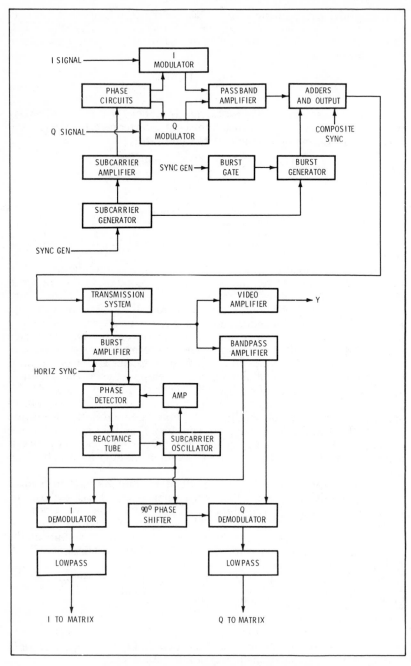

Fig. 13-26. Chrominance modulation system.

suppressed carrier at the transmitter. The suppression of the subcarrier is necessary in the formation of the sideband components at the transmitter because of the eventual use of the sidebands in producing a phase-modulated resultant.

The subcarrier sine wave, through the action of a burst gate, is added to the back porch of the horizontal sync information. The burst gate permits the addition of the subcarrier sine wave at proper intervals which enables the sine wave to ride in correct position on the horizontal-sync back porch. At the receiver, the subcarrier burst on the horizontal sync back porch is keyed off by a pulse (from the horizontal-deflection circuits) and, after amplification, is applied to a phase detector. The receiver contains a subcarrier sine-wave generator that, in conjunction with a phase detector and reactance tube, evaluates the incoming sine-wave burst in order to form a subcarrier frequency of proper phase to permit its reinsertion as the subcarrier of the chrominance information.

The I and Q resultant chrominance signals are applied through a bandpass amplifier to the I and Q demodulators at the receiver. To these same demodulators we now apply the locally generated subcarrier (the subcarrier insertion for the Q demodulator must be shifted 90 degrees in phase). The demodulators at the receiver are often referred to as *product demodulators* or *synchronous detectors*. The term *synchronous detection* is used because proper operation requires insertion of a locally generated subcarrier that has previously been synchronized by information from the transmitter.

In the demodulator the combined I and Q signals are compared with the injected subcarriers and produce difference-frequency signals in the output, the phase and amplitude of which are determined by the phase relationship between the subcarrier sine wave and the individual I and Q subcarrier components (the Q demodulator subcarrier sine wave has been shifted 90 degrees with respect to the I demodulator subcarrier). The demodulator output contains the original I and Q video information. A low-pass filter output circuit ensures the suppression of the higher order of sideband components of video information, as well as of signal components in the subcarrier frequency range. The I and Q signals at the output of the low-pass filters pass into the matrixing circuit.

13-13. TELEVISION CAMERAS

The camera tube converts the image focused on its photosensitive screen to a sequential signal variation (video signal) that corresponds to the brightness pattern of the image. Modern television cameras for studio, remote, or film telecasting use the vidicon, or variation thereof (Fig. 13-27). It is a small camera tube, 1 inch in diameter and 6 inches in length, or even smaller. The ⅔-inch diameter camera has become increasingly popular. The vidicon is capable of generating a video signal of good resolution and stability at low ambient light levels. It is a very sensitive camera tube, consisting of an electron gun, deflection and focusing system, and image section.

In the basic vidicon the image section is a photoconductive layer and a signal plate. The image of the scene is focused through a lens system onto the photocathode surface. The presence of light energy determines the degree of conductivity through to the signal plate for the hundreds of thousands of individual elements that comprise its surface. A bright spot establishes a higher conductivity than a dark spot. Thus each signal plate element is charged in proportion to its related light intensity.

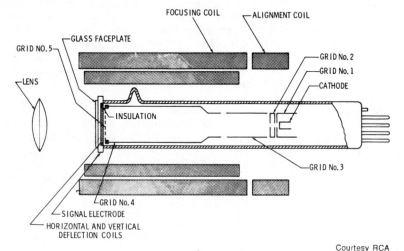

Courtesy RCA

Fig. 13-27. A vidicon camera tube.

A scanning beam, under control of a deflection system, is brought to focus at the charged signal plate. The scanning beam deposits electrons on that surface in accordance with the charge pattern. As each element is restored to equilibrium during the scanning process, a sequential signal flows from the signal plate, via the signal electrode into the output circuit. A bright element causes high conductivity. Hence, the presence of the scanning beam over the element causes a great many electrons to be deposited, and a strong output current flows. For darker spots there is a lower conductivity and a lesser output current. As the scanning beam moves across the elements, the changing signal produced in the output represents the light pattern of the image.

A modification of the basic vidicon and used extensively for color telecasting is the plumbicon shown in Fig. 13-28. The major difference between this tube and the basic vidicon is the photosensitive layer (Fig. 13-29). The photosensitive layer is composed of lead-oxide and has properties that are different from the photoconductive layer of the vidicon. The lead-oxide layer is part of a semiconductor pin junction diode. This has been reverse-biased by a target voltage of approximately 40 volts.

The pin diode consists of heavily doped p and n end materials separated by an intrinsic region. The charge carriers in this latter region

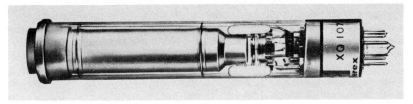

Courtesy Amperex

Fig. 13-28. Plumbicon camera tube.

are not the result of impurity atoms but a function of the material itself.

When light strikes the photoconductor, electron-hole pairs are generated within the intrinsic region and move toward the respective n and p ends. This results in the photoconductor being partly discharged with the pattern of positive charges being a function of the light pattern focused onto the area. Note that a positive charge pattern appears on the scanning-beam side. As it is scanned, the beam deposits enough electrons to replenish the charge loss due to the photocurrent.

The video signal is the result of the current variation flowing within the series circuit consisting of the pin junction layer, scanning beam and target voltage supply. In effect, the photoconductor layer is discharged by the photocurrent and recharged by the beam, resulting in an equilibrium potential close to the cathode potential. Any change in the photocurrent results in a change of the equilibrium potential.

The characteristics of the lead-oxide photosensitive layer provide a low dark current, unity gamma, a high sensitivity, and a favorable lag performance. As a result an accurate black level and a lack of black shading results. Sensitivity is improved and a near unity gamma obtained. There is some reduction in sensitivity to red radiant flux and some loss of resolution in this region. Red resolution can be improved

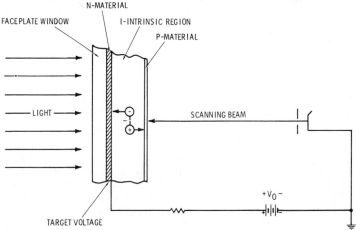

Fig. 13-29. Basic plumbicon construction.

by using a thinner photoconductor layer with some sacrifice in sensitivity. Lag refers to the drop in the output current with a change in the illumination from light to dark. This lag is less for the lead-oxide photosensitive surface.

A disadvantage of the unity gamma is its difficulty to respond to a wide range of light levels. Because of its high sensitivity some means must be included to control signal current at a very high brightness level. The resolution is lower than that obtainable with high-resolution vidicons.

An example of modern RCA cameras using a plumbicon 30-millimeter camera tube is shown in Fig. 13-30. Mounted in front of each camera is a zoom lens. These are followed by the mirrors and reflectors that focus the image on the lead-oxide photosensitive surfaces of the three camera tubes. There are no technical controls at the camera and the operator is able to concentrate on picture composition and artistry. Red, blue, and green video are sent separately to the processor (Fig. 13-31).

The camera processor unit corresponds to the functions included in a camera control unit except it also is free of operational controls. It serves as the interface unit between the camera and the external system. Video signal processing is done here and the unit includes the video processor, encoder, sync generator, and system power supply. Auto-

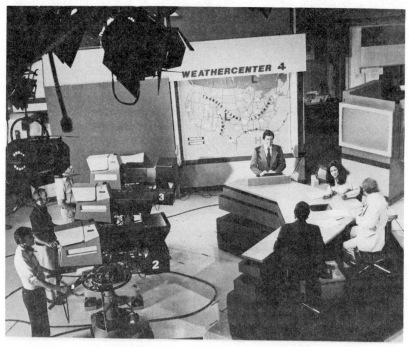

Courtesy RCA

Fig. 13-30. Color cameras picking up a newscast.

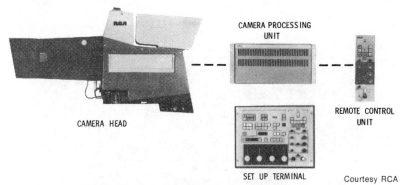

Fig. 13-31. Color camera and associated units.

matic compensation for high-frequency loss in the camera cable is taken care of automatically. The functions of scores of potentiometers employed in older cameras are now handled by solid-state digital memories. The rear of the unit is a centralized junction panel for interconnecting the cables for a camera chain. The actual camera processing unit can be mounted at any convenient location in the station. In a camera chain, one sync generator takes over as a master and locks the other sync generators in synchronism with it.

Operator control is provided by a small compact remote-control unit (Fig. 13-31). Up to four of these small remote-control units may be mounted side by side in a frame which can be fitted into either a console housing or rack. The four cameras can be controlled by an operator from this small console. A joystick on the remote panel permits control of iris and black level. In fact, automatic or manual adjustment of iris, white balance, and black balance is possible. There are individual controls for the three channels as well as a master gain control that operates simultaneously on all three color channels. The remote-control unit can operate as far as 1000 feet from the camera processing unit.

The setup terminal, which is not used in normal operation, functions as a setup technical control center. It houses all the control adjustments related to the camera and the camera processing unit. A single setup terminal can provide central control for as many as twelve individual cameras. As shown in Fig. 13-32 the setup terminal not only includes the various controls but the required monitors such as waveform monitor, vector scope and picture monitor. In a typical setup any one of six camera systems can be switched in at the touch of a button. The advantage of this arrangement is that one setup terminal can serve a number of cameras.

An example of an ENG camera is given in Fig. 13-33. This is a shoulder-mount, self-contained camera, and weighs 14.8 pounds. The camera mounts all the required circuits including encoder and sync generator.

Accessory units are available if the camera is to be remotely controlled in a field production. In fact, the remote-control point can be

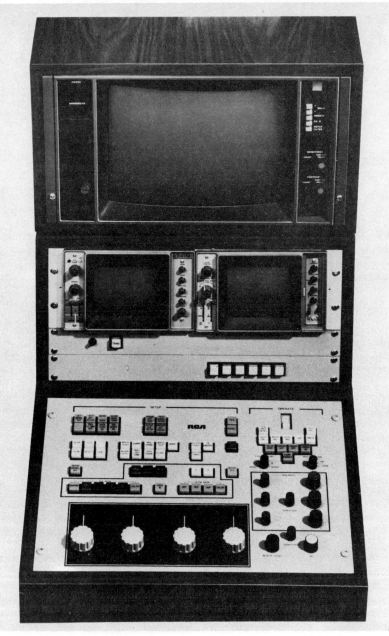

Fig. 13-32. Camera setup terminal.

Courtesy RCA

Fig. 13-33. ENG camera.

spaced as far as 3000 feet from the camera. The separation can be even greater using additional ancillary equipment. Even a microwave link can be used between the ENG camera and the remote-control panel. Additional information on microprocessor-controlled television equipment is given in Chapter 15.

13-14. VIDEO TAPE RECORDING

The video tape recorder has brought about great changes in telecasting. A high-quality video tape recording defies detection from the live telecast. An understanding of the video-tape recording process can best be gained by first considering the limitations of the conventional audio tape recorder. In an audio tape recorder, variations in the audio signal at the tape head magnetize the coating on the tape as it is moved past the head gap.

The high-frequency response is limited by the speed of the tape and the width of the head gap. The higher the frequency that must be reproduced, the narrower the gap required, and the faster the tape speed. Tape speeds of 7.5 inches per second and higher are used in the reproduction of a 15,000-Hz signal. To make a similar magnetic impression of a 4-MHz video component would require a tape speed of 2000 inches per second—or 113 miles per hour! It is apparent, therefore, that the conventional method of tape recording used for audio is certainly not feasible for recording and reproducing high-frequency video components.

13-14-1. The Quadruplex Video Tape Recorder

A quadruplex video tape recorder uses four video tape heads mounted on a rotating drum. These heads are moved across the tape, rather than, as more conventionally, moving only the tape past the head. Hence the combination of moving head and moving tape provides a much higher head-to-tape velocity at a substantially lower reel-to-reel tape speed. This fast effective motion of head and tape permits the recording of high-frequency video components.

As each head moves across the tape transversely it records a track 10 mils wide as shown in Fig. 13-34. There is a separation of 5 mils between each recorded track. In conjunction with the rotational speed of the head drum, a reel-to-reel tape speed of 15 inches per second supplies proper track separation as well as 64 minutes of playing time from a reel of tape 12.5 inches in diameter.

It is important to recognize that, as each head rotates, it picks up one track across the tape. The forward speed of the tape and the rotational speed of the tape head are such that a tape head moves into position just 5 mils away from the previous track. In fact, before one video head leaves the tape, the succeeding head has made contact on the opposite side. Thus there will be some identical information recorded at the bottom of one track and the top of the next track.

The subsequent longitudinal magnetic recording of audio and control information on the same tape destroys some of this duplication. However, enough is retained so that electronic switching from head to head (Fig. 13-35) must be made in the associated circuitry of the tape recorder, to prevent signal overlap in reproduction. The audio signal is recorded in the conventional manner. Of course, there must also be associated control information, to make certain the video tape machine is synchronized correctly with respect to the television signal.

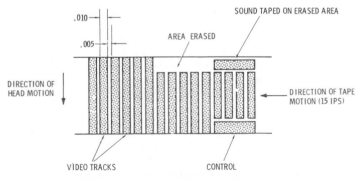

Fig. 13-34. Video tracks on a video tape.

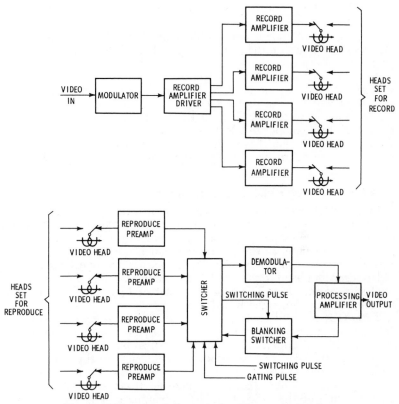

Fig. 13-35. Functional diagram of a video tape recorder.

To counteract some of the problems of recording very-low frequencies with such a very fast head-to-tape velocity, a frequency-modulation process is employed. The modulator converts the incoming frequency range of the video signal (10 Hz to 4 MHz) to a sideband spectrum that extends between 7.06 and 10 MHz. This frequency-modulated signal is amplified and applied to the record amplifiers, which supply drive signals to the video heads. Each head is moved over the tape by the rotating drum and makes its contribution on one track. It is then inactive for three tracks while the three remaining heads are moved into position. Inasmuch as all four heads are supplied with an identical signal, the information is placed on the tape in the proper order.

In the reproduce position, the motion of the video tape beneath each of the reproduce heads generates a signal that is applied to its associated reproduce preamplifier. One of the heads is always in position over the tape; consequently, each track supplies a signal to the reproduce preamplifier section. The four separate signals are applied to a switcher unit which has the responsibility of preventing any signal overlap. As a result, the switcher output signal is the same continuous signal that was supplied to the record-amplifier driver.

This signal component must be demodulated to recover the original video signal for use in the processing amplifier. The video output then constitutes a reproduction of the original video signal.

As the tape moves, audio and control signals are also recovered. By so doing, the motion of the tape and tape heads is made to coincide with their activities during the recording process. The video output signal complies with the FCC standards for a television signal. In fact, the reproduced composite television signal is a good replica of the television signal as would have appeared if it had been applied directly to the video program line of the station, instead of being used in the intermediate taping step.

13-14-2. One-Inch Helical Tape Recorder

In the television broadcast industry the quadruplex recorder is being replaced by the much lower-cost helical tape recorder, using only a one-inch tape. This more flexible machine consumes about one-third the amount of tape. In the basic arrangement (Fig. 13-36A) the one-inch wide tape is pulled in helical fashion around a rotating drum. The video recording head rotates with the scanning drum and makes a diagonal scan of the tape. The type-C format of Fig. 13-36B is the most common among American broadcasters.

Type C is referred to as a continuous field arrangement because a full field of video information is recorded by each scan, except for ten to twelve lines dropped out during the vertical blanking interval. However, a second head can be incorporated to pick up this sync interval as shown in Fig. 13-36B.

In operation the fact that a complete field image is evaluated with each rotation of the video head has advantages. The system can be slowed down very easily to provide a slow-motion rendition of sporting or other events. Even a complete-stop can be shown. Of course, the speed can also be increased above the normal level for special effects or, in particular, for fast cuing and editing. These above operational activities are used mainly in playback operation.

In addition to the video and the vertical-sync tracks the format includes four longitudinal tracks that are used for audio and control. There are three audio tracks with identical characteristics although track 1 is usually used for program audio. Audio track 3, which is located near the reference edge of the tape, is most often used for timecode applications. The control track and its associated circuits provide all the signals required to operate the control facilities of the tape recorder.

An *Ampex* portable recorder is shown in Fig. 13-37. In this portable construction the takeup reel is mounted above the supply reel. Control panel is located at the bottom right and includes two meters for monitoring both the video and the audio signals. The drum for the helical scan operation is at the lower left.

Major components of the scanner are its servo-controlled dc motor, rotating drum assembly and the entrance and exit tape guides. The

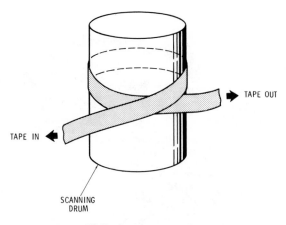

(A) Basic arrangement.

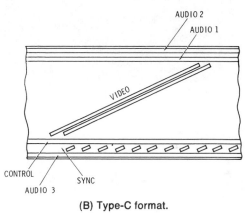

(B) Type-C format.

Fig. 13-36. Helical scan and type-C tape format.

scanner can mount six heads. For active video there are three positions, spaced at 120-degree intervals, for record, playback and edit-erase heads. There are three similar heads for record, playback and erase of the portion of the vertical interval picked up by the sync-track activity.

Two longitudinal head assemblies are a part of the tape transport system (Fig. 13-38). The upper assembly (7) is the video and sync erase assembly. The lower assemblies (15 and 16) take care of the audio channel and control track, record, playback, and erase activities. The path of the 1-inch tape between the supply reel and the takeup reel can be followed in the diagram of Fig. 13-38.

An RCA deluxe studio installation is shown in Fig. 13-39. The type-C tape recorder and its control panel is mounted at the center left. This compact section can be transported to a telecasting site, rolled on a cart, or installed in a standard studio rack assembly. Its features are

Courtesy Ampex
Fig. 13-37. Portable 1-inch video tape recorder.

playback capability for variable-speed broadcast pictures, slow-motion, and instant-replay capability. It includes an elaborate editing system and monitoring capabilities. The use of computerized control is possible.

The frequency response is flat to 4.2 MHz with a tape speed of 9.6 inches per second. The actual writing speed is 1008 inches per second. A 6000-foot length of tape mounted on an 11.75-inch diameter reel provides approximately 127 minutes of program material.

The studio console mounting of Fig. 13-39 provides extensive monitoring facilities including color monitor, waveform monitor, vector scope, and monochrome picture monitor.

13-15. TELEVISION TRANSMITTERS

Television transmitters are available with power output levels ranging from several kilowatts to fifty kilowatts or more. Two basic arrangements of modern transmitters are shown in the functional block diagrams of Fig. 13-40. In both examples the initial modulation occurs in the 40-MHz spectrum. Like the video if spectrum in a television receiver, the picture carrier is on 45.75 MHz and the sound carrier on

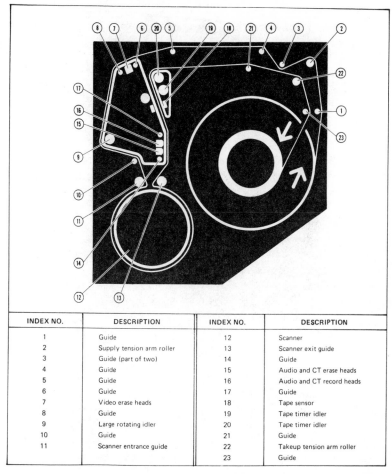

INDEX NO.	DESCRIPTION	INDEX NO.	DESCRIPTION
1	Guide	12	Scanner
2	Supply tension arm roller	13	Scanner exit guide
3	Guide (part of two)	14	Guide
4	Guide	15	Audio and CT erase heads
5	Guide	16	Audio and CT record heads
6	Guide	17	Guide
7	Video erase heads	18	Tape sensor
8	Guide	19	Tape timer idler
9	Large rotating idler	20	Tape timer idler
10	Guide	21	Guide
11	Scanner entrance guide	22	Takeup tension arm roller
		23	Guide

Courtesy Ampex

Fig. 13-38. Tape path and components.

41.25 MHz. Transmitters are solid state up to the final visual and aural power-amplifier stages. In Fig. 13-40A the video signal is applied to the modulator through a video processor section. The visual oscillator supplies the 45.75-MHz carrier component to the video modulator. Actually the visual and aural oscillators are usually interlocked in a pll synthesizer arrangement to maintain an exact separation of 4.5 MHz according to FCC specifications. FCC difference-frequency tolerance is ±1000 Hz.

The output of the video modulator is applied to an amplifier and vestigial-sideband filter (vsb) which suppresses part of the low-frequency sideband spectra as shown previously in Fig. 13-6. The 1.25-

Courtesy RCA

Fig. 13-39. One-inch recorder mounted in console.

MHz calibration corresponds to the 45.75-MHz picture carrier if frequency.

The output then proceeds to an up-converter mixer which, in conjunction with a local-oscillator signal, raises the frequency of the modulated if signal to the transmit frequency. The local oscillators of both the picture and sound systems are usually tied in with the frequency synthesizer system to maintain the very best carrier frequency stability.

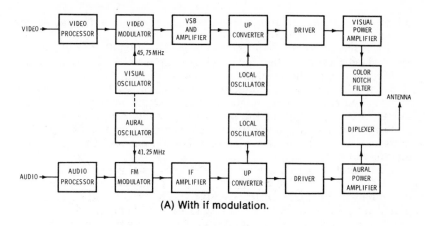

(A) With if modulation.

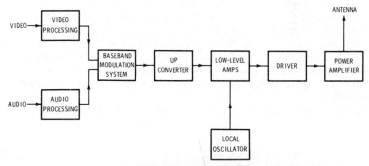

(B) With if diplexing.

Fig. 13-40. Basic tv transmitters.

The visual signal is then built up in level by a solid-state driver. Output level is adequate to drive the vacuum-tube visual power amplifier. One or two tubes are used, depending on the rated visual power output of the transmitter. Before application to the diplexer the visual signal passes through a color notch filter. The responsibility of this filter is to attenuate greatly the low-frequency sideband of the chrominance subcarrier frequency. This undesired frequency component falls at approximately 3.58 MHz on the low-frequency side of the transmitted picture carrier frequency.

In most modern television transmitters the driver and preceding stages are all broadband solid-state stages and no tuning is required. The power amplifier stages must be tuned for resonance, matching, and proper operating conditions.

The sound transmission section is straightforward beginning with an audio processor and frequency modulator. After if amplification the frequency-deviated sound signal is applied to an up-converter. The mixer and oscillator combination raises the frequency to the final transmit sound frequency. Solid-state driver and vacuum-tube power amplifier stages follow. Through the diplexer the visual and aural signals are applied to the antenna system.

In the second basic plan, as shown in Fig. 13-40B, the video and audio signals are processed separately and applied to a baseband modulation system. In this exciter system the amplitude-modulated picture signal and the frequency-modulated sound signal are formed. They are then combined into a complete baseband signal in the if frequency range. Thus the output of the modulation system consists of the complete picture and sound spectra in one complete signal. This method of formation avoids the necessity for a diplexer between the final power amplifier and the antenna.

After suitable amplification the combined signal is applied to an up-converter mixer/oscillator combination. This raises both aural and visual signals to the final transmit frequency. The broadband signal is amplified by solid-state broadband low-level amplifiers and driver. As a function of the required transmitter power outputs the final power amplifier uses one or two vacuum tubes.

Television broadcast transmitters are usually designed with a visual power output that is approximately five times greater than the sound power output. In so doing the coverage of the two transmitters is equalized. Thus the sound signal is usually not sent out any further than the distance over which an acceptable picture can be transmitted. The video bandpass is of course many times wider than the sound emission bandwidth.

An *RCA* three-rack television transmitter is shown in Fig. 13-41. Vis-

Courtesy RCA

Fig. 13-41. Television transmitter.

ual power output is 17-kW; sound output, 3.75-kW. All circuits preceding the finals are solid state delivering 800 watts of video drive and 100 watts of audio drive. The video power amplifier and the audio power amplifier each use a single tetrode vacuum tube. Broadband solid-state amplifiers are used and in the case of the vhf high-band transmitter they cover channels 7 through 13 without tuning adjustments. The three cabinets house the exciter-driver, power amplifier, and power supply. A functional block diagram of the transmitter is given in Fig. 13-42.

To the left is the self-contained solid-state exciter which generates the amplitude-modulated visual if signal and the frequency-modulated aural if signal. The video processor has a number of functions in addition to signal amplification. Some precorrection is needed because of the characteristics of the driver and the tuned visual power amplifier stage. There is a clamp at the blanking level and an adjustable circuit for white clipping.

The picture modulator is a doubly balanced diode type which provides proper linearity and low phase distortion. The carrier is derived from the frequency-synthesizer system.

Frequency control is maintained by a pll synthesizer arrangement using a temperature-compensated crystal oscillator as a reference frequency. The synthesizer is programmed to the assigned channel by making appropriate jumper connections. Since all frequencies are phase-locked to the reference the aural-to-visual carrier frequency separation is stable within ±5 hertz.

The output of the picture modulator is supplied to a vestigial-sideband filter which is in the form of a surface acoustic wave filter (SAW). Such a device is a no-coils, solid-state, piezoelectric device. It provides an almost ideal bandpass filter response as shown in Fig. 13-43. It has an extremely flat frequency response over the passband and very sharp skirts. There is a little group delay distortion at the edges of the passband.

Basically the SAW filter consists of a nonpiezoelectric substrate on which has been deposited piezoelectric film layers. Sandwiched between the two are interdigital metallic electrodes. There are two sets of these, input and output, and an intervening metallic strap coupler. A video rf signal applied to the input side places mechanical strain on the piezoelectric film. Such action activates the nonpiezoelectric surface and surface acoustic waves move along the coupled nonpiezoelectric surface toward the output. At the output the acoustic waves are converted back to an electrical signal by the output transducer.

The passband frequencies depend on the spacings and lengths of the fingers that comprise the interdigital metal electrodes. There are no inductor-capacitor circuits and the performance is entirely a function of the manufacturing process. It is an ideal way of obtaining a stable and ideal vestigial-sideband transmission characteristic.

The incoming audio signal is pre-emphasized and processed and applied to the fm exciter. The carrier is derived from the frequency synthesizer. The visual and sound if signals are now applied to the radio-frequency processor (Fig. 13-42). Individual pin-diode attenuators are

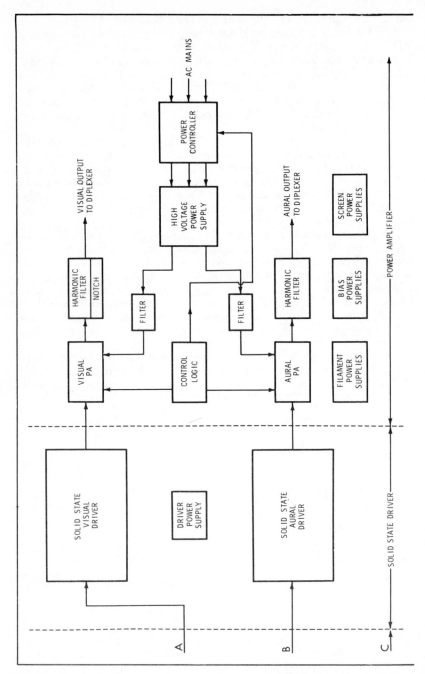

Fig. 13-42. Functional plan of

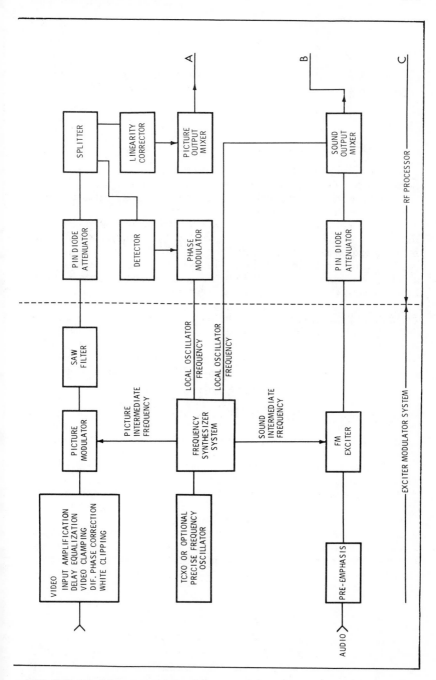

RCA TTG television transmitters.

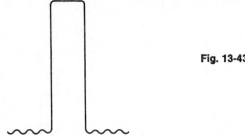

Fig. 13-43. Response of SAW picture sideband filter.

used to set the signal levels properly providing power level control for both signals. Distortion and linearity corrections are made in the visual section for such defects that occur in the process of radio-frequency amplification to the final power level.

Up-conversion is taken care of by the picture output mixer which receives its local-oscillator frequency from the frequency synthesizer through a phase modulator. Phase correction is made by using the splitter to take a sample of the modulated if signal and applying it to a detector. Compensation is then made to the local-oscillator frequency as it proceeds through the phase modulator to the picture output mixer. This step reduces interference between vsiual and aural components (sync buzz), improves sync tip shaping, and minimizes hue shift.

The sound signal is also applied to an up-converter. Again the local-oscillator frequency is derived from the frequency synthesizer. Visual and aural signals at the transmit frequencies are applied to individual solid-state drivers. The drivers supply 100 watts of aural output and 800 sync-tip watts of visual power.

The solid-state drivers are cooled in a unique manner. In addition to an elaborate heat sink, there is an embedded heat-pipe system, that employs a fluid that can be vaporized by heat. When this occurs it rises to the top of the sealed container which is cooled by the heat sink. The vapor will then condense and recirculate to maintain the cooling process. A small blower is used to cool the heat sinks. The visual signal is sent through a harmonic filter and the color notch filter to the diplexer. Sound signal is applied to the same diplexer through an associated harmonic filter.

Power levels are maintained by sampling picture and sound outputs and using an error signal to operate the pin-diode attenuators located in the intermediate-frequency signal paths. A control logic system provides solid-state driver protection against high standing-wave ratios, tube arcs, and overdrive conditions. There is SCR control of the ac input to the anode supply to provide slow turn-on and fast turn-off.

13-16. TELEVISION ANTENNA

As in fm broadcasting, horizontal polarization is used in tv broadcasting. The radiating elements are stacked on a tower. Usually the horizontal-radiation pattern must be essentially omnidirectional; the vertical radiation is concentrated at low vertical angles.

A television transmitting antenna must radiate a broadband signal. Consequently the basic dipole is modified in a manner that will permit wideband operation. A popular television transmitting antenna uses the bat-wing shown in Fig. 13-43A. The quarter-wave sections, on each side of the feed point, add parallel resonance to the basic series-resonant characteristics of a dipole. This damping extends the bandwidth, and the special taper of the element provides a uniform radiation over the desired bandpass.

To obtain a more uniform horizontal-radiation pattern, television broadband dipoles are usually mounted in a turnstile arrangement (Fig. 13-43B), the two perpendicular dipoles being fed in quadrature to obtain a good omnidirectional pattern. The necessary power gain is obtained by stacking the turnstiles in bays.

Several other types of broadband dipoles and antenna styles are used in television broadcasting. The helical-antenna principle is used with one type. Slot dipoles and traveling-wave construction can also be used for vhf and uhf telecasting.

The technique of circular polarization is now being employed on the television broadcast channels. Such technique provides a more uniform coverage and when circular polarization is used at both the transmitting antenna and the receiving antenna there is a noticeable reduction in reflections (ghosts). Such a circularly polarized antenna by RCA is shown in Fig. 13-44. The batwing fan elements provide the horizontal polarization while the V-shaped dipoles provide a vertically polarized field. The fans and V radiators are fed in quadrature to obtain uniform circular polarization and equal radiated signal strength in all directions from the antenna system.

A single television antenna is fed both picture and sound signals through a diplexer. The diplexer provides the proper impedance match between both transmitters and the antenna and prevents interaction between the two transmitters.

A diplexer is made up of sections of coaxial transmission line which along with the pair of antenna elements displays the bridge-like characteristic shown in Fig. 13-45. The antenna itself becomes an actual part of the bridge arrangement. The sound transmitter is connected across diagonally opposite points (one point is ground) of the bridge, while the picture transmitter is connected across the two remaining diagonally opposite points. It is the balanced bridge arrangement that prevents interaction between the transmitters providing an ideal way of feeding two transmitters to the same antenna.

13-17. TRANSMITTED TEST SIGNALS

There are a variety of special test signals that can be transmitted by television broadcast stations or sent along the network line simultaneously with the regular program material. These test signals are transmitted during the vertical interval and in no way interfere with program transmissions.

There are a number of inactive lines transmitted between the last equalizing pulse and the end of the vertical-blanking pulse (Fig. 13-

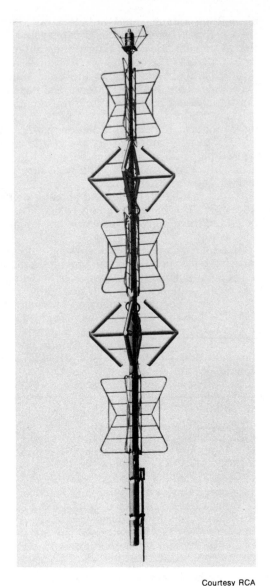

Courtesy RCA

Fig. 13-44. Vhf television antenna with circular polarization.

17). Some of these lines can be put to use transmitting test signals. A number of these test signals are suggested in Section 73.699, Volume III of the FCC Rules and Regulations. Most often these signals occupy the horizontal scanning lines 16 through 20 which occur during the vertical-blanking period.

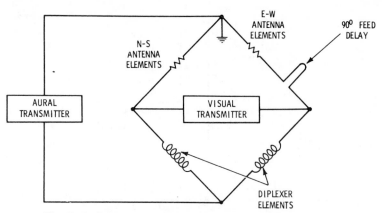

Fig. 13-45. Bridge-type diplexer feed to a television antenna.

An example of a *vertical-interval test signal* (VITS) is the multiburst test signal of Fig. 13-46. This signal occupies line 17 of field No. 1. At the bottom left, in order, is shown the horizontal-sync pulse, color-sync burst and remainder of the horizontal-blanking back porch. The actual test signal begins at T_0. First a white bar is transmitted that matches the 12.5-percent level of the composite waveform. Refer to the calibration of percentage of peak current level shown at the right. Signal corresponds to the white reference level of a transmitted television signal. The left calibration is in terms of IRE (IEEE) units for which a value of 100 is assigned to the white reference level.

Sine-wave bursts of key frequencies follow the white bar extending from 0.5 MHz to 4.1 MHz as shown. Each color burst signal has an amplitude of 60 IRE units peak to peak. There is a short-interval breezeway between bursts.

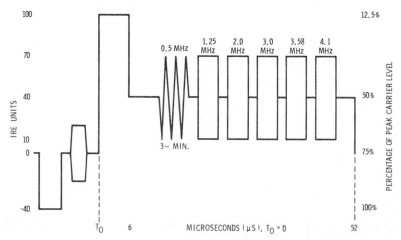

Fig. 13-46. Multiburst test signal.

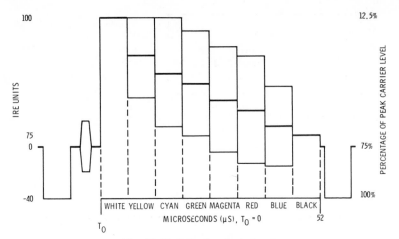

Fig. 13-47. Color-bar test signal.

These frequency components can be used in a similar manner as a video sweep and by observing the test signal waveform at various points in on-line television equipment, waveform monitors, or a home television receiver, operating conditions can be checked. A good quality oscilloscope that can sort out individual lines of video must be used as the test indicator.

The flatness of the frequency response of a video amplifier that must convey the entire frequency spectra of the composite television signal can be judged. All bursts should be of the same amplitude. Also the relative amplitudes of the multibursts can also indicate the performance of chrominance-alone and luminance-alone segments of a television system. For example at the output of a chrominance bandpass amplifier it would be the latter three bursts that would appear emphasized and the 0.5-, 1.25-, and 2.0-megahertz bursts would not be present. In many television receivers and some picture monitors the chrominance components are blocked from the luminance amplifiers. Therefore the 3.58- and 4.1-megahertz components should not appear because they have been trapped out.

A color-bar test signal can be transmitted during the vertical interval (Fig. 13-47). The first bar transmitted is reference white, again conveyed at the 12.5-percent level. The final bar represents reference black and is transmitted approximately 7.5-percent below the blanking level. In between are a range of hues between yellow and blue. The phases and amplitudes of the color bars are in accordance with the FCC Rules and Regulations for 100-percent saturated colors of 75-percent amplitude. Each color bar has a minimum duration of 6 microseconds. Test signal can be displayed on the screen of a waveform monitor or high-quality oscilloscope.

The VITS of Fig. 13-48 is more complex. It consists of a riser staircase with chroma. The subcarrier frequency of the staircase is in phase with the color-sync bursts. There are two short-duration $\sin^2$ pulses, one

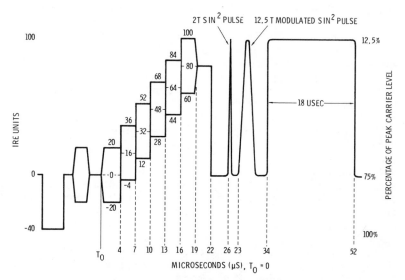

Fig. 13-48. Composite radiated signal.

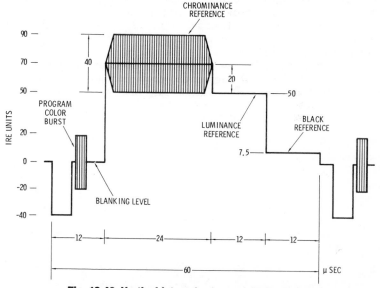

Fig. 13-49. Vertical interval reference (VIR) signal.

of short duration and the other a modulated one of somewhat more than double the duration of the first one. These are followed by a long-duration line bar.

Just several of the many tests that can be made with this signal are mentioned. The staircase can be used to check out nonlinear distortion, especially from the staircase configuration. Other defects shown are luminance nonlinearity, differential phase and gain, and possible intermodulation between chrominance and luminance components. Pulse response can be checked with the 2T pulse. A comparison can be made between the pulse response and the bar response. The 12.5T pulse can make comparisons between chrominance and luminance gain and delay factors. Low-frequency response can be checked with the 18 microsecond bar.

Of course, all of the various VITS signals provide a means of observing and measuring the horizontal-sync pulse and the followup color-sync bursts.

The final test signal (Fig. 13-49) is called the *vertical interval reference signal* (VIR). This test signal conveys a chrominance reference signal at the burst frequency. In fact, the chrominance reference signal and the color-sync bursts have exactly the same phase. This signal can be sent along network lines and/or transmitted for television receiver application. It is used by network and broadcast station engineers to evaluate and correct undesirable changes in color hues (tints) when station programming changes. As a result there is better color uniformity along the stations of a network.

Circuitry is available for taking advantage of this incoming chrominance reference signal and making the necessary hue changes automatically. Also some television receivers include automatic control circuits that operate off the VIR signal to provide truer and more uniform hue reproduction when programs change or when switching between program sources and channels.

The chrominance reference signal has a duration of approximately 24 microseconds. The VIR signal also conveys a luminance reference level of 50 IRE units as well as the standard black reference component.

CHAPTER 14

Digital Electronics

Digital electronics is becoming an important part of modern radio-communications including broadcasting. Presently digital circuits augment the linear systems basic to modern broadcast equipment. Digital emphasis is on control, switching, measurement and display functions. Experiments continue with digital audio and digital video systems.

14-1. DIGITAL BASICS

A first step in understanding digital circuits is to learn just a bit about the binary numbering system. In a binary system, you can count with only two numerals, zero and one. In both the binary and decimal languages, *nothing* is zero or 0. Likewise the quantity *one* is the same for both languages and is written as one or 1. From this point on, things differ. In decimal language, the quantity two is written as 2; in binary language, it is written as 10. Very often the binary code used is in the form of a four-bit series, and the quantities zero, one, and two are set down as follows:

$$zero = 0000$$
$$one\ = 0001$$
$$two\ = 0010$$

The four-bit expression for zero is telling us that there is no eight, no four, no two, and no one. For the quantity one, it is saying that there is no eight, no four, no two, and one one. Likewise, for the quantity two, the expression says that there is no eight, no four, one two, and no one.

In four-bit binary language, the quantity nine is written as 1001, telling us that there is one eight, no four, no two, and one one. One 8 plus one 1 equals the decimal quantity 9. Table 14-1 makes a comparison between the decimal and binary presentations. It also shows the four-bit presentation method along with the quantity or weight represented by each digit of the four-bit sequence. Higher-value decimal quantities can be represented in binary form by adding more bits. For example, the quantity 16 in binary form using a five-bit sequence would be expressed as 10000; decimal 17 would be 10001; and so on.

Table 14-1. Decimal-Binary Equivalents

Decimal	Binary	Four-Bit	Weight 8, 4, 2, 1			
0	0	0000	(0) 8,	(0) 4,	(0) 2,	(0) 1
1	1	0001	(0) 8,	(0) 4,	(0) 2,	(1) 1
2	10	0010	(0) 8,	(0) 4,	(1) 2,	(0) 1
3	11	0011	(0) 8,	(0) 4,	(1) 2,	(1) 1
4	100	0100	(0) 8,	(1) 4,	(0) 2,	(0) 1
5	101	0101	(0) 8,	(1) 4,	(0) 2,	(1) 1
6	110	0110	(0) 8,	(1) 4,	(1) 2,	(0) 1
7	111	0111	(0) 8,	(1) 4,	(1) 2,	(1) 1
8	1000	1000	(1) 8,	(0) 4,	(0) 2,	(0) 1
9	1001	1001	(1) 8,	(0) 4,	(0) 2,	(1) 1
10	1010	1010	(1) 8,	(0) 4,	(1) 2,	(0) 1
11	1011	1011	(1) 8,	(0) 4,	(1) 2,	(1) 1
12	1100	1100	(1) 8,	(1) 4,	(0) 2,	(0) 1
13	1101	1101	(1) 8,	(1) 4,	(0) 2,	(1) 1
14	1110	1110	(1) 8,	(1) 4,	(1) 2,	(0) 1
15	1111	1111	(1) 8,	(1) 4,	(1) 2,	(1) 1

The intriguing part of the binary presentation is that numbers can be represented by combinations of binary 0 and binary 1. Furthermore, it is very easy to understand how to use a simple switch to see a binary 1 or a binary 0. For example, a closed switch could represent a binary 1; the same switch when open, a binary 0. A sequence of switches could then be used to demonstrate a binary counting system (Fig. 14-1). The closed position of the switch in the circuit is customarily called the on position; the open position is the off position. In digital vernacular, the closed position could designate true or binary logical 1, while the off position of the switch would be designated false or logical 0. In representing the decimal quantity twelve, switches 1 and 2 would be closed, while switches 3 and 4 would be open, setting up the sequence of 1100.

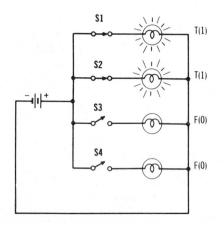

Fig. 14-1. Binary number representation using switches and lamps to show the decimal number 12.

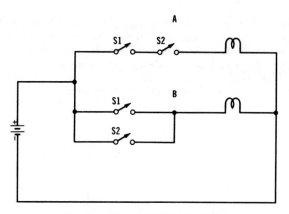

Fig. 14-2. AND and OR switching.

In other switching possibilities (Fig. 14-2) series or parallel closings would be needed to set the binary output. In example A switches S1 *and* S2 must be closed to obtain an output binary 1. In example B the closing of either switch S1 *or* S2 will result in an output binary 1.

14-2. BASIC LOGIC CIRCUITS

In an actual digital system, the switches would be electronic and not mechanical. They operate at very high speeds causing many operations to occur simultaneously and at a high repetition rate.

Some considerable confusion exists because of the several ways of designating a logical 1 and a logical 0. In general, the terms yes and no, true and false, as well as 1 and 0, are identical. In actual circuits, logical 1's and 0's are represented by voltage levels. In a negative logic circuit, the most positive voltage level (high) is 0 and the most negative level is 1. Conversely, in a positive logic circuit, the most positive level (high) is defined as a logical 1, while the most negative voltage level (low) is a logical 0.

It follows, then, that in a positive logic circuit, the following terms are one and the same:

$$
\begin{array}{lll}
1 & \text{and} & 0 \\
\text{yes} & \text{and} & \text{no} \\
\text{true} & \text{and} & \text{false} \\
\text{high} & \text{and} & \text{low}
\end{array}
$$

Conversely, for negative logic circuits the identities are:

$$
\begin{array}{lll}
1 & \text{and} & 0 \\
\text{no} & \text{and} & \text{yes} \\
\text{false} & \text{and} & \text{true} \\
\text{low} & \text{and} & \text{high}
\end{array}
$$

The most common method used is positive logic.

In digital circuits using positive logic, inputs and outputs are either high (logic 1) or low (logic 0). There is no in between. Circuits act like fast switches changing over between high and low at the output in response to high and low conditions at their inputs.

A basic bipolar digital circuit is given in Fig. 14-3. This is a very simple inverter that demonstrates the supply/saturation voltage con-

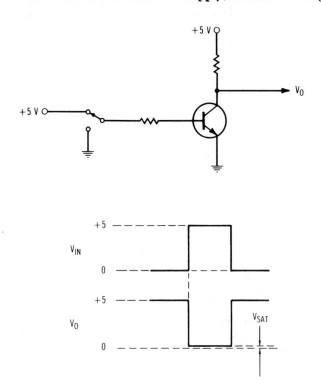

Fig. 14-3. Basic bipolar digital circuit.

cept basic to digital systems. In digital circuits there are only two input/output states. These are logic 0 and logic 1. Assume that the input switch is set to logic 1 (represented by +5 volts). The base bias current will then be such that the transistor operates at saturation. Thus the output voltage drops to near 0 volts (the voltage saturation point). Were the input switch set to common, or logic 0, the bipolar transistor would not conduct. As a result the output voltage equals the supply voltage (again +5 volts) or a voltage level of logic 1.

The waveforms show the operation with the application of 5-volt pulses. When the input pulse is high or logic 1, the output pulse is low or logic 0. Between pulses the input logic is 0 and the output logic is 1. Input and output logics invert and the circuit is acting as a logic inverter. Actually the output waveform is the complement of the input waveform. Note that the output waveform swings between the supply voltage and the near-zero saturation voltage of the bipolar transistor.

The same conditions occur with a field-effect transistor as shown in Fig. 14-4. In normal operation the circuit swings between two definite voltage levels. In the circuit shown, it is again between the supply voltage and saturation voltage. Again the output logic is inverted.

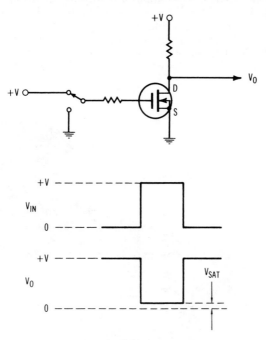

Fig. 14-4. Basic fet digital circuit.

The building-block of modern digital circuits is the so-called *logic gate.* Although gate circuits can be built using discrete components they are usually in the form of multiple gates that are a part of a digital integrated circuit. The two most common families of digital integrated circuits are TTL (transistor-transistor-logic) and CMOS (complementary metal oxide semiconductors). The TTL device responds to voltages between 0 and +5 volts. Maximum supply voltage to a TTL device is +5 volts. The logic 0 voltage falls between 0 and 0.8 volt; the logic 1 between 2.4 and 5 volts. Thus a dc voltmeter or popular logic probe can be used to ascertain if input and output levels are at logic 0 or logic 1.

A CMOS digital integrated circuit will also operate at the same level as the TTL. However, supply voltages may extend between 4 and 15 volts. In most applications logic 0 would fall between 0 and 0.8 volt. The logic 1 value would be between 3 and 15 volts depending upon the supply voltage.

In addition to gates there are other digital ICs that perform a variety of functions. Some of these will also be discussed in this chapter.

14-3. LOGIC PROBE

A key test instrument in locating faults in digital circuits is the logic probe (Fig. 14-5). The logic probe contains light-emitting diodes (LED) which turn on according to the logic of the point in the digital circuit to which the logic probe is connected. If it is touched to a logic 1 point the high LED will come on; a logic 0 point, the low LED will light. The instrument can be used to check out either TTL or CMOS circuits.

Courtesy Continental Specialties Corp.

Fig. 14-5. Logic probe.

A pulse LED also indicates the presence of square waves or pulses in the digital system. Each time the input signal changes to the logic probe the pulse LED is activated for 0.1 second. When observing low-frequency, low duty-cycle signals, the pulse LED provides an immediate indication of the pulse activity in the circuit. Also by observing the high and low LEDs the polarity of the pulse train can be ascertained. If the high LED is on, the signal is normally high and pulsing low. If the low LED is on the signal is normally low and pulsing high. High-frequency signals cause the pulse LED to flash at a 10-hertz rate. The incorporation of a pulse stretcher in the logic probe makes this possible.

The logic probe can be moved from circuit to circuit in a digital system and by checking the logic at key test points proper or faulty operation can be ascertained. Measurements can be made under steady-state dc condition as well as with pulses present in the digital system.

14-4. CODES AND NUMBERING SYSTEMS

Various codes based on the binary 1 and 0 concept have evolved to meet the requirements of digital equipment operation and objectives. A simple code that has been extensively used is known as the binary-coded-decimal (BCD) method. Four binary bits are employed. Each is said to have a weight of 8, 4, 2, 1 in the order of digits from left to right. Each digit position has a definite value (weight).

In the true binary case, it is simply 8, 4, 2, 1 as shown in Table 14-1. Conversion to decimal values involves the simple addition of the weights of the digits as shown previously. For special needs, there are various other types of codes, some involving more than four digits or characters. In the case of BCD, however, a simple four-bit number is used to express all decimal quantities zero through nine. Although a four-bit number can designate higher numbers (up to 15 as shown in the chart), the BCD code restricts each four-bit character to decimal numbers from zero to nine.

Table 14-2. Numbering Equivalents

DEC	BINARY	BCD	OCT	HEX
0	0000	0000 0000	0	0
1	0001	0000 0001	1	1
2	0010	0000 0010	2	2
3	0011	0000 0011	3	3
4	0100	0000 0100	4	4
5	0101	0000 0101	5	5
6	0110	0000 0110	6	6
7	0111	0000 0111	7	7
8	1000	0000 1000	10	8
9	1001	0000 1001	11	9
10	1010	0001 0000	12	A
11	1011	0001 0001	13	B
12	1100	0001 0010	14	C
13	1101	0001 0011	15	D
14	1110	0001 0100	16	E
15	1111	0001 0101	17	F

When a higher number is to be indicated in binary form using the BCD code, additional four-bit characters are conveyed. For example, the number 35 in the BCD code becomes 0011 0101.

3 5
0011 0101

Note that the first four-bit character is the binary representation of three while the second is the representation of the decimal quantity five. Thus, the number 6751 would be written:

0110 0111 0101 0001

The *BCD* code is a popular one because of the ease with which its 4-bit binary sequences can be used to activate a digital display. For example, the previous 4-bit binary numbers when applied to a four-place digital display would read out as 6751.

In addition to numbering to the base two (binary), and numbering to the base ten (decimal), there are two additional numbering bases used widely in digital and microprocessor systems. These are *octal* and *hexadecimal* (hex). Octal uses a base 8; HEX a base 16.

In a binary system there are only two numbers, 0 and 1. In a decimal system there are numbers 0 through 9. As you well know, after the number 9 in a decimal system, the sequence repeats 10 through 19. After number 19 there is another set of 9 numbers, 20 through 29, and so on.

In an octal numbering system there are 8 basic numbers, 0 through 7. The next set of 8 numbers extends between 10 and 17 (Table 14-2). The next set of 8 numbers is represented by 20 through 27, and so on.

A hexadecimal numbering system has sixteen basic numbers, 0 through 9 and, then, to represent the decimal equivalents of 10 through 15, a sequence of letters A through F, as shown in the last column of Table 14-2. The next set of hex numbers after F would be 10, 11, 12, 13, 14, 15, 16, 17, 18, 19, 1A, 1B, 1C, 1D, 1E, and 1F. This demonstrates how the hex counting repeats itself as one moves on into higher values. It is a fact that the following all represent the same equivalent value:

$$1100_2, \quad 0001\ 0010_{BCD}, \quad 14_8 \text{ and } C_{16}$$

Stated another way the equivalent of decimal 12 in binary would be 1100, in BCD 0001 0010, in octal 14, and in hex C. The usefulness of codes and numbering systems clarifies as you learn more about digital and microprocessor circuits.

14-5. LOGIC GATES

There are six basic logic circuits that come under the general heading of logic gates. These are inverter, AND gate, NAND gate, OR gate, NOR gate, and Exclusive/OR gate. These gates are found built into digital integrated circuits with usually four or more gates of the same type included in the same chip.

14-5-1. Inverter

A digital inverter has an output logic which is the inverse of the input logic. Output Y is the complement of input A (Fig. 14-6). Shown is the inverter symbol, truth table, and diagram.

It can be seen that if the input logic is 0, the output logic is 1. An input logic of 1 drives the output to logic 0. A clock pulse or other sequence of pulses applied to the input A will appear inverted at the output Y. The truth table is a manner of expressing the logic conditions of a digital circuit. It shows the logic output for every possible combination of input logic.

Data is given for the TTL 7404 hex inverter. There are six independent inverters included in this single IC chip. Note that there are twelve separate pins for the various inputs and outputs. Supply voltage is connected to pin 14, while pin 7 is grounded.

A simple demonstration circuit using just one of the inverter gates in the 7404 is given in Fig. 14-7. The switch permits a connection of logic

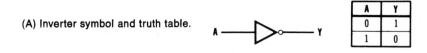

(A) Inverter symbol and truth table.

A	Y
0	1
1	0

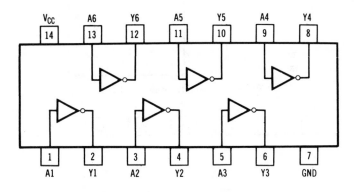

(B) Six inverters are included in one IC.

Fig. 14-6. Symbol, truth table, and schematic diagram of the 7404 hex inverter.

1 or logic 0 to input A. If the switch were connected to the supply voltage it would be the same as connecting a logic 1 to the input. Under this condition the output at Y would be logic 0. A logic probe like the one shown in Fig. 14-5 can be used to make the check. Also a dc voltmeter could be connected at the output pin 2 indicating whether the output logic was 0 (approximately 0 volts) or logic 1 (approximately +5 volts). Note the supply voltage connected to pin 14 and the ground to pin 7.

If a series of positive pulses were applied to input A, they would appear at the output Y as negative pulses, showing the inversion characteristic of an inverter stage.

14-5-2. Two-Input AND Gate

Schematic diagram, symbol, and truth table of a TTL 7408 AND gate are given in Fig. 14-8. Note the symbol for the AND gate and how it differs from the triangle symbol of the inverter. In an AND circuit, input gates A *and* B must be at logic 1 before there can be a logic 1 output. If either or both of the inputs are logic 0 (low), the output Y is logic 0 (low). These facts are again given in the truth table which shows the

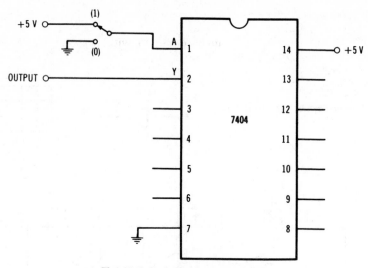

Fig. 14-7. Practical inverter circuit.

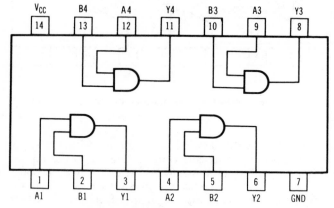

(A) Four AND logic gates in one IC.

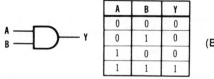

(B) Logic gate symbol and truth table.

Fig. 14-8. Diagram, symbol, and truth table of the 7408 AND gate.

output logic state for every possible combination of input logic states.
Every possible combination of A and B is given, showing the resultant
output state.

The TTL 7408 contains four individual AND logic gates as shown in the schematic arrangement. Supply voltage positive is connected to pin 14; ground, to pin 7.

Truth table verification can be obtained with the simple circuit of Fig. 14-9 using one of the AND gates in the 7408. A logic probe or dc

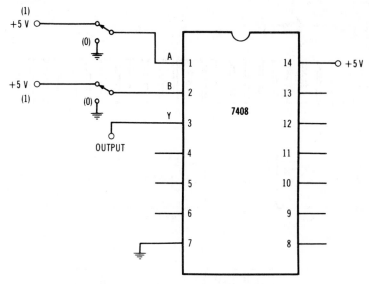

Fig. 14-9. Practical AND circuit.

voltmeter can be used to check the output logic at Y. When both switches are connected to logic 1 as shown, the output Y will also be logic 1. Any other combination of the two switches will result in a logic 0 at the output.

An AND gate circuit as you might find on a schematic diagram is given in Fig. 14-10. If a series of pulses, such as might be derived from a clock pulse generator were applied to input A, their presence at the output would depend upon the setting of the logic at input B. Were the logic at input B set to logic 1, as shown, the pulses will appear at output Y with the same polarity (no inversion). However, if the switch at B is set to logic 0 there will be no output at Y. Recall that in AND gate operation both inputs must be at logic 1 before there can be a logic 1 output.

It should be mentioned that it is customary practice in presenting diagrams of logic circuits that the supply voltages are *not* indicated. It is assumed in this case that the proper potentials are applied to pins 14 and 7 as shown previously in Fig. 14-9.

It should be stressed that the input to gate B is usually a pulse waveform too and is not the simple switch arrangement of Fig. 14-10. The waveforms of Fig. 14-11 show such a possibility. Assume that clock pulses of a particular repetition rate are applied to input A as shown. A low-frequency and longer-duration series of pulses is applied to

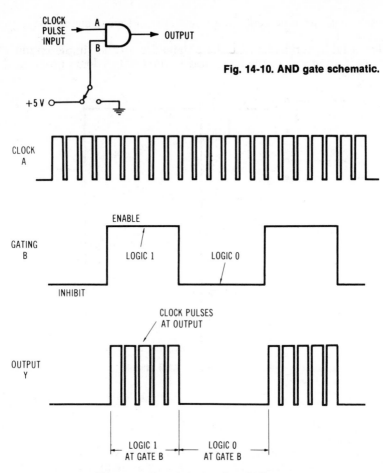

Fig. 14-10. AND gate schematic.

Fig. 14-11. Gated clock pulses AND gate.

gate B which drives gate B between logic 1 and logic 0. Note that when the gate B pulse is at logic 1, the clock pulses applied to gate A appear at the output. Conversely when gate B is set to logic 0 by the applied gating pulse, there is no output pulse present at output Y. This shows how a gate pulse can be used to gate on (enable) and off (inhibit) the AND gate, allowing or not-allowing the pulses at gate A to appear at output Y.

14-5-3. NAND Logic Gate

A schematic, symbol and truth table for a NAND gate are given in Fig. 14-12. Again the integrated circuit houses four individual NAND gates.

In a NAND gate configuration when either or both inputs are at logic 0, the output is at logic 1. If both inputs are high at logic 1, the output

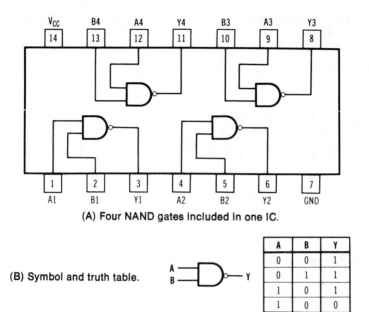

(A) Four NAND gates included in one IC.

(B) Symbol and truth table.

A	B	Y
0	0	1
0	1	1
1	0	1
1	0	0

Fig. 14-12. Diagram, symbol, and truth table of the 7400 quad NAND gate.

is low at logic 0. In fact, the NAND gate is referred to as a negated AND gate.

In comparing Fig. 14-12 with Fig. 14-8, note that the output logics in the Y column of the truth tables are complements. Note too that the two symbols are very similar except for the very small circle at the Y output of the NAND gate. A truth table can again be verified using the simple circuit of Fig. 14-13 and an appropriate logic probe or dc voltmeter.

When input data or a clock pulse is applied to input A there will be no output if the gate B is at logic 0. If gate B is set to logic 1, however, there will be an output signal. However in the case of the NAND gate the output signal will be the complement of the input data. Thus the NAND gate inverts the input signal.

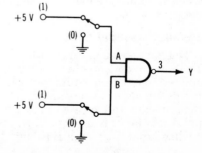

Fig. 14-13. Practical NAND circuit.

When a combination of clock and gating pulses is applied to the input as shown in Fig. 14-14 there is a different output than that obtained when using an AND gate. Note again when the gating pulse at input B is a logic 0 there is no output. However, under the logic 1 condition, there is an output. This output is a series of inverted clock pulses as shown in Fig. 14-14.

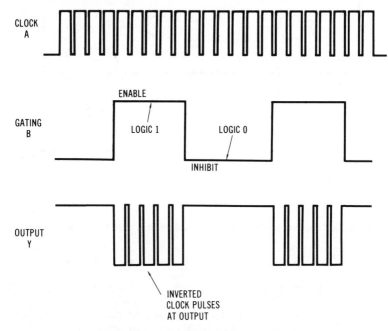

Fig. 14-14. Gated clock pulses NAND gate.

In the previous examples only two inputs were shown. However, logic gates can have more than two inputs and quite often do. An example of the symbol and truth table for a three-input NAND gate is given in Fig. 14-15. Note again that all the possible conditions for A, B and C have been set down. The resultant output is indicated in the Y column. Again for the NAND type of logic circuit the output is logic 0 when all inputs are logic 1. When all, two, or one input is at logic 0, the output is at logic 1.

14-5-4. Two-Input OR Gate

Diagram, symbol, and truth table for an OR gate are given in Fig. 14-16. In an OR gate circuit a logical 1 output results when a logic 1 is applied to either or both input gates. The output is logic 0 when both inputs are logic 0. Compare the truth table of the OR gate with that of the AND gate. In the case of the AND gate the output is logic 1 when input A *and* input B are logic 1. In case of the OR gate the output is logic 1 when input A *or* input B is logic 1.

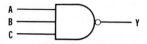

Fig. 14-15. Three-input NAND gated.

A	B	C	Y
0	0	0	1
0	0	1	1
0	1	0	1
0	1	1	1
1	0	0	1
1	0	1	1
1	1	0	1
1	1	1	0

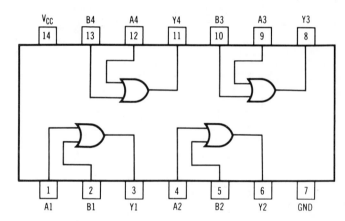

(A) Four OR gates included in one IC.

(B) Symbol and truth table of OR gate.

A	B	Y
0	0	0
0	1	1
1	0	1
1	1	1

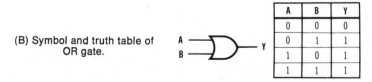

Fig. 14-16. Diagram, symbol, and truth table of the 7432 OR gate.

If a clock pulse or other input data is applied to input A and input B is at logic 0, the input data is transferred to the output without inversion. Conversely, a logic 1 state at input B blocks the data applied to input A, and it does not appear at the output.

A gating signal applied to input B can be used to switch the output data on and off at the rate of the gating pulse. However, the transfer is made to the output whenever gate B is set to logic 0. This is the converse of the activity of an AND gate as detailed previously.

14-5-5. Two-Input NOR Gate

Diagram, symbol, and truth table for a NOR gate are given in Fig. 14-17. Note that the NOR gate symbol is the same as that for an OR gate with the exception of the small circle at the output. In NOR gate circuit operation when either or both inputs are at logic 1 the output is logic 0. The output is logic 1 only when both inputs are at logic 0. Compare the NOR and OR gate truth tables, observing that the Y columns are complementary. The NOR is in fact referred to as a Negated OR gate, hence the name of NOR gate.

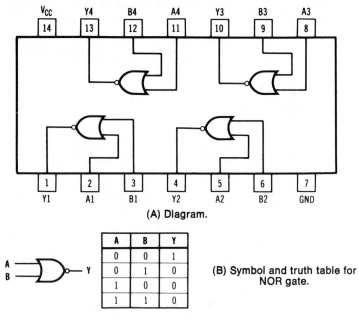

(A) Diagram.

A	B	Y
0	0	1
0	1	0
1	0	0
1	1	0

(B) Symbol and truth table for NOR gate.

Fig. 14-17. The 7402 NOR gate.

If input data or clock pulse is applied to A gate and a logic 1 to B gate there will be no output. If a logic 0 is applied to the latter gate, however, the input signal appears in inverted form at the output. The output is, in fact, the complement of the input.

If required, a gating pulse can be applied to the B input. In this case the output is switched on and off and clock pulses appear in the output whenever the input gating pulse swings to logic 0. Output pulses are, of course, opposite in polarity from the input pulses applied to gate A.

14-5-6. Two-Input Exclusive/OR Gate

The Exclusive/OR gate is unique as shown in Fig. 14-18. When gates A and B are both set to logic 0 the output is logic 0. Furthermore when gates A and B are both set to logic 1, the output is also logic 0. If logic A is zero and logic B is 1, or logic A is one and logic B is zero, the output is logic 1. Symbol and truth table are given.

The Exclusive/OR gate is unusual in its response to input data or clock pulse. Assume that input data is being applied to gate input A. If gate input B is set to logic 0 the input data is transmitted directly to the output and is of the same polarity. However, if gate B is set to logic 1 the input data will also appear in the output but will be in inverted form.

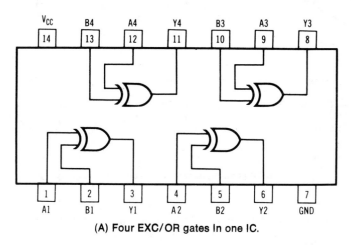

(A) Four EXC/OR gates in one IC.

(B) Symbol and truth table for EXC/OR gate.

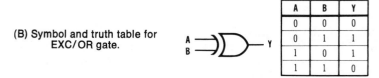

A	B	Y
0	0	0
0	1	1
1	0	1
1	1	0

Fig. 14-18. The 7486 EXC/OR gate.

It would be advisable to review all gate circuits. Pay particular attention to their symbols and truth tables. You may wish to set them down side by side and make appropriate comparisons. Memory can be aided by considering the relationships between AND and OR gates, AND and NAND gates, and finally OR and NOR gates.

There is also an exclusive/NOR gate. For the XNOR gate the output is logic 1 whenever both inputs are logic 0 and whenever both inputs are logic 1. If input A is logic 0 and input B is logic 1, or A is logic 1 and B is logic 0, the output is logic 0. The XNOR gate is unusual in its response to input data. If input data is being applied to input A and input B is set to logic 1, the input data is transmitted directly to the output and is of the same polarity. If, however, input B is set to logic 0, the input data also appears in the output but it is in inverted form.

14-6. BOOLEAN ALGEBRA

The boolean expressions for an inverter and the six logic gates are given in Fig. 14-19. Whatever logic is applied to input A of an inverter appears in complementary or inverted form at output Y. A small circle at the output side of the symbol indicates that inversion. The boolean

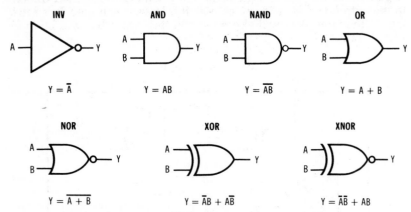

Fig. 14-19. Boolean equations for inverter and logic gates.

equation for the inverter is: $Y = \overline{A}$. The short line above the A indicates that the output is negated (not A) or inverted in polarity.

The AND gate provides a logic 1 output whenever inputs A and B are at logic 1. The boolean expression for the AND gate is:

$$Y = A \cdot B = AB$$

In this case the multiplication dot does not mean multiply. Rather it means "and." Usually in writing boolean expressions the dot is not used and, as in conventional multiplication, the two quantities are just brought close together as shown.

In the case of the NAND gate a logic 0 appears at the output when both input A and B are logic 1. This can be expressed in the basic equation:

$$Y = \overline{AB}$$

The line above AB indicates a "not," or negated output. The equation is the same as that for the AND gate with the exception that the not sign appears above the output.

For an OR gate circuit the output is logic 1 whenever input A or input B or both are at logic 1. The boolean equation that expresses the OR gate is:

$$Y = A + B$$

The plus sign in this case does not mean add; it means "or." The three common boolean algebraic signs you have been introduced to are the negation or "not" sign over a letter, the "and" sign which is a multiplication dot (usually not shown) and the "or" sign which is the conventional plus sign.

The NOR gate has a negated output. The output is logic 0 whenever either or both inputs are logic 1. The basic equation is:

$$Y = \overline{A + B}$$

In this case, too, the equation for the NOR gate is the same as that of the OR gate with the exception of the output negation.

In the case of the XOR gate the output is logic 1 when either input A or input B is at logic 1. Stated as a boolean equation:

$$Y = \overline{A}B + A\overline{B}$$

The XNOR gate is a not-form of XOR. The output is logic 1 whenever the two inputs are both logic 1 or logic 0. Boolean expression is:

$$Y = \overline{A}\overline{B} + AB$$

In the previous discussions some of the basic boolean equations were introduced. Also given were the boolean representations of "not," "and" and "or." Next several additional boolean concepts and manipulations are introduced. Although the introduction is brief, it will give you a better comprehension of the activities that occur in the digital circuits associated with digital control and microprocessor circuits.

When several gates are interconnected the resultant boolean expressions are more complex than the simple ones representing the individual gates. The two most important categories of more complex boolean expressions are known as *sum-of-products* and *product-of-sums* relations. Two simple samples are shown in Fig. 14-20.

Example A consists of two AND gates and their individual outputs applied to an OR gate. The equation for the AND gate in Fig. 14-19 shows that the outputs of the two AND gates would be represented by the products AB and CD. This information is applied to the separate inputs of the OR gate. However, the equation of the OR gate shows that its output is a sum quantity. Thus the complete equation for the three gates is:

$$Y = AB + CD$$

This is a *sum-of-products* expression.

Example B comprises OR, NOR, and AND gates. The inputs again are A, B, C, D. As shown in Fig. 4-19 for the OR and NOR gates the outputs are sum quantities. The NOR gate output is a negated sum. The A + B and negated C + D quantities are applied to the two inputs of the AND gate. The output of an AND gate is a product quantity. As a result the expression for the circuit is:

$$Y = (A + B)(C + D)$$

This is a *product-of-sums* boolean expression.

The more complex the functions that are to be performed, the greater is the number of digital devices required and the more complex becomes the boolean equation for these activities. The circuit designer

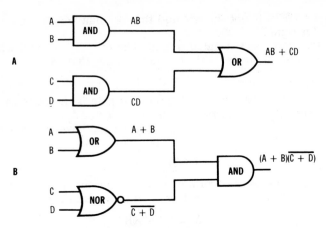

Fig. 14-20. Sum-of-product and product-of-sums expressions.

with his knowledge of boolean algebra is able to simplify the various boolean expressions and eventually come up with a digital system of fewer circuits and devices that will perform the same operations more economically and, in many cases, more efficiently.

There are any number of boolean theorems and equivalents that are of benefit. Several important ones are mentioned here to give you just a very basic understanding of the processes.

There is a boolean rule of *intersection*. This applies to the AND gate (Fig. 14-21A). When a logic 0 is applied to the lower input, the output will be 0 regardless of input A. This is inherent with the AND gate which has a logic 0 output except when both inputs are at logic 1. Thus:

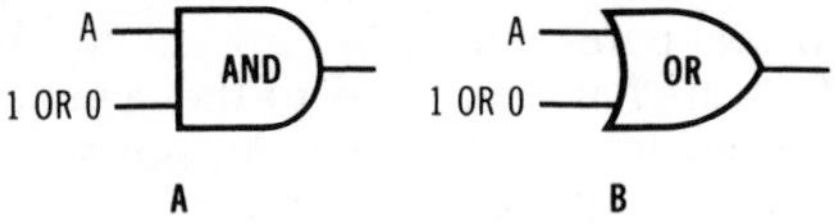

Fig. 14-21. Logic of intersection and union rules.

$$A (0) = 0$$

If the logic at the lower input is 1, the output will be A. Recall that in the operation of the AND gate the data applied at A appears at the output whenever the second gate is at logic 1. Hence:

$$A (1) = A$$

There is a boolean rule of *union*. This one can be proven with the characteristics of the OR gate (Fig. 14-21B). In an OR gate circuit, as discussed previously, the data applied to input A is transferred to the output whenever the second input is at logic 0. Stated as a boolean expression:

$$A + 0 = A$$

If the second input to the OR gate is at logic 1, the output will be logic 1, regardless of the logic at input A. Remember that for an OR gate the output is logic 1 when either or both inputs are at logic 1. As a boolean expression:

$$A + 1 = 1$$

There is a boolean rule of *complements*. When a logic signal and its complement are applied to the inputs of an AND gate, the output is 0. This is apparent from the AND gate truth table. Stated as a boolean expression:

$$AA = 0$$

If a logic signal and its complement are applied to the inputs of an OR gate, the output becomes logic 1. This too is basic to the operation of the OR gate and is proven in the truth table. Stated as a boolean expression:

$$A + A = 1$$

There is a boolean rule of *sameness*. When identical signals are applied to the inputs of a gate, output is the same as input. If the same input A is applied to both inputs of an AND gate, the output is A. Boolean expression is:

$$(AA) = A$$

In like manner if the same signal is applied to the inputs of an OR gate, the output is the same. Stated as a boolean expression:

$$A + A = A$$

Again these relations are proven by the respective truth charts.

There is a boolean rule called the *DeMorgan theorem*. One version states that the complement of a product equals the sum of separate complements. Stated as a boolean expression:

$$AB = A + B$$

The second form states that the complement of a sum equals the product of separate complements. The boolean expression is:

$$A + B = AB$$

These relations can be proven with appropriate truth charts and boolean manipulations. There are any number of other rules appropriate to boolean algebra. The above and several additional ones are given in the following list.

$$A(0) = 0$$
$$A(1) = A$$
$$A + 0 = A$$
$$A + 1 = 1$$
$$AA = 0$$
$$A + A = 1$$
$$AA = A$$
$$A + A = A$$
$$AB = A + B$$

$$A + B = AB$$
$$(AB)C = ABC$$
$$(A + B) + C = (A + B + C)$$
$$AB + BC = A(B + C)$$
$$A(A + B) = A$$
$$A(A + B) = AB$$
$$A + AB = A + B$$
$$A + AB = A + B$$
$$A + AB = A + B$$

Some of the equivalents are basic rules while others can be derived by using two or more of the basic rules. One example is the relationship that states:

$$A + AB = A + B$$

The proof is as follows:

   ① $Y = A + AB$
   ② $Y = A (B + 1) + AB$
   ③ $Y = AB + A + AB$
   ④ $Y = A + B(A + A)$
   ⑤ $Y = A + B$

In the second step note that the A term is multiplied by the quantity $(B + 1)$. By the rule of union this is permissible because $(B + 1)$ is equivalent to 1 and multiplying any number by 1 does not change its value. In step three the first quantity is multiplied out. In the fourth step the B term is factored out of the first and third terms. By the rule of complements the $(A + A)$ term equals 1. The result is shown in step five. The equivalent in the list has been proven. If you wish to pursue these design techniques there are any number of books on the subject.

14-7. LED AND 7-SEGMENT DIGITAL DISPLAYS

The light-emitting diode (LED) is a semiconductor diode that emits light when forward-biased (Fig. 14-22A). A series resistor is used to limit the diode current to a safe value. The most common LED color is red; yellow and green versions are available.

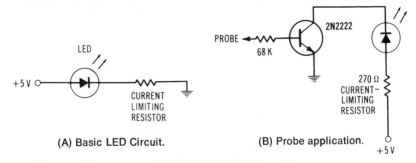

(A) Basic LED Circuit.   (B) Probe application.

Fig. 14-22. LED probe.

LEDs are used widely in digital and analog electronic systems. They are reliable and have a long life. In TTL systems the supply voltage is usually 5 volts. An appropriate resistor must be placed between the 5-volt source and any LED that is operated in the circuit. Resistor values usually fall in the 100- to 470-ohm range. In most cases the LED current should not exceed 50 mA and an actual current of 20 to 30 mA is typical. Common series resistor values are 180, 220, 270, and 330 ohms. Of course, the lower value resistors provide the brighter glow. In CMOS circuits using higher-value supply voltages, Ohms law can be used to calculate the higher value of series resistance required.

Illustration B shows how an LED circuit in conjunction with a bipolar transistor can be used as a simple logic probe or lamp monitor. The LED circuit has a low impedance and could load down a particular higher resistance digital or analog circuit. The purpose of the bipolar transistor is to provide current amplification at the same time it presents a very much reduced load to the circuit to which the probe is connected. A very low input base current will result in the significant current needed to light the LED connected in the collector circuit.

This circuit can be used as a very simple probe for checking or monitoring TTL circuits. If the probe is connected to a logic 1 point (+5 volts), the LED will light. If connected to a logic 0 point (0 volts) it remains unlit.

The LED is the basis for digital number displays. A 7-segment display consists of seven LED slits, two or more of which are illuminated to display the numerals 0 through 9 (Fig. 14-23). For example, if segments f, g, b, and c are lit the number 4 will be displayed. The illumination of segments a, b, g, c, and d reproduces as the numeral 3. This typical 7-segment display plugs into a 14-pin DIP mount.

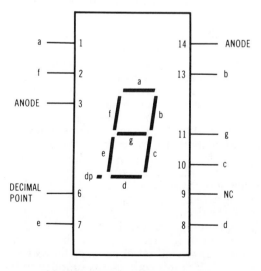

Fig. 14-23. Seven-segment display.

Anode voltage can be supplied to either pin 3 or pin 14. A specific LED slit is illuminated by connecting its associated pin to ground through the appropriate current-limiting resistor. Note in Fig. 14-23 that the individual slits are connected to pins 1, 2, 7, 8, 10, 11, and 13. Decimal point illumination is made via pin 6.

The simple circuit arrangement of Fig. 14-24 shows how the number 5 is illuminated. In this case slits a, f, g, c, and d must be connected to ground through current limiting resistors. This involves physical connections to pins 1, 2, 11, 10, and 8.

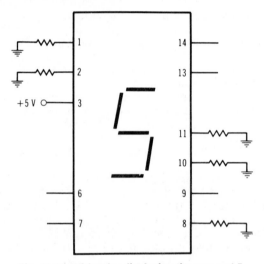

Fig. 14-24. Wiring for displaying the numeral 5.

To operate the 7-segment display electronically a 7-segment decoder is required. The TTL 7447 integrated circuit, Fig. 14-25, is an example of such a decoder. It is able to convert a positive logic BCD input signal to a proper sequence that lights a 7-segment display.

Recall that the BCD code is a 4-bit digital signal that represents the numerals 0 through 9 as a proper sequence of logic 0 and logic 1 bits. Refer back to Table 14-1. It is this coded signal, when supplied to pins 1, 2, 6, and 7, that provides the proper 7-segment illumination. The individual seven segments that connect to the 7-segment display involve pins 9 through 15. A schematic showing the decoder and 7-segment display properly interconnected is given in Fig. 14-26. Note the links between decoder output and display input by way of current-limiting resistors. If the digital logic signal applied to the 7447 is 0100 the b, c, f, and g output of the decoder will be placed at logic 0 and current will flow in the appropriate segments to illuminate the numeral 4.

Truth tables are given in Fig. 14-27. The first column is the actual decimal numerals. The second set of columns shows the BCD code for the various numerals. It is this code that is supplied to the input of the 7447 decoder. The final set of columns shows the individual segments

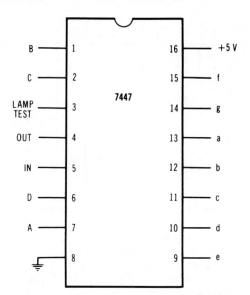

Fig. 14-25. 7447 BCD to 7-segment decoder.

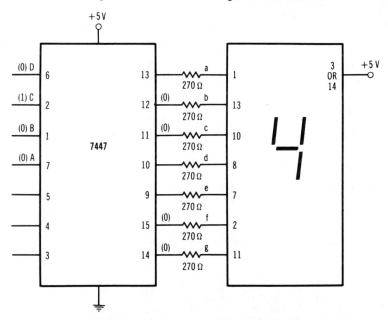

Fig. 14-26. Decoder and display connected together.

of the display. When an individual segment is connected to logic 0 by the decoder it will glow.

Pin 3 of the decoder (Fig. 14-25) can be used to test all of the seg-

	"8"	"4"	"2"	"1"							
NUMBER	D	C	B	A	a	b	c	d	e	f	g
0	0	0	0	0	0	0	0	0	0	0	1
1	0	0	0	1	1	0	0	1	1	1	1
2	0	0	1	0	0	0	1	0	0	1	0
3	0	0	1	1	0	0	0	0	1	1	0
4	0	1	0	0	1	0	0	1	1	0	0
5	0	1	0	1	0	1	0	0	1	0	0
6	0	1	1	0	0	1	0	0	0	0	0
7	0	1	1	1	0	0	0	1	1	1	1
8	1	0	0	0	0	0	0	0	`0	0	0
9	1	0	0	1	0	0	0	0	1	0	0

Fig. 14-27. BCD-to-decimal decoding.

ments of the display. When it is connected to logic 0 (grounded) all of the slits will glow if they are operating properly. Pins 4 and 5 are used for blanking purposes and to provide a link to other 7447 devices that are connected when a multiple readout display is required. For example, if a 4-section numeral display is desired each individual display has its own decoder.

In a digital display system the decoder is preceded by a counter. The purpose of the counter is to convert a series of input pulses (clock) to the BCD output code. The TTL 7490 is an example of such a decade counter (Fig. 14-28). The decade counter can be considered to have ten stable states made available at pins 8, 9, 11, and 12. These ten states match the 4 bits of the BCD code through the sequence from 0 through 9. After a complete sequence has been made there is a return to the 4-bit 0000 that represents the numeral 0.

The purpose then of the decade counter is to count in sequence between 0 and 9 as the pulses arrive at pin 14 of the 7490. For each ten pulses coming in, in sequence, the BCD output will follow the sequence

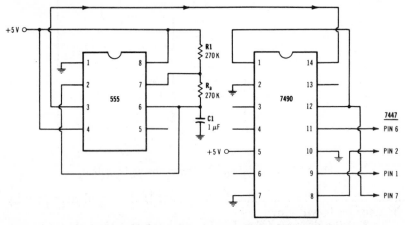

Fig. 14-28. BCD decade counter and clock generator.

between 0000 and 1001 of the BCD code. After this sequence of ten pulses, the next arriving pulse will result in a 0000 output and the count sequence will resume again.

The Fig. 14-28 circuit includes a 555 clock pulse generator which is generating the sequence of pulses applied to the input pin 14 of the decade counter. If you combine Figs. 14-26 and 14-28 into an actual circuit you will come up with a demonstration counter that will continue to sequence between 0 and 9 and back to 0 and so on, as long as the clock generator is in operation.

In an actual digital display system other circuits and pulse sources are required. It may be that some analog quantity has to be measured. If so, circuits must be incorporated that will illuminate the display only for a given numeral as a function of the information being interpreted by the digital display system.

The circuit of Fig. 14-29 shows how a NAND gate can be used to control the number of clock pulses or other data that is applied to a counter. If the duration of the gate pulse is known one can determine how many pulses are applied to the counter during this interval of time.

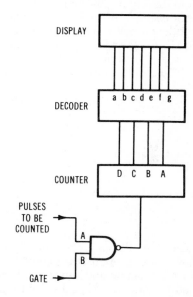

Fig. 14-29. Use of NAND gate to enable the count sequence.

For example, if the duration of the positive gate pulse applied to input B is one second and the counter counts up to 7 during this interval of time it means that the pulses to be counted are arriving at a rate of 7 per second. This is the first step in understanding how a frequency counter operates.

Recall that for the operation of a NAND gate the application of logic 1 information to gates A and B results in an output of logic 0. Refer back to the waveforms of Fig. 14-14. When the gate pulse at B is positive (logic 1) the gate is said to be *enabled* and the pulses applied to gate A will appear in the output. They will be of negative polarity which is correct for applying the information to the counter.

The sequence of pulses applied to the counter results in the generation of the BCD code signals that correspond to the number of pulses that are applied from the gate. This BCD signal is decoded and converts to the 7-segment signal that operates the LED display. When the gate B signal is at logic 0 the gate is said to be *inhibited* and no pulses applied to gate A are able to reach the counter.

This very simple counter is only capable of counting between 0 and 9 and is just a single-digit display. If a higher count is desired, individual counters can be added in series. If the series of pulses applied to the first counter exceed ten in number the excess pulses leave the first counter and are supplied to the second counter. In fact, one pulse is sent to counter 2 for each ten pulses that are applied to counter 1. The combination of the two counters in series will permit a total count of 99.

A third counter can be added to the chain and will become active if there is an excess of 99 incoming pulses. Thus with a three digit display the total possible count jumps to 999. A fourth counter permits a maximum display of 9999 and so on.

An example of such a four-digit display is given in Fig. 14-30. Note that the output of the count gate at the lower right is applied to counter No. 1. Furthermore there are interconnections that join counters 1 through 4 in series. In such an arrangement 4 digits will be displayed with the first counter displaying the lowest significant digit and count No. 4 the maximum significant digit.

If we assume that the count gate pulse applied to the count gate is 1 second in duration, and the signal input has a frequency of 2564 hertz, this is the number of pulses that will be applied to the counter chain in the one second period. Therefore the display at counter 4 will read 2, that at counter 3 will read 5, that at counter 2 will read 6, and counter 1 will display the numeral 4.

If the frequency of the signal input changes a different number of pulses will be applied during the 1-second interval of the count gating pulse. Therefore the display will read a new frequency, either higher or lower, depending on the direction and extent of the frequency change at the signal input.

Consider the operation of the major blocks of the 4-digit display shown in Fig. 14-30. It is important that the count gating pulse be of an exact frequency and duration. Therefore a crystal-oscillator system is used to generate this calibrated pulse. Usually the crystal oscillates at a high frequency and a series of dividers brings down the frequency to the desired clock frequency. Timing and control circuits generate the various pulses required by the frequency counter. Three basic pulses are usually generated with specific durations and time positions. These are shown in simplified form in Fig. 14-31.

The count gate pulse was mentioned previously and is applied to the count gate along with a signal processed from the input signal. The input signal, more than likely, will be a sine wave. This sine wave is converted to a square wave by the signal processing block. This square wave has the same frequency as the input sine wave and is applied to the count gate.

The count gate permits a certain number of these pulses to pass through to its output as a function of the duration of the calibrated gating pulse. In our previous discussion we mentioned that the count

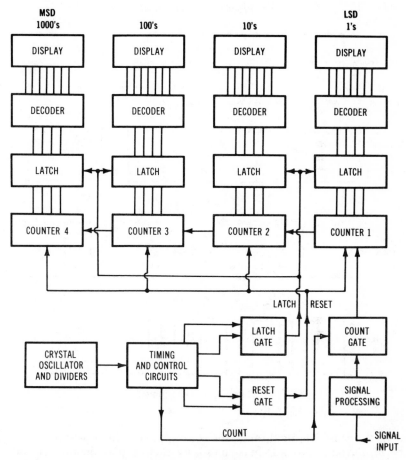

Fig. 14-30. Four-digit display system.

gating pulse had a duration of 1 second. It could be some other known duration depending on the frequency range to be measured by the counter. A typical figure might be a duration of 100 milliseconds. At any rate it is an exact and known quantity and permits a certain number of the processed input pulses to pass through to counter 1. These pulses pass along the counter chain. They are said to *ripple* through the counter and the series connection of counters is referred to as a *ripple counter*.

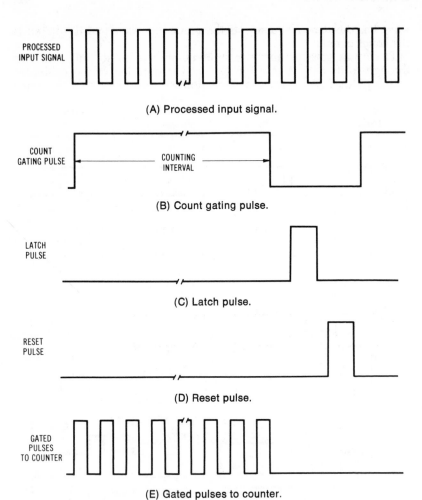

(A) Processed input signal.

(B) Count gating pulse.

(C) Latch pulse.

(D) Reset pulse.

(E) Gated pulses to counter.

Fig. 14-31. Key digital display system waveforms.

As the pulses ripple through the counters, the entire operation would be displayed as the numbers run-up on each display, finally reaching the desired final count for each individual section of the four. This would result in an annoying display and it would be more satisfactory if the only numerals displayed would be the last ones representing the actual frequency of the incoming signal. Blanking out of the run-up of the displays is handled by a series of latches and a latching pulse as shown in Fig. 14-30. The pulse counting in each of the individual counters keeps building up to the desired value as they are applied to the individual latch circuits. However, the final number is not passed to the decoder until a latch pulse is applied to each of the individual latches. Despite the fact that the ripple counters are very active during the count interval, only the final count number is seen, because this data is not passed to the decoder until the latch pulse arrives. Therefore the actual number that is displayed is the final count and you do not see the actual counting process visually on the displays.

After the numbers are displayed for a specific interval of time, a reset pulse arrives and restores each of the individual counters to its zero, and a new cycle of activity begins. This activity repeats itself at a fast rate and a continuous display appears and, at the same time, a change in the signal input frequency is recorded immediately. Thus the counter very quickly follows each change in the input frequency.

The waveforms of Fig. 14-31 tell us much about the operation of the display system. Waveform A is the processed input signal, the frequency of which is to be measured. Waveform B shows the count gating pulse. Counting occurs when this pulse is at logic 1. After a precise interval of time the count gating pulse goes to logic 0 and the counting ceases. At this time the latching pulse (waveform C) arrives and passes the last count number of each chain on to the decoder and to the 7-segment display. After the count has been displayed for an interval of time, the reset pulse arrives and quickly returns everything to zero, ready to begin a new count.

Waveform E shows the pulses that are gated to the first counter. Note that this activity occurs during the duration of the count gating pulse. No pulses are gated to counter 1 during the times that the latching and reset pulses are active. All of these activities occur at a fast rate but the eye sees a continuous display that does not flicker or show a count run-up.

14-8. DIGITAL IC CIRCUITS

There are many types of digital ICs with numerous applications and functions. Several important CMOS types and associated circuits are described.

14-8-1. D-Type Flipflop

The flipflop is a bistable two-element device. It has two stable states. An appropriate input signal causes a changeover from one state to the other.

In a so-called D-type flipflop (Fig. 14-32A) the logic applied to the

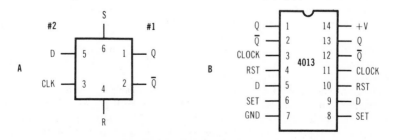

Fig. 14-32. Dual D-type flipflops.

D input is transferred to the Q output whenever the clock makes a positive transition (edge) from logic 0 to logic 1. The D input initiates a delay activity because the logic at the D input is held until the clock signal makes the positive transition. Note that the flipflop has two outputs, Q and not-Q. They are complementary outputs. When Q is logic 1, the not-Q output is logic 0 and vice versa.

Assume input D is set to logic 0. The output at Q and not-Q does not change until the clock input changes from logic 0 to logic 1. When this happens assume the Q output becomes logic 0 and the not-Q output, logic 1. If the D input is now set to logic 1, the circuit will flipflop upon arrival of the next positive transition of the clock from 0 to 1. At this moment the Q output changes to logic 1; the not-Q output to logic 0.

The *set* and *reset* potentials also influence the output. A positive *set* results in a logic 1 at Q and a logic 0 at not-Q, regardless of previous output logics. Conversely a positive *reset* results in a logic 1 at not-Q output and a logic 0 at Q output. These latter set and reset functions are dominant and overrule the output logic that has been established by the D logic.

An example of a D-type flipflop is the 4013 digital IC. In fact, it contains two separate flipflops in the same package (Fig. 14-32B). A test circuit for checking out the operation of the flipflop is given in Fig. 14-33A. Four switches permit you to set the logic of the D, clock, set, and reset inputs. A transistor and LED permit you to observe the logic at the Q output.

As shown, a logic 1 is applied to the D input. The set and reset inputs are at logic 0 because of the link to ground through the 10K resistors. If you momentarily connect switch S4 to logic 1, the Q output will be logic 0 (LED off) and the not-Q output will be logic 1. Now momentarily connect the clock input switch S3 to logic 1. Q output is 1 (LED on); not-Q output is 0. Connect switch S2 to ground, applying a logic 0 to the D input. The output will not change. However, if switch S3 is momentarily connected to logic 1, the output will flip and the LED will turn off. Connect switch S2 back to logic 1. Nothing will change until switch S3 is momentarily connected to logic 1. Then the output will flip again. Whenever the LED is off it can be overruled by momentarily connecting switch S1 to logic 1. This is the set function.

The basic circuit can be made to flipflop on a continuous basis by making a feedback connection between the not-Q output and the D input as shown in Fig. 14-33B. Under this condition there will be a change in the output logic every time the clock voltage swings positive. Now the logic at the not-Q output changes the D input each time the output logics change. In other words, the not-Q output takes the place of switch S2 in circuit A. Each time switch S1 is momentarily connected to logic 1, the output logic will change.

Assume that the Q output is logic 0. The first time switch S1 is momentarily connected to logic 1, the Q output will become logic 1. The next time switch S1 is momentarily connected to logic 1, the Q output changes to logic 0. The next time switch S1 is connected momentarily to logic 1, the Q output will be back at logic 1. Note that it required

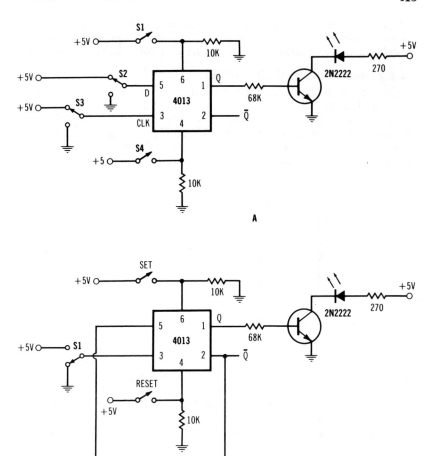

Fig. 14-33. Type-D flipflop circuits.

two positive voltage changes of the clock input to produce a complete cycle at the Q output (1 to 0 and back to 1). There is one output cycle for each two input cycles. If a square wave were applied to the clock input, the square wave at output Q would be one-half the frequency of the input square wave. The same applies for the output of the not-Q output. In this application the D-type flipflop is dividing the input frequency by a factor of 2. It is said to be acting as a *binary counter*.

It is possible to connect the output of one flipflop or binary counter to the clock input of the next. In this case the total division would be 4 (a × 2). The combination is said to be acting as a divide-by-four counter. Four such binary counters connected in series string would produce a total division of 16(2 × 2 × 2 × 2). Furthermore by the proper choice of feedback links among the individual binary counters it is also possible to establish other counts such as 5 or 10 or some other whole count. There are many applications for flipflops and counters in digital systems.

14-8-2. Hexadecimal/BCD Counter

The CMOS 4029 is a versatile digital IC counter. Pinout diagram is given in Fig. 14-34. The package contains a series of D-type binary counters. Depending on the logic applied to pin 9, the total count can be made 16 (hexadecimal) or 10 (BCD). The logic applied to pin 10 determines whether there is an up-count or a down-count. In the case of BCD setting, then, the count can be 0 *up* to 9 or 9 *down* to 0.

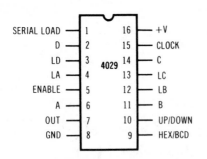

Fig. 14-34. Versatile counter CMOS chip.

The connections for division-by-ten counting (decade BCD) and division-by-16 (hexadecimal) counting are shown in Fig. 14-35, along with associated tables that show the DCBA binary output logic as a function of the arriving clock pulse. Circuits are connected for up-counting. If down-counting is desired pin 10 must be connected to ground (logic 0).

There are many possible counting methods. Our accepted method is decade counting which involves numbering to the base 10. Binary counting is, of course, to the base 2 as introduced earlier in the chapter. Another popular counting method in computers and microprocessor systems is called hexadecimal meaning counting to the base 16. For that reason the counter just described has applications in hexadecimal systems because of its division-by-sixteen capability.

In the hexadecimal system both numbers and letters are used. In counting from 0 to 16 in hexadecimal it would be 0-1-2-3-4-5-6-7-8-9-A-B-C-D-E-F. In hexadecimal all decade numbers between 0 and 15 can be represented as a single symbol. Equivalents of binary, decade and hexadecimal counting are shown in Table 14-3. Additional details on counting methods can be found in Reference IV.

14-8-3. CMOS Decoder/Driver

The Motorola MC14495B (Fig. 14-36) is a versatile driver for a 7-segment display. In fact, it is a combination latch, decoder, and driver in a single package. Furthermore the driver output can be supplied directly to the 7-segment display. No current-limiting resistors are required. Another attractive advantage is that it can be used for both

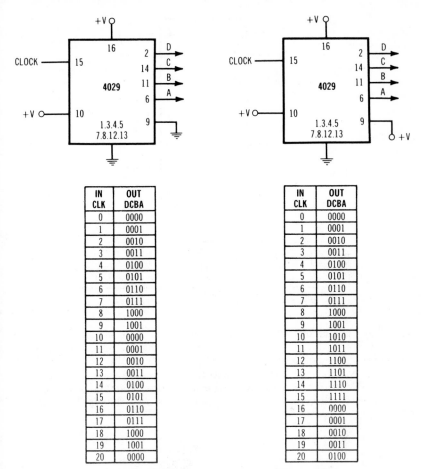

Fig. 14-35. Connections for BCD and HEX counting.

BCD and HEX displays. The decoding is such, that the same 7 segments of the display can also be used to reproduce the hexadecimal numbers A through F. The actual display capability is shown in Fig. 14-36. The A, C, E, and F are upper case. However, hex upper case B and hex upper case D are displayed as lower case b and d.

Input and output are shown in the pinout diagram. A latch pulse can be applied to pin 7. Its leading edge will latch whatever binary number is being applied to the DCBA input. This number will be displayed so long as the latch remains high. When the latch is made low, the display will continue to count. An LED connected directly to pin 4 will turn on whenever the six numbers A, B, C, D, E, and F are displayed.

An interesting demonstration circuit is given in Fig. 14-37. The clock can be derived from a 555 timer using components that will provide a

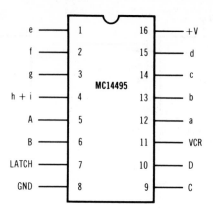

Fig. 14-36. Decoder/driver pinout diagram.

very low frequency output. The output should be a conventional 7-segment common-cathode display. Note that the DCBA output lines of the counter are connected to the DCBA inputs of the 4495. The three switches can be used to demonstrate the versatility of the circuit. Switch S1 permits you to switch between up-count and down-count. As connected the circuit will up-count. Switch S2 selects BCD or hex

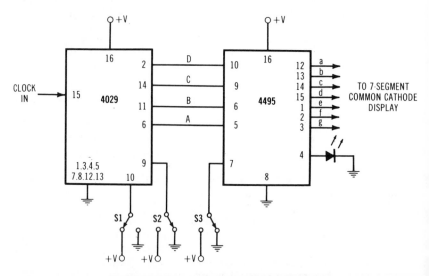

Fig. 14-37. Counter/decoder combination.

counting. As connected it will count BCD. Switching over to logic 0 (+V) will result in hex counting and the display of the numbers A through F. Switch S3 provides a latching demonstration. As connected there is no latching. When switch S3 is connected high (+V) the binary DCBA signal applied to the 4495 input at that moment will be locked and displayed continuously. Changing switch S3 back to low will restore normal counting.

14-8-4. CMOS Data Selector

A data selector has several inputs that supply data to a single output on a scheduled basis which is determined by the binary addressing supplied to its control circuit. The 4512 chip is an example of such a selector. There are eight inputs (Fig. 14-38) that can be selected one by one according to the 3-bit binary signal applied to pins 13, 12, and 11. The highest number that can be represented by a 3-bit binary is 7, establishing proper selection for the maximum number of 8 inputs. Thus the inputs from 0 through 7 are selected in sequence when the

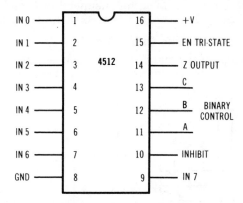

Fig. 14-38. Eight-channel data selector.

3-bit binary signal steps from 000 to 111. Of course, inputs can be selected at random according to the changing values of the CBA applied.

Output is removed at pin 14. If the logic at input 3 were 1 when the CBA code is 011, a logic 1 appears at output pin 14. Were the logic 0; the output would be 0. If the CBA address is changed to 110, the output at pin 14 would match the logic present at input 6.

The 4512 data selector is said to have a tristate output. Pin 15 provides tristate enabling. When pin 15 is low, the selector operates in normal fashion. However, if pin 15 is switched high, the output pin 14 is switched to a high-impedance state. Thus the three possible outputs are 0, 1, and high-impedance disconnect. An advantage of a tristate output is that pin 14 can be connected to a multiaccess interconnecting line (bus) along with similar circuits having tristate outputs. As a result there is minimum loading and interaction among chips connected to the bus line. Only the chips which are to be activated at the moment are placed on line with the tristate enabling facility.

Circuit connects are shown in Fig. 14-39. The eight inputs are shown at the top left. With all the switches closed, a logic 0 is being applied to each input. Whenever a switch is opened for a particular channel, that input sees a logic 1 because of the connection of the input through its resistor to the supply voltage.

Output is removed at pin 14. A transistor and LED will cause the LED to turn on whenever the output is logic 1. Switches S1 through S3 can be used to provide a specific binary address. Tristate enabling can be checked with switch S4.

To transfer the logic at input 5 to the output you must use the CBA address of 101. By opening and closing the switch associated with input 5, the LED at the output will turn *on* for a logic 1 input and *off* for a logic 0 input. When the input switch of input 5 is open the LED is on.

If you now connect switch S4 high, the LED will turn off, indicating that a disconnect has been made at the pin 14 output. For this setting of switch S4 there is really no output, neither 1 or 0, and the transistor and LED have been completely disconnected from the 4512.

14-8-5. CMOS Addressable Output Latch

The performance of the output latch is complementary to the output of a data selector. In this circuit the input data is channeled to a specific

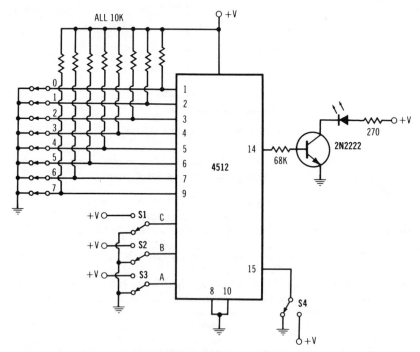

Fig. 14-39. Data selector circuit.

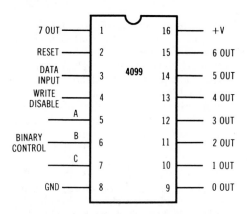

Fig. 14-40. Addressable-output latch.

output. The output selected is again determined by a binary addressing system. Furthermore the logic supplied to a specific output is latched and remains there until it is cleared by a reset pulse.

An example of an 8-output latch is the CMOS 4099 (Fig. 14-40). There are eight outputs and a single data input. The output is selected by the 3-bit binary control. Data is transferred to the output only when the WRITE/DISABLE pin 4 is low. Reset pulse is applied to pin 2.

Assume that there is a logic 1 on the data input when the binary

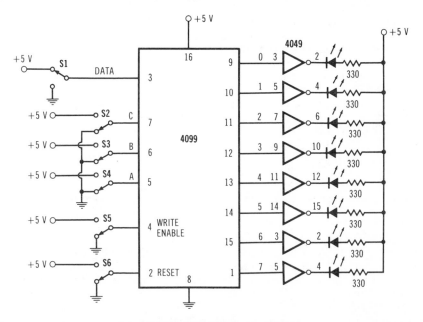

Fig. 14-41. Addressable-output circuit.

address is 101. If at the moment pin 4 is also low a logic 1 will appear on the number-5 output (pin 14). Once latched this output data will not change regardless of the logic applied to pin 4. Thus one or more outputs can be activated, and, in effect, serial input data is presented as parallel output data. Outputs can be deactivated by setting the chip disable or reset (pin 2) high.

A demonstrating circuit is shown in Fig. 14-41. A group of switches on the left permits setting of the data logic, CBA addressing, WRITE/ENABLE, and reset. The output level of the 4099 is weak and is built up with the use of an amplifying inverter. In this case the output of the inverter supplies current to individual LEDs.

When the circuit is connected exactly as shown, the address is 000, the WRITE activity is enabled and, therefore, the 0 output LED turns on. This output remains high even though switch S5 is set to logic 1. If another CBA address is now used, such as 111, the number 7 LED will turn on as soon as switch S5 is returned to low. Now both the number 0 output and the number-7 output LEDs are on. Output can be deactivated by setting switch S6 high. Of course, in an actual circuit these activities would take place very quickly because of the digital signals being applied to the data and address inputs, as well as the WRITE and reset inputs. The circuit does show how appropriate digital signal can be used to turn on and off outside devices which could be attached to the output system of the latch.

14-9. DIGITAL ANTENNA SWITCHING

The wireless microphone receiver was described previously in Chapter 4, Section 4-6. This receiver includes an antenna logic circuit that sums the combined signals from two antennas. However, the two signals are automatically phase-shifted to obtain the best signal-to-noise ratio. Digital circuits handle this antenna phasing under control of a rectified noise component.

The antenna logic circuit consists of three digital IC chips and an operational-amplifier chip. One of the chips used is the D-type flipflop described in Section 14-8-1. The two other chips are shown in pinout form in Fig. 14-42. One is the versatile 4017 counter. The simple connection of example A shows the 4017 connected as a 10-to-1 counter. However, the 4017 has additional attributes as shown in example B. Any frequency division between clock frequency divided by 1 through clock frequency divided by 9 can be obtained at the output of pin 3 when a suitable connection is made between pin 15 and the count desired. For example, if the clock frequency is to be divided by 6, pin 15 is connected to pin 5.

It is possible to connect the 4017 in various circuit configurations to obtain output pulses of various durations, divisions, and relative timing. Such a counter is shown at the left center of the block diagram of the antenna logic system (Fig. 14-43). The clock pulse is applied to pin 14 and outputs are derived at pins 2, 7, and 10. Note that pin 15 and pin 10 are joined, establishing a 4-to-1 count. This output is used to set the 4013 flipflop.

Table 14-3. Count Systems Equivalents

DECIMAL	BCD	BINARY	HEX
0	0000	0000 0000	0
1	0001	0000 0001	1
2	0010	0000 0010	2
3	0011	0000 0011	3
4	0100	0000 0100	4
5	0101	0000 0101	5
6	0110	0000 0110	6
7	0111	0000 0111	7
8	1000	0000 1000	8
9	1001	0000 1001	9
10	0001 0000	0000 1010	A
11	0001 0001	0000 1011	B
12	0001 0010	0000 1100	C
13	0001 0011	0000 1101	D
14	0001 0100	0000 1110	E
15	0001 0101	0000 1111	F
16	0001 0110	0001 0000	10
17	0001 0111	0001 0001	11
18	0001 1000	0001 0010	12
19	0001 1001	0001 0011	13
20	0010 0000	0001 0100	14
21	0010 0001	0001 0101	15
22	0010 0010	0001 0110	16
23	0010 0011	0001 0111	17
24	0010 0100	0001 1000	18
25	0010 0101	0001 1001	19
26	0010 0110	0001 1010	1A
27	0010 0111	0001 1011	1B
28	0010 1000	0001 1100	1C
29	0010 1001	0001 1101	1D
30	0011 0000	0001 1110	1E
31	0011 0001	0001 1111	1F
32	0011 0010	0010 0000	20
33	0011 0011	0010 0001	21
34	0011 0100	0010 0010	22
35	0011 0101	0010 0011	23
36	0011 0110	0010 0100	24
37	0011 0111	0010 0101	25
38	0011 1000	0010 0110	26
39	0011 1001	0010 0111	27
40	0100 0000	0010 1000	28
41	0100 0001	0010 1001	29
42	0100 0010	0010 1010	2A
43	0100 0011	0010 1011	2B
44	0100 0100	0010 1100	2C
45	0100 0101	0010 1101	2D
46	0100 0110	0010 1110	2E
47	0100 0111	0010 1111	2F
48	0100 1000	0011 0000	30
49	0100 1001	0011 0001	31
50	0101 0000	0011 0010	32

The antenna logic circuit uses several inverters, a NOR gate and a NAND gate. All of these, inverters and gates, can be found in a single 4572 integrated circuit chip as shown in Fig. 14-42C.

In operation, a high-frequency noise component is derived from the receiver proper, the amplitude of which varies inversely with the am-

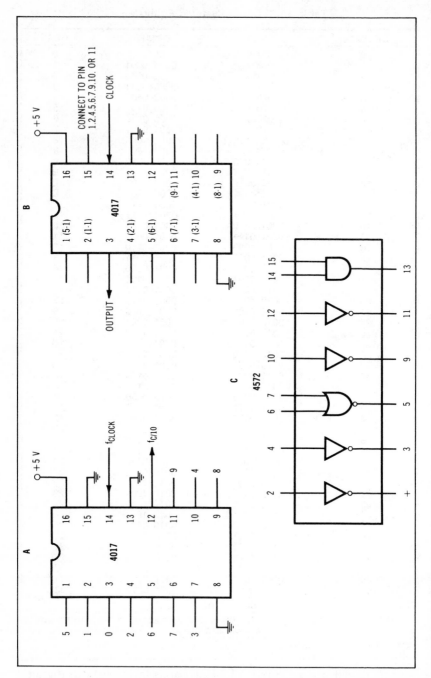

Fig. 14-42. Pinout diagrams for digital chips used in antenna logic circuit.

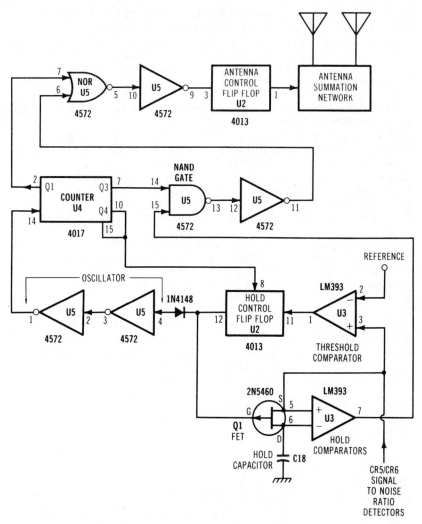

Fig. 14-43. Block diagram, antenna logic.

plitude of the received carrier signal. This component is rectified by two diodes (CR5 and CR6) and is applied to one of the inputs, pin 3 of comparator U3; one input (pin 5) of the second U3 comparator; and the source of the sample-and-hold FET (Q1) as shown at the bottom right of Fig. 14-43. This dc signal is a measure of the signal-to-noise ratio of the system. The antenna logic system responds to the level of this rectified noise component.

The two U3 operational amplifiers develop an output logic of 0 or 1 depending upon the relative levels of their inputs. For example, the dc level at pin 2 of U3 is set by the reference diversity-level control when the input signal level to the receiver falls between 1 and 3 microvolts. When the input signal level is increased by a factor of 10 dB the logic level at the pin 1 output of the antenna control flipflop U2 shifts 10 volts. This output will be either 0 volts or 10 volts and will flip from one level to the other with the 10 dB up and down changes of the input signal level. It is this change in the flipflop output level that shifts the relative phasing of the signals picked up by the two antennas, maintaining the most favorable signal-to-noise ratio in the signal delivered to the receiver radio-frequency input stage.

If antenna 1 or antenna 2 is receiving a good signal, the pin-7 comparator output would be low and the pin-3 comparator output low as well. If one or the other or both of the antennas receive a poor signal, the pin-1 comparator output goes high, which causes the hold-control flipflop to store the charge on capacitor C18 by way of the FET. (Note that pin 12 of the flipflop is connected to the gate of the FET.) The FET is now off. This charge is a measure of operating conditions just prior to signal deterioration.

The hold-control output at pin 12 is also applied through a diode to a timing oscillator that generates the gate pulses applied to the counter U4 (pin 14). The Q1 output of the counter is applied to pin 7 of the NOR gate, the output of which flips (or toggles) the antenna control flipflop through the inverter. This causes the output at pin 1 to go high or low depending on its prior condition. As a result the phasing-line transmission characteristic of the two antennas changes. If the two antenna signals happen to be out of phase, the network puts them in phase and vice versa. The phase switching always works to supply the strongest signal to the radio-frequency amplifier.

The output of pin 7 of the counter is supplied to the NAND gate. If the signal at pin 5 of the U3 comparator is better than it was previously, its pin-7 output will be held low and the gate U5 output condition will remain unchanged. However, if the signal-to-noise ratio has worsened, the gate output through inverter U5 will apply a logic change to the input (pin 6) of the U5 NOR gate. This will again toggle the antenna control flipflop and restore the original operating conditions. Thus the gating from pin 11 output of U5 and the Q1 output of counter U4 control the flipflopping activity through the U5 NOR gate. In this activity it is to be noted that the comparison level for this change, or no-change, activity is referenced by the charge originally put on capacitor C18.

The Q4 output of the counter sets the U2 hold flipflop which stops the U5 oscillator and also releases the stored voltage on capacitor C18. The activity begins again when antenna 1 or antenna 2 receives a poor signal that results from weak signal or phasing problems. The digital system continues to supply the best signal possible from the pickup of the two antennas.

14-10. DIRECTIONAL ANTENNA MONITOR

The *Delta* antenna monitor (Fig. 14-44) measures the operating parameters of a directional am broadcast antenna array. It measures the phase of the antenna current in a selected tower relative to a refer-

Courtesy DELTA ELECTRONICS
Fig. 14-44. Digital antenna monitor.

ence tower over a range of ±180 degrees in 0.1-degree increments. The monitor also measures the ratio of magnitude of the current in a selected tower relative to the antenna current in a reference tower in 0.0001 increments. The resultant readings are displayed simultaneously on two 4-digit, 7-segment digital displays. The relative current in any tower can also be measured.

Tower selection is made by the front-panel pushbuttons. A ratio/amplitude switch is included. In the ratio position, the readout indicates sample current ratio of the selected tower compared to the reference tower. In the amplitude position, the relative amplitude of the sampling current for the selected tower is displayed.

Appropriate connections are available at the rear of the monitor for setting up a remote control and digital readout position up to 1000 feet. An accessory unit is also available for remote control and digital display over a telephone line or radio link.

The day/night/remote switch accommodates power changes and selection of a different reference tower if required by differing day and night directional patterns. This changeover can be handled remotely when the switch is set to the remote position.

A functional block diagram of the monitor is given in Fig. 14-45. At the top left are the required attenuators and relays to which samples from the reference tower and measured tower are applied. As many as six towers can be accommodated. Day/night switching is handled by the function-select block. This can be done locally or by remote control.

In making a phase comparison the signals from the two towers are supplied to separate mixer-amplifier and zero-crossing detectors. The actual phase reading is obtained by counting the time interval between negative-going zero crossings of the two selected samples. A digital signal that results from this comparison is counted and displayed as a phase angle.

To obtain a current ratio, rectified samples of the signals from the two towers to be compared are applied to the separate voltage-to-fre-

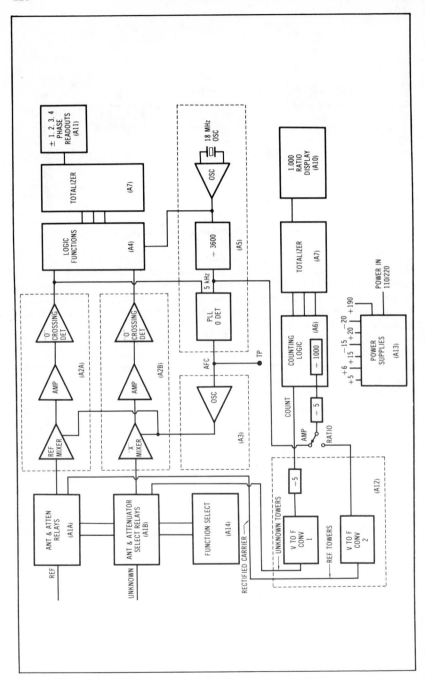

Fig. 14-45. Block diagram of antenna monitor.

quency converters shown in the lower left of Fig. 14-45. These two digital signals of differing frequency are processed in a counter and totalizer system. The output is counted and displayed in relative amplitude or as a ratio. Additional circuit details follow.

14-10-1. Phase-Measurement Circuits

The A2A and A2B input blocks develop two 5-kHz square wave signals which are phase related in accordance with the phase relationship between the two tower signals being compared. The input mixer converts the input radio-frequency signals to a 5-kHz sine wave. Local-oscillator injection is derived from block A3 which operates on a phase-locked loop frequency that is 5 kHz below the transmit frequency of the am broadcast station. The reference frequency for the pll system is derived from a crystal oscillator and f/3600 divider. The pll detector compares this local reference with the 5-kHz square wave at the output of the A2A zero-crossing detector. The 5-kHz sine wave at the output of each mixer is increased in level and applied to the zero-crossing detector.

A zero-crossing detector produces an output that has a transition from 0 to 1 or 1 to 0 whenever the input signal changes direction. In the case of a sine wave this change in direction occurs each time the sine wave passes through its zero. When the applied sine wave is going through zero in a positive-to-negative transition there will be a change in the output logic. Output logic may go from 0 to 1. The next time the sine wave passes through zero will be when it changes in voltage from negative to positive. As a result the output logic of the zero-crossing detector will then swing from 1 to 0. The next swing of the sine wave through zero will cause the output logic to change from logic 0 to logic 1, and so on. As a result the output of the zero-crossing detector will be a square wave with a frequency that is double the input sine wave.

The important feature of the two output square waves of the zero-crossing detectors is that there is a phase displacement between the two that corresponds to the phase difference between the two applied sine waves. This is obvious because the two input sine waves do not have the same phase and their zero crossing occur at different times. The logic function A4 and totalizer A7 evaluate the time displacement of the two outputs of the crossing detectors to develop a digital readout of the phase displacement.

The A4 circuit (Fig. 14-46) makes the phase comparison and generates a pulse train for application to the totalizer and display sections. The timing signals are first applied to the JK flipflops (U8 and U12). Both signals are divided by two because the flipflop output logic change only occurs when the input waves are making a negative-going transition. Frequency is halved.

The waveforms of Fig. 14-27 show the digital relations. The first two waveforms correspond to the output of the zero-crossing detectors when there is a 60-degree phase displacement. The third waveform shows the B output of U8. Note that its timing is coincident with the negative-going transitions of the first waveform. The number-4 and number-5 waveforms are the E and E outputs of U12. They are time

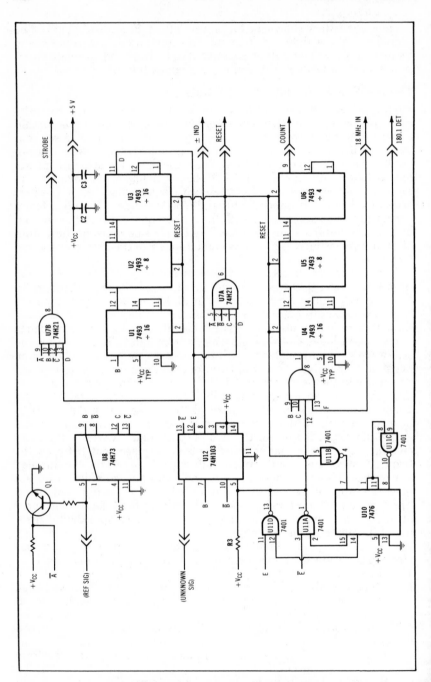

Fig. 14-46. Phase-measurement logic (A4).

coincident with the negative transition of waveform number 2. These latter two waveforms, you will note from Fig. 14-46, are applied to the inputs of the so-called steering NAND gates (U11). This circuit permits the automatic choice of an output logic that is properly related to the output logic of U8. From the schematic note that the B and C outputs of U8 are applied to the top two inputs of the four-input AND gate U9B. The C output of U8 that is applied to the number-3 input of U9B is the output of the second counter of U8 and has encountered an additional division-by-two as shown in waveform 7. Applied to the third input of this gate is the output of the steering gates. The fourth input of U9B is derived from the 18 MHz crystal oscillator circuit. U9B produces a high output when all of its inputs are high.

When waveform 3, 4, 6, and 7 are logic 1, there will be a logic-1 output at U9B as demonstrated by waveform 8. In the example of Fig. 14-47 this will produce 600 18-MHz pulses. It is these pulses that will be counted to determine the phase relation. Note that the duration of the series of pulses corresponds to the 60-degree time displacement between waveforms 3 and 4. The U9B output is supplied to a series of three counters, U4, U5, and U6, to obtain a division-by-512 ($16 \times 8 \times 4$).

The U1, U2, and U3 dividers are supplied with logic from the B output of U8. As a result the output at pin 11 of U3 has been divided by 2048. This output is supplied to the bottom input of the 4-input AND gate (U7A). When its inputs are at logic 1 there will be a logic-1 reset pulse available from its output. This reset determines the count period. During this period 512 cycles of the U9B output, each containing 600 pulses, occur. Output is, in effect, the average of 512 phase measure-

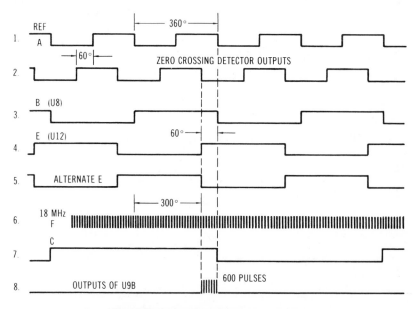

Fig. 14-47. Formation of count waveform.

ments, which are delivered to the totalizer and display section producing a reading of 60.0 degrees.

The four-input AND gate U7B develops the strobe pulse which causes the contents of the totalizer to be displayed on the digital readout.

In summary, three key logic outputs are developed. These are strobe, reset, and count. The count output is in a series of pulse groups corresponding to the phase relation between the two towers. The strobe signal permits the count to be displayed on the digital readout. The reset pulse renews the count sequence, providing a continuous display that can follow any phase change between the two antenna signals.

The waveforms that show the formation of the strobe and reset pulses is shown in Fig. 14-48. In the case of the strobe the four inputs to AND gate U7B are shown. The A waveform is derived from transistor Q1 at the upper left of Fig. 14-46. It is formed by a bipolar inverter. The input waveforms to the reset AND gate (U7A) are shown. Time coincidence of all four inputs produce the logic-1 reset output. A logic output for operating the +/− display is derived from the second flip-flop in U12. The B and B pulses are used as a reference while the selected E and E are applied to clock inputs. If the unknown signal leads, the flipflop output at pin 8 is high, thus illuminating the plus sign. If the unknown signal lags, U12 output is low, and the minus sign turns on.

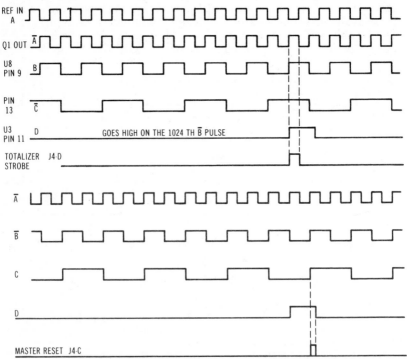

Fig. 14-48. Formation fo "Strobe" and "Reset" waveforms.

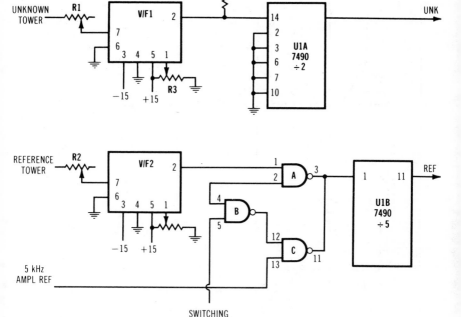

Fig. 14-49. V$_{co}$ ratio circuit.

The operation of the totalizer is similar to that discussed in conjunction with Fig. 14-30. TTL 7490s and 7475s are used as counters and latches, respectively. DD 700s function as decoder/driver combinations for the displays.

14-10-2. Ratio/Amplitude Logic

A similar technique is used to measure the current ratio between unknown and reference towers or to determine the relative amplitude of the current in a given tower to the reference. The first step in using logic circuits for such measurements is to make a conversion between voltage and frequency. Initially a dc voltage is rectified in the antenna and attenuator blocks at the top right of Fig. 14-45. Voltage components have a magnitude that is determined by the radio-frequency current sampled in the reference tower and the current in the tower to be evaluated.

The above two dc voltage components are applied to the voltage-to-frequency conversion oscillators as shown in Fig. 14-49. Each 1-volt change in *voltage* produces a 1-kHz change in output pulse *frequency*. Potentiometers R1 and R2 are calibrate adjustments; potentiometers R3 and R4 provide zero set.

The generated pulses are stepped down in frequency. In the case of the unknown tower a direct division-by-two is obtained. In the case of

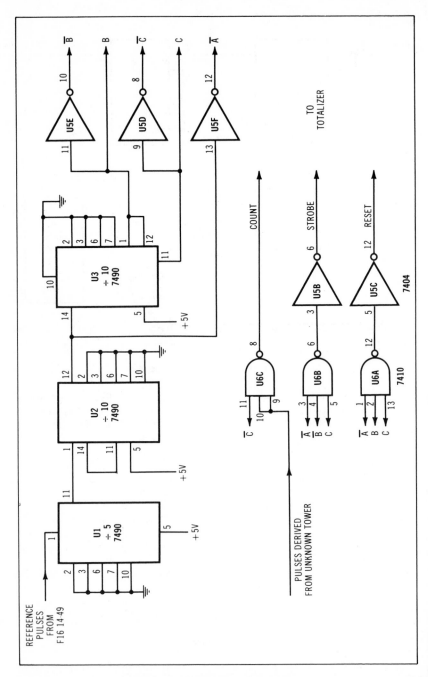

Fig. 14-50. Ratio/amplitude logic.

the reference tower a division-by-five is required. However, steering gates U2 are required to permit a choice of a ratio display or a relative amplitude display. The pulse outputs that represent the reference tower output and the output of the tower to be measured are applied separately to the logic circuits of Fig. 14-50.

A series of three counters results in a further division of the reference pulse frequency as in the case of the frequency dividers used for phase measurement. These dividers also form the necessary pulse trains for generating the three basic logic waveforms required by the totalizer. The application of these five waveforms to the three 3-input NAND gates forms the totalizer data. In the case of NAND gate U6C a specific number of pulses from the tower current to be evaluated appear at the output because of the gating activity of waveform C which has been derived from the reference tower. Proper strobing of the digital display and the reset pulse is generated directly from the five waveforms generated by the series of counters. Activity is similar but not identical to the waveforms shown in Figs. 14-47 and 14-48.

When the relative amplitude of the unknown tower is to be measured rather than the current ratio as in the previous paragraph, it is only necessary to supply the appropriate reference pulse. The reference for relative amplitude measurement is derived from a 5-kHz reference square wave derived from the reference oscillator block (A5, Fig. 14-45). This reference frequency is applied to the NAND gate steering circuit of Fig. 14-49 and after a division-by-five appears at the input of the reference counter chain of Fig. 14-50.

CHAPTER 15

Microprocessor Systems

In elaborate, and not so elaborate, broadcast systems, the micro-processor has become a popular control and organizing device. It is capable of monitoring complex facilities and making appropriate changes when necessary. Microprocessors are also found in test equipment. This chapter gives you a brief introduction to the major sections of microprocessor systems and several practical applications.

15-1. MICROPROCESSING SIMPLIFIED

The microprocessor unit (*MPU*) is the control center of a micro-processor control system or microcomputer. Its awesome capabilities are housed within a small integrated circuit chip. Size varies from a standard 16-pin chip up to a 64-pin configuration. To carry out its activities the MPU must be surrounded by other devices, within or without, that can supply its input needs and respond to its output controls. A very simple diagram of an MPU plan is given in Fig. 15-1.

Each MPU type has its own so-called instruction set. Depending on size and power, a processor may have anywhere from sixteen, to scores, to hundreds of individual instructions that it is capable of carrying out. At a given instant a proper instruction is selected by a program stored in memory.

First, a programmer with a knowledge of the capabilities of the MPU instructions sets down such a program, which the system will fulfill in an orderly sequence to meet the needs of a microcomputer broad-cast or operational control system for which it has been designed. The program is then stored in the memory. The system can be made to run the program whenever necessary, or it can be made to go through the program endlessly, depending on application.

The timing or sequencing of the microprocessor activities is under control of a clock. The clock is a pulse generator that permits very fast switching of the activities of the MPU and associated chips. Clock rates may be as high as 2 million pulses per second. This gives you some idea of the speed with which a system can go through a program and

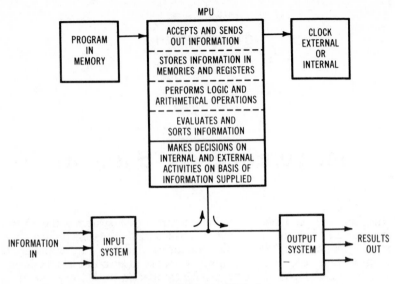

Fig. 15-1. MCU simplified plan.

the speed with which information can be evaluated and result in output activities. No human could begin to react so quickly to the vast quantity of information that can be supplied, evaluated, and responded to. It may take a long time to prepare a program and check the validity of such a program. However, once set in operation the speed with which information can be gathered and acted upon is phenomenal.

In an MPU system there must be an input system to gather the desired information and an output system to carry out the dictates of the MPU evaluation.

In general, an MPU accepts and sends out information. Incoming information is placed in registers for short storage and immediate use. There are also memories that provide somewhat longer storage facility to allow enough time for manipulation. Each microprocessor includes an arithmetical logic unit (*ALU*) that solves logic functions and performs mathematical steps just like a calculator. Information must be evaluated, sorted, and distributed inside and outside the microprocessor proper. On the basis of the information supplied, decisions must be made and the proper internal and external activities must be initiated. No sorcerer ever matched the magic semiconductor brew in these tiny black boxes.

15-1-1. A Work Example

A simplified plan of an MPU in a work situation is shown in Fig. 15-2. In this application, the microprocessor system is to monitor, measure, and control a broadcast activity. There are input sensing lines and output control lines that extend to the broadcast equipment. The sensing devices are called *sensors* or *transducers*. They are capable of measuring

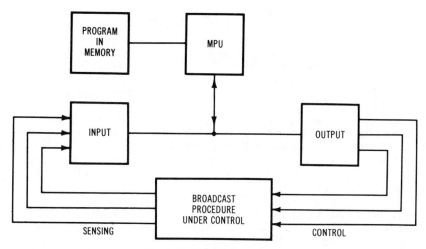

Fig. 15-2. The MPU at work.

equipment performance and monitoring the outputs. There may be three sensors, or scores of them, depending on the complexity and exactness of the task. There can be as many controls over the operating procedures as are required.

Displays can be associated with the process indicating where defects arise and what corrections are being made. Faults can be anticipated and corrections made automatically. In the case of a serious fault a procedure, or the entire process, can be stopped automatically by the microprocessor system.

In a critical, or precision procedure, a tremendous advantage of a microprocessor control system is the speed with which it responds to a situation. An operating maladjustment can be identified and corrected long before a human operator would recognize that such an adjustment was needed, not even considering the time that the operator would require to react and make the necessary correction.

Sensors of many types are available. Their responsibility is to change over a reading or measurement to an electrical representation which is applied to the input of the microprocessor system. Likewise, the output of the system is an electrical one that manipulates switches and electronic controls to bring about the electrical and mechanical changes that the microprocessor has deemed necessary.

In addition to being the decision-maker of all computers, a microprocessor has may other applications. Their application in broadcast programming is just one. They can operate a broadcast transmitter or a color-television camera. Sublime to silly, they can control the study of Saturn's rings or be the brain of an elaborate arcade game. They can be part of an electronic toy or an automatic pilot, or control an entire manufacturing procedure. Present and future applications are so many that the microprocessor is sure to stay.

15-2. BITS AND BYTES

Microprocessors and microprocessor systems are supplied with input signals in bits, evaluate and act upon information in bit form, and deliver output signals in the form of bits. A bit is short for binary digit. A binary digit or bit can only be one of two quantities, a 1 or a 0. Information presented in bit form is called data. A simple example of the use of bits is in order.

Each microprocessor system has a memory which locks-up the program procedure. The memory information is stored in many locations like the rows and columns of the individual compartments of an elaborate shelf. However, only two types of information are stored; these are 1s and 0s. Each storage system has a specific address. Even the address is expressed in binary form.

For example the address of the first row in a microprocessor program may be 00000000. The second program address would be 00000001. Each one of the 0's and 1's in an address is called a bit. The 8-bits of a complete address is called a byte. Refer to Fig. 15-3.

Not only is the memory address given in bits but the data stored at each address is given in bits. Lets assume that the first address stores

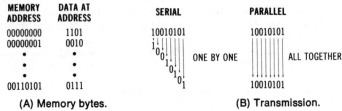

(A) Memory bytes.   (B) Transmission.

Fig. 15-3. Bits and bytes.

four bits of information. The data stored might be 1101. This quantity when delivered to the microprocessor might cause it to perform one of the activities of its instruction set. If the data stored were 1011, some other instruction would be performed by the microprocessor.

In the second storage place or memory address you might find the data 0010. This might cause the microprocessor to respond in a specific way to the instructions just given previously. It might pick up some incoming digital data or deliver some digital data to the output. As in the case of the memory address each 0 and 1 stored by the memory is called a bit. The 4 bits of the data together are called a byte. If you wish to be more specific, you state address bit and address byte, or data bit and data byte.

Binary information is conveyed from one circuit to another in one of two ways. These are serial and parallel. In a serial transmission system the byte is conveyed one bit at a time as shown in Fig. 15-3B. For example the quantity 10010101 would be conveyed in the sequence 1-0-0-1-0-1-0-1 on one line.

If the information is to be conveyed in parallel form, the entire byte would be conveyed at one time. It is apparent that with the latter method, information can be conveyed at a much faster rate and the microprocessor will respond more quickly to operating conditions. However, the path of transmission would require eight individual conducting paths. In the serial conveyance method only a single line would be needed. Sometimes the latter is the more economical and simpler procedure when speed of action and evaluations must not be made as quickly.

15-3. MORE ESSENTIALS OF A MICROPROCESSOR SYSTEM

The principal activities of a microprocessor system were introduced in Figs. 15-1 and 15-2. However, additional circuits and signals are required if these activities are to be implemented. Additional essential circuits and interconnections are given in Fig. 15-4.

You learned previously that a memory must be addressed. There must be a means of moving the activity step by step from one memory byte position to another. This sequencing is accomplished with a

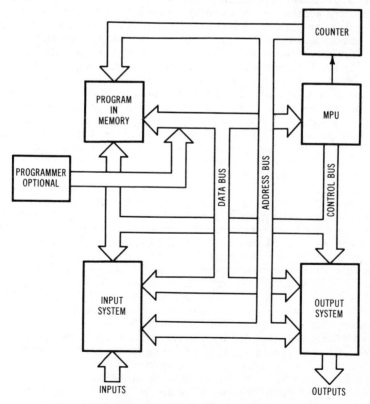

Fig. 15-4. Functional plan of a microprocessor system.

counter as shown at the top right. Often the counter is a part of the MPU proper although it is shown externally in Fig. 15-4. The counter is driven by the MPU clock which acts as the timing center for all MPU activities. If the memory has an 8-digit address there must be eight lines connected between the counter and the memory. Such a multi-conductor interconnection is called bus. Bus lines are drawn as shown in Fig. 15-4.

Address information goes out to other parts of the system as well. In particular the input/output (I/O) system must be addressed in such a manner that a particular input is chosen at a particular time and a particular output is selected at a particular time. This important address information is said to be distributed among the sections of a microprocessor system by an *address bus.* Note the interconnections among counter, memory, input system and output system are shown. Address information flows in a single direction out of the MPU to the various circuits where it is needed, inside of and outside of the MPU.

Data lines, or *data bus,* must also interconnect the MPU with the memory and I/O systems. The data bus line is a bidirectional facility because data must be exchanged among the devices of the microprocessor system. As the program is sequenced by the step-by-step change of memory address, the information in each memory byte is released to the data bus. In Fig. 15-1 this was shown as a single line connecting the memory and the MPU. In all but the very simplest of processors a data bus interconnects the memory and MPU. Also the data bus connects to the I/O systems as well as other devices depending on the complexity of the system. Thus there are several types of information exchanged among units of the data bus line. Instructions go out from memory to the MPU in accordance to the MPU instruction that the program selects. Another memory byte will provide the information as to where particular data can be collected and how it is to be executed by the MPU. Thus data is delivered from the input system to the MPU. Furthermore data must leave the MPU and go to the output system. The data bus is indeed a two-way path.

In a design microprocessor system, or in a system that permits the program to be changed by the user, there must also be a data bus connection between the programmer and the memory. Such a facility permits programs to be programmed, changed, and checked out for performance validity. Memories are used to store the digital 1s and 0s of a program. Actually there are three basic memory types—permanent, temporary, and a semipermanent version that can be erased with suitable facilities and replaced with a new program. A temporary memory chip is called a *RAM* for random-access memory. The data stored in a RAM is lost whenever its supply voltage is removed. A permanent memory chip is called a *ROM* for read-only memory. Information stored cannot be destroyed by loss of supply voltage. ROMs are prepared by the chip manufacturer according to the programs submitted by the users. An example of a semipermanent type is the *EPROM* or erasable-programmable read-only memory. An ultraviolet light can be used to erase a program from this type and then the chip can be reprogrammed.

Operations in a microprocessor system must be synchronized and special information must be sent out to the various segments as a function of the particular instruction activated in the MPU. This is a function of the information sent along the conductors of the control bus. One such type of information is the clock pulse which goes out to synchronize operations in other circuits with the sequencing of the program memory. A pulse must go out to select input or output operation, depending on whether data is to be delivered to the MPU from the input system or supplied to the output system. There are other special pulses sent out in accordance with the activated instruction set of the MPU.

The typical microprocessor is rated on the basis of the number of lines on the data bus. It is said to be a 1-bit, or 4-bit, or even a 64-bit microprocessor. The four most common values are 4 bits, 8 bits, 16 bits, and 32 bits. The higher the number of bits, the higher is the so-called power of the microprocessor. What this really means is that data can be transferred and acted upon faster with the parallel movement of a high number of bits. Also a system is able to respond to a greater volume of data because of the higher number of bits.

15-4. SIMPLIFIED PROGRAM SEQUENCE

In a microprocessor system there are two activity phases. These are known as fetch and execute. In the fetch phase the instructions or operational code (OP CODE) is brought from memory and enters the MPU. In a typical microprocessor system the fetch would involve the time interval of one clock cycle. The execute phase might require one or more clock periods depending on the nature of the information required to execute the instructions. In the execute activities the data must be gathered that is to be acted upon. This data is known as the OPERAND. In the usual programming activity the address of the OPERAND must first be obtained from the memory. After the address is obtained then the OPERAND must be gathered from that address. This particular type of execute then would require two clock periods. The combination fetch and execute phases in this case would equal the time interval of three clock periods. Remember that the OP CODE is the instructions to be followed and the OPERAND, the data upon which the instructions are to be performed. All of the above activities are timed and synchronized by the clock pulses.

Usually there are two clock pulses of the same frequency but differing polarity. One might be referred to as clock and the other as inverted clock. The two clock components are of the same frequency but may differ in polarity and duration.

Two clock components are shown in Fig. 15-5. The clock pulses are not square waves. Thus in comparing A and B clock intervals the negative portion of the B clock begins ahead of the positive portion of the A clock. The A clock has its trailing negative transition occur ahead of the positive transition of the B clock. These relative timings are set to properly augment for fetch and executive activities.

The activities for the three clock-pulse intervals of the previous ex-

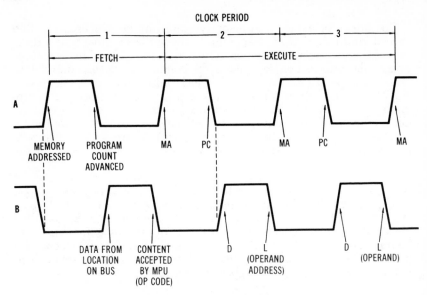

Fig. 15-5. Program activities.

ample are shown. The first positive transition of the A clock addresses the first position in the memory. The trailing transition of the A clock simply advances the count in preparation for the next memory address. The first positive transition of the B clock places the data present in the first memory address on the data bus. The negative transition of clock B causes the MPU to accept this data. The data in this case is the OP CODE. This OP CODE data is now latched into the MPU and causes it to evaluate what must be done and then to execute the instruction. This concludes the activity of the first clock period and the appropriate OP CODE has been fetched.

Next the second memory position is addressed and according to OP CODE instructions it is necessary to determine the address of the OPERAND. The positive transition of the second B pulse causes this address to be placed on the data bus. The negative transition of the same pulse latches the OPERAND address to the MPU.

The third line of memory is addressed by the positive transition of the third clock A pulse. As in previous cases the program count is advanced by its trailing edge. The positive transition of the B clock third pulses places the OPERAND data on the data bus line. Its trailing edge latches the OPERAND to the MPU and the appropriate operation is performed in response to the OP CODE instruction supplied to the MPU during the fetch period. Note that the execute time required two clock periods. The speed with which the instruction was fetched and executed is revealing. Assuming a clock frequency of 500 kHz or 0.5 MHz, the clock period would be 2 microseconds (1/.5). Thus the entire procedure required only 6 microseconds.

The previous instruction OP CODE may have told the MPU to store this OPERAND in the ALU register (sometimes called an accumulator). Other instructions are now supplied from the program asking the MPU to add this stored data to the data supplied to one of the inputs of the microprocessor system. After the addition the new result is stored in the accumulator.

Now the MPU might be provided with instructions to compare this sum with the data on some other input line. The instructions might tell the MPU to place a logic 1 on output line 2 if the two quantities are of the same value. If they are not the same, then the MPU should put a logic 1 on output line 4 and so on.

In the above manner a short program of perhaps 12 instructions or a longer one with 200 instructions can be sequenced at a high rate of speed. The program can be repeated many times per second, demonstrating how quickly a microprocessor system can respond to input changes, transcribing them to output decisions.

15-5. INTERFACING

Previous paragraphs covered the fundamental makeup of the microprocessor system. Such a system has input and output facilities that must be interfaced with a variety of input sensors. Likewise its output must be interfaced with the systems and devices under its control.

On the input side (Fig. 15-6) there might be a mechanical or digital switching panel that is used to supply the microprocessor system with specific operational sequences. The microprocessor installation could be involved in the measurement of electrical and/or physical parameters to which the system must respond. So-named sensors or transducers are able to evaluate a variety of parameters such as voltage, temperature, current, frequency, velocity, pressure, etc. Their primary responsibility is to form an electrical output current that is a measure of the parameters to be evaluated. Since a microprocessor is a digital device, these analog signals must be converted to digital data. This changeover is handled by an analog-to-digital converter, or ADC. These interfacing

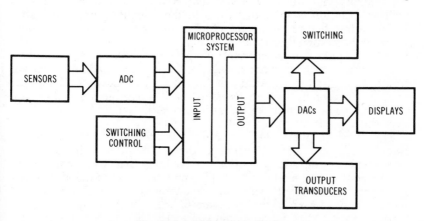

Fig. 15-6. Interfacing methods.

circuits, then, process a great variety of possible information to digital representations that can be acted upon by the microprocessor system.

Digital information is also developed at the output of the microprocessor system. As a result, it must often be supplied to a digital-to-analog converter, or DAC. The analog data is then used to operate a visual display, switch electrical/electronic devices on and off, change a frequency, operate an electromechanical valve, activate emergency equipment, etc. Interfacing is indeed an important segment of microprocessor control systems.

Additional knowledge and practical experience with solid-state devices can be gained by studying and building the demonstration circuits included in the microprocessor fundamentals book of Reference IV, Chapter 1.

15-6. REMOTE CONTROL ATS SYSTEM

The *Delta Electronics* remote control and automatic transmission system permits unattended monitoring and control of standard am, fm, and tv broadcast stations. A complete installation can be made to operate in the remote-control mode or complete ATS operation. In case of an ATS shutdown it will revert to remote control mode. If desired the initial installation can be remote-control only and, at a later date, can be expanded to full ATS. The system employs microprocessor technology. A functional plan of the complete system is given in Fig. 15-7. Several of the items are auxiliary units that provide convenience but may not be necessary.

A remote-control panel with modulation display is shown for the remote-control position at the studio and for the transmitter. These two locations are interconnected with a voice-grade telephone circuit and appropriate 1200 baud modems.

In the diagram an auxiliary video display for the chief engineer is shown as well as a printer, which may be installed at the studio or the transmitter. An appropriate printer can be used for automatic logging. An auxiliary video display is also indicated at the transmitter site as well as a station coupler that links to the telephone line. The latter could be installed to permit the chief engineer to dial into the system from his home or other location. Using an appropriate security code, he can dial into various channels of the microprocessor system and a programmed voice synthesizer will provide a voice readout of various transmitter parameters. Although the FCC does not permit remote-control operation by such an access as yet, it is feasible to install equipment that could even make the necessary adjustments by instructions over this type of telephone route.

The input/output (I/O) assembly is located at the transmitter. A shielded ribbon cable interconnects the I/O system with the microprocessor, control, and programming facilities that are a part of the remote control and modulation display unit. The I/O unit and its interfaces provide the bidirectional links to antennas and monitoring equipment as well as each of the transmitters or auxiliary equipment under remote control. Modulation monitors are also connected to the remote-

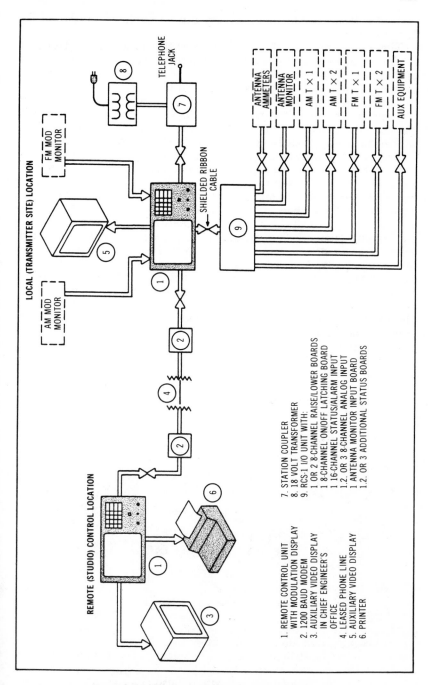

Fig. 15-7. DELTA ELECTRONICS RC/ATS system.

control unit and modulation readings can be displayed on the oscillo-scope screen.

There are a number of special modules that make up the I/O unit. There are input and output circuits used to measure station parameters and control station functions. There are switching-relay circuits and circuits that convert analog data to digital format.

There are one or two 8-channel raise/lower boards. When a certain channel is activated, it is possible to raise or lower a specific circuit parameter in response to instructions from the control panel. There is an 8-channel on/off latching module that can be used to control on/off activities in the operation and monitoring of the transmission system.

One or more 8-channel analog input modules can be used in the I/O unit. These are required to make the conversion between the analog signals being monitored and the digital format required by the micro-processor system. There is a 16-channel status/alarm assembly. This assembly is linked to the 16-event channels that can be displayed on the screen. Channel values are always displayed and are kept updated. When appropriate, alarm capability can be incorporated that will re-spond to a parameter that exceeds its preset limit.

An antenna monitor interface is necessary to display the antenna tower phasings and ratios. All of these activities are in response to the programs loaded in the memory chips of the microprocessor system and the front-panel keyboard pad of the remote control and display unit.

The front panel of the control and display unit is shown in Fig. 15-8. The hexadecimal keypad is shown at the top right. Note the lettering from 0 to F. The four longer buttons at the far right are for control, raise/on, lower/off. and normal operations.

From the video display observe that an am station and an fm station are being monitored. In the case of the am transmitter, channel 01

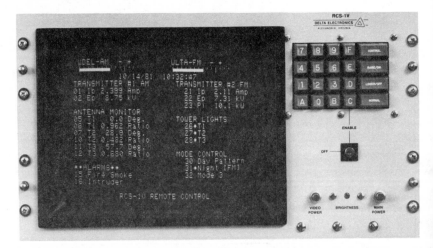

Courtesy DELTA ELECTRONICS

Fig. 15-8. Remote control panel with video display.

measures plate current and channel 02, plate voltage. The phase and current ratios of three antenna towers are monitored by channels 05 through 12. The plate current, plate voltage, and power input are displayed for the fm transmitter.

An illuminated star indicates tower light on for each of the three am towers. There are fire/smoke and intruder alarms as well as an indicator for day, night, and operating modes.

The duty operator needs to touch the system only when a control command is required. He is alerted to this requirement by the appearance of a reverse video flag in the particular channel. For example, if the plate current of the transmitter increases above the preset limit, the 01 channel would be displayed as a black-on-white rather than a white-on-black as is shown in Fig. 15-8. In this case he depresses the CONTROL button to enter the control mode and then depresses the 0 and the 1 buttons of the hexadecimal keyboard. Now the channel number 01 will display in reverse video confirming the channel selection. He will then depress the LOWER button to return the parameter to the desired value. As soon as correction is made, the I_p will return to the normal black-on-white condition. Then he depresses the NORMAL button to restore normal operation.

A special key-lock switch activates keypad buttons C through F. This will permit an authorized person to call up a second page of video display containing additional parameters and events not displayed to the duty operator. These keys are used for setup and formatting of the video display. Other activities are the storage of parameter limits, calibration, clock setting, etc. The actual video display format is usually programmed in by the chief engineer. The overall operation of the installation is under control of the microprocessor and its associated permanent memory (ROM) chips. This is the system brain.

15-6-1. Microprocessor Assembly

A detailed circuit discussion of the entire system as given in the block diagram of Fig. 15-7 is not possible. However a few key assemblies and circuits are described briefly. They have been selected to give you a better understanding of system performance. The description of the microprocessor assembly itself is in some detail (Fig. 15-9). First there is a brief discussion of the individual chips found in the microprocessor assembly (Fig. 15-10 through Fig. 15-12).

The ROM, RAM, and decoder pinouts are given in Fig. 15-10. The ROM has ten address lines. These are connected to the first ten address bits of the microprocessor as shown in Fig. 15-9. There are eight data lines which are supplied with the 8-bit data outputs of the ROM. This 8-bit binary number corresponds to the information stored in the ROM at the particular address selected by the input address. These data lines connect to the data bus of the microprocessor system as shown also in Fig. 15-9.

The total number of binary addresses would extend between ten binary 0s and ten binary 1s. This corresponds to 2048 individual addresses into which 8-bit binary data can be stored. Stated in another way, the particular ROM can store 2048 8-bit bytes. It would be a

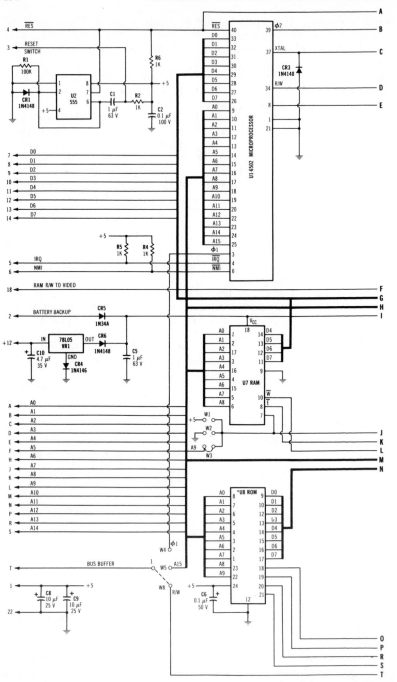

Fig. 15-9.

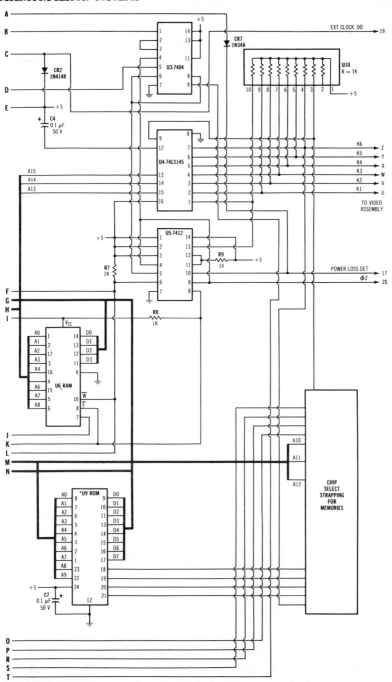

Microprocessor assembly.

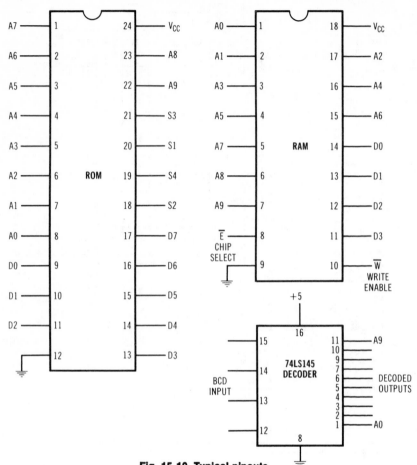

Fig. 15-10. Typical pinouts.

2048×8 ROM. The total number of individual bits that can be stored would be 2048×8, or 16,384 bits. Total storage is said to be 16K.

There are four select-chip pins (S1 through S4). Various ROMs can be connected to a microprocessor system and through the logic applied to these chip-select pins one and only one particular ROM is activated at that moment.

The RAM pinout (Fig. 15-10) shows that it has ten address lines and four data lines. This would be 2048×4 memory RAM.

A particular RAM is enabled (made active) when a logic 0 is applied to pin 8. Whether data is to be inserted into memory (WRITE) or withdrawn from memory (READ) depends on the logic applied to pin 10. A logic 0 at pin 10 prepares the RAM for the application of a 4-bit binary byte to be stored at the particular address. If a logic 1 is applied to pin 10 the binary information stored in memory is to be released to the data lines. This data corresponds to the information stored in memory for the applied address.

The 74LS145 chip is a one-of-ten decoder/driver. One of ten outputs will be activated (in this case set to logic 0) corresponding to the BCD 4-bit binary signal applied to its inputs. For example if the BCD input is 0101, the A4 output will be at logic 0. All the other outputs will be at logic 1.

The pinouts for the inverter and three-input NAND gate are shown in Figs. 15-11 and 15-12. These two chips can be seen in Fig. 15-9. Their logic connections will be described in succeeding paragraphs.

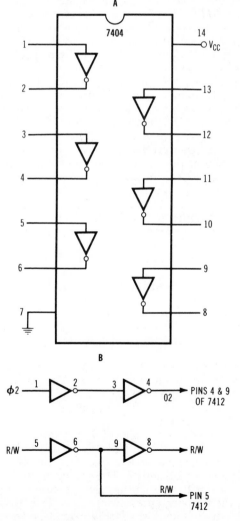

Fig. 15-11. Inverter IC and logic of Fig. 15-9.

Take a close look at the microprocessor assembly schematic (Fig. 15-9). Most of the pins of the 6502 microprocessor involve the 8-bit data lines and the 16-bit address lines. The address lines are distributed about the microprocessor assembly and go out to other parts of the complete system (A through S). Data lines are interconnected with the RAMs and ROMs and also go out into other units of the system (pins 7 through 14). The ROMs store permanently the operating program of the entire system. The 1-MHz clock is derived from the clock generator of the video assembly. It is applied to pin 37 of the microprocessor. The phase-1 and phase-2 microprocessor clock components are available at pins 3 and 39. They are distributed wherever needed.

The *READ/WRITE* (R/W) logic is taken off at pin 34. This waveform controls the READ and WRITE activities of the system RAMs. In Fig. 15-9 this component is applied to the U6 and U7 RAMs. These are called scratch-pad RAMs. A scratch-pad memory is one that stores temporary results in the microprocessor system.

The resetting of the program activity occurs when a logic 0 appears at pin 40. In addition to normal operating reset this logic 0 can be applied from a reset switch or from the power loss detector.

Pins 4 and 6 are used for interrupt services. An *NMI* (nonmaskable interrupt) activity takes care of an event that requires the microprocessor to jump off to another routine. It will do so when there is a logic 1 to logic 0 transition at pin 6. After the interrupt sequence is satisfied the microprocessor returns to the main program. The *IRQ* (interrupt request) is said to be a maskable one. The interrupt occurs when the IRQ line is low. However, the interrupt routine does not begin unless there is a proper condition met. If the microprocessor internal mask bit is set, the microprocessor ignores the interrupt request. If it is not set, the interrupt is initiated.

When active the U3 inverters form the RAM R/W signal under control of the phase-2 clock. The activity is shown in Fig. 15-11B. Phase-2 clock from the microprocessor is applied to pin 1, while the R/W signal from pin 34 is applied to pin 5. The phase-2 clock signal at pin 4 is the same polarity as at pin 1 because it has passed through two inverters. However, its power level is now capable of driving the NAND gate U5. The R/W component is inverted and applied to pin 5 of the same NAND gate chip.

The NAND gate logic is shown in Fig. 15-12B. Clock 2 and R/W components are applied to the lower NAND gate. When they are high, a logic 0 component appears at pin 6 for activation of the WRITE function at the scratch-pad RAMs, pin 8. The circuit also removes the memory chips when there is a power loss.

The 74LS145 decoder (U4), Fig. 15-9, generates the signals required by the CRT (cathode-ray tube) controller of the video assembly. The selection of the proper signal is determined by the 3-bit binary address data applied to pins 13, 14, and 15. The source of this signal is the A13, A14, and A15 address lines from the microprocessor. Only seven of the ten outputs of the decoder (previously shown in Fig. 15-10) are used. Thus the binary input signal need only extend between 000 and 111.

The large block at the bottom right of Fig. 15-9 contains the chip-

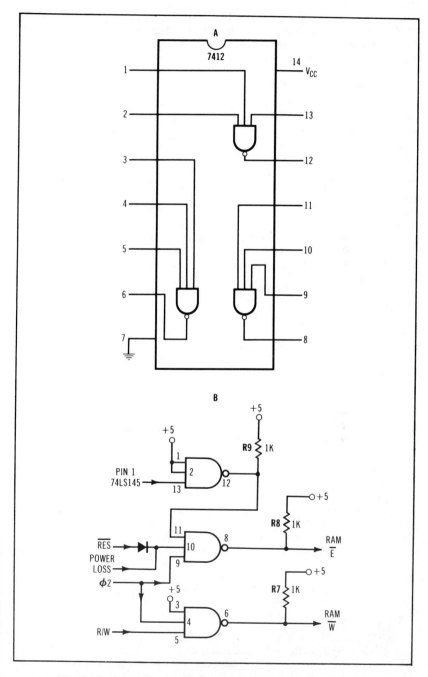

Fig. 15-12. Three-input NAND gates and logic circuit of Fig. 15-9.

select strapping for the two ROMs. The selection of a particular ROM in the microprocessor assembly or at some other location in the system is under control of the microprocessor addresses available on address lines A10, A11, and A12.

15-6-2. Keypad Assembly

The keypad assembly is an interesting segment of the microprocessor system (Fig. 15-13). The keys of the pad are connected in a 4-by-5 matrix as shown at the top left. When a particular pushbutton is depressed there is a row connection and a column connection that determines a specific letter or numeral. For example, if switch S8 is depressed it joins the row column Y2 with the column connection X3. Thus pin 2 of the encoder U1 is connected to pin 8. In making this connection a binary representation of the decimal 6 appears on the data output lines. These lines are D0 through D4. The five-digit binary number that results is 01010.

If pushbutton S9 is depressed a binary E appears on the data line. If switch S10 is depressed there is a resultant binary signal that will handle the raise/on operation of the microprocessor system. You will recall that the lettered rows C through F can only be made active when the panel T switch is closed. The connection to this switch is by way of pins 3 and 4 of J2.

Connections to other assemblies of the system are made by way of J1 at the top right. Note the input data lines D0 through D7. The top five lines carry the keypad binary data. The data on the latter three lines takes care of other electronic changes that must be made in the system to fulfill the operations that must take place when the keypad is operated.

Pins 3 through 7 of J1 carry other signals necessary for the operation of the keypad function. There are chip-select signals on pins 3, 4, and 5. These are applied to NAND gate U2 at the lower right. The proper sequence of signals will generate the output enable OE signal that is applied to pin 14 of the encoder. This signal activates the output data lines and transfers the data to output J1. U2 functions as an address decoder.

The tristate buffer at the lower left passes the required digital signals to data lines D5 through D7 of J1. It allows the decoder signals to be added to the processor data bus when the keypad is operated. It is the DAV output of the encoder that activates the tristate bus (U3). This output is also supplied through capacitor C4 to transistor Q1. An appropriate logic at the collector of this transistor serves as the IRQ that interrupts the normal microprocessor programming for the addition of information that is supplied by the keypad assembly.

15-6-3. Analog/Digital Converter

In the microprocessor system there must be a method of converting the analog signals to be measured (such as current, voltage, power, phase, etc.) to a digital representation. This is the responsibility of the A/D converter. The basis of A/D operation are demonstrated in Fig.

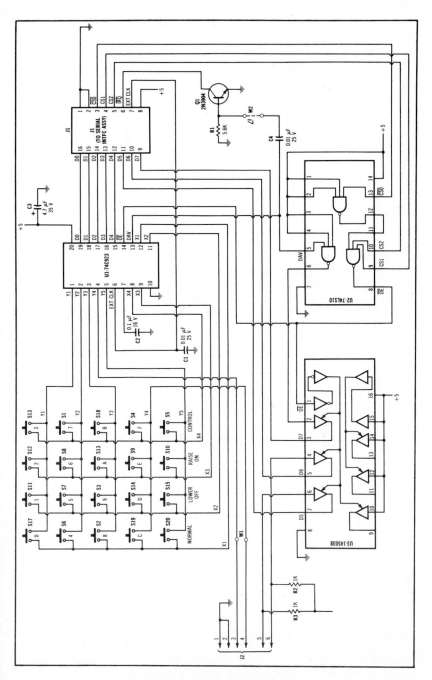

Fig. 15-13. Keypad assembly.

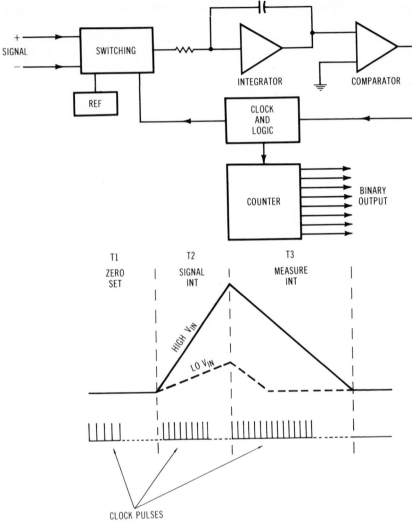

Fig. 15-14. Basic A/D operation.

15-14. There are various types of such converters, one of which is known as a dual-slope integrating circuit.

In operation the input signal is allowed to charge the integrator for a specific time interval as preset by logic pulses. A changeover is now made to a reference voltage that is applied to the integrator. The integrator now discharges to 0 toward this reference. During this measurement interval the clock pulses are being counted. The number of counted pulses is proportional to the input voltage.

The three critical time periods are shown on the waveform drawing of Fig. 15-14. Time T1 represents a reset period when operations are reset to 0 and error information is compensated.

During the T2 interval the input is switched to the signal and the integrator is charged for a specific number of clock pulses. The charge on the integrator is proportional to the input signal level. When a lower level signal is received as indicated by the dashed-line slope, the integrator charge is not as high.

At the beginning of time T3 the integrator input is switched to an opposing-polarity reference voltage. Its polarity and stability are such that the integrator now discharges to zero at a constant rate. The number of clock pulses that occur between the beginning and end of the T3 period produces a digital measure of the magnitude of the input voltage. Note that the discharge time to zero for a lower input voltage requires less time and fewer clock pulses as compared to the higher input signal.

In the operation of the counter system the counter is said to be permitted to reach overflow (a logic of all 1s). At this point the counter resets to all 0s and the T3 interval begins. When the integrator discharges to zero, the output of the comparator changes logic and the pulse count is stopped. This is the reading that is latched on to the display. Of course, all of these activities occur very quickly and changes in input signal level are followed by the binary output logic. Since the clock timing and reference voltage are precise, known quantities, the binary data is an accurate measure of the level of the input signal.

The converter used in the microprocessor system is shown in Fig. 15-15. The *Intersil* ICL-7109 is a 12-bit, dual-slope type. Its responsibility is to measure the analog input samples taken from the antenna monitor interface. There is a 12-bit binary output—pins 5 through 16. The logics on pins 3 and 4 indicate polarity and overrange, respectively. The data from all 14 pins is not conveyed simultaneously. The lower byte pins (9 through 16) are transmitted first and then the higher byte pins (3 through 8) are conveyed.

The switchover between bytes and the enabling of the converter depends on the logics applied to pins 18, 19, and 20. The status of the converter operation is made known to the microprocessor by the logic of pin 2. Actually the status output goes high at the beginning of integrate time T2 and continues high until the latch time at the end of the measurement period (T3).

Input signals to the converter are applied to pins 34 and 35. The reference voltage is made available by U3 and associated resistors, appearing between pins 36 and 39. Capacitor C6 is the reference capacitor, while the integration system is involved with capacitor C4 attached to pin 32 and other components associated with pins 30 and 31. The clock-frequency crystal is connected between pins 22 and 23. The very high clock frequency permits seven to eight conversion measurements to be made each second.

15-6-4. Peripheral Interface Adapter

The *peripheral interface adapter* (*PIA*) permits a convenient means of interfacing the input/output (I/O) channels of a microprocessor

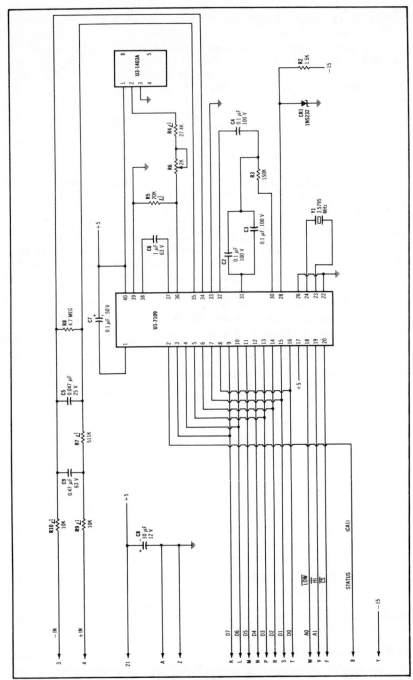

Fig. 15-15. A/D converter.

system to the equipment to be sensed, monitored and controlled. The PIA replaces many conventional logic circuits that could undertake the same responsibilities with the use of a combinational logic and many individual chips. The PIA can perform control tasks that free the microprocessor for other responsibilities. The PIA includes some decoding circuits as well as temporary memory capability in the form of registers. Its circuits can be controlled by the program.

Previous sections gave brief discussions of microprocessor, keypad, and analog/digital converter. The final description covers the use of a PIA in the control of external relay circuits. A simple diagram of this capability is given in Fig. 15-16.

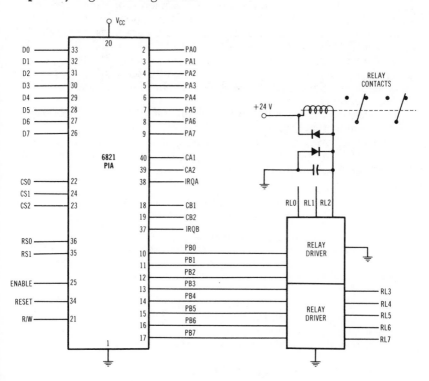

Fig. 15-16. PIA and output circuit.

The 6821 PIA is a 40-pin chip. It has an 8-bit digital input and two 8-bit outputs. However, the device is bidirectional and data can be transferred in either direction between microprocessor and PIA in response to the data to be delivered to or extracted from the PA and PB lines.

In addition to the logic on the data bus, logic from the address bus can be supplied to pins 22, 23, 24, 35, and 36. The logics on pins 22, 23, and 24 are used for chip selection. For the particular PIA shown pins 22 and 24 must be high and pin 23 low. Pins 35 and 36 are register lines. Pin 35 determines which side of the PIA (A or B) is selected. Pin 36 selects the register on the appropriate side. As in the case of a microprocessor the logic placed in registers provide enabling/disabling instructions and logic to be acted upon by the PIA.

The timing of the PIA is set by the logic applied to the enable pin 25. Usually this is the phase-2 clock. The logic on the READ/WRITE line determines if the PIA is to send data to or receive data from the microprocessor. Master reset is applied to pin 34, resetting microprocessor and PIA.

An interrupt logic is made available for each output section, pins 38 and 37. This logic can be used to initiate a microprocessor interrupt of programming when it is required by the PIA responsibility.

In the simplified circuit of Fig. 15-16 the PB data lines are connected to two relay drivers. As many as 8 relays can be controlled by the PB outputs and associated relay drivers. In the example, the logic present on the data line connected to pin 12 operates relay RL2. Single-pole double-throw relay contacts are shown. Diodes and capacitors provide transient protection for the relay drivers.

The PIA shown interfaces relay circuits. The PB section controls 8 latching contactors through appropriate drivers. The PA outputs operate the raise/lower assembly and associated relay. All these activities are controlled by the microprocessor program that supplies the proper logic to the data and address lines.

15-7. MICROPROCESSOR-CONTROLLED AUDIO CONSOLE

A *Harris* microprocessor-controlled audio console is shown in Fig. 15-17. The keyboard at the far right can be used to program switching, sequencing, timing, and program transitions. These programmable activities are augmented by additional data stored in the permanent memory of the console. The general plan of the console is given in Fig. 15-18 which shows the bus interconnections among input, submaster, output, timing, and monitoring segments of the console.

There can be as many as sixteen input modules. Each input is able to select one of two audio sources. Therefore the total input capability is 32.

An attenuator is used to control the input amplifier gain. This attenuator has but one moving part and is digitally scanned (no wiping contacts), developing a digital output signal according to its physical position. This digital signal is converted to an analog control voltage which sets the gain of a voltage-controlled amplifier. The physical sensing of the attenuator is the responsibility of detectors and LEDs. There is noiseless control of amplifier gain. The gain change is linear in one dB steps for the first 40 dB of gain control, then rolls off quickly to the off-position maximum. Each amplifier also has a cue capability.

Each input channel can supply signal to three submaster bus lines A, B, and C. Each module has its own on, off, input, and output pushbuttons. Input facilities can be established for monophonic and stereo-

Courtesy HARRIS BROADCAST PRODUCTS
Fig. 15-17. Microprocessor-controlled audio console.

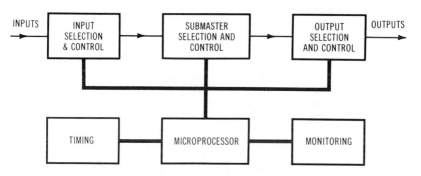

Fig. 15-18. General plan of microprocessor-controlled console.

phonic sources, low level and medium level. There are also program and control interfaces for cart players, reel-to-reel tapes, and turntables.

The three bus assignment switches permit grouping of the various source types. Each of the A, B, and C buses also permits insertion of external units such as audio processing, filter, equalizer, special effects, or reverberation and other signal-enhancement equipment.

The bus lines supply signal to the submaster control group. Each submaster channel has an individual attenuator as well as a trio of output switches. This section can be seen at the right of Fig. 15-17, immediately to the left of the programming pushbuttons. Note that there is an attenuator control for each submaster bus. The three pushbuttons at the top of each bus control permit an individual bus to be transferred to either program, auditioning or auxiliary outputs. Appropriate output amplifiers follow depending on the stereo and monophonic needs of the station. Output amplifiers are transformerless.

The first three pairs of meters on the console measure the stereo output levels for the auxiliary, audition and program lines. The single meter at the right is for measuring monophonic level. Although not shown distinctly in the photograph, there is a digital real-time clock at the far left. This display can also show month, day, and year. There is a second time digital display at the far right for program timing. It is capable of up-timing, down-timing, and also capable of giving a warning after a specified elapse. Edit information can also be displayed. Carefully timed operations and required displays are handled by the pushbuttons of the keyboard at the far right. Furthermore preset programs can be edited and changed from this panel. It is convenient to make time checks of commercials, music selections, announcements, and talks.

Programs can be set up according to program sources. Cart lock-outs can be prevented. This means it is impossible to replay a cart that has just been aired. Timing can be adjusted to prevent cart cue-ups from being aired. Appropriate cutoffs and delays can be inserted in relation to reel-to-reel cue operations.

Versatile cue, monitoring, and muting capabilities are included. Appropriate facilities can be wired into the system and activities controlled by the monitoring keyboard which is positioned immediately below the program keyboard at the far right. There are individual gain controls. Proper muting assignments can be set up with the programmable keypad.

15-8. VIDEO PRODUCTION SWITCHER

The *Echolab* SE/3 is a production video switcher that includes microprocessor control and a variety of transition possibilities between cameras and other special effects. Changeovers can be made manually or automatically. The changeover can be made manually with a hand lever or automatically with a time-adjustable control system.

The switcher includes preview facilities. Hence a changeover can be rehearsed and previewed before it is placed on the program output. Furthermore such a changeover can be placed in memory and a simple operating procedure used to use it in the program channel when required. When on the air such sequences can be initiated by a single key stroke. Also it is possible to set up the next special effect and preview it while another special effect is being aired.

There are twelve inputs: ten for cameras, a special black background pattern, and a color background generator. These twelve inputs are arranged in two preview buses and one program bus as can be seen on the left side of Fig. 15-19. The bus connections are shown in the simplified block diagram of Fig. 15-20. Three separate colors are generated for background mattes. Also the keyboard can then be used to set up a specific color according to hue, luminance, and saturation.

The program input bus selects the input that is placed on the air.

In the cut mode of operation an abrupt changeover between sources can be made by depressing the appropriate program pushbuttons. The program channel can be set for a manual changeover or dissolve in which one camera is faded down while the other camera is brought up. This is accomplished by using the TAKE lever shown at the bottom right of Fig. 15-19. Such a dissolve can be made automatically without the use of the lever by proper setting of the rate time sequence using the information stored in the take-rate register as previously set with the keypad control at the top right.

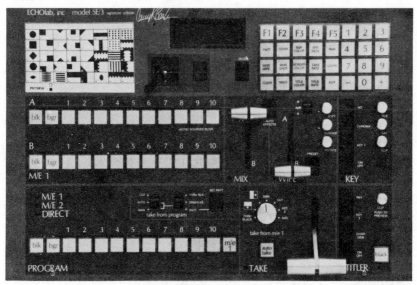

Courtesy ECHOlab, Inc.

Fig. 15-19. Microprocessor-controlled switcher.

A wipe transition can also be made in accordance with the patterns shown at the top left. Each pattern has a number and is activated by depressing the corresponding numbers on the keypad. An automatic wipe can be made or the TAKE lever can be used. Titler controls are included at the bottom right.

The pair of pushbuttons and controls along the center of the switcher (Fig. 15-19) is used for setting up and previewing mixes, wipes, and keys or combinations thereof. The results of such previewing can be stored in memory temporarily and then inserted into the program in a single stroke. Furthermore it is possible to store as many as ten of these changeovers permanently if they are used often in programming. By depressing a single pushbutton these changeovers can be brought back from memory and inserted into the program. They can be used time and time again without having to go through the setup procedures.

The mix lever permits one to make dissolves between the cameras and inputs along the A and B buses. For example, if camera 3 is active along bus A, it is possible to activate camera 2 along bus B by moving

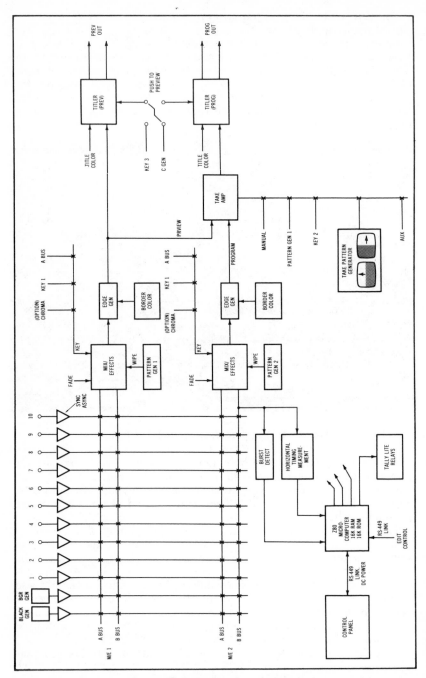

Fig. 15-20. General plan of switcher.

the mix lever from top to bottom. The time of the dissolve depends on how quickly you move the lever from A to B. If desired the dissolve can be timed automatically and the lever need not be moved.

The wipe lever performs wipe transitions from the two sources selected along the A and B buses. These wipes can be made according to the pattern chart at the top left which must be preset by using the keypad at the top right. Wipes can be made manually with the lever, or automatically. Various edge, border, and rotate procedures can be set up using the controls associated with the wipe section of the panel. Mix and wipe activities can be used together in special transitions.

A joystick is also located at the top center and can be used to move the wipe pattern about the screen to create other special effects. The joystick can also be used to create color effects. A full range of background hues and saturations can be established with white being the joystick center position.

The key section at the center right can be used to create many special effects and superimpositions. Three sources are needed for key effects. These are a source of video program such as camera, tape, or basic colored background video. Second there is a key source such as a character generator or art card. Finally there will be the so-named fill video that will appear in the background as seen through the holes cut into the primary video signal by the key source.

A great advantage of a microprocessor-controlled switcher is that after great care is used to set up a special effect by preview activities it can be placed on the air with a simple switchover, or it can be stored for an interval of time, and then placed on the air. Furthermore if it is to be used frequently it can be stored permanently for use whenever necessary. This storage means that the preview facilities can then be used to set up other transitions and special effects. Even in normal programming it is possible to set up a new changeover while a previous changeover is being followed in the program channel.

The two mixing facilities are shown in Fig. 15-20. These are followed by an edge generator and border color capability which can be used to create colored border effects in connection with the wipe procedure. Note that both the preview and program channel supply signal to the take amplifier. This simply indicates that the switcher can be used in normal program switching activities as well as an operating procedure which inserts a preview transition that has been preset in the preview channel. Note the separate preview and program outputs pass through the titlers. Inputs for various generators are shown as well as the Z80 microprocessor and associated control and timing circuits. The block diagram location of the control panel is lower left.

In a given changeover it is the responsibility of the microprocessor system to be aware of the exact position of each lever, control, and switch of the front panel. A simple switch can provide a digital result for evaluation while a lever is an analog device and an analog-to-digital conversion is needed to indicate its exact setting. This indicates the vast amount of data that must be evaluated and stored in memory for a particular special changeover. Timing information must also be stored on long-time and short-time basis. Creativity is the responsibility of the operator. However, such creativity is enhanced and simplified with microprocessor-controlled techniques.

15-9. VIDEO CONTROLLER

The *RCA* multirate video controller permits microprocessor-controlled remote operation of the TR-800 helical video tape recorder described in Chapter 13. The only interconnection required is a simple two twisted-pair cable which can be a maximum length of up to 500 feet. This type of controller is often called a *slow-motion controller* and is typically used for live sporting events because of its instant replay capability and ability to slow motion. It is just as adaptable to other creative production techniques. In a second mode of operation it can function as a playback device for off-air or on-air use of previously recorded material.

Its small size permits unobstructed viewing of events and provides the normal video tape recorder functions of play, wind, rewind, and record from its panel, Fig. 15-21. It has the previously mentioned advantage of variable playback control as well as frame-by-frame jogging that can be used to show a single frame still picture. There are also pushbuttons for pre-fixed-rate replay speeds of 30, 15, and 6 frames per second in addition to the continuously variable control.

Courtesy RCA Broadcast Division

Fig. 15-21. Multirate video controller.

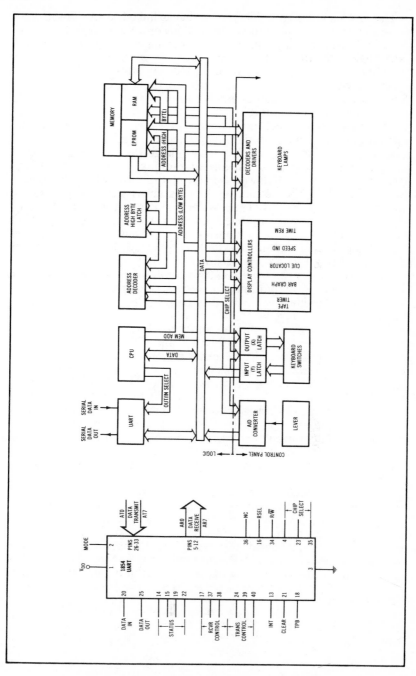

Fig. 15-22. UART pinout and microprocessor system.

The unit includes an LED display that is linked to the TR-800 tape timer. Thus it is possible to locate sections of a video tape for replay. A second LED display shows time remaining on a specific playback regardless of the playback rate. Arrangement can be used conveniently to log the start times and durations of memory-stored programming. A special bar-graph display can be used to show either 60 seconds or 6 minutes of elapsed time. There is a horizontal cue-point locator displayed below the bar graph.

The linear slider mechanism at the lower left provides continuous motion control from one-third to two times the regular playback speed. The output of this slider is an analog voltage that is changed over to a digital representation by an analog-to-digital converter. Lever and converter are shown at the lower left of the basic block diagram of Fig. 15-22. Along the bottom of the diagram is shown the keyboard as well as the display and lamp systems that are interconnected with the data, address, and chip-select buses. The microprocessor and the associated address systems and memories are shown along the top row. Scratch-pad RAMs and erasable ROMs are included. The link between the controller and video tape recorder is a UART.

UART is short for the *Universal Asynchronous Receiver/Transmitter*. This is another key chip of many microprocessor systems and provides a bidirectional method of communications. In the example it is the key link between the controller and the recorder.

A UART includes a transmitter and a receiver section. It accepts an 8-bit parallel input (pins 26 through 33) and changes it over to a serial output that leaves at pin 25 and carries data to the video tape recorder. Conversely data input (serial) can be accepted from the tape recorder and the UART will convert it to 8-bit binary (parallel) data (pins 5 through 12) for use by the controller. Information can be carried back and forth continuously under control of the control logic applied to the UART from the microprocessor. Chip-select data is applied to pins 4, 23, and 25, while transmit and receive control logics are applied to pins 17, 24, 37, 38, 39, and 40. Various other logics for clear, interrupt, R/W, etc., have appropriate pinouts that provide connection to the 40-pin UART chip.

The nine pushbuttons at the top of the control panel (Fig. 15-21) can be used to establish nine permanent cue memories. The cue start points and durations can be stored here. Beneath them is the "clear" button as well as three A, B, and C cue memory pushbuttons that are used with the scratch-pad RAMs. Each time the manual cue control is pressed there is a memory shift. Thus only the last three cue points are retained in first, second, and last order. This facility permits short-time storage as a tape is recorded or played and provides easy access for an instant replay.

Index